PATTERN FOR
WORLD
REVOLUTION

By YPSILON

CHICAGO ZIFF-DAVIS PUBLISHING COMPANY NEW YORK

Preface

THIS BOOK ATTEMPTS TO PRESENT TO THE AMERICAN READER THE
political psychology of those men and women who, since the
foundation of the Communist International, have fought for
its aims in all corners of the globe. The history of this organization
and its relationship to the Soviet Republic is treated only as a background for the story of the book. For this reason only a few of the
most important points of contact between Soviet Russian foreign
and domestic policy and the international Communist movement
could be touched upon.

The problems that confront such an undertaking involve difficulties
of a peculiar kind. Political personalities imprinting themselves
on a period of nearly thirty years in the bright as well as the obscure
corners of the world are to be described in change and development.
Such description cannot be infused with data and accounts of an
equally authoritative character for the whole of the period. From
1918 to 1928 the relationship of the Soviet government to the Communist International was clear and open. Russian and International
Communists did not try to conceal the impulses they were giving
the history of their times. They presented themselves as the executors
of an inevitable development toward world Communism. They
stated their revolutionary purpose with complete candor. Their
publications are therefore historical documents and source material
with no unusual obstacles to interpretation. After 1928, however,
it becomes more and more difficult to understand and to follow the
interconnections of international Communist politics. No longer
can one infer Communist policy from its doctrines. Turn follows
turn. The words of Communist leaders vaporize into confusion.
One of their most important aims has become the concealment
of their aims.

Documents of the Communist movement of this period are evidence only for those who know the inside story of the Comintern.
To the distant observer they are nothing but an unintelligible abraca-

dabra. Communist language of these years has become a sort of totalitarian Esperanto—with meaning for the totalitarian directing center only, and confusion for the rest of the world.

This confusion in the outside world came to a climax at the time of the Comintern's dissolution in May, 1943. Three explanations of the event were offered. Some saw in it only a shrewd and audacious war move. Others interpreted it as a turning away of the Soviet Republic from Communism and the beginning of its definitive conversion to the principles of liberal democracy. A third group maintained that the Soviet Republic was not changing its domestic policy but that it would no longer interfere with the international labor movement or domestic affairs of other countries.

Today, three years after the dissolution, it has become clear to practically everybody that the dissolution represented a much more complex historical affair than the various interpreters of 1943 supposed. For now it is evident that it was more than a war move; and that the Soviet Union has turned in the direction of democracy only the most stubborn of Stalin's ardent admirers maintain. What has really happened is that the Soviet Republic has been transformed into a state of a new type, not known in the usual dictionary of political formulas. Such transformation and the subsequent imperial development of the Russian state required for its vehicle in foreign politics something more fit for its purposes and aims than the Comintern.

The purpose of the authors was to portray this transformation in the psychological transformation of the men and women participating in it. The lack of homogeneous literary form in the book has its source in the nature of the material. For the first fifteen years of the Comintern the authors could fall back upon personal notes, memories, notes of participants, biographies, reports of important officials of the general staff of the "world revolution." The intimate character of this material permitted a presentation in the form of diaries although it was not originally conceived and recorded in this form. Reasons of an obvious nature forced the anonymity of X and Y. Beginning with 1928 the authors had to rely chiefly on their ability to decode the secret language of published documents and their personal acquaintance with the personalities of the various Communist leaders as they put in their appearance on the stage of the drama, only to vanish in the dark of the backstage and make room for their successors to step into an equally treacherous spotlight.

The last section of the book, the "Stalintern" as the authors have chosen to call the successor organizations to the dissolved Comintern, is a personal and subjective interpretation of the motive power and background of Stalin's policy in the world—whether right or wrong only the future will show. It might not be without significance to state that the manuscript of the book was finished in the winter of 1943 and had only to be supplemented in the spring of 1946.

Finally, a few observations on the concluding chapter, "Era of Stalinism?" To present, particularly in this extremely sketchy form, an analysis of Russia today is an adventure and a risk. But it was essential to take this risk, for the "Stalintern" will rise or fall with the new state that has arisen in Russia. What we are offering here are conclusions from an analysis, not the analysis itself. In our opinion the Soviet Republic of today is not the end product of a historical development, as for instance—with due regard for the limitations of such an analogy—was the British Empire of the second half of the last century. The gigantic social eruption beginning with the October revolution of 1917 has not yet come to a standstill in Russia. Everything there is still in flux and in transition. Russian society and social structure has not yet taken an ultimate and fixed form. The Russian Vesuvius is still rumbling. There is no way of telling when new eruptions will burst forth, but that they will come seems certain to us.

The reader may legitimately ask for supporting evidence for such an interpretation. Undoubtedly it has a conjectural quality. But even if space permitted a more elaborate documentation, no elimination of this speculative quality could be expected. For nobody knows the real situation with all its ramifications in Russia except a small circle around the dictator. The mystery surrounding the nature of developments in Russia is one of the most important political monopolies in the hands of the Stalin dictatorship. To eliminate this monopoly would mean to eliminate the dictatorship itself. To define this God is to defy him. *Le dieu défini est le dieu fini.*

Contents

CONTENTS

PART II: PROFESSIONAL REVOLUTIONARIES

PART III: DECLINE OF WORLD REVOLUTION
THE END OF THE COMINTERN

CONTENTS

Part I

GENERAL STAFF IN MOSCOW

CHAPTER I

Enter Ye! Here Live the Gods

BIRTH OF AN IDEA

FOR SEVENTEEN DAYS WE HAVE BEEN ON OUR WAY FROM Vienna to Moscow. Like tramps we have travelled the entire distance—on coal cars, on locomotives, on couplings, on freight cars, on foot—through the lines of counter-revolutionary troops in Poland and the Ukraine—always in danger of our lives! But always too with a longing in us—to Moscow we want to go, to Moscow we have to go, and nothing will keep us from getting there! . . . ."

Thus in the dark days of early March, 1919, spoke one of the few delegates who had succeeded in getting through to Russia from the West, to the founding Congress of the Communist International.

* * * * *

The Third or Communist International was born in two minds at one time—in that of Vladimir Ilyitch Ulianov, called Lenin, who at the outbreak of World War I was living in a small village on the Austro-Russian border; and in that of Rosa Luxemburg, leader of the radical wing of the German Socialist movement, who then as during most of the war years was in a German prison cell.

It was not a big step for Lenin to break with the Second or Socialist International in the early days of the outbreak of the First World War, and to call for the establishment of a Third. In doing so he was drawing the conclusions from the theories for which he had fought his entire lifetime. For him war and the collapse of the Second International represented a logical outcome of the social and political structure of capitalist society. The Bolshevik party under his leadership had split the Russian Social Democracy many years before. Now the same split had to be applied to the Inter-

1

national organization of the Socialist movement. Those Socialists who really wished to break down the barriers that separated the old world of capitalism from the new world of Socialism should, in Lenin's view, use the dictatorship of the proletariat as a lever and unite in a new international organization of their own. But the others—the believers in a democratic transition from one system to the other—should be dealt with as traitors and deadly foes of the society to be born.

Rosa Luxemburg had a different concept of a new, a Third International. She hated the reformist leaders of the Second International as passionately as did Lenin. But to her way of thinking, to split the old working class parties would produce at best a blunted weapon. Only after the masses had changed their old patterns of thought and had acquired a new Socialist consciousness should a new International be formed. The split of the old organizations was to occur, to her way of thinking, at the end of such a process and not at its beginning. Fundamentally, there would really be no need for such a split because with the death of the old reformist spirit in the masses the old organizations would decay and collapse of their own weight.

Destiny willed that Lenin and Rosa Luxemburg were not to meet again after the outbreak of the First World War. Their followers met at the conferences in Zimmerwald in 1915 and Kienthal in 1916, in neutral Switzerland. Rosa Luxemburg, however, did not participate in person. The greatest mind of western Socialism never received an opportunity to test her concepts of revolution in the fire of actual experience.

Lenin's concepts, however, were further confirmed by the outbreak of the Russian Revolution: the East took upon itself to restore the idea of a socialist world revolution born in the West, to give form to it in an International and embody it in a living reality.

WORLD REVOLUTION ARRIVES IN RUSSIA

The Russian revolution of February, 1917, did not develop according to the pattern of the democratic revolutions in the West. Alongside the "legal" government which derived its authority from the old Czarist Duma, embryonic forms of a new government—of a

2

new principle of government—began to grow. The striking workers and mutinying soldiers in St. Petersburg, in Moscow, and elsewhere, established their own might that had already swept away the old authority, and formed Workers' and Soldiers' Councils—Soviets, at first on a local, then on a regional, and finally on a national scale. So a new central power, a plebeian democracy, a state within a state, was silhouetting itself against the background of the old.

Lenin, who, with a few Russian revolutionary emigré Socialists, had found political asylum in Zurich, immediately realized the tremendous opportunity presented by these new Soviets for his theories and hopes. His first efforts were directed towards organizing the return of himself and his political friends from Switzerland to Russia. But all attempts to get permission for transit from the Allied English and French governments failed.

Lenin knew that the Central Powers saw victory in the elimination of the "second front" in Russia. If, thought Lenin, the Prussian generals expected the return of the Russian refugees to contribute to a further military weakening of Russia, they might persuade themselves to agree. He was well aware that his enemies in Russia would brand him a German agent, but he accepted only one tribunal to judge his actions: the revolution of the working class and the coming International.

"The undersigned are aware of the obstacles and objections raised by the Allied governments to the departure of the Russian internationalists. . . . . They are aware that the German government is permitting the trip of the Russian internationalists only in the hope of intensifying by these means the movement against the war in Russia. . . . . Nevertheless they are of the opinion that the Russian internationalists have not only the right but the duty to use the opportunity offered them of returning to Russia."

This was the statement made public by some of the pioneers of the coming International on April 7, 1917, in Berne, Switzerland. Among its signers were the German Paul Hartstein; the Frenchmen, Henri Guilbeaux and F. Loriot; the Pole, Bronsky; the Swiss, Fritz Platten; and the Swede, Lindhagen, Mayor of Stockholm.

Lenin's reasoning squared with the facts. His negotiator, Fritz Platten, secretary of the Socialist party of Zurich, succeeded in his talks with the German minister, Romberg. The German General Staff was so eager to have Lenin and his revolutionaries return to Russia that all their demands without exception were met. This was the first of the many rencontres between the Russian revolution and the German army.

When word was received that permission for passage had been granted, Lenin decided to take the first train to Berne, where the journey was to start. In less than two hours the little household and all the small things accumulated during the long war years in Switzerland had to be disposed of, bags packed, and farewells exchanged.

Lenin and his friends had spent their years in Switzerland always at the edge of poverty. Krupskaya, Lenin's wife, had inherited about 2,000 rubles from her mother during the war, and now when they were moving back to their old home in Petrograd she was still carrying some of this inherited money with her, money that, seized in a raid on their room in Petrograd a few months later, was to serve as evidence to their enemies that Lenin had been paid by the Germans.

In Berne many friends went to meet the travellers and send the sealed car off on its unknown destiny. Onlookers at the station would have taken Paul Hartstein, the tall and elegant German, for a conservative aristocrat rather than a dangerous revolutionary. Yet during the war years he had frequently risked his liberty on revolutionary missions. After the German revolution Paul Levi, for that was Hartstein's real name, was to become the outstanding leader of the first big Communist party outside of Russia. Lenin had tremendous respect for Levi's great knowledge, his ability as an orator, the power and brilliance of his literary style, his loyalty to Rosa Luxemburg and the cause she represented.

Among those who rode with Lenin and his wife were three men destined to play leading parts in the establishment of the new International: Yevsey Radomislsky, named Grigori Zinoviev, who was to become the first president of the Third International; Karl Radek, one of the outstanding propagandists and journalists of the Soviet Union and of the coming world organization; and Fritz Platten, the Swiss Socialist who accompanied the Russian revolu-

4

tionaries as the responsible neutral mediator of their agreement with the German government.

During the war years in Switzerland, Zinoviev, a pale, fat man with light blue eyes and the nervous slim hands of a woman, had been one of Lenin's closest associates. Zinoviev had never had an idea or thought of his own—he was always completely satisfied to repeat in a thousand different ways the thoughts of the man whom he considered his superior in all respects. Radek called him "His Master's Voice." But Zinoviev was more: he possessed the strength and power of a revolutionary conviction that he was able to transmit to others. His high voice gathered dramatic force at mass meetings, as well as in conferences, denouncing enemies and lukewarm friends of the revolution. With tireless energy he kept up contacts with friends in France, Italy, and Germany whom he hoped to make into comrades. The left wing of the conferences of Zimmerwald and Kienthal in Switzerland was largely his work.

But neither Radek nor Zinoviev knew the thoughts that were passing through Lenin's mind while the sealed car was rolling through Germany. Lenin hardly uttered a word during the entire trip. So many years separated him from the home country, from his comrades in Russia, from the workers, from those friends who had remained in Russia after the revolution was lost in 1906 and who, during the war, had been deported to Siberia—he knew that his ideas were different from theirs.

When they crossed the Russian border into Finland on sleighs, everyone was silent.

One of Lenin's companions, seeing the first group of Russian soldiers on the other side of the border, cried out: "Long live Socialism and the world revolution!" But there was no response. Lenin seemed as far from the Russians as he had been during the war years in Switzerland, without an echo in the hearts and minds of his fellow countrymen to whom he was returning with his message of their mission in the world:

. . . Immediate peace and fraternization of the working classes of the world; a working class republic like the Paris Commune of 1871; Socialism and a dictatorship of the proletariat; end of the imperialist war all over the world and overthrow of capitalism

5

as its source, even at the risk of civil war; and finally a working class Communist International to accomplish and bring to an end the work begun in Russia: the foundation of the Socialist Republic of the world. . . . .

When back in Petrograd Lenin explained his political program to his party comrades and leaders of other Socialist groups, his audience remained unconvinced, amazed and astonished at the words of a man who, after a few hours of sojourn on Russian soil, believed he knew exactly what was needed. Next morning the newspapers in the capital sighed with relief and Miliukov explained to the French Ambassador that Lenin "came absolutely to grief yesterday before the Soviet" because he "defended the peace idea . . . with such shamelessness that he had to withdraw amid shouts of abuse. . . . . He will not recover from this reverse."

Kamenev, chief editor of *Pravda*, the party newspaper, wrote a few days later: "The general scheme of Comrade Lenin's political ideas is unacceptable."

The February Revolution had excited the hopes of the Russian people for peace, bread, freedom. The ruling groups in the government told the masses—Yes, peace—but after victory over Germany; bread and land, yes—but after an orderly agrarian reform; freedom—that is the only thing you may have immediately.

Yes, said Lenin, Russia is now the freest country in the world, but Russia and the Russian people should use their freedom. Peace, bread, land—it is yours for the asking. Make an end to the war; drive out the present government of democratic warmongers who continue the imperialist policy of the Czar. Russian soldiers! fraternize at the fronts with the German soldiers. Extend your hands to them. Build a Socialist government of peace by your own councils, the Soviets of workers, peasants, and soldiers. Don't be afraid of the struggles, the battles, and the sacrifices. The victims of the Revolution will be fewer than those of a world war.

This program of the new Russian revolution, of the world revolution, of the new, the Third Communist International, Lenin expounded with tireless energy.

Again, as in Switzerland during the war, Lenin was in a minority. Yet here in Petrograd he was free to move, to act, and to proclaim

6

his message of salvation to the Russian people and the people of the world. He appealed to the Bolshevist members of the Petrograd Soviet: You still have confidence in the provisional government. You still are willing to back the government that is backing out of its promises to deliver peace to Russia and the world. I will not walk this path with you! One *Liebknecht* who raises his voice in the wilderness, alone, against the slaughter committed by his imperialist government on the battlefronts is worth more than a hundred Socialists who defend their countries. A parliamentary republic that continues this war betrays all the ideals of Socialism. I fight for a state ruled and governed by its workers and peasants. I fight for a state that will abolish the standing army and organize a militia of the people in its place, that will elect all its officials directly with the right to recall them, and with salaries that do not exceed those of skilled workers.

In this way did Lenin begin to reconquer his own party, which he had helped to create nineteen years before, and to build on these foundations the world party that was his aim.

On the twenty-third of May, 1917, Trotsky arrived in Petrograd from the United States to become immediately Lenin's closest associate, his most determined follower, and the most brilliant executor of his program for the conquest of power. Since 1903, when the first split in the Russian Social Democracy occurred, Trotsky had frequently belonged to groups opposed to Lenin and his friends. He had always preferred to live the life of a lone wolf.

But now he made himself the most powerful and efficient fighting machine for the aims and objectives of the Bolshevist revolution. His energy was dynamic. He would drive himself on for endless hours of the day and night, weeks and months on end, without showing any signs of exhaustion.

While Lenin and Trotsky demanded peace, the provisional government conducted an offensive against the Germans in the South and withdrew its armies in the North. There were rumors among the masses that the government was deliberately exposing Petrograd to the German armies, in order to have the breeding ground of the Bolshevist infection burned out. The governmental campaign against Lenin became more and more open. The newspapers were shrieking "German spy!" On the sixth of July the government signed a warrant for the arrest of Lenin, Zinoviev, and Kamenev. Trotsky had been arrested earlier. Once more Lenin had to go into hiding—this time to Finland, where he finished *State and Revolution,* a book that restored the doctrine of Karl Marx on the state and its functions, and proclaimed as the final aim of Socialism the liberation of the individual from the coercive chains of state power.

The masses continued to demand peace. Entire regiments at the front returned to their homes and villages. More and more the authority of the Duma and its government waned, while the hold that the workers' and soldiers' Soviets had gained on the minds of the masses of the country tightened.

From his hiding place in Finland Lenin slowly approached closer and closer to Petrograd till finally he sheltered himself in the house of a railroad worker in the city itself.

In October, 1917, the Central Committee of the Bolshevik party agreed, upon the insistent demands of Lenin and Trotsky, to an armed insurrection against the government in power under the slogan "All power to the Soviets." But again Lenin's closest friends vacillated. Zinoviev, the future first president of the Communist International, and Kamenev, the chief editor of the party newspaper, openly denounced the secret decision of the party to participate in the coming armed rebellion. Stalin, who after his return in March, 1917, from Siberia had become an editor of *Pravda* and, as a member of the Central Committee of the Party had been delegated to its military council, hesitated, as did Kalinin and many others. The Central Committee remained undecided until the workers and soldiers of Petrograd, particularly the organization of the military revolutionary Soviet under the leadership of Trotsky, took matters into their own hands. Then the insurrection swept aside all obstacles with an ease and suddenness that surprised even Lenin and Trotsky.

In the morning there was still doubt and hesitation. By nightfall all the signposts of the old power had been surrendered to the new masters. Lenin and Trotsky were the heads of the new government—the Soviet government.

On the morrow the victorious revolution turned to the entire world, proclaiming its aims and calling on everyone to follow: Immediate

8

peace; publication of the secret treaties; no more bloodshed; workers of England, France, Germany—unite with us, the workers of Russia; do away with war, imperialism, and capitalism, and build upon the ruins of the old system a new world of Socialism and peace. This was the language of the victorious revolution in Petrograd: it was the language of Lenin's new International.

WORLD REVOLUTION STEPS INTO THE ARENA

It was impossible to form and organize a Communist International during the first few weeks after the victory of the Revolution, with the very existence of the Bolshevik government still being threatened from all sides.

The war in Europe continued to be waged with unabated fury. Although the munitions workers of many of the warring countries had gone out on strike, there had been no response to the call for revolution from Moscow. Russia's allies had received new encouragement in their fight against Germany, from America's entry on their side. The appeal of the Soviet government for a democratic peace, without territorial or financial retribution, went unanswered.

Yet Lenin was aware that the Soviets could remain in power only if they fulfilled their promise to bring the war to an end. The Allies determined to continue the war. Lenin turned to the Germans.

Thus in the beginning of 1918 peace negotiations between Germany and Soviet Russia were initiated in Brest-Litovsk. The German High Command, which had granted transit rights through Germany to the Russian revolutionaries twelve months before, expected to meet willing and agreeable peace negotiators in Brest-Litovsk. Instead they found a team of determined foes who opened up the meeting rooms of Brest-Litovsk for all Europe to witness the unfolding of a dramatic revolutionary spectacle.

The players were, on one side, Lenin, who overshadowed the whole scene, and Trotsky, the People's Commissar of Foreign Affairs; on the other side the German supreme commander, Ludendorff, with his chief general in the East, Hoffmann. Both sides had staked much on this play—Lenin and Trotsky everything, in the knowledge that nothing else was left to them, Russia not being in a position to continue the war; Ludendorff and Hoffmann their hope for a victory

9

on the Western front which would permit them to deal with Bolshevik and revolutionary impertinence later.

But men do not know the future. The peace treaty victory of the German generals in Brest-Litovsk appears today as the knell of their defeat. The troops that Ludendorff and Hoffmann had to use for the occupation of the Ukraine were lacking in the West. Pushing towards the Marne and closing in on Paris, they had not enough reserves to make their push effective. With their defeat the currents of revolution that were gathering in the West were free to flow and to unite with those that had arisen in the East.

What the Soviet government announced as its credo at the beginning of negotiations with representatives of the German Kaiser was in all essential points identical with the political program of the Communist International that was officially founded one year later:

"In negotiating for peace, the Soviet government has set itself a double task; first to set an end in the speediest possible way to the shameful and criminal slaughter laying Europe waste, and second to assist the working class in all lands, with all means at our disposal, in its efforts to seize political power, in order to effect a democratic and Socialist reconstruction of Europe and the whole of humanity."

Never in their negotiations with the Germans did Trotsky, Kamenev, or Joffe disclose to the Germans by word or even gesture what the real situation in the Russian army was. The Russian peasants had already decided the question of war or peace. They simply quit the trenches and hurried home not to miss the distribution of land. But all the political parties, hostile to the new revolutionary regime, violently opposed peace negotiations. They were well aware that the Bolshevik government had promised peace to the country. They knew the army was in no condition to fight. If there are no peace negotiations, they thought, shrewdly, and the army does not fight, the Germans will move in and take over. Let them! At least they will rid the country of this Bolshevik plague. They were supported by the French and English embassies and military missions in Petrograd. The country was seething with unrest. A new civil war seemed knocking at its doors.

10

Yet Trotsky and his comrades acted as if the Soviet republic were a rock. They negotiated for and demanded peace without annexation or contribution, and self-determination of the small nations, particularly those whose territory had been occupied by Germany. Trotsky used all means at his command to prolong the negotiations and to concentrate the attention of the workers of Europe on what was happening in Brest-Litovsk. He asked for the transfer of the conference to Stockholm and even for a trip to Vienna in order "to negotiate directly with representatives of the Austrian working class." At the conferences he hurled his speeches with indefatigable energy into what he hoped was the open arena of Europe and the revolution of its working class.

On the eighteenth of January, the Germans put a stop to Trotsky's tactics. Hoffmann, in an ultimatum, asked for immediate acceptance of his peace conditions, the severance of Poland, Lithuania, and the Ukraine. Lenin was willing to bow to his demands.

What happened after that in Russia seemed to be the beginning of the end. All parties from the monarchist to the social revolutionaries united against Lenin. Now Lenin's enemies seemed to have definite proof that he was a German agent. In all cities there were anti-Bolshevik demonstrations demanding the overthrow of the "government of traitors."

To make matters worse, a conflict disunited the ruling party itself. While Lenin favored immediate acceptance of the German ultimatum, he found himself in a small minority. The left wing of his own party, under the leadership of Bukharin and Radek, demanded the organization of a revolutionary war against the Germans and an overwhelming majority followed their leadership. It seemed impossible to them that the revolution should sign such an ignominious peace after so glorious a victory.

In these dark days of distress, Lenin never wavered.

Finally the Germans terminated the armistice, occupied Finland, massacred thousands of revolutionary workers there, and threatened Petrograd as well as the Ukraine. Now the opposition ran to cover behind Lenin's broad back and pleaded for immediate peace. The opposition to Lenin's policy vanished overnight. Everything that was happening seemed to justify what he had said, and the Soviet

11

government signed a peace even harsher than that offered at Brest-Litovsk.

But Lenin had accomplished what he wanted—he had saved the revolution and prevented the Germans from crushing it. He had demonstrated his right to lead a revolution, to guide a state, and to head the new International. To the enthusiasm of the war-weary European masses for the Russian revolution and its ideals, he had added the feeling of confidence, a nearly blind confidence, in himself. When one of the leaders of the new International exclaimed, "Enter ye—here live the gods!" he gave voice to the feeling of the entire Bolshevik party.

A STAR SINKS IN THE WEST

The revolution inundated Germany in November, 1918, sweeping away the entire political structure. Enthusiasm ran wild in Petrograd and Moscow. At long last the hope that had guided Lenin's entire strategy seemed to materialize. He himself had said the German revolution was so much more important and essential than the Russian for the final victory of Socialism. Now it was knocking with strong hands at the gates of Europe. The Kaiser had abdicated—Ludendorff was fleeing—red flags were floating high above the battleships of the German navy. Karl Liebknecht, symbol and leader of an unbreakable opposition to war, together with Rosa Luxemburg, founder of the Communist-Spartacus group, were released from prison and were proclaiming that Germany was going to be a free Socialist republic. The entire Western sky seemed alight with the fire of the revolution.

Moscow immediately sent Nicolai Bukharin and Karl Radek as its emissaries to Berlin. Radek had been expelled from Germany before the outbreak of the war and therefore travelled with the papers of a German war prisoner in Russia. Soon after his arrival, however, he was arrested. Bukharin established himself in the building of the imperial Czarist embassy, as helpless to direct the swelling tides of events in Germany as were the German Communists, the members of the Spartacus group, themselves.

The power and authority of the old German regime were gone with the first gusts of the revolution. But the Spartacus group, consisting in the fall of 1918 of only a few thousand men and women, possessed no organization such as the Russians had had to direct and to lead the hundreds of thousands of soldiers returning home from four years of war, and to guide the working masses of the country to a new revolutionary destiny.

The first government of the revolution consisted of a coalition between the Independent Socialist party, a vaguely revolutionary mass with incapable leaders, and the old-time Social Democrats who had supported the old regime during the war, but were led by intelligent men opposed to disorder and revolution. Karl Liebknecht refused to participate in this government. His slogan was the same slogan that had carried Lenin to victory—"All power to the German Soviets!" In Germany, however, things moved in the opposite direction. Already in December, the workers' and soldiers' councils refused Karl Liebknecht the right to participate in their deliberations.

The German Revolution of November, 1918, was hurled with overwhelming power at the country. But it receded just as quickly. The groups that made it recede were led by Friedrich Ebert, a solid saddlemaker with good nerves and both feet on the ground, who through long years of effort had climbed into leadership of the Social Democratic party and who, as he said himself, hated the revolution "like a deadly sin." Ebert delegated the War Ministry to his party comrade, Gustav Noske. "Somebody had to do the bloody job"; Noske didn't hesitate. He organized regiments of officers who used all the paraphernalia of the trenches to extinguish the revolution. In January he provoked an open rebellion of the Spartacus group and their followers among the Berlin workers. A few days later Karl Liebknecht and Rosa Luxemburg were dead—killed by officers of the Social-Democrat Noske.

The death of Rosa Luxemburg was a tragedy for the German Communists. With Rosa Luxemburg the party lost its one great leader before it had time to evolve from a formless mass into an organized party.

She and her closest collaborator, Leo Jogiches, were born in Poland. There, in early youth, they founded the radical Social Democratic party, in violent opposition to the Socialist party of Pilsudski, who

13

later became dictator of Poland. Both participated in the Russian revolution of 1905 and cooperated closely with the Russian Social Democracy. In the years before the outbreak of the World War, both had belonged to the left wing of the German Social Democratic party. Jogiches had worked behind the scenes. He knew all the threads that bound the underground organization together during the war. He made the most daring escapes from Czarist jails, and ran the safest of the underground printing presses.

Rosa Luxemburg embodied in her very person and nature the internationalism of her aspirations. She was an accomplished master of the Russian, Polish, German, and French languages, and blended within herself the best of these civilizations. She was at home in the Socialist movement of all these countries, and was bound to them with a thousand threads. Although on the fourth of August, 1914, she had denounced the acts of the Second International as treason to Socialism, in December, 1918, she refused with great determination to heed Lenin's call for the immediate founding of a Third International. The time did not yet seem ripe to her.

But there was more that troubled Rosa Luxemburg. In bygone years she had already fought violently with her Russian friends. The centralized organizational party advocated by Lenin and his friends, that had accomplished such brilliant results during the October Revolution, was always foreign to her conception of Socialism. Socialism to her was not something that one could impose from above—even if it were accomplished by an organization of revolutionaries like the party of Lenin, sincerely devoted to the cause.

She was afraid that the founding of the International in Moscow would give the Russian Bolsheviks a complete hegemony in its affairs, that all the other Communist parties would become pawns in the hands of the strongest group. She did not want a Russian; she wanted an international International.

Lenin and his friends were aware of Rosa Luxemburg's objections. They knew she and her opinions commanded profound respect within the entire revolutionary labor movement of the West. But they hoped to be able to convince her and overcome her objections in personal discussion. Therefore they sent out an invitation for a preparatory conference.

14

In those days of confusion and revolutionary upheaval, none of the four chief leaders of the German Communist party felt justified in leaving the field of battle—not Karl Liebknecht, nor Leo Jogiches, Paul Levi, nor Rosa Luxemburg. They decided, therefore, to send two young party members as their representatives to Moscow, Hugo Eberlein and Eugene Leviné. Both were given binding orders to vote against the immediate founding of the Third International. Both were devoted followers of Rosa Luxemburg.

Eugene Leviné, who did not succeed in leaving the country, was shot a few months later as a leader of a Soviet republic in Bavaria. Hugo Eberlein departed on the dark dreary day after Rosa Luxemburg had been crushed to death by Noske's officers.

Two months later, Leo Jogiches, her closest friend and organizer of the Spartacus group, followed her into death. After his arrest by the authorities, he was "shot while trying to escape."

Rosa Luxemburg's body was lost for many months in the water of a canal in Berlin. When it was recovered, tens of thousands from all the lands of Europe thronged the streets of the city to bow their heads in a last tribute of respect. The purity of her heart and the nobility of her mind were like a symbol for the longing of untold millions.

In March, 1919, the Communist International was founded in Moscow.

THE FOUNDING FATHERS

The manifesto calling for the founding of a new International had been signed by George Chicherin, Trotsky's successor as People's Commissar of Foreign Affairs. This gesture was meant to demonstrate to the entire world that the young Soviet Republic and the rising new International were one.

Lenin had little choice other than to make Zinoviev president of the Communist International. He himself was chairman of the Council of People's Commissars and of the Politbureau, the highest party authority. On his shoulders weighed the whole burden of building up the new state.

Trotsky was the organizer, the supreme commander and the leader of the Red Army. He conducted its operations against the

15

armies of the civil war and of foreign intervention, on all war fronts, living in armored trains, traveling from one front to another.

Bukharin was too young, too gentle, too emotional, and no organizer.

Radek—smart, intelligent, shrewd—was not a leader sufficiently integrated into the organism of the Bolshevist Party to be entrusted with such a task.

Stalin had never been involved in the international labor movement, and in addition to Russian knew only the Georgian of his Caucasian Mountains.

So Zinoviev became the logical candidate, being at home in the international labor movement perhaps even more than in the Russian. He was a peculiar man, full of contradictions—sentimentality that would quickly turn into sharp irony, amiability that would suddenly change into an insulting harshness, dynamic energy that would abruptly stop in complete passivity. With his fine instinct for mass psychology, he would, nevertheless, make the most fundamental mistakes in his judgment of individual men.

The founding Congress was a Russian-German affair. Because of the delayed arrival of the German delegate, the opening of the Congress had been postponed for two weeks. When the German Eberlein finally arrived, he was taken straight to Lenin. He was acclaimed at mass meetings: the German Communists represented the great hope of the young Soviet Republic, and this lank, blue-eyed German was as enthusiastic, believing, and naive as was the German revolution itself. But he had brought with him an order, issued by Rosa Luxemburg, leader of the German Spartacus group. At the conference Eberlein defended not merely an order—he defended a last will.

Rosa Luxemburg had declared: We agree! The Third International should be founded. But not now! The time is not yet ripe. Outside of Russia, there are as yet no Communist parties in existence. The masses in Europe feel deep enthusiasm for the Russian revolution. But they do not yet know what its real objective is. Wait until the struggles in Germany, in France, in Italy, have borne fruit!

The Russians translated the order into their own language, to

16

read: We do not want a Russian International. You are too strong and we are too weak. You have achieved victory in a country where the working class represents an insignificant minority. Therefore the Russian revolution is full of danger—danger for you, danger for us!

"We have to proceed," Lenin said to Zinoviev; Zinoviev to Bukharin; Bukharin to Kuusinen, leader of the defeated Finnish revolution; Kuusinen to the other delegates. These represented the Russian border states—the small remnants of Austria after the war—tiny groups in Switzerland, Sweden, and the United States; German, Austrian, Hungarian, and Czechoslovakian prisoners of war in Russia, and a few revolutionary tourists like the two Frenchmen—Jacques Sadoul, military attaché of the French embassy, and Henri Guilbeaux, a revolutionary poet and friend of Barbusse. Italy was not represented.

In face of these delegates who were not delegates—Eberlein alone represented a real movement, and he stood for opposition to the founding—Lenin hesitated as little as he did in the critical October days. He was sure that the Communist International would grow into an avalanche during the next months. All objections, and all respect for the wishes of Rosa Luxemburg vanished in his firm conviction that the immediate founding of the Comintern was essential to utilize the greatest revolutionary chance that world history had ever offered.

This firm and audacious Bolshevist conviction was accompanied by the naive and enthusiastic choir of the new converts. "The world revolution knocks at the door!" said the European and American delegates who did not know precisely whom they represented.

"The United States of America are as ripe for world revolution as are the old countries of Europe, if not riper!" said the American.

"The Soviet system is winning in England," said a Russian who had been released from a British prison only a year before.

"The Bolshevik leaders are like a lighthouse for the masses, its beacon illuminating the path ahead," exclaimed the Frenchman Sadoul.

"Moscow has become the center of Communism, a center that is indestructible," chimed in the Austrian.

Zinoviev tried to persuade the Germans: "Our party counted not even ten thousand before the revolution. Now it numbers five hundred

17

thousand! In Germany you have a party that is preparing to seize power and that, in a few months, will form a proletarian government. And you want us to hesitate?"

The metallic voice of Trotsky joined in: "When once the time comes that our brothers from the West call for our help, we will answer: 'We are here!' In the meantime we have learned how to use arms, and we are prepared to fight and to die for the cause of world revolution!"

Thus the Communist International was founded. The German delegate abstained from voting.

Trotsky read a flaming manifesto: "Humanity whose old culture now lies in ruins is facing the danger of complete destruction. There is only one power which can save it—the power of the proletariat. It is the proletariat which must establish real order, the order of Communism. It must end the domination of capitalism, make war impossible, wipe out state boundaries, transform the whole world into one cooperative commonwealth, and bring about real human brotherhood and freedom."

Zinoviev concluded: "Old Europe is dashing at mad speed towards the proletarian revolution!"

The delegates departed, leaving in the hands of their first president the task of assembling an executive committee for the new International, a general staff to plan and direct the coming attacks of the army of world revolution.

A few days after the close of this founding Congress of the Communist International, the Hungarian revolution broke out. The first Soviet republic outside of Russia in Europe was established. This was in the spring of 1919.

SECOND WORLD CONGRESS

In July, 1920, when the Second World Congress of the Communist International assembled at the winter palace in Petrograd, the Hungarian Soviet Republic had long since gone under. An admiral, Horthy, had become successor to its leader, Bela Kun.

Yet the Hungarian defeat was only a passing episode in the eyes of the High Command of the world revolution. Had not the Bolsheviks won a complete victory in the civil war? Had they not forced the withdrawal of the English, French, and American troops of inter-

18

vention? The demonstration seemed final proof: Lenin and Trotsky could not be defeated in Russia.

In Europe the first great postwar depression was threatening new misery and insecurity. The European labor movement took a tremendous turn towards Moscow.

This time hundreds of delegates came from all countries of the world: real labor representatives elected and re-elected a hundred times, revolutionaries and opportunists, workers from the factories and shrewd attorneys, terrorists and elegant Socialists from the salons of Europe; everybody was on his way to Moscow.

With poetic enthusiasm Zinoviev welcomed the dawn of victory: "We have in front of us a picture that is perfect and commands adoration in its simplicity. What could be simpler? The workers of the capitalist countries unite in order to liberate themselves from the weight of oppression. What could at the same time command more adoration? Comrades, listen to the wingbeat of victory! Our earth will be free! Wage slavery will disappear and Communism will triumph all over the world!"

MASS THEATER ON THE NEVA

On the Champs de Mars in Petrograd, the marriage of the European millions with the Russian workers was feted. Multitudes, mad with joy, cheered the members of the coming revolutionary governments of Europe. Never had the world seen so moving a spectacle.

On the eve of the opening of the Congress, a tremendous show was staged on the square in front of the Bourse, before all the delegates and an audience of eighty thousand people. It presented the history of the labor movement from 1848 on.

The huge stage was illuminated by searchlights from the cruisers anchored on the Neva. The cannons of the Peter and Paul fortress announced the beginning and end of each act. From an immense banner stretched over the whole square, Marx' and Engel's words blazoned forth:

"Workers of the world, unite! You have nothing to lose but your chains!"

Scene after scene rolled over the stage: The Paris Commune of

19

1871 with its masses dancing the Carmagnole; counter-revolutionary troops from Versailles, with the help of Bismarck's Prussian regiments, destroying the Commune. Fat capitalists clipping coupons, and chained workers; trumpets blowing—World War, 1914 vintage, beginning. Karl Liebknecht crying "Down with the war!" and raising the Red Flag that had been torn to shreds by the leaders of the Second International. The revolution in Russia commencing; the Czar with his court—hungry and weeping women with their children—hunted soldiers. Automobiles with armed workers speeding right through the audience, storming the stage and throwing the Czar from his throne. Out of the darkness Kerensky emerging. Shouts ringing out from the warships on the Neva: "Lenin! Lenin!"

And now, out of the black night, illuminated by powerful searchlights, rose the picture of Lenin. The provisional government disappeared. The Red Flag was hoisted; Trotsky's picture raised. The masses on the square cried out:

"All power to the Soviets! Long live the Soviet government!"

Then the final scene: The civil war began. The cavalry of Budyenny galloped across the square. A choir of many hundred voices sang the songs of the Third International. The leaders mounted the stage; the Red Army returned victorious from the fronts.

Giant skyrockets burst overhead: Long live the Third International! Workers of all countries, unite!

The march into the world revolution began.

LENIN'S VISION

Russia at the time of the Second World Congress was even hungrier than a year earlier. Grain was taken by force from the peasants. The ruble was without value. Industry was not moving. Masses of workers had returned to the villages in order not to starve to death in the cities.

When Lenin took the floor to explain to the emissaries of the masses from Europe and Asia his vision of the new world of Communism, and the strategy necessary to establish it, his face was pale, haggard. He did not need or use oratory—his voice held the quiet assurance of his spirit.

He presented to the assembly his vision of a capitalist order that was collapsing, and whose heritage would fall to Communism—if the

Communists would act with determination, faith, and willingness to sacrifice.

The Allies have won the war, he said. They have divided the world between themselves. But they are losing the peace. From the war have arisen everywhere, even in their own countries, conditions that are unbearable to the masses. These conditions cannot be improved without abolishing private property, without a Socialist revolution.

They have made the war debts an insoluble problem. None of the debtor countries is able to pay and the creditor countries have gotten themselves into a position where they can neither buy nor sell. The mechanism of capitalist world economy is in disintegration.

The ideals of Wilson have become illusions. The Treaty of Versailles has made a farce out of the promise to end wars. The bourgeois world and the parties of the Second International supporting it have nothing to offer the masses of mankind any longer.

Versailles and the League of Nations do not bridge the conflicts within the camps of the victors. They have not even been able to act in unison against Bolshevism.

"Weak and ruined Russia, this backward country, has won out against all nations, against an alliance of the rich and powerful states that dominate the entire world. We were not in a position to oppose them with forces equal to theirs, and we have won out nevertheless.

"Why? Because between them there was not even the semblance of unity; because one power opposed the other. France wished Russia to pay her debts and to threaten Germany. England attempted to divide Russia and to lay her hands on the oil of Baku. . . .

"A small minority has enriched itself during the war, but even this small minority is now dependent on America. More than three-quarters of all the men and women alive on this planet have suffered misery, ruin, injustice, through this war. Germany is living in conditions such as have never yet been endured by a civilized people.

"These are the conditions from which only a world revolution can save the world. Nevertheless the situation is not beyond repair for the bourgeois world. There exists a tremendous crisis of the bourgeois order, and only the victory of the revolution will represent the final proof that the sickness of the bourgeois world has become irreparable . . . . ."

A breathless stillness pervaded the vast hall when Lenin assured the delegates that the Socialist dreams of centuries now had become plans, and that their action would make the plans into realities.

Lenin finished. The delegates had heard the wingbeats of victory.

For the first time at an international labor congress, the peoples of the Far East were represented—China, Korea, Indo-China, India; with them the Mohammedan tribes of Middle Asia, the Persians and the Turks, all following the lead of the Indian, Manabendranath Roy.

Lenin's vision encircled the entire globe. His ideas about the East were as sweeping as those about the West had been on his return from Switzerland in 1918. He proclaimed the alliance of the revolutionary workers of the advanced capitalist countries with the revolutionary masses of the countries of the East, where no modern working class yet existed.

World imperialism will definitely be destroyed if the hundreds of millions of the Far East, who have taken no active part in history and have been only its pawns, unite with the revolutionary armies of the West.

Now the Communists of Europe and America knew what the Bolshevists meant when they talked of world revolution. Now they understood that the conquest of power in one separate European country was only a detail in a total revolutionary plan of more sweeping proportions than ever before conceived: to the West of the Russian Soviet Republic, a chain of proletarian revolutions carried forward by the industrial workers; to the East, the Soviet movement of the Chinese and the Indians; the Russian Soviet Republic as a foundation for a world federation of Soviet Republics; and the Comintern as the High Command and executor of this plan.

LEAP TO THE WEST

Lenin meant what he said. He was ready to risk the very life of the Russian Soviet Republic when he saw a chance of taking a step forward towards the realization of his ideas.

Before the Second Congress opened, the Ukraine had been invaded by the armies of Pilsudski. Pilsudski had become the leader of the Polish national army, and wanted a Greater Poland. He thought that revolutionary Russia was weak and without defense, that the Red Army—whose generals had only yesterday been factory workers or cadets; whose commander-in-chief knew the art of war only from books; whose soldiers were without shoes, carried only rusty bayonets, and had but a small piece of bread in their sacks—would be an easy prey. But this army drove Pilsudski's troops back, far beyond the Russian borders.

In the midst of the Second Congress' negotiations, the Bolshevist leaders had to decide: accept the Polish offer of peace or continue the war?

Trotsky was opposed to taking the campaign beyond the Russian borders. He did not believe in the offensive power of the Red Army. Radek, who knew Poland better than the other Bolsheviks, warned: if we come to a stop at the border, then the demoralized Polish army will flow back into the country. Pilsudski will be buried in the ignominy of a war provoked and lost. Maybe then the proximity of the Red Army will incite the Polish workers and peasants to revolt. If we cross into Poland the country's traditional hatred for Russia will be in Pilsudski's favor. We will lose the sympathy of the Polish masses. We can help a revolution to victory—we cannot carry it at the points of our bayonets into other countries.

"You have learned your lesson of 1918 too well!" Lenin replied sharply. "When you have an enemy on the run, you should destroy him. We must not allow Pilsudski the breathing-spell that he needs, until the French arrive. Weygand is on his way to Warsaw. We can take the city before his arrival."

Radek and Trotsky were right. The Polish workers did not revolt when the Red Army approached Warsaw. Pilsudski got his breathing-spell because the Red Army was out of breath.

Yet at the Congress, Radek talked the party language: "Comrades," he said, "I express my firm conviction that our Red Army in Poland will be assisted by iron divisions of Polish workers. They will fight with us to victory."

THE ARMY OF INTERNATIONAL REVOLUTION

Lenin's vision of world revolution moulded the shape of the new International that was to be its instrument. The Bolsheviks could have organized an International with the major part of the European labor movement in it. All the big labor parties of Europe, with the exception of the old German and Austrian Social Democracies as well as of the English Labor Party, were there. Together with them and the representatives of the colonial East, a world-embracing Socialist organization could have been formed.

But Lenin and Trotsky had a different objective. They wanted more than an international federation of revolutionary parties. Their aim was a Communist World Party, an army of soldiers of the revolution, officered by experts of insurrection and rebellion, directed by a High Command in Moscow. Not for one moment did they yield to the temptations of triumph. They remained hard and uncompromising.

To them it seemed perfectly clear: To achieve final victory in the world, one thing only was lacking, a Bolshevist party modelled on the Russian. Zinoviev expressed this in the following words:

"We need a centralized Communist Party with an iron discipline, an international organization made from the same metal. There is no other way during the civil war that we are undergoing. You should accept from us Russians only what really merits imitation. The best that we have given the Russian workers is devotion to the Party. The Party is for the progressive Russian worker something sacred, something more dear than life. . . . . And in this respect, the workers of the entire world should follow the Russians."

Now Lenin and Zinoviev were no longer afraid that the new International might be too small. They feared rather the opportunists who were streaming towards Moscow.

Their first action was to protect the Third International from the disintegration that had befallen the Second. Never again would they commit a blunder like the one in Hungary. They reproached themselves bitterly for having given in to Bela Kun and agreed to the unconditional merger of the Hungarian Communists with the Social Democrats. In this merger they found the decisive cause for the defeat of the Hungarian Soviet Republic.

Lenin and Zinoviev formulated twenty-one conditions for admission into the Communist International. The conditions were hard. Without a continuous merciless fight against opportunism, without removing all reformist and vacillating elements from important posts and excluding them from membership—no admission to the Communist World Party.

24

Without creating an underground organization alongside the legal one, without fighting militarism and pacifism, without building a centralized party whose leadership would consist of dependable Communists only, with complete control over parliamentary delegations and newspapers—no admission to the Communist World Party!

Without accepting unconditionally the authority of the Executive Committee of the Comintern over all member parties—no admission to the Communist World Party.

"The Russians are resolved to stay alone rather than agree to unite with traitors of Socialism," Zinoviev said. "The Socialist leaders may behave as they please. The hearts of the workers in all countries of the world are ours!"

Zinoviev called all the parties that had joined the Communist International since its first Congress mercilessly to task. The Italian Socialists had refused to expel the reformists from their party. The French and Swiss Socialists were pacifists and placed their faith in Wilson, permitting the enemies of the revolution to write for their newspapers. The Swedish comrades had failed to exclude Lindhagen, Lenin's enthusiastic adherent in 1917, but now advocating entry into the League of Nations. The leader of the Norwegian labor party, Tranmael, had accepted entire trade union organizations into the party without giving a thought to their political convictions.

With the exception of the German Party, all parties were immersed in an acid solution of Bolshevist criticism.

GERMAN-RUSSIAN UNITY

The Germans and the Russians were one heart and one soul. Although the German Communists had not yet seized power, by the time the Second Congress convened, as Zinoviev had so confidently predicted at the first Congress in March, 1919, nobody doubted that what had not yet happened would happen tomorrow.

In reality, after the defeat of January, 1919, they had suffered a second much more devastating defeat. In March, 1920, the German monarchists had risen against the government of the Social Democrat, Ebert. In the West of the Reich, in the Ruhr district, resistance to the monarchist rebellion had swelled into a huge revolutionary movement. A German Red Army had sprung up sponta-

25

neously without party organization and without leadership—a movement that made the earth tremble underneath the German Republic. In Russia only one inference was drawn from the movement: Just as Lenin had succeeded Kerensky, Paul Levi, Rosa Luxemburg's successor, would follow Ebert. Everything focussed on Germany. German was the language of the Congress. Lenin, Trotsky, Zinoviev, Radek, and Bukharin made their speeches in German. The poor English and Americans were unsuccessful in having English admitted as an official language.

The German Communist delegates were enthusiastic. This was really their Congress. The Russian comrades were conducting themselves as true internationalists. Rosa Luxemburg had been too suspicious. Had she been alive, not the slightest misunderstanding could have come into their brotherly alliance with the Russians.

Lenin was heard to say: "Without Russia and without Germany, Europe cannot rise again."

"If crucified and suppressed Germany is not permitted to live, to feed itself, and to work, it will rise against French imperialism," thundered Trotsky.

"When the Red Army fighting the White Army of Poland approaches the borders of Germany, it will hear from the other side above the bayonets, the cry of the German proletariat: 'Long Live Soviet Russia!'" Paul Levi, the German leader, replied.

LATIN MISUNDERSTANDINGS

French delegates were little seen and less heard. They had come with empty hands, they had nothing to offer—no hope for a revolution, not even for a general strike against the French shipments of arms to Poland.

Marcel Cachin, a typical Frenchman from Normandy—quick, temperamental, a brilliant orator, and a favorite of the mass meetings in Paris—had made this journey to Moscow as a real trip to Canossa. In 1915 he had visited Italy as representative of the French government, in order to persuade his party friend, Mussolini, to begin a campaign for the entrance of neutral Italy into the war on the side of the Entente. In April, 1917, he had visited Russia, together with the French Munitions Minister Thomas, in order to persuade his Russian party friends to keep revolutionary Russia in the war. Now he was sitting among the most steadfast opponents of the imperialist war which he had supported.

Lenin had received him coldly and briefly. "Comrade Cachin, today a world separates us. Whether we will march together in the future depends entirely on your behavior."

Cachin was not too happy. He found solace with Froissard, a lawyer from Alsace who had worked his way up to the leadership of the French Socialist parliamentary delegation. Well versed in all the political tricks of the game, he took Moscow, the civil war, and particularly this Congress, as an amusing pastime.

"*On se debrouillera,*" he counselled the melancholy Cachin. "Here in Moscow we will accept Bolshevism, lock, stock, and barrel. When we return home, everything there will still be the same!"

Radicalism was a wonderful thing, a good preliminary to becoming a minister in the French government later on. Nothing simpler than to sign a statement: Agreed, agreed! Zinoviev could get the French to accept anything he wanted.

With Serrati, the leader of the Italian Socialists, it was different. Serrati's long beard had become as popular as his beautiful tenor, in Moscow. He was a proud and self-assured man. His party had always taken a decided stand against the war. Its deputies had greeted the King in parliament by singing the International, and afterwards had left the hall. When Cachin went to Italy during the war, Serrati had treated him as a traitor. And now Cachin was to be admitted to the new International.

The Italian Socialists had been the first big party to apply for membership in the new International, after the founding Congress. But now, in Moscow, the roles were changed, and Serrati found himself suddenly condemned as a stubborn sinner!

Probably nobody among the delegates loved the Russians as did Serrati. Only he could not understand them. To split the party, to separate from the old Socialist leader Turati, and to expel him as a traitor—how was that possible among brothers? Exclude Turati who had opposed the war, and admit Cachin? Incomprehensible. Trick and lie your way into reactionary unions in order to gain influence? Serrati was a gentleman without fear: a lie is a lie, unworthy of

27

Socialism. It was unthinkable not to trust a comrade! "We do not possess a *'sincéromètrè,'* " he complained.

"You want a Communist World Party? We are with you. But we are not to blame that we are Italians and you are Russians. Nor is it our merit." They did not understand each other.

"Let us not talk about Turati, but let us organize the revolution. The situation in Italy is favorable!"

Serrati had to admit that never had he felt as weak and powerless as here in Moscow. Lenin and Zinoviev showed no more mercy to him than to the representatives of the German Independent Social Democracy, Dittmann and Crispien, who had come only because their own party members had insisted upon this trip. The Bolshevik ideology of organizing the revolution was foreign to them. It was but another term for ultimate command by Moscow.

Yet even had they been inclined to accept, it would have been of no avail. "I do not concede you to have revolutionary conviction— not in the sense that you are not prepared to act as revolutionaries, but in the sense that you are not able to think as revolutionaries!" Lenin said to them.

The twenty-one conditions of Lenin and Zinoviev had become an absolute ultimatum to every labor leader who wanted to join Moscow, and who had failed to move all the way into the Kremlin.

FLAMING ORIENT

The summer and fall of 1920 were a culmination point in Zinoviev's life and career. During these months he became Jupiter on the Olympian heights of the Bolshevist world revolution. Even Lenin's and Trotsky's glory paled against his. Both West and East echoed with his powerful shrill voice, calling confidently for world revolution.

At the beginning of August, the Second World Congress of the Comintern closed. On the first of September, Zinoviev went to Baku to attend a Congress of the peoples of the Orient. At the beginning of October, he went to the Congress of the Independent German Social Democratic Party at Halle.

Already in 1919, the Soviet government had solemnly renounced all extraterritorial privileges in China and Persia and had recognized the nationalist governments of Sun Yat Sen in China, of Riza Khan in Persia, and of Kemal Pasha in Turkey. It had published the secret contracts between the Czar and the British government, promising the Dardanelles to Russia. It had annulled all debts of Persia to Russia, transferred to Persia the railroads the Russians had built there, and proclaimed the right of the Turkish people to the straits between the Black Sea and the Mediterranean. It had supported Kemal Pasha in his struggle for national reconstitution with money and weapons.

In the Asiatic districts of the Soviet Republic inhabited by Mohammedans, a vigorous anti-imperialist campaign had been conducted. Moscow had sent a propaganda train of twenty cars to Tashkent. These cars were decorated with flaming symbols calling the Moslems to fight against England. They carried vast quantities of propaganda material to be handed out to the people of Turkestan. Wherever the train stopped, revolutionary moving pictures were shown under an open sky. Most of the spectators had never seen or heard of pictures moving across a screen. The magicians of Moscow could easily dislodge the Emir of Buchara and chase him out of the country. In Tabris, the capital city of Persian Azerbaijan, a movement for autonomy took hold.

Now the time seemed ripe for Zinoviev to pick the fruits of Soviet anti-imperialist policy.

From Turkey and Persia, from Afghanistan and Buchara, from China and Korea, from India and Java, Oriental revolutionaries had come in droves to Moscow. To these delegates from the Orient, Moscow became a wonder garden from the books of the Koran. By the white sahibs, they were received as brothers.

They were conducted into the Kremlin where they were welcomed by the greatest of all sahibs, Zinoviev. Their interpreter needed all his powers of persuasion to prevent them from bowing to the dust before this great white man. Never had there been such a meeting of West and East.

It was then that Zinoviev conceived the idea of a Congress in Baku.

After her victory in the World War, Great Britain had subjected the world of Mohammed to her rule, but had been unable to prevent the Bolshevik conquest of the Caucasus, whence the roads open ahead to the Middle East and India. Zinoviev's Congress in Baku,

29

the capital of Russian Azerbaijan, was to establish itself as a triumphant challenge to the British Empire.

The prologue to Baku had been Lenin's speech on the world revolution and the revolution of the colonial peoples of the East, at the sessions of the Second World Congress. Lenin had asked for the alliance of the revolutionary working class movement of the West with the revolutionary movement of the colonial peoples of the East, for their liberation from imperialist suppression. He advocated a broad anti-imperialist movement in the Far East and in the colonies, comprising all classes and groups of the population, and the support of such a movement by the revolutionary parties of the West. He had been seconded by Manabendranath Roy, the son of a wealthy Brahmin family, whose arrival in Moscow he had regarded as a great achievement for the Comintern.

Lenin's respect for Roy had increased, when the latter with the self-assurance of a born leader had presented a viewpoint independent to his own.

"I agree with what Lenin says," Roy had exclaimed, "but in India and China as well as in the countries of the Near East, a national bourgeoisie is arising that regards the movement of the peasants and the industrial workers with suspicion. Only an independent Communist Party, supported by the industrial workers in the East, will safeguard the nationalist revolutions of the colonial peoples. The nationalist bourgeoisie is an unreliable ally."

The Congress had merged the viewpoints of Lenin with those of Roy. The Comintern was to support only those national revolutionary movements that fought without compromise against imperialism and for Soviets.

Almost two thousand delegates from the Mohammedan tribes of the Middle East had arrived in Baku, half of them from the areas of the Soviet Union, the others from Persia, Afghanistan, Turkey, the Near East, and the Orient.

Zinoviev came to Baku accompanied by Radek and Bela Kun, and delivered one of the great speeches of his life. He promised the revolutionary Orient a grand future.

"The world revolution will begin to flourish only when the eight hundred million people of Asia, when the African continent, marches with us! We will find the right path to victory only if the hearts of the millions of suppressed in the world open to the true and pure words of truth!"

At the end of his speech, the delegates went wild with enthusiasm. From thousands of throats came mad shouts of hatred for the infidels. Swords flashed to greet the white man, the Messiah of whom the Koran had spoken, who would appear to lead the holy war against the enemies of the green flag of the Prophet.

Ostrovsky, the organizer of the Congress, had succeeded in attracting Enver Pasha, Turkey's dictator during the war, who was now living as a refugee in Turkestan. Enver Pasha, slaughterer of hundreds of thousands of men, women, and children, who had aroused the horror of the entire world, was trying to form an army in Russian Turkestan and adjoining areas, to fight Kemal Pasha, the leader of the new Turkey. The Bolsheviks expected to utilize his authority among the Mohammedans of the Near East, and in this way to increase their influence in Buchara, Afghanistan, and adjacent territories. They had no particular objection to supporting him in a small, private war of his own, as long as he was willing to submit to them.

But they did not want to be involved in any conflict with Kemal Pasha. So, when Kemal's representative, Ivrahim Tali, assured the Communist International of Turkey's friendship, Zinoviev barred Enver from appearing in person at the meetings of the Congress. Enver had offered his services to the revolution, and sworn that in the future he would use all his strength not only against Great Britain, but also against France and Germany, and that he would fight for an alliance of the Mohammedan world with the Soviet Union.

Enver Pasha left the Congress disappointed and bitter. In his talks with Zinoviev and Radek, he had realized that these were no European diplomats, but men who knew all the tricks of the Orient as well as he. He got neither money nor weapons.

It was only a short time after Baku that he started a holy war— against the Soviet Republic. He was lured into a trap by the Red Army and shot.

The Congress of Baku did not demand that Kemal Pasha choose between the wealthy and prosperous classes in Turkey and the poor peasants. After its close, he remained what he had been before its opening, a leader of rich and poor alike. The Comintern did not see in this compromise a contradiction to its own existence. Because of its support of Kemal Pasha, it refused to permit Turkey's Communists to appear openly in Moscow after Baku.

In Baku there had been no revolutionary proletarian groups. There had been only the chaotic wild flaming Orient.

Baku was just a dress rehearsal for the coming drama of the Orient, presenting the leaders of the world revolution to the Near and Far East.

ZINOVIEV'S TRIUMPH

From the East Zinoviev rushed to the West. At the beginning of October he was already on his way to the party Congress of the German Independent Social Democracy at Halle.

Everybody was surprised that the German Social Democrats, who represented the government in Germany at the time, gave Zinoviev, president of the Communist International, permission to enter their country. Radek was sure that the Social Democrats favored the coming split in the Independent Social Democracy in order to become again the sole Social Democratic organization in the country. He was certain that those who did not join with the Communists would soon return to the Social Democratic fold.

Zinoviev went by train to Reval, and from there by boat to Stettin, accompanied by a few powerful GPU men. Shortly after his arrival, the party Congress at Halle opened. Zinoviev again surpassed himself. His triumph was even greater than at Baku. Even his bitterest opponents admitted that they had never heard so powerful an orator.

He did not seek appeasement. He did not try to convince the enemies of Moscow, but to destroy them. For four hours his voice filled the huge hall. He talked like a god of revolutionary vengeance, denouncing the mortal sins committed against the holy spirit of Socialism, driving the reformists mercilessly from the temple of the labor movement.

The most thorough-going skeptics among the German Communists, men like Paul Levi, were enthusiastic. The newly won Communists among the Independent Social Democrats, who had shied away from a split in their party before this Congress, were now in

32

"seventh heaven." Zinoviev's flaming picture of victory was for them victory itself.

The Congress concluded in a frenzy of enthusiasm: a Communist mass party had finally been formed in Germany. The few thousand German Communists of the Spartacus group were now to be joined by the hundreds of thousands from the Independent Social Democracy.

Returning to Berlin, Zinoviev was so hoarse that he could not talk at the mass meetings where thousands upon thousands awaited his appearance. But his appearance alone was sufficient to bring out the same rush of acclaim as had greeted him in Baku and in Halle.

The cheers continued in Moscow and Petrograd. Zinoviev had risen to a place third in rank, after Lenin and Trotsky. His vacillation during the revolution of October, 1917, was forgotten. The entire Bolshevik party as well as the Communist International accepted him as an ideal chief of the High Command of the World Revolution.

A few months after Halle, the French Socialist Party in Tours and the Italian Socialist Party in Leghorn were split. Serrati, who in Moscow had voted for the twenty-one conditions, fell into the same conflict at home as had troubled his conscience in Moscow: fraternal unity among Socialists or obedience to the strictures of Bolshevist discipline?

After a long inner struggle, he decided to remain what he really was, a brother to his Socialist comrades. With the help of Zinoviev's agents, the Communists split off from the Socialist Party as a minority and formed a party of their own.

In Tours the picture was different. Cachin and Froissard knew no conflicts of conscience. The majority was on their side. Léon Blum and his followers, the minority, had to found a new Socialist party of their own.

All revolutionary dreams seemed to be realized: the Socialist state, the springboard of the world revolution; a powerful High Command guided by the most daring revolutionaries ever known to history; the Red Army of Trotsky burning with desire for action; mass parties in Germany, France, Italy, and Czechoslovakia; the capitalist world in the throes of the postwar depression.

The ultimate victory of Communism was as certain as the amen after a prayer. . . .

CHAPTER II

Giants and Pigmies

(From the Papers of Comrade X)

CALL TO MOSCOW

February, 1921

LATE AT NIGHT A COURIER OF THE CENTRAL COMMITTEE OF OUR French Communist Party brought me a wire they had received from Moscow:

"Insist on immediate departure of Comrade X for Moscow. Further delay impossible. (Signed) Secretariat of the Executive Committee."

Our Central Committee concurred. It is essential, they said, to keep the promise we made at the Second World Congress in Moscow, to cooperate with the Russian comrades by sending them experienced European collaborators.

I am sitting now in a compartment aboard the train to Berlin. There I am to receive my Russian visa.

I did not even have time to see Jeanne before I left. She is visiting her mother in Provence. I am really ashamed of myself—my thoughts are so full of Moscow. It is even a little difficult for me to call Jeanne's face to mind. . . . If she could only be with me on this trip into the land of my desire.

At the border my eyes are caught by the headlines in the German paper: "Famine in the Volga district! Hundreds of thousands starving to death!" Exaggerations of a cheap journalist. I know Russia is poor and hungry. For that I only love her the more. She is the home my heart has always longed for.

These pages—I write them to help keep my direction. I need a check on myself. When a life swings out on such sudden curves as mine, one is in danger of losing oneself. I have to become hard—hard against my own self.

I ought to think of my father as my model—he was as harsh to himself as he was kind to his fellows. My heart is filled with memories of the old man. How he helped and supported the tiny parish in the mountains of Haute Savoie, where he spent his life as minister. For thirty years he tolled the little bell of our village church. Had he forgotten even once, the very breath of our mountain valley would have been suspended.

For a man who has faith, it doesn't matter whether his faith is in God or in Communism. One has to understand faith. Comprehend it with the head. Feel it with the heart. One has to tempt one's heart through the labyrinthian paths of reason. To achieve the jump from Calvinistic theology to atheistic Communism, one must be hard with oneself.

While I was still wearing my minister's robes, the workers made me their comrade, and gave me their full confidence. The poorest of the poor persuaded me to become one of them. I have to prove my gratitude.

*   *   *   *   *

A few days' stay in Berlin. The social contrasts here are much stronger than in Paris. In the middle-class western end of the city, luxury without reticence or shame. In the working class quarters, hunger and misery, and a strange hopelessness in the eyes of the people.

In the Soviet Embassy on Unter den Linden, I received my visa from Mirov, the Comintern's technical agent. I like the Russian comrades. Mirov cares for me as though I were a child trying to take his first steps. He brought me warm underwear.

"You're going from the warmth of France into the cold of Russia and," he added jokingly, "you're not Russian: you won't be able to keep warm on vodka!"

As a sign of his confidence, he has entrusted me with a package of confidential letters to Zinoviev. I am sure that I will justify this confidence. I am happy.

RIDDLE OF KRONSTADT

March, 1921

On the first of March, I arrived in Petrograd. One of Zinoviev's secretaries, a peculiar creature with Mongolian eyes and head always held to one side, called for me at the station. She took me to the Hotel Continental, where all the Comintern delegates are quartered.

Today is gray and very cold. A strange heaviness spreads over the city. We pass groups of people talking excitedly. In front of all the public buildings I notice soldiers with bayonets. At the Neva bridges, machine guns. Automobiles crowded with armed workers speed through the streets.

My heart is heavy. I can't understand all this! The civil war came to an end long ago.

When can I see Zinoviev, I ask his secretary.

"Oh, I am afraid you will have to have patience for a few days. Zinoviev is very busy just now."

Next morning the sailors of Krondstadt revolt. I am depressed and confused. The same sailors whose armored cruiser Aurora, in October, 1917, directed their fire against the Winter Palace—are they turning their guns now against Lenin and Trotsky? This is impossible to understand.

Nobody bothers about me. I speak no Russian and am left entirely to myself. I walk around the streets; the cold penetrates my thin coat. At the Neva bridges, wood fires are burning, and I warm my hands at them like many others. Like thousands of others, I stare through the wintry fog that hovers over the river.

A distinguished-looking old gentleman addresses me. I shrug my shoulders, not understanding. The old gentleman addresses me in fluent French, saying how happy he is to see a real European.

"Do you know what is happening over there?" he asks, pointing to the fortress of Kronstadt whose contours are dimly visible through the fog. "That is the Third Revolution. The sailors are putting an end to Lenin and Trotsky. It is the just vengeance of fate! They will fall by the hands of those who raised them to power."

The next morning. It is still pretty dark. I am awakened by the sound of guns in the distance. I rise quickly. It is impossible to wash, the water is frozen in the basin.

I run to my observation post on the Neva. This time the bridge is blocked. I show the pass Zinoviev's secretary has given me. "Comrade X is a guest of the Soviet Government. All Soviet authorities are directed to give their brotherly support to Comrade X."

The soldier takes the paper and walks over to a group standing on the middle of the bridge, looking through field glasses towards Kronstadt. They consult each other, and then I am permitted to pass. As I approach the group I recognize Trotsky, very pale but calm; and Zinoviev, gesticulating in great excitement.

Only at the railing of the bridge do I notice the extraordinary panorama unrolling on the ice of the Neva. Thousands and thousands of soldiers and armed civilians are marching over the ice towards Kronstadt. From time to time, the fog is illuminated by spurts of yellow fire. Those are the guns of Kronstadt.

I can hear the heavy cracking of the ice. The sun is rising like a dim red ball. The fog lifts. Now the ice seems to be moving back and forth. More and more masses of soldiers march down the banks of the Neva and on to the ice. I am told later that delegates of the Tenth Congress of the Russian Communist Party, which happened to be in session at this time, were leading the storming soldiers. Among them were Voroshilov, Satonski, and Bubnov.

Over the whole scene an unspeakably somber atmosphere prevails. All faces are drawn. The guns of Kronstadt fire faster and faster. The cracking of the ice grows louder and louder. From a distance one can hear the storming troops roaring "Urra!"

Had I not seen all this myself, I would have declared it impossible. Infantry with bayonets storming a fortress surrounded by armored cruisers, across a frozen sound!

A few days later the rebellion is beaten. Across the ice of the Neva the defeated and captured sailors of Kronstadt are marched into the Peter-and-Paul Fortress. Thousands are court-martialled and shot, other thousands sentenced to long years of prison. There is not a hostile move among the masses of people who line the streets as the captured sailors march by.

Who has won here, and who has been defeated? I cannot answer the question.

* * * * *

A few days after my arrival in Moscow, I was asked to present myself to Zinoviev. He received me in his spacious study in the

Kremlin, and explained the details of my work in the Secretariat of the Executive Committee of the Communist International. Several times he emphasized the desirability of intimate cooperation between Russians and foreigners.

"Abroad there is frequent talk about a Moscow dictatorship over the Comintern. You will see for yourself that we would be overly happy if the foreigners would take upon their shoulders part of this dictatorship. It is too bad that they do so little of it. I hope some day we will be able to transfer the entire dictatorship to you foreigners, and shift the Executive Committee from Moscow to Berlin or Paris."

Zinoviev drowned me in a flood of questions about my impressions of the French and German Communist movements. His intimate knowledge of French affairs surprised me again and again. There was not a single important French Communist whose name he did not know, and whose articles in *l'Humanité* he had not read. He knew all the various political nuances. Obviously his memory was excellent.

After a few hours of talk, I had the feeling that Zinoviev had sucked me completely dry. I was just going to take leave of him, when he called me back from the door.

"You have come from Petrograd," he cross-examined me, squinting at me with one eye. "You must know the extraordinary difficulties we are having. I have a favor to ask you. Certain comrades will be traveling to Berlin within the next few days. There, things are taking a significant turn. It is not impossible that a new revolution is in the offing."

I interjected that, during my short stay in Germany, I had not heard a single word of this nature. Zinoviev paid no attention to my remark.

"In reality, Radek, Bukharin, or I should go to Germany immediately. But the risk is too great. We've all been expelled from Germany. Besides, none of us should leave Russia now while we're fighting here for our very lives. So we've decided to send Bela Kun to Germany. Will you accompany him?"

"I am ready to obey any order of the Executive Committee, but I can't see what good I'll be in Germany. I know neither the

38

country nor the German Communists sufficiently well to undertake any responsible action."

"No, I am not asking that of you. This is something different. Go to Berlin and report to me directly, as frequently as possible, your personal impressions. The situation is so complicated and our responsibility so vast that we need all the information we can get."

I agreed. But I was afraid that the task was beyond me. Zinoviev impressed me as a strong and shrewd man. But I would not say that he attracted me personally.

MISSION TO BERLIN

End of March, 1921

I first met Bela Kun on board the ship that took us from Petrograd to Stettin. In his entourage were two Hungarian comrades, one of them Pogany, the former War Minister of the Hungarian Soviet Republic, and a young German with a slight stutter who spoke an excellent French. They all knew about me. The German welcomed me in a friendly way, the Hungarians with much reserve.

Bela Kun did not show up the first day. He is seasick, they told me. The afternoon of the second day he appeared on deck.

"You are X. Zinoviev has told me about you. We will work well together. You will always do what I tell you. You know who I am!"

He looked at me, half mocking, half patronizing. He did not wait for my reply, but drowned me with such a rapid flood of words that it was impossible for me to understand. As he talked, he kept running up and down the deck.

"Yes, I'll show them how to make a revolution." He rubbed his hands. "Yes, I'll show them."

His Hungarian comrades ran along the deck beside him. Two little dogs running after their master.

In the evening we ate together in the big cabin of the ship. There I had even a better opportunity to observe Kun than during his monologue of the afternoon.

I had heard much about Bela Kun before this meeting. When he was People's Commissar of Foreign Affairs in the Hungarian Soviet Republic he was in the center of attention in Europe. Evidently he had the special confidence of Zinoviev who had sent him in his own stead to Germany.

How is it possible, I wondered, that a man with so little control over himself can be a real leader? Not that I judge a man by his table manners—although I have never met a plain worker who behaved as badly at table as Bela Kun.

The next day passed uneventfully. Every few minutes Kun ran inside to the radio room where cables were received. His Hungarian friends talked excitedly and with great rapidity. Together with the young German, I stretched out on the top deck and let the warm spring sun shine on my face.

By the time we arrived in Stettin, Kun's excitement was intense. He had dressed very carefully to resemble the Dutch exporter on whose passport he was traveling. The German customs and passport control was short. Nobody paid any attention to us.

We got into a big car waiting at the pier and drove towards Berlin at great speed. Kun seemed very dissatisfied. His face was scarlet, and he talked vehemently with a German comrade who had met us at the pier. In spite of all his efforts, he failed to pacify Kun.

In a few hours we reached Berlin. It was already dark and we stopped before an elegant house located in a sort of park. In the big dining room some German comrades, leaders of the Communist Party, were already awaiting us. After a quick meal, the conference began, and lasted into the early morning.

The Germans gave a short report. Under all circumstances it seemed necessary to them to dislodge the German government. Everything was prepared for action. The masses are ready to fight. Only the conditions in the party leadership are unfavorable, as the former party president, Paul Levi, and with him some other leading comrades, oppose our plans. But the masses in the party demand action!

Bela Kun opened immediately with a disagreeable personal attack on Paul Levi and the other opponents of immediate action. When one of the Germans intimated it might be desirable to win over at least the pillar of the party, old Klara Zetkin, who had been an intimate friend of Rosa Luxemburg's and enjoyed great popularity among the working masses of the country, Bela Kun fumed at him:

"You're a fool! Have you ever heard of hitching an old cow to a cart when you want to make quick progress?"

I knew Klara Zetkin personally. She had been the delegate of the Communist International in 1920 at the Party Congress in Tours, where the Communist Party of France originated. She was a great speaker and a great human being.

I decided to report Kun's rudeness in my first letter to Zinoviev.

I explained my mission to the German comrades who were very friendly and promised me all the assistance I wanted. I asked them to get me an interview with Paul Levi, who had resigned from the Party presidency. I wanted his opinion firsthand, to report to Moscow. But it took several days before I could accomplish my plans.

In Kun's quarters there was constant coming and going. Couriers were at his beck and call all the time. He dictated long manifestoes, orders, and articles. Everything was swinging into action.

Paul Levi lived in an elegant apartment house in the West End of Berlin. An elderly lady opened the door. Some time passed before Paul Levi received me. Time enough to observe the fine antique furniture, the tasteful rugs, and the glass closets containing beautiful old china.

Paul Levi wore a handsome morning gown, and had evidently just stepped out of his bath. Everything about him was cool, reserved. I repeated my name and asked for his interpretation of affairs, so that I might report it to Zinoviev. Levi spoke calmly and slowly—a man accustomed to weighing his words.

"Please write Zinoviev that I refuse to negotiate with his gray cardinals. After my experiences with Rakoczi, his last agent, who turns my every word around but isn't prepared to stand up for his own words, I will use only the written form of negotiation!" He arose and dismissed me with a brief nod.

"But, Comrade Levi, you misjudge me. I don't merit your suspicion. In all my life I have never yet uttered an untrue word!"

I spoke indignantly. This was the first time anyone had ever doubted my trustworthiness. Levi hesitated a moment, then sat down again.

"Excuse me if I have insulted you. My remarks were not personal. I don't know you. But my experience with Zinoviev is such that I have to proceed with utmost caution."

"I assure you I will report our conversation accurately and truthfully in Moscow."

Levi appeared to believe me, and went on to explain his conception in sentences that excited my admiration by their assurance and clean logic.

"Unbelievable things have happened. Our Central Committee has proclaimed a general strike and has attempted to drive the workers who do not follow their slogans by force out of the plants and factories. This sort of policy can lead only to a complete collapse.

"In the *Rote Fahne,* our main Communist daily in Berlin, insanity prevails." He took a newspaper from his desk and read: "No worker gives a hoot or a damn about the law. He picks up a gun where he finds it."

Bitterly he continued. "And this sort of language, mind you, after the party has asked for a general strike to assist the miners in Central Germany, without response. Write Zinoviev that this time I will turn to the public. I will not tolerate that his dilettantism and the tricks of the adventurers he is sending to Berlin, together with the idiots in the German Central Committee, shall completely destroy the Communist movement in Germany."

Returning to Bela Kun's headquarters, I confessed to myself that Paul Levi had made a deep impression on me. The self-assurance of his behavior, the logic and determination of his arguments, were much more impressive than Bela Kun's hysterics. On the other side, I wondered about Levi's elegance, the comfort and distinction of his living arrangements, that seemed to contradict my idea of a working-class leader. I could not conceive of such a man as the leader of a party consisting largely of half-starved unemployed.

Bela Kun pounced on me like a savage. "What did he say?" I reported briefly.

Kun yelled. "That scoundrel! That traitor! He should be shot like a mad dog!" He shouted and shrieked. I was disgusted and decided to avoid him as much as I could in the future.

The next morning there was a meeting with the leaders of the German Communists. The insurrection was coming to an end.

Hundreds of workers in Central Germany had been killed; thousands arrested by the police. Yet the masses in the country did not move. The German leaders vacillated and wanted to retreat. Only Bela Kun's wild authority prevented it.

For the first time I understood the mysterious power he was able to exert on the German Communists. Nobody could have remained unaware of the human frailties of Bela Kun, whom a peculiar fate had destined to become a revolutionary leader. There could not be the slightest doubt that most of the German Communist leaders were far superior to Kun, politically and morally. Yet they listened to him as to a high priest because behind him was the shadow of Zinoviev.

After a few days a complete retreat had to be called. The insurrection suffocated in its own smoke.

Kun went from one fit of hysterics into another. Frequently his yelling changed into weeping. Everybody stayed as far from him as possible, even his Hungarian friends.

My German friends had gotten me a room alone elsewhere. I could not bear Kun any longer. I stayed on for two weeks in Germany and collected material and information about the catastrophe that had befallen the working classes after the insurrection. I took a train for Central Germany and saw the unending misery in the mining villages. The few Communists who had not been arrested did not dare lift their eyes. The womenfolk cursed them.

I visited the courts and listened to Prussian judges, after a few minutes of hearings, sentencing revolutionary workers, or even men who had been arrested accidentally, to five, ten, or fifteen years of prison. The defendants were not permitted to say a word in their own defense.

I had another talk with Paul Levi, who had written an impassioned accusation against his comrades of the Central Committee. He compared them to the German general, Ludendorff, who had sent thousands and thousands to a senseless death.

I had won Levi's personal confidence although he knew I belonged to Bela Kun's delegation (whom, by the way, he called Genghis Kun). In saying goodbye, he pressed my hand.

"Try to give your report to Lenin, not to Zinoviev. Zinoviev's is the main responsibility for the disaster you have seen. Lenin is the only one who can take things in hand."

Only on board the ship back to Petrograd did I see Bela Kun again. To my great astonishment he was in good spirits. He conversed with animation. Among his companions were several leading German Communists who had participated directly in the insurrection. He behaved like a general returning from victorious battle. He seemed not to notice me. I was not unhappy about this.

CONFUSION IN THE HIGH COMMAND

May, 1921

Our delegation entered Petrograd in triumph. Bela Kun gave his report at a big meeting of the Petrograd Soviet with Zinoviev presiding. Workers of a textile factory presented him with a few yards of fabric and the message that, from now on, the plant would operate under the name of Bela Kun. Glowing with happiness, he told everybody who did or did not want to listen:

"You know, already the textile factory in Y is running under the name of Bela Kun!"

The man exhibited a ridiculous vanity. At the meeting he talked as if he had been a victor. It appeared that the defeat was only the first step to an inevitable tremendous victory. Zinoviev seemed to agree with him. I was treated by him with great reserve, and was told, at the end of a short conversation: "You understand, Comrade X, your mission was of an entirely confidential nature."

In Moscow I fought with myself for a while, whether to keep silent or to try, as Levi had counselled, to see Lenin. Radek cut my doubts short. In the dead of night, the telephone in my room at the Hotel Lux rang:

"Radek speaking. I just learned that you have been in Berlin. Please come over at once. I have sent a car for you—my secretary will pick you up."

At that time I did not know the Russian custom that made day out of night with perfect naturalness. I rose quickly and was glad of the invitation. In a few minutes we were at the Kremlin.

Radek's room was at the end of a long hall, in one of the massive old Kremlin buildings. The walk through that endless hall took much longer than the drive from the hotel to the Kremlin. Radek's room was dark and had a musty smell.

He came to the door, and a light shone through from the next room. "Come in quickly! I haven't much time."

Not very courteous, I thought. From the floor of his studio rose little mountains of books, periodicals, newspapers. One had to wind one's way through them, trying not to upset one while avoiding the other. I apologized, and Radek laughed heartily.

"Yes, of course, you're a Frenchman! You wouldn't forget your manners even among ruffians like myself." His French was somewhat crude and unpolished, but comprehensible. He looked as if he hadn't used soap in a week. Below his fingernails one could see black dirt. His beard was unkempt, his teeth yellow and discolored. Between his thick lips was a short pipe that gave out a suffocating cloud of smoke.

He offered me a seat on a turned-over bookcase, and a cup of coffee that tasted abominable. He himself sat on the floor, his back against a pile of books.

"All right. Now tell me everything you know."

When I stopped the first gray light of morning was filtering through the windows. In the cold air, the biting smoke stood as if frozen. I shivered. Radek had listened to me attentively and had made quick notes from time to time. Now he rose.

"I thank you very much," he said in a friendly voice. "You have rendered us a great service by your report."

"Would you be kind enough to arrange a conversation with Lenin for me?"

"With Lenin?" He looked at me surprised. "Do you doubt that your report will get to Lenin? Lenin hasn't much time for conversation. He works eighteen hours a day!"

"Maybe you could tell him of my wish to see him."

"If you insist, but I don't know whether Zinoviev's affection for you will be so warm afterwards."

I took my leave.

The very next evening I received an invitation to go and see Lenin. I was terribly excited when I was ushered into the reception room. There is no man in the world whom I adore more than Lenin. Now I was to see him face to face!

Lenin's secretary was a small, shrivelled woman with pale cheeks. "Comrade X?" she said. "You have fifteen minutes. Be as short as possible."

I had memorized everything I wanted to say, and in as brief a fashion as possible.

When I entered the room, Lenin immediately got up from his desk, came towards me, shook my hand, offered me a chair, and drew up another for himself alongside. My nervousness vanished. A feeling of absolute confidence came over me. I realized right away that I could talk with this man as with a father confessor.

His countenance was open and wholly good. His eyes studied me, clear and penetrating. In ten minutes I had finished my report. In Lenin's face there had not been the slightest change, nor had he interrupted me a single time. Now he rose.

"Please write a comprehensive report as quickly as possible. The entire affair is exceedingly important."

I replied that several detailed reports were already in the hands of Zinoviev. Lenin looked at me surprised.

"So? M-m . . . . . Then naturally it is not necessary."

I took my leave.

How is it possible that Zinoviev has kept my reports from Lenin? Because I expressed an opinion different from Bela Kun's? Is he trying to extricate himself from responsibility in this matter by petty tricks like that? What are the relationships among the Russian leaders, if such things are happening? In the hands of this group of men lies the leadership of the greatest revolutionary movement the world has ever known.

JEANNE AND THE BESPRIZORNY

June, 1921

Jeanne has arrived. I am overjoyed! I expressed my thanks to Comrade Piatnitsky for having arranged her trip so quickly. I am so full of thanks as to embarrass him.

Jeanne is more beautiful and charming than ever. She wins over all these people in Moscow immediately. In the hotel, she is already the favorite of the many children who swarm the halls, with their noise and shouts and games.

"Our little Parisienne," says the sinister GPU man stationed at the entrance to the hotel. "Our little Parisienne" is served first in the restaurant, and nobody complains when the waitress serves her a double portion of dessert.

Even Piatnitsky smiles with pleasure when he meets my little Jeanne. His secretary whispers to me: "Jeanne is a magician. Piatnitsky smiles only once in five years." Jeanne has conquered Moscow overnight.

In the first few days after Jeanne's arrival, I am very busy. One meeting after another. Endless discussions. Usually I get home so late that Jeanne is already sleeping. Jeanne does not make any comments, but I already see in her eyes the shadow of a reproach.

"You have too little time for me." My Jeanne is not a spoiled woman. She knows the hardships and difficulties of life. She has worked since early childhood. She is not curious, but she wants to know all my thoughts—everything that goes on inside me, because her tenderness wants to take all the burdens off my soul. . . . .

Living with Jeanne, I discuss everything with her. She is not a Communist and has never been a member of the party. "I do not want to concern myself with politics. I do not like conflict and fighting." But Jeanne is my confessor. I depend on her instinct, to judge good and evil in men and events.

When the week end comes, I throw aside all responsibilities and phone to Jeanne: "Darling, tomorrow we will have a whole day together! Tomorrow we will drive out to Sokolniki. The woods there are just like Fontainebleau."

On the way home I buy her a bouquet of spring flowers, gay, a can of fresh gray caviar, and a bottle of golden Crimean wine that tastes something like our Haute Sauterne at home.

Jeanne adores the flowers, and wants to taste the wine right away. Yet somehow I sense a change in her. Her voice is uncertain, her eyes damp as if she had been crying. I take her on my lap.

"Tell me what happened?"

Her eyes fill with tears.

"This morning I was crossing the street to do some shopping, when a wagon stopped in front of the hotel, delivering bread. Two policemen guarded the wagon. Passersby stared at the bread as at a mirage. They devoured it with their eyes.

"Then a terrible thing happened! A mob of abandoned children was circling around the wagon. I really can't say what happened. I'm ashamed that a thing like this is possible . . . . . When they were carrying the bread into the hotel, one loaf fell and broke into pieces. The children threw themselves like wolves at the pieces. A policeman immediately moved in on the mob of fighting children, and hit into them as if they were wild animals! One of them was a little girl not more than seven or eight years old. Her left arm was crippled. She had on a tattered man's coat over her little body that was covered with dirt. The policeman hit her so hard with his stick that she fell down as if dead. I ran towards him, yelling at him to stop.

"I carried the little girl into the hotel, to take her up to my room. But the doorman absolutely refused to let her in—this was strictly prohibited. I tore upstairs to get some bread and chocolate and bandages for the poor child. When I came down, she was gone! The doorman said she had run away.

"I'll never forget that child. I just can't stay in Moscow—I want to go home to France."

Jeanne clings to me sobbing, herself like a deserted child. I am terribly moved. These abandoned children in the streets of Moscow have been like a bad dream for me. I search for words to pacify Jeanne and to explain.

"In Russia there is a terrible famine now. Great parts of the country have been suffering from a severe drought. The peasants are starving by hundreds of thousands.

"In the Volga and Ukraine, there's not even a crumb of bread to be had. Hordes of peasants are running away from the hunger districts. In their flight, they lose their children, and often the children run away by themselves after their parents have died of hunger. Those are the abandoned children you have seen.

"The Soviet government is doing everything in its power, but there are many tens of thousands of them. There aren't sufficient

damned always to be misunderstood by the Comintern, that not only he himself, but many of the delegates as well were shocked.

Lenin listened to every word Lazzari said. In his face no muscle moved. Even when poor Lazzari addressed him directly. When Lenin spoke, he did not answer Lazzari, although the old man's eyes were looking to him for help. He left the reply completely to Zinoviev, who dealt with Lazzari in his attack on the Italian Socialist party.

I learned later that Lenin kept inquiring again and again about the health of his greatest political enemy in the Russian labor movement, Martov. Martov had emigrated to Berlin where his health had broken down. Yet he had not given up his sharp attacks against Lenin. Lenin replied in the same vein, but secretly directed the Soviet embassy in Berlin to give Martov all the material support and assistance that he might need.

How does the harshness against Lazzari fit in with the behavior of Lenin toward Martov? Has any other leader felt the horrible contradiction between the longing for humaneness and the inhumaneness of the statesman's task, more than Lenin? Once, in a conversation with Gorki, he said:

"Do you think that all this is not hard on me? It is very hard! But it is better to suffer than to fail."

I studied the Russian leaders as they finished their talks and received the customary storms of applause.

Zinoviev ended all his speeches with a shrill and enthusiastic "Long live the world revolution!" or "Long live the Communist International!" During the applause, he would toss back his curly hair, hesitate an instant, then walk back slowly to his seat, his face mirroring his triumph.

Trotsky denied himself all the rhetorical banalities of Zinoviev. His speeches were so powerful, he needed no artificial finale. His face remained unmoved, untouched, by the applause. He would stand like a general, home from victorious battle, accepting the people's thanks as his due.

Lenin always concluded his speeches in a logical, never a rhetorical way. Sometimes he would add a final sentence like: "If we act this way, then we will have a chance to win," or "That is all I have to say." Frequently there was not even such an ending. But whatever the ending, the ovations never ended, and unfailingly Lenin suffered the same painful embarrassment each time. Quickly he would gather his papers together. Eyes lowered, face closed, he would disappear as fast as possible from sight.

Of the same Lenin it is said that for his adversaries he has a deadly bite. When he wants to destroy an adversary or an enemy, he never lets go! His logic then is a sharp dagger, his humor a tight hard clamp. He does not know mercy until he thinks the enemy destroyed. Attacking, his precision brain functions as if emptied of all emotion.

On the surface it appears as if Lenin were full of contradictions. Yet actually he is always in balance, because he has the strength to keep his emotions within the core of his being, and prevent them from penetrating to the outside. He does not allow his personal sympathies to conflict with the political exigencies of his statesmanship. With nearly all of his intimate associates he has had sharp political conflicts. Yet all of them surround him with the same personal devotion, devoid of ulterior motive.

He has the ability to destroy the ideas of a man without touching the man himself. He himself does not hesitate to admit a blunder that he has committed, with complete frankness. There is no trace of personal vanity in him.

Frequently I ask myself whether I am not building too ideal a picture of Lenin. Yet I notice that he always makes the same impression on others. When he leaves the hall, all eyes follow him as if afraid to lose sight of his slight figure. . . . .

"WE ARE NOT TO BLAME THAT WE ARE ITALIANS!"

Zinoviev told the Congress about an incident at the conference of the Italian Socialist Party in the fall of 1920. The delegate of the Comintern had been received with cries of "Long live the Pope!" This was a demonstration against the categorical commands of Moscow which were likened to papal edicts. Some delegates had let loose a pigeon in the halls to caricature Zinoviev's ambassador as a message carrier without will of his own.

Early in 1921 the Italian workers had occupied plants, factories, power houses. Their revolutionary activity was no less energetic than that of the Russian workers in October, 1917. Throughout all of this, Serrati succeeded in maintaining his majority in the Socialist Party in opposition to Moscow's insistent demands to form a revolutionary, centrally directed Bolshevik organization, to rid it of the hesitant reformist elements, and to utilize it for a speedy accomplishment of revolutionary victory.

Mussolini and his Fascist gangs were threatening Italian democracy at the very time that the Comintern suffered this defeat. Zinoviev placed the blame for the failure of the Italian workers to push the revolution to a victorious end entirely on Serrati, for his having refused to split the party. His words were scornful and angry.

I talked to Serrati's friend Maffi. Maffi is a physician with a great name in Italy. He is adored by the Italian workers. I asked him to explain to me why Zinoviev's friends in Italy do not want to separate from Turati, who is an open enemy of the Communist International. Maffi showed me an election manifesto written by Turati:

"Read that and you will understand why, although it was easy for Zinoviev to throw the enemies of the Communist International out of the Independent Social Democratic Party in Germany, it is so difficult to separate the revolutionaries from Turati in Italy."

I read Turati's manifesto directed against the brutality of Mussolini and his Fascists: "Do not despair, brothers! Do not be subdued but do not become enraged. I give you my oath, brutal force will not bring fruit to those who use it against you! When the storm is past, you again will be the strong! Do not give them an opening. Do not respond to their calumnies. Be good! Be patient! Be holy! As you have been for a thousand years, continue to be.

"Be tolerant. Be conciliatory. Do not despair! The less intent you are on vengeance, the more you will be revenged. Those who are lighting the flames of terror against you will tremble before their own works. There is still war—the war that does not want to die, the war that continues its contemptible existence, the war that nonetheless will die!

"You are the peasants of Italy, its labor and its peace. That is

55

why you are their enemy, but that is also why you are the certain victors and the future!"

Maffi explained this strange document to me: "Turati is not a tumor that we can cut out of the body of the party, as Zinoviev wants. Turati is an attitude of mind, a sickness of the soul, if you like, that can be overcome but that cannot be operated upon.

"I know it is incomprehensible in Moscow to oppose to the wild terror of the Black Shirts of Mussolini only submission and suffering. But the Italian masses know that Turati is sincere—he believes what he says, and that is why a great part of our workers believe in him.

"To try to remove Turati by force would mean to cut into the revolutionary heart of our party. We are innocent, and we cannot be blamed for being Italians."

Many of the foreigners who come to Moscow carry with them the traditions of their homelands. If they defend their traditions, they immediately run into conflict with the icy logic of the world revolution. They retain their traditions and lose their homes. For the home now has become Moscow.

*　*　*　*　*

Lenin is deeply concerned with developments in Italy. Reports come in daily that the workers' cooperatives and trade union buildings have been raided by gangs and destroyed. Many Communist and Socialist functionaries have been tortured and killed by the gangs. The name of the leader of these gangs, that call themselves *"arditi populo,"* is mentioned more and more often; a former editor of the Socialist paper *Avanti*—Benito Mussolini!

Radek told me that Lenin continues to ask for reports about the new Fascist movement. One day there was an extended discussion between Lenin, Zinoviev, and Radek about this new counter-revolutionary organization. Zinoviev compared them to the Russian Black Hundred, a pogrom gang that had frequently been exploited by the police.

"No, this isn't the same. This is a different phenomenon, something very much more dangerous," said Lenin. "How would it be to have this Mussolini killed? He is apparently a talented and

56

dangerous bandit. The fact that he started his career in the labor movement makes him even more dangerous!"

Radek and Zinoviev didn't know what to reply. The Bolsheviks in general refused to have anything to do with individual terror. Lenin did not insist.

They decided to have a talk about this with the Italian comrades. Lenin didn't forget. At frequent intervals he inquired whether Zinoviev and Radek had done anything against Mussolini.

Several things were tried. But the Italians did not have the matter at heart, and besides they were not organized properly for such undertakings. Lenin's suggestion evaporated.

KARL RADEK, MEPHISTOPHELES OF THE COMINTERN

One of Zinoviev's main concerns during the sessions of the Congress was to prevent public discussion of his responsibility for the March events in Germany. It was not easy. Klara Zetkin was difficult to silence. Her personal respect for Zinoviev was below zero. Zinoviev therefore preferred to let her give vent to her anger in small closed conferences and to avoid replying at the open sessions of the Congress.

At the committee meetings Bela Kun was the scapegoat and the target for all attacks.

For the plenary sessions Zinoviev proceeded according to a well-defined plan. He removed discussion of the March events from his own report, and handed this task to Radek whose speech was scheduled for a day or two later. Consequently a vote of confidence on the past activity of the Executive Committee was taken before there had been any discussion about the March events in Germany.

This caused a conflict with Loriot, a simple and sincere man who hated this sort of diplomacy. He was the most important figure of the French delegation to the Third Congress and had been Lenin's friend during the difficult war times in Switzerland. He was a silent introspective man, the very opposite of Vaillant-Couturier, one of the other French delegates, whose oratorical powers made the delegates of the Congress forget that during the war Vaillant had been an enthusiastic patriot. At that time a captain in the French army, he had received several military decorations and medals for his heroic

57

deeds. Loriot had passed many of the war years in prison for his anti-militarist propaganda.

During the sessions of the French delegation, Loriot had already announced his intention to put the problem of the German March events and Zinoviev's responsibility for them directly to the plenary sessions of the Congress.

"We are lost if we permit the introduction of such methods!" He moved to defer the vote on Zinoviev's report until after the discussion of the March events. Zinoviev, who felt the move was directed against himself, replied sharply:

"If you, Comrade Loriot, want to express your lack of confidence, then please do it openly. Vote with 'Yes' or 'No.' "

Zinoviev knew that he would have the majority of the delegates on his side, most of them knowing nothing about the background of this dissension. Loriot was pushed into a cul-de-sac by Zinoviev's way of putting the question. If he insisted on his move he would have to vote against the entire Executive Committee, therefore also against Lenin. He did not give in to Zinoviev, however, nor did he enter the cul-de-sac that Zinoviev had prepared for him. He evaded the issue and retreated.

From then on he did not say another word throughout the discussions, and his calm and thoughtful voice was replaced by the resounding tenor of Vaillant-Couturier.

But what did Radek do? When Loriot made his motion he called so loudly into the hall that everyone could hear: "Why this motion? The Executive Committee did not make the March events!"

Zinoviev had used a parliamentary trick; Radek an arrogant lie. I was even more amazed when I saw Radek, perhaps an hour after this little episode, in a corner of the huge hall surrounded by a group of delegates laughing hilariously at one of his well-known stories.

Is this man really a thorough-going cynic as some people have it? His life might have made him into one.

His satire knows no inhibitions. He directs his satirical arrows against the hostile bourgeois world—but uses even sharper ones against his own friends, the revolution, and particularly against his own self.

REVOLUTIONARY LAUGHTER

A few days ago I heard Radek tell one of his satirical stories. Some foreign comrades had asked him to explain to them the principles of Soviet justice. Radek began at once.

"You are aware that we have discarded the principle of bourgeois law, to regard a crime as something in itself and to condemn it as such. For us the social motive of the crime is decisive. We attempt to fight crime by destroying the social milieu that produces it.

"Some time ago a habitual murderer was being tried by the people's court in Kharkov. Dumb and indifferent, he was standing in front of his judges.

"But his attorney, a young lawyer who had just graduated and was completely engrossed with the revolutionary spirit of our reforms of criminal law, would not give up so easily.

" 'Comrade Murderer,' he asked, 'what was your father?'

" 'My father? My father, Comrade Lawyer, was a murderer like me.'

"The attorney turned to the judges. 'Look here, Comrade Judges, his crime is to be explained by inheritance. As you all know, this is the result of the social milieu.'

"The judges were not very impressed. Yet our attorney did not give up. 'Comrade Murderer,' he asked, 'what was your mother?'

" 'My mother? A pickpocket.'

"Now our attorney saw a new chance. 'Comrade Judges,' he said, the case becomes clearer from moment to moment. You cannot possibly sentence this man to the highest punishment. Even his poor mother was driven by this damnable capitalist social order to thievery, in order to protect her children from hunger!'

"The attorney felt that the judges softened a bit. He pushed further. 'Comrade Murderer, have you any brothers or sisters?'

" 'Yes, a sister.'

" 'What is your sister?'

" 'My sister? My sister, Comrade Lawyer, is a prostitute.'

"Now our attorney knew the turning point of the trial had come. 'Comrade Judges, you see,' he said, 'you will have to acquit this man. There is not the slightest doubt the social milieu alone is responsible.'

"The judges were nearly won over. One of them, wishing to acquaint himself further with the defendant, asked him: 'Have you any other sisters or brothers?'

" 'Yes, a brother.'

" 'What does your brother do?'

" 'He is in Moscow at the Workers' University.'

"The game was won now. Was not the brother in Moscow a confirmation of the correctness and progressiveness of a theory of criminal law based on the social milieu?

" 'You see, Comrade Judges,' interjected the lawyer, 'the brother of the defendant has found his way back to us. Our Soviet order has helped him to overcome the social milieu which is responsible for these crimes.'

"The judges were convinced. The president of the court turned with sincere benevolence to the murderer. 'Tell me, Comrade Murderer, what does your brother do at the Workers' University?'

" 'Oh,' replied the murderer proudly, 'my brother's a phenomenon! His head has been cut off and put into alcohol. He was born without ears.' "

What is back of this satirical urge of Radek's? Does he use it as a device to increase his popularity? He is one of the most popular speakers in Moscow. The listeners at all his meetings wait for his celebrated anecdotes and jokes.

Such an interpretation, however, would be banal. A man whose essays and articles exhibit not only biting satire but also deep pathos does not seek popularity like a barker at a fair. Once I heard Radek talk at a school of young officers who were about to leave for the front. He talked about the meaning of death with such sincere emotion and such profundity that he completely enthralled his young listeners.

It seems to me Radek's entire character is different from what it appears to be. He is to Bolshevism what Chaplin is to the movies. . . . . His life in reality is a painful grimace. It is the revenge for a childhood spent in misery between physical dirt and the monotonous abracadabra of the Talmud. Revenge against the bourgeois world that made a pariah out of him. Revenge against

60

his revolutionary friends who did not want to share their table with this still uncouth Bohemian.

Sometimes Radek's satire changes suddenly into blind hate. This happened during the Congress, when he was making Paul Levi his target. All at once, trembling with rage, he cried out to the defenders of Levi: "When did anyone ever see this man in a revolutionary trench?"

But it was not the trenches of the revolution that Radek really had in mind. Levi had stood up under the difficulties of the underground work as courageously and bravely as had Radek. Radek was really thinking of the trenches of life, where one is placed through no merit or fault of one's own. Radek hates not Levi, but the culture, the family background and assurance—everything that he himself has never possessed.

Radek's satire is the instinctive gesture of a revolutionary Ahasuerus afraid that his wanderings will come to an end in a world at rest, that the revolution itself will cease to move and will become a norm and a standard. Most of all he is afraid to stand still and feel his loneliness.

Radek seems to me the most tragic and unhappy figure of Lenin's circle.

NICOLAI BUKHARIN

Bukharin is altogether different from Radek. In the Party he is endearingly called Bukharchik. He comes from a comfortably situated family of intellectuals and has never suffered privation, not even during his exile. From him emanates the real atmosphere of Russia—of its landscape, its literature, and its music. Bukharin is completely adjusted and harmonious. He is in favor with everyone.

It is impossible not to love him. Even in dissensions he disarms his opponents by the sincerity of his convictions and the charm of his humor. After the sharpest political fight there is never the least personal animosity against him.

He enjoys sketching finely drawn caricatures of the various Communist leaders on scraps of paper, but they end up in the waste basket before they can hurt anyone's feelings.

Bukharin alone among the Bolshevik leader-team does not permit his scientific and artistic inclinations to be submerged in his political tasks and functions. His knowledge is encyclopedic. He is at home in political economy and philosophy, in literature and in the natural sciences.

In the garden of his little frame house near Moscow, where he spends his days of rest, he has a collection of snakes that he studies as attentively as his material for the theses he writes for the sessions of the Congress.

He knows the Latin and Greek classics as well as the old and modern Russian, German, French, and English literatures.

Bukharin is gentle and does not like to stand alone. He never tries to dominate anyone. He seeks everybody's friendship—his entire character is a direct negation of any claim to authority.

One day the chauffeur at the Kremlin garage whom he had asked by telephone to send up a car and who had misunderstood his name, refused his request rudely. Bukharin as a member of the highest Russian political authority, the Politbureau, had the right to have a car at his disposal at all times. But it did not occur to him to insist on his right. He preferred to walk a long way home with a heavy burden of books.

None of the Russian leaders is seen as frequently in the streets of Moscow as Bukharin. He always looks the same—high boots of Russian leather that suit his short figure badly; a Russian blouse, blue in winter, gray in summer. On his head always a cap tilted as if it wanted to say: Look how smart I am! His light blue eyes look out from under the cap, a friendly small blond beard frames a face that wins everyone's liking immediately. It is to Bukharin among all the Bolshevik leaders that I feel myself most drawn.

HIGH COMMAND WITHOUT LENIN

May, 1922

After the close of the Third Congress the atmosphere in Moscow changed. Crops were better than in past years, famine began to die down. Slowly the starving children disappeared from the streets. Foods one hadn't seen for years made their appearance on the markets.

Moscow was a convalescent taking his first slow faltering steps after a long illness.

In the Comintern the feverish activity of the Congress days subsided. Piatnitsky modernized the Comintern building from top to bottom and equipped the headquarters of the world revolution with up-to-date business machines.

Zinoviev, Bukharin, and Radek worked in their offices in the Kremlin whose high red walls were just a few steps away from the Comintern building. Every two weeks the entire Executive Committee of the Comintern got together at Zinoviev's office to discuss important questions in detail. These sessions were like Congress meetings in miniature, with representatives of all Comintern parties participating. It was only at such plenary sessions that final decisions could be made.

These sessions were always held in the huge hall belonging to Zinoviev's offices. Before the revolution the secret council of the Czar had met there. The hall was spacious and elaborately furnished. The heavy wooden doors were hand carved, the floor mahogany. The great arched windows and the glistening crystal chandeliers were heavily draped in red silk.

In the beginning of May, 1922, such a session was in progress. The members of the Praesidium of the Communist International sat around a long conference table. As usual, Zinoviev was presiding. Bukharin was speaking, when suddenly the telephone rang. Zinoviev took up the receiver.

His face drained of color as he listened. He was trembling. Everyone jumped up frightened. Bukharin too grew pale when Zinoviev whispered into his ear.

Finally Zinoviev said with effort: "I must ask to be excused. I don't feel well. I have to leave."

He hurried out with Bukharin. Radek took the chair. But he also was nervous, and a German comrade moved to adjourn the meeting.

I and some others were asked by Radek to stay behind. Our eyes were fastened on him, everyone knowing something terrible must have happened. But no one was prepared for what he told us.

"Lenin has suffered a severe stroke. He is completely disabled."

* * * * *

Lenin recovered. In July he was able to work again. But the nervous

63

tension that had set in that afternoon in May did not recede.

The Fourth World Congress which gathered in November, 1922, showed all signs of having been improvised. Lenin appeared only once for a short talk. His face was haggard, and unspeakable fatigue showed in every movement. When he left the meeting hall the delegates rose and gave him an ovation that did not end. Nobody thought this would be a parting farewell.

After the sessions, groups of delegates marched past his rooms and sang the revolutionary songs of their home countries. The Italians were the most diligent, singing their *"Bandierra Rossa,"* happy when Lenin appeared at the window.

Spring 1923

In March, 1923, Lenin suffered a second stroke, which disabled him permanently. Although he had never participated in our current work, it seemed as if everything had come to a standstill.

Zinoviev, Bukharin, and Radek were frequently absent from our meetings, so that no important decisions could be made. Often weeks went by without the president of the Executive Committee having been available.

Once Zinoviev asked me to give him a report in person. I had to wait about an hour in his reception room. At the door of his studio, I ran into a stocky man with coarse features, a narrow forehead, and dark piercing eyes. Somewhat later I learned that this was Stalin. I had not met him before in Moscow.

Unfortunately, while the work in the Comintern was in disorganization, new tension arose in Germany. France had occupied the Ruhr, the German government having sabotaged reparation payments. Inflation in Germany was moving ahead in a wild swing. This time all signs pointed to a revolutionary crisis!

German comrades came to Moscow more and more often, to seek advice and assistance. Yet the Russian leaders had very little time for them. Lenin was on his deathbed. It was now impossible to organize any conferences.

The German comrades ran from Zinoviev to Trotsky, from Trotsky to Bukharin, from Bukharin to Radek, and back again! Radek went to Germany on missions several times. Each time he returned, his attitude became more mysterious. Nobody among us foreigners in the Comintern could have said what the policy of the International during the German crisis was.

Summer 1923

In July, 1923, I was sent to Paris with the task of urging the French Communists to intensified activity against the Ruhr occupation. I was happy to return to Paris. Jeanne accompanied me, feverish with excitement and joy when we crossed the French border and saw the first French customs official.

In the dining car she immediately ordered a glass of Pernod, and was a little tipsy by the time we reached Paris. It was a hot and sticky summer day. The air at the Gare du Nord was unbearable. We inhaled it with deep breaths.

I found the French Communist party greatly changed. There was much more activity, courage, and determination in it. The masses were embittered and excited about Poincaré's Ruhr invasion. They desired real peace at last.

"Poincaré, c'est la guerre! A bas la guerre!" I heard these cries night after night at mass meetings filled to overflowing from the suburban workers' districts.

Shortly after my departure on a last leisurely walk on the Boulevard St. Michel, I met a friend whom I had not seen since my university days. He had chosen a path altogether different from mine. He worked as editor of the *Matin,* one of the most reactionary newspapers of Paris.

Knowing that I had been employed in Moscow during the last few years, he observed ironically: "Your Russian friends are again working hand in glove with the Prussian generals!"

I replied angrily: "Your newspaper reported some time ago with as much truth that parents in Soviet Russia eat their children!"

Unperturbed, he answered: "You just investigate carefully. The Russians are secretly shipping arms to the Germans, arms that the Treaty of Versailles does not permit to be made in Germany."

We parted cold and hostile. This time it was more difficult for me to leave Paris than two years before.

On my return to Moscow, I gave a detailed report, and in conclusion added a joking word about my meeting with the *Matin* editor. To my great surprise, Radek pounced upon me.

"Comrade X, please do not concern yourself with matters that you do not understand!"

I replied with even greater aggressiveness: "Up to this moment I have regarded the tale of that man as a typical Parisian *'bobard.'* If there is really some truth in it, I demand an explanation!"

Radek already regretted his faux pas.

"Naturally it was only a *'bobard.'*" But my suspicions had been aroused. From that day on, I began to look at Comintern policies with rather changed eyes.

CHAPTER III

Financial Agent of the Comintern

(From the Memoirs of Comrade Y)

Y FATHER WAS A SOCIALIST UNDER BISMARCK, A SUFFERER
from the Iron Chancellor's anti-Socialist laws. He was forced
to move from his home and begin anew in the hills of Thuringia, where I was born. As a boy of fourteen I joined the Socialist
Youth Movement. Long before the World War, I had become an
ardent supporter of the left wing of the Social Democratic party in
Germany.

When I was still a small boy I became a printer's apprentice. I
loved the trade—particularly the meticulousness that my master insisted upon. He was an old man with long years of trade union
experience.

After my apprenticeship, I worked in many cities. In Berlin, the
Social Democratic party sent me to a party school. That was where
I first met Rosa Luxemburg who was then head of the school. She
inspired in me, as in everyone who knew her, a deep devotion.

When war broke out in 1914, I was in my early twenties. I joined
in Rosa Luxemburg's fight against the betrayers of Socialism and the
patriots who were leading the masses to slaughter at the battle fronts.

At the end of the war, Rosa Luxemburg was released from prison.
I helped her bring out the first issue of the *Rote Fahne,* the paper
of the Spartacus group that she founded in Berlin.

This group established itself as the Communist party of Germany
in December, 1918. I was proud to be one of the delegates at this
meeting. I was even prouder of the confidence Rosa Luxemburg
placed in me when she asked me to represent her group in Moscow
and to explain her attitude towards the founding of a new International.

I managed in weeks of travel, of escapes, of hiding, to make my
way through the White Guards blocking the routes into Russia.

In Moscow, Lenin often invited me in the evenings to visit him and his family in their room in the Kremlin. So it was through Lenin that I met my wife. She was the daughter of Inessa Armand, a French Communist who had become a close friend of Lenin and his wife, Krupskaya, in Switzerland, and had followed them to Russia. After the mother's early death, they took the daughter into their household and loved her like their own child.

OPEN SESAME

March, 1919

I was sitting in a small hall of the Kremlin, listening to one of the speeches at the founding Congress, when Peters touched me on the shoulder. "Come on, let's leave!" he whispered. "I'll take you to the treasure chamber of the Kremlin."

Together we crossed the wide cobblestoned courtyard of the Kremlin. An old man opened the heavy iron gates for us. I drew back: What a blinding hoard of riches—golden thrones, coronation chairs, tables, couches, mirrors. Before a diamond throne Peters stopped me. "Look here! The throne of Alexei Michailowitch, Czar of all the Russias in the seventeenth century. Little did the old bandit dream that one day he'd help pay for the world revolution. Fools! They left all those jewels here when they took to their heels; simply didn't think of them as capital. Of course not: the treasure chamber of the Czars . . . . the Holy of Holies. . . . ."

An expression of pain crossed the wrinkled face of the old keykeeper. "Don't worry, old fellow," said Peters, "nobody's going to take those keys away from you." He laughed. "He's kept those keys for more than thirty years; he's immune to the temptation of gold." Turning to the old man, he said: "I trust you more than my own men anyhow. . . . ."

Peters was a Lett, tall and lanky, with disagreeable piercing eyes. He was one of the chief officers of the Cheka and headed the Department of Internal Espionage. When the Cheka was rechristened GPU, he remained at the top of the organization.

The day after our visit to the Kremlin, he took me on a trip to Troitza-Lavra, one of the Russian cloisters that I had heard much about. On the way out I noticed some heavily armed Red Guardists following our car. Peters explained that jewels had been smuggled out of the cloister—a famous diadem from Troitza-Lavra had been found on a White officer. "I will teach them a lesson!"

The treasure chamber of the cloister was even more splendid than the one at the Kremlin. Hundreds of icons covered the walls of the vast cellar, which was dimly illuminated by a few glowing petroleum lamps. The frames of the icons were laminated with gold and jewels. The eyes of many of the bizarre saints were shining diamonds and rubies as big as marbles.

Peters stepped in front of one of the most beautiful of the icons, specially lit by a small golden lamp. The eye sockets of the saint were dark holes! "Who has gouged out the shining eyes of your honorable saint?" The Russian priest who accompanied us trembled and murmured incoherently into his long beard. Peters drew his pistol. The priest sank down on his knees crossing himself and swore by all the saints and the life of the Czar that he knew nothing.

Peters ordered a guard to stay in the treasure chamber, and we went on to the chapel in the second interior courtyard, followed by the abbot who had joined us in the meantime. Ignoring the protestations of the abbot, he parted the heavy velvet drapes, embroidered all over with gold and jewels, and disappeared into the darkness.

In a few minutes he returned, some large rubies in his hands. "Are these the eyes that you gouged out, you damned. . . . . I'll teach you . . . . to smuggle the jewels out to the Whites. . . . . Return everything immediately to the treasure chamber . . . . nothing but the objects that you need for your religious services stays in the sanctuary!"

I disliked the scene I had witnessed. Peters swore: "These damn priests, they have plundered the entire countryside for centuries— hoarded tons of gold in their treasure chests. Now the gold is ours, and we'll use it—whether it comes from a throne or a monstrance!"

DIAMONDS IN TRANSIT

April, 1919

Before I returned to Germany, Zinoviev asked me to get in touch with Rudnyansky, Secretary of the Communist International, to discuss with him the money I was to take along to Berlin. This was the first time anything about money was mentioned, and it came out only casually at the close of a long conversation.

It caused me some embarrassment. I had received no authority from my party to ask for or to accept money in Moscow. I regarded it as my duty to speak to Zinoviev about it. He smiled in a friendly and superior fashion.

"Comrade Y," he said, "these are really *petit bourgeois* objections. We are members of one party! Our money is your money. You should realize that the Soviet government decided as early as a year ago to set aside in its budget two million rubles to support and further the international revolutionary movement."

This was completely new to me. Zinoviev continued: "And anyhow, what we are really doing is paying debts. During the past years we often got money from the Social Democratic party of Germany; many of our party conferences abroad got under way only because old man Singer furnished us with the wherewithal."

Singer had been the powerful comptroller of the German Social Democratic party. I had known the friendly old man very well.

"You don't expect us to return the money to the Social Democrats! Those counter-revolutionaries! We give it to you—we give it to Rosa Luxemburg's friends."

The following morning I asked Zinoviev's secretary, Pikel, to show me the decree to which his boss had referred. I studied it with the greatest care. It ran as follows:

> Decree of the Sovnarkom, December 26, 1917. Taking into consideration the fact that Soviet power bases itself on principles of international solidarity of the proletariat, and on the brotherhood of the toilers of all countries; that the struggle against war and imperialism can lead toward complete victory only if waged on an international scale, the Soviet of People's Commissars considers it necessary to offer assistance by all possible means, including money, to the left international wing of the labor movement of all countries, regardless of whether these countries are at war or in alliance with Russia or neutral.
>
> For this reason, the Soviet of People's Commissars decides to grant two million rubles for the needs of the revolutionary international movement and to put it at the disposal of the foreign representatives of the Commissariat of Foreign Affairs.

I thought and thought: Two million rubles! That's the equivalent of five million gold marks. For what purpose were these small Communist parties to use this tremendous sum? And why hadn't the Russian comrades asked us what we thought about this? I was utterly confused.

At that time I was still completely immersed in the tradition of the German labor movement. I had learned that a Socialist labor party should support itself; that it should be built financially from the savings of its members, so that the workers would regard it as their own. I recalled also how my mother used to take half a mark each Friday evening out of the wages my father brought home, and say: "Don't forget to pay the party and trade-union contribution." I myself had been overjoyed when I paid my first twenty pfennig dues, as a fourteen-year-old apprentice, out of my first week's wage of three marks.

Doubt and irritation remained with me. Why was this not discussed at the Congress? Why was this taken up with each delegate individually? I decided to present my doubts to Lenin.

I was even more confused the next day, when Rudnyansky came to see me. He was a former officer in the Hungarian army, a captain in one of the proud Honved-Regiments, and had been a prisoner of war in Russia. Trained there for Bolshevism in Bela Kun's school for Hungarian war prisoners, he was now one of the secretaries of the Communist International. He brought with him a pretty heavy bag filled with diamonds.

"What shall I do with this?" I asked. "The Spartacus group does not run a jeweler's shop. What will the workers say?"

"Nothing, because they won't know anything about it," answered Rudnyansky. "We can't give you anything else. Gold is too heavy to carry along, so you will have to take these jewels. They are worth about a quarter of a million." I was flabbergasted. "What do you expect us to do with a quarter of a million?" Rudnyansky laughed: "You'll be surprised how quickly you will spend this money. A big party needs money. You will have to have newspapers, you will have to pay salaries. Without money there is no conquest of power."

In spite of my intention, I did not take the matter up with Lenin. The evening before my departure I saw him for a few minutes. He

71

looked so tired and worn that I had not the courage to disturb him with my questions.

Rudnyansky turned out to be a good prophet. The money was quickly spent. In the storm of events that swept Germany at the time, nobody even raised the question whether it was right to accept this money. We had other problems. The revolution seemed just around the corner.

Everything had changed. During the war we had spent very little. A leaflet cost next to nothing: my printer friends printed them secretly in one of the big Berlin printing establishments. If we needed money for some purpose, we collected it among ourselves. We all had jobs—nobody even thought of expecting money from the party.

Now we had no time for jobs any more. The party needed our entire time.

March, 1920

I had a hard time. With no experience in the diamond trade, we had to pay dearly for our lessons. One of our men trying to sell a big stone to a jeweler had to take to his heels, leaving the stone behind, when the jeweler summoned a policeman to identify the seller. Another time, we had given a diadem to a shop to be sold. The shopkeeper displayed it in his window, and a few days later a Russian prince claimed it as his property. The shop had to turn the diadem over to a court. Naturally our man did not return to claim the diadem.

Finally I was relieved of the diamond business. A representative of the Executive Committee of the International, Comrade T, arrived in Berlin from Moscow, and took all financial matters into his hands.

One day I chanced to ask him about Rudnyansky. "Forget that name!" he frowned back. "That scoundrel was sent a few months ago to open some large accounts for the Comintern in Paris, London, and Rome. Many hundreds of thousands of dollars were involved. He disappeared with the money."

I was dumbfounded: Rudnyansky had been one of the secretaries of the Communist International, an intimate of Zinoviev and Radek. Many years later I heard that Rudnyansky had purchased a huge estate in Rumania.

Berlin now became the center for Communists from all Western countries, on their way to Moscow. T received them, examined their papers, and equipped them generously with money. In grand style he took charge of the financial matters of all Communist parties in the West, and organized a publishing house that spread Communist literature in millions of copies throughout Europe.

For all its splendor, Comrade T's reign didn't last long. After two or three years of absolute rule, he was shorn of some of his powers. Finally only his publishing ventures remained, and these too were taken from him at the end of 1924.

THE GUARDIAN OF THE FINANCIAL GRAIL

March, 1922

When I returned to Moscow in March, 1922, I found everything changed from 1919. Only Zinoviev still had his offices in the Kremlin. The Comintern had moved into a tremendous building directly adjacent to one of the gates of the Kremlin on the Machavaya. All financial affairs were now in the hands of a new man, Ossip Piatnitsky. He was a man of few words, relatively young but already gray —a man completely devoted to the Communist movement. Piatnitsky became the good spirit of the Comintern in financial matters.

He explained to me at great length the new financial policies of the Comintern. "Just as our party now emphasizes precise accounting in Russian affairs, so the Comintern will have to proceed. The period of 'war Communism' is past. If we had won out quickly in Germany, then you Germans would have put order into the finances of the Comintern. Now we have to do it ourselves."

The Finance Committee responsible for Comintern affairs was composed of Zinoviev; Solz of the Control Commission; Grinko of the State Bank; Dzierzynski, the head of the Cheka; and Piatnitsky. From now on, each Communist party was to hand in, semiannually, a budget plan which would be examined by this Finance Committee. The Executive Committee of the Comintern would receive a fixed amount of money on the basis of these budget plans, as well as extraordinary sums for extra-budget purposes as, for instance, election campaigns and other unpredictable and incalculable events. All budget plans were to be drawn up in terms of dollars.

Piatnitsky, a former tailor, had modern bookkeeping machinery installed. System and order reigned everywhere.

"Don't think," said Piatnitsky, "that the Comintern will continue to be the good uncle, with pockets full of money for you to put your hands in. We have little foreign exchange. Even the biggest store of jewels and art objects finally comes to an end. European and American markets are saturated with our diamonds and pictures. Prices are low . . . . we need foreign exchange for the import of machinery and the installation of scientific laboratories. In a word, each Communist party should attempt to be self-supporting, and ask from Moscow only such sums as it cannot raise itself but urgently needs. The gold stream from Moscow cannot run forever!"

This turn of events made me very happy. "The gold stream from Moscow" had been a source of constant worry to all of us. The atmosphere of financial carelessness that surrounded us was disturbing.

I proposed as small a subsidy from Moscow as possible and drew up a minimum budget. When we finished, we found to our great surprise that it was higher than the average subsidy we had been receiving during the last two years! The party had expanded; we had bought many buildings and printing establishments; we employed double the number of people from the year before. We had to hand in a request for tens of thousands of dollars more than last time!

That was a hard blow; we couldn't rid ourselves of doubts and worries. We knew that in France, Italy, and Czechoslovakia, Moscow money was used to overcome political differences.

I asked Zinoviev what his opinion was in regard to such methods, but he was evasive. I realized that among many of our own comrades a servility towards Moscow was developing that had nothing to do with enthusiasm for the Russian revolution. After our merger with the left wing of the Independent Social Democratic party, many new elements had entered the party, and some had pushed into its leadership. With them a new atmosphere of careerism had grown up.

November, 1923

Since July we had been preparing an armed insurrection. We needed millions for the purchase of arms which were offered to us from all sides. A representative of the Dynamit-Nobel Company offered us several carloads of munitions. The Thuringian arms plants indicated that we could buy light guns without difficulty. A French captain of the Inter-Allied Military Commission offered us tremendous amounts of confiscated German Reichswehr material. Moscow held unlimited means at our disposal. Every morning I went over to the Soviet embassy on Unter den Linden. There I received from Mirov, Piatnitsky's representative, packages of dollars neatly bound together with paper bands—$100, $500, and even $1,000 notes. We were at the peak of inflation in Germany. All foreign notes, original and falsified, were quickly snapped up!

When the Berlin shoe store, Salamander, got the bright idea of printing a facsimile dollar bill on the back of an advertising circular, a swindler got the equally bright idea of pasting two such circulars together, and sold thousands of these "dollars" in villages and small towns.

From July to October, I alone had received more than one million dollars from Mirov. This money moved out of our hands so fast that the stamp of the Soviet embassy on the paper band frequently went with it. Did we receive the arms we paid for? Nobody knew.

Once one of my arms buyers, a deputy to the Thuringian Diet, came to me and explained that he had concluded a big deal with some middleman. Twenty baskets of army revolvers were stored in a warehouse. He needed ten thousand dollars immediately for this purchase. When we took over the baskets, we discovered that only the top layer consisted of revolvers. The rest was stones and cabbages.

In the end we were defeated ignominiously and devastatingly. The organization that we had built for the insurrection distintegrated. Financial control was impossible, and we didn't bother anyway. You do not pick up your purse when your veins have been cut open.

CHAPTER IV

A Game of Bolshevik Poker

GERMAN-RUSSIAN PACT OF 1921

URING THE INTERMISSION OF THE GERMAN-RUSSIAN PEACE negotiations of Brest-Litovsk, the French military mission in Moscow offered the Bolsheviks armed support against Germany. The Soviet government at that very moment was calling for a revolution in France.

Within the Bolshevik leadership a discussion arose whether a revolutionary party was justified in accepting help from an imperialist power. Lenin answered the question in the affirmative. But the French offer was rejected for special reasons, at that time.

The German collapse in November, 1918, changed the situation. France now sent her arms to the armies of intervention who were attempting to put an end to the life of the Soviet Republic.

At the end of 1921 the Bolsheviks received another "imperialist" offer, this time from Berlin. The chief of the German Reichswehr, an army of one hundred thousand soldiers permitted to Germany by the Treaty of Versailles, was General von Seeckt. At the time of Germany's defeat he had conceived a plan for the military resurrection of his country. Each private of this new army was to become a future sergeant, each sergeant a future lieutenant, each lieutenant a future captain, each captain a future general. The small army was to be trained as a cadre for the army of millions to come.

To accomplish this, however, he needed modern arms, the production of which was prohibited by the Treaty of Versailles. In 1921, the German aviation industry had to be closed down because of an ultimatum of the Allies. So Seeckt turned to Moscow, saying:

"Our military engineers will install and equip munitions and aviation plants. We will claim only a portion of the output. Our main aim is not to forget the 'know-how' of the production of modern weapons. In addition, we will send military instructors who will show the Red Army how to use these weapons."

The Bolsheviks accepted this offer without much hesitation. Their own arms industry was insignificant. Their own engineers were few and poorly trained. The Red Army was in urgent need of modern weapons.

In this way a secret pact between the Red Army of Trotsky and the Reichswehr of General von Seeckt was consummated. Now the interests of the Soviet Union demanded segregation from those of the Communist International. No longer was there complete harmony between the two as at the time of the founding Congress. Now the Comintern had been relegated to the servant quarters of revolutionary policies.

In the winter of 1919, when Brockdorff-Rantzau, the German ambassador, arrived in Moscow to present his credentials, Germany was the first European state since the war to take up diplomatic relations with the Soviet Republic. No other government, with the exception of the Turkish government of Kemal Pasha, had yet recognized the Soviet Union, for all were convinced that the days of the Soviets were numbered.

When the Bureau for Revolutionary Propaganda was changed into a foreign office—the Narkomindel—Chicherin, Trotsky's successor, demonstrated his ability to run its affairs with the same efficiency as Trotsky was exhibiting in creating a modern ministry of war out of nothing.

Brockdorff-Rantzau and Chicherin fell in love at first sight. The German ambassador had been chairman of the German delegation at the Peace Conference at Versailles and had refused to sign his name to the treaty. He was the prototype of a Prussian aristocrat. He and the Bolshevik intellectual who was now heading Russian foreign affairs had many likes and dislikes in common. Both were excellent historians, passionate lovers of Beethoven, and talented pianists. Both preferred the society of men, and avoided women. Both loved heady red wines that have to be imbibed slowly for one to appreciate the secret of their bouquet.

Chicherin's spirits came alive at night. His working hours would begin in the late afternoon and run into early morning. His diplomatic rendezvous with Brockdorff-Rantzau usually took place around the midnight hour. Frequently Chicherin would visit at the German Embassy for his midnight talks, particularly after the Count had just received a new case of the finest French red wines.

Together they organized German-Russian cooperation after the first World War. Together they began a game of revolutionary poker that went on intermittently over a period of years. Chicherin was aware that Brockdorff-Rantzau had come to Moscow in order to prepare Germany's revenge against the Allies. Brockdorff-Rantzau was equally aware that the Soviet Government regarded Germany only as a springboard for world revolution.

He was one of those for whom the stakes could never be too high —for they were always sure the last card would remain in their own hands.

After the first few rounds of the game, a third player joined them at the poker table—the Comintern—in the person of Karl Radek.

Nobody in the High Command could have filled this role as well as did Radek. Trotsky once said of him: "Radek is irreplaceable. He can always be repudiated without insult to his person or damage to the cause." His nature as well as his training permitted him to act as Jack-of-all-trades for the revolution.

His exceptional gifts as well as his revolutionary devotion gave him a supreme value in the ranks of the Bolshevist leadership. Nevertheless, he never was accepted on a completely equal footing in Lenin's and Trotsky's circle. His peculiar cynicism did not diminish his devotion to the revolutionary movement, although it made it impossible for him to become a revolutionary statesman and leader in his own right. He always remained an instrument for the accomplishment of the political objectives of others.

He had grown up in a Galician ghetto in the poorest and most miserable conditions imaginable. As a half-grown boy he had run away from home to study in Warsaw. There he earned a living giving lessons, but only rarely did he have enough to eat.

Like so many Polish-Jewish intellectuals, he was attracted by the revolutionary movement. His brilliant gifts notwithstanding, he was very unpopular among its leaders. To Rosa Luxemburg and Leo Jogiches who came from well-situated bourgeois families and had

had a good upbringing, his bohemian carelessness was repulsive. Their personal antipathy accompanied him to Germany, to where, in the end, all three had to escape.

In Germany, Radek soon developed into a brilliant publicist and journalist of the radical wing of the Socialist movement. Yet personally he remained always alone.

In revolutionary Russia he succeeded with surprising ease in playing himself into the footlights. He became the unofficial propaganda minister of the Soviet and the Comintern. His ability to work was inexhaustible: he could dictate articles and essays for twelve hours at a stretch without pausing. He could write on any subject, always with esprit and knowledge.

In addition to his activity in the Comintern, he served the Soviet government as a Cicerone for celebrated foreign visitors. He amused them and informed them. He had endless discussions with them, whether they were pacifists, conservatives, diplomats, big industrialists, or spies. By the end of such discussions they had left neither the energy to draw breath nor a spark of argument in their brains.

If after their departure from Russia, their attitude abroad did not please or satisfy him, he exposed them in biting epistles not quickly to be forgotten. So did he treat H. G. Wells, Bertrand Russell, and many others.

Radek had little time to stay with one adversary: there were too many of them in the world needing his satirical attention. He omitted none of his well-known contemporaries; not Winston Churchill nor Lloyd George nor Woodrow Wilson—nor Friedrich Ebert. The more famous a European statesman, the more certain he was of becoming the target of Radek's poisonous arrows.

Strangely enough, the relationship between the Prussian aristocrat and the Polish Jew became one of great mutual warmth and respect. If Radek had discussed with Brockdorff-Rantzau the intensive preparations of the Comintern for the next insurrection in Germany, the Count might have found the association with the journalist less to his liking.

At first Radek saw in the Count only an ideal source of information about the plans and intentions of the German Reichswehr. Later, in 1922, when German-French relations became so strained that war appeared a possibility, Radek attempted to involve Brockdorff-Rantzau in his own game.

In the intermissions, the Polish Jew discussed Prussian history with Brockdorff-Rantzau, explaining his interpretation of the role of Stein and Hardenberg, the two Prussian noblemen who had conducted the Prussian wars of emancipation against Napoleon in the spirit of a poker game of a hundred years earlier! If Seeckt and Brockdorff-Rantzau were to play the roles of a modern Stein and Hardenberg, thought Radek, and involve Germany in a war of "national liberation" against France, Bolshevism would inherit Germany, destroyed by their folly!

Radek knew that the German ambassador himself was playing a double role in regard to the German Democratic Republic, and so might be ensnared into the Bolshevist maneuvers against the German Democracy.

The Count, Chicherin, and Radek were united as much in their hatred for France as in their contempt for the German Social Democracy. The first president of the German Republic, Ebert, a former saddlemaker, symbolized for Brockdorff Germany's utter humiliation after the war. To Radek and Chicherin, Ebert was the butcher of the Spartacus rebellion, the man whose party was responsible for the murder of Rosa Luxemburg and Karl Liebknecht, the head of a party that obstructed all efforts at a German-Russian collaboration, and whose objective in foreign policy was a coalition with hostile democratic England and France.

But there was more than just a political game in all that. Brockdorff-Rantzau embodied in his person and his behavior an aristocratic negation of the democratic bourgeois world, and found a diabolical pleasure in studying and discussing the adventuresome ideological exploits of Radek. As he got to know Radek's game in all its details better and better, he enjoyed more and more the latter's biting revolutionary skepticism as a source of spiritual rejuvenation. The postwar world of bourgeois-democratic mediocrity he found boring and expected to have as little traffic with it as possible.

"You are Mephistopheles in person!" he said to Radek. "When Goethe wrote his Faust, he must have anticipated you!"

Radek was grateful. He, in turn, knowing the Count's absorption with the times and personality of Bismarck, would often drag from the archives of the Narkomindel voluminous files on the relationship between Bismarck and Russia and together they would indulge their passion for history and argument.

In the spring of 1922 a fourth player joined the game, the German Minister of Foreign Affairs and multi-millionaire, Walther Rathenau. Walther Rathenau was the first and only Jewish Minister of Foreign Affairs in Germany. His father had been the founder and chief share-holder of the Allgemeine Deutche Elektrizitaetsgesellschaft, the German General Electric, one of Germany's most modern giant enterprises. During the war, Rathenau had become the organizer of the German war economy. Germany owed to his efforts its ability to last until 1918.

Rathenau participated in the German-Russian poker game with plans and objectives far removed from those of each of the three other players. Personal, political, and cultural inclinations drew him toward Paris and London. He had become a convinced pacifist after the war, and joined in the play only in the hope of becoming an acceptable partner for the West with the profits from the game in Moscow.

"As soon as Paris and London realize that in our despair we are willing to ally ourselves with the Bolsheviks, they will be ready to take us into their own circles. Then my dream of a reconciliation between Germany and the West will be close to realization . . . . ."

So it came about that Rathenau, early in 1922, invited Chicherin to visit Berlin.

Before the arrival of the Russian delegation a little formality had to be taken care of. Radek's expulsion from Germany had to be rescinded. Radek had spent several months in 1919 in a Berlin prison cell, the first few days in heavy chains. But this memory disturbed nobody in Berlin any longer. Radek was the hero of the day.

Now he played the part of his life. With the heads of the German bourgeoisie he negotiated a pact of friendship, in strict observance of all diplomatic formalities. With the heads of the Communist Party he negotiated the means to bring the same government down in the shortest possible way. With the chairman of the German General Electric, Geheimrat Deutsch, he discussed the improvement of German-Russian business relations. With the Communists he went into the chances of a strike in German industry. With General Seeckt he conferred on how to expand the secret military connections between Germany and Russia.

The Communists he reminded of the principles of the Third World Congress: to win the confidence of the Social Democratic workers and not to forget the construction of underground military organizations. And in the meantime, he did not neglect his rendezvous with Count Reventlow, through whose hands ran all the threads of the extreme nationalist conspiracy against the Weimar Republic.

Geheimrat Deutsch arranged a brilliant reception for the Russian delegation in his luxurious house in an elegant suburb of Berlin. For the first time in his life, Radek moved in such surroundings. Everybody who counted in Berlin society was present—the heads of the great banks, the leaders of industry, diplomats, the chief editors of the big newspapers, beautiful ladies. Radek did not take a false step. He moved around on the parquet floor as if born to the manor.

"Mr. Radek," he was interrogated by Geheimrat Deutsch, "if we conclude a commercial treaty with your government, isn't it possible then that instead of paying your debts you might elect to make a revolution for us in Germany?"

"Mr. Deutsch," replied Radek, "if you elect not to send us your machines and your goods, you will be scourged by an even greater amount of unemployment in Germany than you already have. Then it might happen that you will relieve us of the trouble of making a revolution in Germany."

At the secret negotiations with General Seeckt, it was not possible to play hide and seek. Here one had to put one's cards on the table. In respect to the secret military relations between the two countries, there did not exist the slightest difference of opinion. But Seeckt stated unequivocally that he would not permit a victory of the Communist Party in Germany.

Radek was well aware that the old soldier whose body still showed the resilience of that of a young man said exactly what he meant. So he replied:

"We will not ask for your support, General, if we decide to start a revolution in Germany. The stronger will win. We will not ask for mercy if we are defeated and are sure you will do likewise.

"However, if the German people should decide for Communism, and your army should attempt to suppress it, you may give up the hope of ever again seeing a German people's army!"

"The time of a people's army is past," Seeckt replied. "In the wars to come, highly qualified and skilled cadre armies will decide the issues. You missed your chance in 1919 and 1920. It is possible that Germany, allied with your Red Army, may fight a war against France, but not with a German Red Army."

RADEK'S ROYAL FLUSH

In April, 1922, another round of the poker game was played, this time in Genoa. The conference in Genoa was the first great diplomatic discussion that England and France had with revolutionary Russia. It closed the period of the armed intervention against the Soviets, and opened the new period of their diplomatic recognition.

Lloyd George and Poincaré regarded an understanding with Lenin as impossible. But they had decided a conference without results would demonstrate this to the public of their own countries which had begun to doubt the wisdom of their Russian policy. As the conference was to have a European character, Germany had to be included.

Chicherin celebrated a great personal triumph. He came, saw, and conquered. His magnificent mastery of all Western European languages, his personal charm, and his accomplished diplomatic assurance immediately captivated this brilliant diplomatic gathering. He surmounted the walls of hatred and prejudice that had stood between the Soviet Republic and bourgeois Europe since 1917.

Radek did not accompany Chicherin this time. In Moscow Radek was not considered the right sort of partner in negotiations with the all-powerful Lloyd George and Barthou. In Radek's stead, therefore, was Rakovsky, president of the Ukrainian Soviet Republic, a man whose appearance and background had predestined him for the role of a successful diplomat.

Chicherin shared Lloyd George's and Poincaré's opinion that a real reconciliation between the West and Russia was impossible. The English-French conditions, recognition of the Czarist government's debts and of foreign property in Russia, were unacceptable to the

Bolsheviks. As far as England and France were concerned, this was a *conditio sine qua non.*

Rathenau attempted in vain to accomplish a German reconciliation with England and France. Lloyd George did not even grant the German delegation the favor of a personal conversation. Rathenau saw his game was up, and so accepted Chicherin's and Brockdorff-Rantzau's countermove; the Treaty of Rapallo between Germany and Russia was the consequence.

For the Soviet Union, Rapallo was a great diplomatic victory— the first diplomatic penetration into the capitalist West; for Germany it was the first step into the arena of world politics prohibited by the peace treaty of Versailles. From now on, her relationship to the Soviet Union became the most important instrument of pressure against France and England.

A few months later Rathenau paid for his participation in the German-Russian poker game with his life. A member of a terrorist nationalist secret organization shot him, because he believed Rathenau wished to deliver Germany up to Bolshevism.

After Rathenau's death the German-Russian game was continued, but with certain complications added for the Russians. The fact that they were preparing a revolution in a country with which they had just concluded a pact of friendship was not a matter of concern. In any case the revolution had not yet ripened.

But in the meantime, German-French relations had worsened from day to day. Maybe before the outbreak of a German revolution there might be a German-French war. Either of these two eventualities naturally required a different revolutionary policy.

The Russian leadership, however, could not decide on what eventuality to base its policy, whether to count on a revolution in Germany or on a war between the French and Germans.

Up to this time Bolshevist tactics in Germany had been under the close personal scrutiny and supervision of Lenin. Now, however, Lenin's severe illness and the bitter factional fights that disrupted the Russian party permitted Radek to act completely on his own, with Zinoviev as his hesitant consultant and Trotsky as a distant spectator.

In 1923 Radek was certain that at last he held the royal flush in this interminable poker game. Poincaré had occupied the Ruhr dis-

trict in January. Large sections of the nationalist movement had begun
to advocate publicly a war of alliance with Red Russia against France.
Masses of workers driven by hunger and unemployment had turned
from the Social Democrats to the Communists.

Now Radek put his royal flush on the table. The *Ace* was the
Soviet Union which had always fought the Treaty of Versailles and
had never signed it, which had always regarded France as Enemy
Number One of the world revolution.

The *King* was the German Communists, the chief enemies of the
Social Democracy and of the Catholic Center Party—both of which
were held responsible by the people at large for the humiliation of the
nation as well as for the misery of the postwar period.

The *Queen* in Radek's hand was the leadership of the left Social
Democrats in Saxony and Thuringia.

The *Jack* was the underground insurrectionist military organization
of the Communist Party.

The *Ten* was the nationalist leadership—such men as Count Reventlow; the revolutionary romanticist Moeller van den Bruck; the
General von Lettov-Vorbeck, conqueror of the German colonies in
Africa; the terrorist Schlageter, who had been arrested by the French
in the Ruhr, court martialled, and shot to death.

This last trump Radek played out in sensational fashion in a
speech to the plenary session of the Executive Committee of the Comintern on June 20, 1923. Here he made an open offer to the extreme
Nationalists like Reventlow, whom he called "Fascists" according
to the Italian example, to support the Communist revolution in Germany, in exchange for cooperation in a common effort to erase the
German defeat of the World War. The immediate occasion for his
speech was the execution of the German terrorist, Schlageter.

"This brave soldier of the counter-revolution merits an honest and
manly appraisal by the soldiers of the revolution! . . . . "

Radek told the Fascists that they were "wanderers into nothingness," that their ideals were an illusion; that they believed themselves
to be fighting for the emancipation of Germany, but in reality were
instruments of world capitalism. "The cause of the nation must be
made the cause of the people" in order to enable Germany to fight
against Versailles and the capitalism of the Entente. It is necessary

85

for the Communist and Nationalist masses to unite without reserve.

"With whom do you want to ally yourselves?" he asked the brave soldiers of the counter-revolution. "With the Russian people and the German workers, or with the capitalism of the Entente?

"Schlageter can no longer hear the truth. We are sure that there are hundreds of Schlageters who will hear it and understand it!"

There was great pathos in Radek's speech. He was carried away by his own words. On Zinoviev's lips was an ironical smile. Most members of the Executive Committee were embarrassed. Klara Zetkin expressed her distaste unmistakably.

Radek's "wanderer into nothingness" had been but an adventurer as ready to throw a bomb into a Communist meeting as into a French troop transport, if well paid for his action.

But who were the Nationalist masses whom Radek addressed? They were the young officers who had become unemployed after the collapse of the monarchy, their followers, and thousands of desperadoes who had sworn revenge against France. From exactly these groups had come the brave soldiers of the counter-revolution who had murdered Rathenau just a year before.

The leadership of these "masses" was in the hands of sophisticated Prussian reactionaries like Count Reventlow, or of naive national revolutionary romanticists like Moeller van den Bruck, who had a great influence on the younger idealistic elements.

Reventlow seemed an ideal partner for Radek's adventures. In 1920, when the Red Army was approaching Warsaw, he had actively advocated attacking the Poles from the West and destroying the new Polish state.

From Reventlow and similar leaders thousands of threads led to the Reichswehr and to the higher bureaucracy. Radek's aim was to win these groups and thus to exert pressure on the army command of von Seeckt. So he hoped to add to the active resistance against France.

For the "brave soldiers of the counter-revolution" he had reserved the role of agents provocateurs or maybe that of specialists and experts for the future German Red Army. In 1920 Lenin had warned the Communists, in view of the "National-Bolshevist" currents that were making themselves felt in Germany, against an "unnatural block" of the revolutionary with the reactionary elements. These warnings were now utterly forgotten.

The poor German Communists did not know what to make of Radek's speech. Many accepted it in good faith because it had come from Moscow. Loyally the German Communist newspaper, *Rote Fahne,* opened its columns to von Reventlow and discussed with him Germany's future and the path that Communists and Nationalists might travel together.

One of the leaders of the Berlin Communists, a woman, went from one ecstasy into another about the "heroes like Schlageter who are ready to sacrifice their lives for freedom on the altar of the Fatherland!" Radek had so confused her that she nearly permitted herself to incite a pogrom at a meeting of Nationalist students: "Trample them down, the Jewish capitalists! String them up on the lamp posts!" On afterthought she added, "But don't forget the Aryan capitalists either."

Radek had been fortunate that his "salvation of the German nation" went no further than his speech. The "wanderers into nothingness" would have supported him and the German Communists—with a hangman's rope, had they had the opportunity! (Years later many of them became the organizers and commanders of Hitler's S.S. gangs.)

Radek was so enamored of his game that he forgot to study the movements in the masses with care and attention. The climax of the revolutionary movement in Germany, and in the German districts occupied by the French, came as early as August, 1923.

Radek and Zinoviev wanted to launch their final revolutionary offensive in the beginning of October. By then the revolutionary mass movement was already ebbing.

At the same time the German government had given up its resistance to the occupation of the Ruhr, and had undertaken first steps towards a reconciliation with France. The revolutionary aspirations of the masses had become uncertain, the attitude of the government more certain.

Yet Radek and Zinoviev still believed they could play their royal flush.

The Soviet Government stuck to its word, given to the German

Communists at the Second and Third Congresses of the Communist International. The Red Army was partly mobilized and stood ready to march at the Baltic frontier. In the Baltic and North Sea was a fleet of ships loaded with guns and wheat, ready to move into German ports the instant of the insurrection.

In Berlin a group of first-class Russian military and economic experts was assembled, prepared to lend assistance to the coming German Soviet Republic.

The insurrection was scheduled for October. The German Communists formed a coalition government with the left Socialists in Saxony—the *Queen* in Radek's hand. According to the revolutionary plans of Radek and Zinoviev, this coalition government was to become the springboard for the conquest of power throughout Germany. Saxony, already in the days of the Kaiser, had been called the Red Kingdom, and it was now to take the place of Petrograd in the German revolution.

A few days before the scheduled insurrection, Radek was visited with sinister suspicions. His friend Brockdorff-Rantzau had learned from Seeckt that the Reichswehr had arrived at an understanding with the new strong man of Germany, Stresemann, and was determined to march against the Communists. Radek immediately made for Dresden, this time via underground routes. En route from Warsaw and Prague to Dresden, he realized that he had lost his royal flush. Although the Communist Party was still feverishly awaiting the struggle that had been announced and prepared for such a long time, the masses had already turned completely indifferent. Not even the left Socialist workers were still willing to engage upon the uncertain venture.

At five minutes before twelve, Radek called off his insurrection!

Seeckt kept his word. His troops occupied "red" Dresden and chased the Communist-Socialist government out of the city without a single shot fired. A general strike was proclaimed but did not take place. Radek had lost the great game of his life.

Chicherin had been a spectator to Radek's and Zinoviev's adventure. He accepted the protests of the German government, brought to him by his friend, Brockdorff-Rantzau. He took the documents that condemned the behavior of the Russians as an interference prohibited by the friendship pact between the two countries, and threw them into the waste basket.

Had the German revolution been victorious, the Narkomindel would have been superfluous for a long time anyway. In the case of defeat, the influence of Brockdorff-Rantzau was sufficient to repair the damaged diplomatic bridge. . . . .

The Treaty of Rapallo remained in force. After the revolutionary "misunderstanding" had been eliminated, the secret connection between the Red Army and the Reichswehr came into its own. Even more engineers and military instructors departed from Berlin for Moscow, and there were even more mysterious shipments from Petrograd to Stettin.

CHAPTER V

Giants and Pigmies (Cont.)

(From the Papers of Comrade X)

LENIN'S DEATH AND STALIN'S OATH

January, 1924

O N THE TWENTY-FIRST OF JANUARY, 1924, LENIN DIED.
Jeanne cried bitterly. "People in the streets look as if they had suddenly lost their own father!"

Within me was deep misery. An abyss of despair and pessimism.

Over the Comintern hovered the same paralyzing mourning as over Russia. People said now one ought to work doubly hard. One made an effort to do it, but everything had the stamp of utter hopelessness.

Things in Germany had come to a head in October, before Lenin's death. The high command of the world revolution had again lost a great battle!

Again, as in March, 1921, the fight commenced on whom to place the blame. But this time, Lenin was dead, and Trotsky sick and away from Moscow.

Zinoviev had had a free hand. His responsibility was far greater than in 1921. He had given all directions himself. He had instructed his agents in Germany directly, and there was no scapegoat like Bela Kun at hand.

The leaders of the German Communists had to put their own heads on the execution block. Zinoviev repeated his old game. All his directions had been correct, but the Germans had erred in their execution. Therefore they should be crucified. Those same people who had demanded the head of Levi in 1921, now became Zinoviev's victims.

This time, however, Radek did not play along. He remained loyal to his German friends, defending them, maintaining solidarity with them, and sharing their fate! Zinoviev, all powerful now in the

Comintern, ordered his exclusion from all activity connected with the German Communist movement.

There has been a great change in the Praesidium of the Comintern. In place of Radek is Manuilsky, who has worked in the Ukrainian Soviet government up to now. And Bela Kun, back from his exile, has been entrusted with the direction of propaganda activities.

Our meetings are boring. Discussions short and indecisive. Some of the older foreign members of the Executive Committee have declared their solidarity with the Germans and have returned to their countries or live as "pensioners" at the Hotel Lux. From all parties, new delegates arrive in Moscow.

* * * * *

On the eve of Lenin's funeral, a gathering of mourning took place at the Great Theatre. This huge red-gold hall had seen all the triumphal celebrations of the Russian Revolution! From here Trotsky and Zinoviev had sent their flaming revolutionary manifestoes out into the world. Here the Second World Congress of the Communist International had had its final sessions, and the Third its opening session. Here Lenin had made some of the speeches that laid the basis for the young Soviet state.

Now the Bolsheviks were saying farewell to the man to whom they owed everything.

Men stood shoulder to shoulder, heads bowed in mourning and grief. Even little children, the tiny Pioneer members of the Bolshevik children's organization, lined the stage and stood motionless. The music played the Revolutionaries' funeral march. Its somber tones, into which generations of Russian revolutionaries have poured their suffering, mingled with subdued weeping.

"You have fallen, immortal victims. . . . ."

Then Krupskaya, Zinoviev, Kamenev, Bukharin, Stalin, and many others spoke. Trotsky was absent.

All the sympathies of the people in the great hall went out to Krupskaya, Lenin's widow. A little woman, her head bowed now in pain, her face disfigured by long illness; she spoke a few modest words:

"All Lenin's love was with the masses that work and suffer. Yet he never said a word about it."

Stalin read a speech from a manuscript, attempting to inject emotion into his colorless voice. His speech was in the form of an oath. He talked in the biblical "thou":

"In leaving us, Comrade Lenin ordered us to conserve the unity of our party as the apple of our eye. We swear to thee, Comrade Lenin, to honor thy command!

"In leaving us, Comrade Lenin enjoined upon us fidelity to the Communist International. We swear to thee, Comrade Lenin, to devote our lives to the enlargement and strengthening of the union of the workers of the whole world, the Communist International!"

It seemed that a brotherly bond united the speakers on the platform, the masses in the hall, and the tens of thousands that were listening out on the square. Nobody realized that the struggle for the successorship to Lenin had already flamed high around his sickbed.

When the Politbureau decided to embalm Lenin's body and to exhibit it permanently in a glass coffin in a mausoleum to be built on the Red Square, I was dumbfounded. The idea that Lenin is to be embalmed and put on exhibition is simply inconceivable.

I have never liked the propaganda of the Russian Association of Atheists. I do not believe that a European, be he even a radical atheist, could possibly accept this type of propaganda. These people have attempted to unmask faith in such a crude, disagreeable fashion, admitting no human respect for the faith of one's fellow human beings. Maybe this is necessary among the primitive Russian peasants. The Russian comrades have frequently shown that they know how to talk to the peasants in their own language.

But how does this embalming conform to the atheism of the Bolsheviks?

A few weeks after the placing of Lenin's body on permanent exhibition in the mausoleum on the Red Square, Jeanne told me that one of her favorite children from the creche where she is working said:

"Lenin has not died. He is just resting. He has worked so hard for us children, that he needs a long rest."

Peasants who come from a great distance to have a glimpse of their leader's dead body, carry the legend into the country: "He is only sleeping. But his wise and generous hand still rules our Mother Russia."

Do the Russian comrades who know their country so well want this result? Why has Trotsky, who was one of the instigators of the Atheist Association, permitted this?

I am told the decision to embalm Lenin was made in Trotsky's absence. I asked Bukharin and reminded him that Friedrich Engels, before his death, ordered his ashes to be strewn into the ocean. Bukharin did not answer, but only looked at me with his soft appealing eyes. What I read there was shame and fear. Later I learned that Zinoviev had proposed the embalming and had been supported by Stalin.

STALIN OPENS THE DOOR OF THE HIGH COMMAND

June, 1924

The Fifth World Congress of the Comintern opened in June, 1924. In the Red Square the leaders of the Comintern stood on the roof of the temporary mausoleum that housed Lenin's body. Among them for the first time was Stalin who had not participated in the Congresses in Lenin's time although he had been a member of the Russian delegation to the First Congress.

Now he could sometimes be seen sitting silently on one of the benches of the Russian delegation. The language used by the Congress being, as usual, either French or German, Stalin could not follow the negotiations. The entire attention of the delegates was concentrated on Zinoviev. This time he was the sovereign master, and his controversy with Radek was the focus of attention for all minds.

This Congress, too, took place in the coronation hall of the Czar, the most ideal meeting place imaginable. The Czar's architects had thought of everything when they erected the magnificent structure— except one thing. In the tremendous hall of the Andreyevsky Palace there were only three toilets, two of them cubicles without water, air, or light, that could be reached only by passing through several huge halls. The third was the private toilet of the Czar, and had water.

Next to the coronation hall were the private rooms of the Czar where committees of the Congress frequently held their conferences.

The first room was the bedchamber, completely filled by a tremendous four-poster bed with a canopy. When a conference took place here, one had to sit on the bed, because there were no chairs and no tables.

The next room was the boudoir of the Czarina. One had to pass through both rooms to get into the bath that adjoined the boudoir of the Czarina.

Once, when I passed from the bedroom into the boudoir, and opened the heavy door, I nearly ran into Stalin standing close by the door, talking to two or three dozen delegates. He shot an angry glance at me. I murmured a quick apology. When I returned, Stalin was standing in front of the door, so I sat down on one of the marble windows sills, and listened.

It was a Polish committee, whose members all were talking Russian. In front of the little table, sat Dzierzynski, head of the GPU, a thin man with pale, hollow cheeks and eyes with no light in them. He looked as if he were hovering at the edge of his grave.

Stalin was wearing a gray linen blouse and trousers, the latter tucked into the wide cuffs of his low black boots. He talked without a manuscript, and frequently paused for seconds at a time, apparently thinking and formulating his next sentences. Yet in the short while I listened, I got the impression that his real self was far removed from his words. His sentences had a monotonous rhythm. His gestures were few. Usually his left hand was between the upper buttonholes of his blouse. In his right hand he always held his pipe. His dark, rather squinting eyes moved coldly and indifferently. He never looked directly at anyone and sought no emotional contact with his listeners.

Nobody ever interrupts Stalin—nobody asks a question. Stalin's speaking technique precludes this. He himself formulates his questions and answers them as if talking to himself.

The structure of his sentences is simple, his comparisons primitive and usually taken from the life of Russian peasants. When he wants to emphasize something, he usually says: "It appears completely clear to me that. . . . . "

It is easy to understand Stalin, but he is tiring to listen to. As a speaker Stalin does not compare with the other Bolshevik leaders. He leaves no lasting impression.

In the main meeting hall of the Congress, the German delegates
run wild. Their leader is Ruth Fischer, a short, fat young Viennese
with great oratorical gifts and an overflowing temperament. When
she talks her little fists beat the table like drums. She is a merciless
executioner of her immediate predecessors in the leadership of the
German Communist Party, the pupils of Rosa Luxemburg. Zinoviev
is manifestly taking a great liking to her.

Another leader of the Germans is Ernst Thaelmann, a herculean
worker who roars so loudly that it is impossible to understand his
words. When his huge fist comes down on the table one fears the
table will break.

At this Congress argument no longer has weight. Whoever talks the
most radical language carries the day. When the numerous German
delegation hears a word it does not like, it drowns out the speaker in
jeers and boos, and the chair does nothing. The delegates from the
other countries are surprised and intimidated.

One of Lenin's last words to the Comintern was: "The most important thing for all of us now is to learn." Yet Zinoviev seems to be
sincerely enthusiastic about this Congress.

LUX DECAMERON

August, 1924

The GPU unmasked two East Indians as spies. Both admitted they
were working for the British as well as for the Japanese secret information service. After that, the Secretariat of the Comintern unanimously agreed on a discreet surveillance of the hundreds of delegates
who had arrived for the simultaneous sessions of the Comintern and
the Youth International.

By agreement with Piatnitsky, Trilisser, the chief of the foreign
service of the GPU, put his agents into all of the hotels where delegates were housed. It was their task not only to prevent the activities
of spies but to discover among the delegates themselves any suspicious elements.

Fortunately this measure turned out to be superfluous, after the
incident with the Indians. No more spies were found.

But the surveillance led to a funny episode that caused everyone
in the Comintern building considerable amusement. One of the GPU

agents had the idea of quartering in the Hotel Lux two young women Communists who were to gain the friendship of the delegates. These special agents were the sisters Chiura and Miura. They were particularly fitted for their work, because they had had a good education and were able to speak German and French fluently.

Chiura and Miura plunged with great ambition into their revolutionary work. Neither of them was beautiful, but both were kindhearted and charming girls who quickly became popular in the Hotel Lux. Chiura and Miura took their work very seriously. So it happened that frequently they took up very intimate relations with delegates, in order to get the full truth.

Among the French delegates was a young Communist who, for some reason, had aroused the suspicion of one of the Lux Commissars. Chiura was entrusted with his supervision and she seemed to derive particular pleasure from her task. The suspect was a handsome and intelligent boy.

But all her reports, sent in after a night of service, did not show anything suspicious. The young man told her many things about his life, about his enthusiasm for Communism and Moscow. Nothing indicated that he was a dangerous element.

To everyone's great surprise, the delegate's papers were taken away from the young man one fine morning, and he was brought before Piatnitsky and subjected to a very painful cross-examination. Piatnitsky produced reports of the Lux Commissar, declaring the young man to have engaged in counter-revolutionary conversations, to have condemned the entire Comintern, and to have maintained suspicious contacts in France.

The delegate denied so vehemently ever having said anything along the lines of the accusations, that Piatnitsky finally confronted him with the Lux Commissar and Chiura.

Now it came out: After one or two weeks of intensive observation, Chiura had stopped reporting to the Lux Commissar, because in her opinion there was nothing to observe. Only her visits with the young man she did not stop. In the rush of business, however, the Commissar, with several hundred delegates living at the Hotel Lux, forgot that he had assigned this task to Chiura, and gave the same order to Miura.

Now she began to observe the young man with the greatest diligence. He in turn was very proud of his success as a Don Juan. One night he had the pleasure of being observed by Chiura, the next night by Miura. Both kept their work absolutely secret, according to their instructions which strictly forbade them to talk to anybody but their superiors about their services as operatives.

But then the unexpected happened. Miura fell in love with her victim and dreamed of going to France with him, when one morning she met her sister Chiura coming out of the room of her dearly beloved.

Miura forgot her duty as an eye-of-the-law and sought revenge. He really was a traitor, this fine Frenchman! He'd have something to think about! Never again would he dare risk such counter-revolutionary behavior in Moscow.

So Miura wrote reports about the disloyal young man, describing him in darkest colors.

Piatnitsky's strict demeanor caused her to confess at once and admit the whole truth. The impression she made was so desperate and so comical at the same time, that nobody thought of punishing her. Partly also because Chiura burst into bitter tears at her sister's unhappiness.

The Hotel Lux ceased to be a hunting ground for Chiura and Miura. In future they were permitted to fight only as stenographers in the office of the world revolution.

THE PURE AND THE IMPURE
September, 1924

There are many new delegates in Moscow now—people with new faces and new manners—no longer the serious-minded and pedantic labor leader and the intellectual with a Socialist past, but people whose history begins in 1918 and after.

It is peculiar. We have suffered defeat after defeat everywhere. Yet this new generation in the Comintern seems to believe that life is just beginning. In the Hotel Lux parties and celebrations are carried on as never before.

One morning I was awakened by a terrific noise out in the hall— roars of laughter and loud singing. I opened the door and was immediately encircled by a bacchanalian gang. I recognized the Italian, Bordiga, and the German, Heinz Neumann, with several half nude young girls, all dead drunk.

I was more upset than indignant. I was well aware that the Hotel Lux was no cloister. But what did such lack of inhibition in people who belonged to the inner circle of the Comintern leadership signify?

The Hotel Lux has two different types of residents, one the "pure," who dominate the discussions of the Congress, the other the "impure," leaders fallen from grace with whom nobody talks, who are given no work or duties and who are permitted to live there on the "bread of charity," as it were.

Zinoviev has invented a new form of exile for foreign revolutionaries: the Hotel Lux. They are prohibited from returning to their own home countries so that they will not disturb their successors. By submitting to this form of treatment, they may entertain the hope of some day being allowed to work again in their old parties. Otherwise they have to figure on becoming old and gray in the back rooms of the Hotel Lux.

There are many of these "impure" at the Lux. Germans, Austrians, Czechs, French, Chinese, Indians—the entire International is represented because, after the German defeat of 1923, Zinoviev cleaned out most of the old leaders of the Communist parties.

Bukharin personally has taken the "impure" under his protective wing, helping them in their minor difficulties. I voice my disapproval of Zinoviev's tactics. Bukharin answers, helpless as ever:

"This is only an episode. Zinoviev is not as bad as all that. I believe the comrades should be satisfied to have an opportunity to read and to study. I personally would be happy to be exiled like that for a few months."

Among the "impure" were some who agreed with Bukharin and spent their time at libraries, on the whole amused by Zinoviev's hysterical ambition.

Most of them, however, suffered from their Lux exile. In their own countries, they had known confidence and respect, and had lived in an atmosphere of solidarity. Here they were near pariahs, having no contact with their Russian surroundings. Most of them were profoundly unhappy. To them the Hotel Lux was a genuine exile.

November, 1924

Radek has given me, sub rosa, a brochure that Trotsky wrote recently entitled "The October Events and What They Can Teach Us." Although frequently couched in diplomatic terms, this is an unmistakable polemic against Zinoviev's policy during the German events of October, 1923, interspersed with numerous hints of and allusions to his treacherous attitude in October, 1917. At the bookstores, however, the brochure is not for sale.

We foreigners are aware that backstage Zinoviev, Stalin, and Kamenev are waging a bitter fight against Trotsky. But nobody knows its real reasons or its objectives. Rumors circulate through the halls of the Comintern building and the Hotel Lux. I have tried to call Piatnitsky's attention to this, with the observation that such conduct will necessarily lead to a disintegration of the work of the Comintern staff. He does not reply. His eyes are unsteady and try in vain to conceal the fear and doubts in his mind.

After a session of the praesidium, I ask Zinoviev whether he would object to my making a motion at the next session for an informative report on the discussions within the Russian party. He responds with a cool and surprised look, measuring me from head to foot:

"I would advise you to abstain from such a move."

One morning I call the Secretariat of Trotsky and ask to be received by him. After one hour I get the answer: Comrade Trotsky is sorry; he is still sick and cannot receive visitors.

I know that other comrades have received the same reply.

It is evident: The Russians regard the fight in their leadership as a family affair that does not concern us foreigners at all. In that respect they are united.

The one exception is Radek. But he too talks only in mysterious hints, saying, for instance, that Trotsky will resign soon from the Supreme Command of the Red Army. Or he indulges in witticisms exuding bitter hatred for Zinoviev.

INTERMEZZO IN ESTHONIA

December, 1924

One morning there was an extraordinary scene in the Secretariat. Even before the session was called to order, Bela Kun took the floor and demanded that the events in Esthonia should be made the first point of discussion. He was very excited—there was cause for excitement.

On the first of December, the Moscow evening paper had carried the headline: "Revolution in Esthonia!" Nobody in the Comintern had known, during the preceding weeks, that a "revolutionary situation" had existed in Esthonia, or that preparations had been made for revolutionary action.

On December 2 the papers carried no report. Everyone went around asking the astonished question: What has really happened in Esthonia?

Piatnitsky refused with determination to accede to Bela Kun's demand. The latter raged and pounded the table with his fists, crying aloud: "If Zinoviev believes he can bring about a *putsch* behind the backs of the Executive Committee of the Comintern, he's wrong! I'll show him he's not God!"

Piatnitsky rose and left the room. Kuusinen and Manuilsky followed. I was curious to learn what had happened in Reval, the capital of Esthonia, and asked Bela Kun to tell me the story.

This is what he told me. Zinoviev had instituted a "revolution" in Esthonia on his own account. Up to the end of November he had informed nobody in the Comintern of his plans. Bela Kun had learned of the planned insurrection from a Hungarian friend who was working in the central division of the military information service.

The plan of insurrection was drawn up in the General Staff of the Red Army. It called for the following: At dawn on the first of December, heavily armed units of the Red Army and selected groups of Esthonian and Finnish Communists were to take possession of governmental buildings, the railway station, the post office, the arsenal, and the flying field. Then a general strike was to be proclaimed.

Zinoviev was sure that they would succeed in overthrowing the Esthonian government. As far as the military aspect of it went, the enterprise functioned perfectly. The government in Reval was taken completely by surprise, and the Communists easily took possession of some of the positions mapped out in the plan of insurrection. The guards did not put up any resistance, and those who did were shot.

100

But the political part of the plan of insurrection failed utterly. The Communists had attempted by distributing tens of thousands of pamphlets to the workers, to persuade them to come out in a general strike and support the insurrection. There was no response.

At six in the morning the insurrectionists were already surrounded and cut off. The government troops had no great difficulty in winning, as the city remained passive. By eight o'clock the fighting Communists lacked ammunition. By nine o'clock the insurrection was over, for all practical purposes. Only at the flying field some particularly brave officers of the Red Army continued to defend themselves. Later on they were able to escape by plane.

The total military ensemble of the Communists had amounted to between two and three hundred men. They had suffered about one hundred dead; the government troops approximately double.

Bela Kun, immediately upon hearing of the plan of insurrection, had run to Stalin. Stalin had not been informed either. He advised Bela Kun to wait for developments and force a discussion at the praesidium of the Comintern of Zinoviev's behavior, after the insurrection. Bela Kun had acted accordingly, and the result had been the explosion in the Secretariat. His voice rang so long and loud that it reverberated from the walls!

"He sent me into the wilderness after March, 1921. But this time I'll show him!"

The telephone rang. It was Zinoviev asking for Bela Kun. He shot me a triumphant glance when he took up the receiver. Zinoviev must have said something flattering, for Bela Kun's face lit up with a big smile. He ran out of the room.

An hour later he returned and came into my office rubbing his hands with satisfaction. "Everything is in order. I've given him a good piece of my mind."

I never learned what was in order nor what the piece of his mind consisted of. For the Esthonian insurrection was never mentioned again in the Secretariat of the Comintern nor in the Praesidium.

MANUILSKY'S FOLLIES

March, 1925

In the Comintern building everything seemingly moves in its old

101

routine again. One meeting after another. Manifestoes are written; departments are all completely staffed and functioning well. Couriers come and go.

The Russian Piatnitsky and the Finn Kuusinen insist on order and punctuality. Bela Kun and Manuilsky provide the disorder and the humor. The Communist leaders who were installed by the Fifth World Congress have already been deposed, and many have been expelled. Some have been exiled to the Lux realm of the "impure."

The meetings with Zinoviev become less and less frequent. We foreigners are not told why. When I ask Manuilsky, he answers with an ironic smile:

"We are adults now. We can do without a daddy for awhile!"

In reality, the struggle between Stalin and Zinoviev is already flaming high. A Stalin faction is being organized in the Comintern. They attempt to cut off Zinoviev from his contacts abroad. Important documents and information are kept from him. His secretaries are sabotaged. Even the technical personnel frequently acts with impudence towards the formerly almighty Comintern Pope.

Much malicious pressure is applied to the "impure." Stalin has their complete sympathy. He uses every opportunity to demonstrate to the foreign comrades his contempt for the Comintern regime of Zinoviev. So far he does not act openly against Zinoviev, but from time to time he emits an arrow from his bow—everyone knowing against whom it is directed.

He comes out for democracy and solidarity within the Comintern. He opposes Zinoviev's system of building up and dismissing leaders. He writes a letter to a German Communist that gets circulated through the entire Comintern:

"The leader of a party can be a real leader only if people are not just afraid of him, but respectful and submissive to his authority in the party. To create such leaders is difficult. It is a long and tedious process. But it is necessary."

Bukharin goes along with Stalin on every single question and is instrumental in creating an atmosphere of confidence in the Comintern for him. Kuusinen keeps cautiously silent, not knowing what the outcome of the fight will be. Piatnitsky buries himself in his organizational work. Bela Kun tries to bring Zinoviev and Stalin together, and is scornfully repulsed by both.

Only Manuilsky is always in the best of spirits. He enjoys making fun of friends and foes alike. Particularly of Piatnitsky and old Riazanov, director of the Marx-Engels Institute. Of these two he tells the following story:

One day Karl Marx arrived in Moscow. He immediately walked up to the Comintern building. At the entrance he was stopped by a GPU man.

"Your permit, Comrade!"

"I am Karl Marx."

"That doesn't mean a thing to me. Even if you were Comrade Piatnitsky in person, you'd need a permit!"

"Who is Comrade Piatnitsky?" Karl Marx inquired.

"Comrade Piatnitsky is Comrade Piatnitsky, damn it!"

"I'd like to talk to him."

"First you've got to fill out a questionnaire: What is your name? ....Spell it..... Born where?"

"In Trier."

"Where is Trier?"

"In the Kingdom of Prussia."

"Now I got you! You're really a counter-revolutionary. Don't you know there aren't any kings any more? Who knows whether Comrade Piatnitsky will even want to speak with you. . . . . . What party do you belong to?"

"To the First International."

"Aha! You're not even a member of the Third International!"

Piatnitsky received his guest with great suspicion. "What are you seeking in Moscow, Comrade Marx? Have you a mandate? How did you travel? The Department of Communications has not sent in a report on you. Have you a passport?"

Karl Marx took from his pocket an old yellow paper: "The state authorities confirm . . . . *etc., etc.*"

Piatnitsky snatched it from his hand and called into the telephone: "Mirov, come down right away! I've got an interesting passport . . . . . What? . . . . No, it isn't false. It's an original." Turning to Marx: "Now, tell me, what do you want in Moscow, Comrade Marx?"

"I should like to see what you have done to my teachings here."
Piatnitsky looked embarrassed. "I'm sorry. I'm not competent
in that field. You must talk with Bela Kun in the Propaganda
Department. Or better yet, go over to the Karl Marx Institute,
to Riazanov." He took up a telephone. "Comrade Riazanov, I
have a visitor, Karl Marx. Can he come to see you?"

Riazanov roared: "Have him come right over. I urgently need
a collaborator to decipher Marx's manuscripts."

At the Marx-Engels Institute, Karl Marx was received magnifi-
cently. Riazanov showed him with great pride the many steel
vaults where he was keeping his Marx manuscripts. He invited
him in friendly fashion to enter.

Unsuspectingly, Karl Marx stepped into the steel vault. In a
flash, Riazanov clamped down the door. "At last I've got you, and
here you stay for all eternity!"

And so Karl Marx stayed in Riazanov's vaults and has not been
seen in Moscow since.

A BOMB EXPLODES IN SOFIA

April, 1925

The bomb that the Central Committee of the Bulgarian Communist Party exploded in the Cathedral of Sofia caused an earthquake in the Comintern building on the Machavaya. Piatnitsky
was out of his mind. Kuusinen locked himself up in his office and
was not to be seen. Bela Kun ran from room to room, his thick
underlip trembling with excitement. Nobody risked an opinion.
Even Manuilsky remained silent.

The tension was extraordinary when an invitation to a special
session of the Secretariat arrived from Zinoviev. For the first time
the head of the Foreign Department of the GPU, Trilisser, participated at a session of the Secretariat of the Comintern. Zinoviev was
even more nervous than the other participants at the session. His
face was paler than usual and his voice higher pitched.

He began his explanations with a statement that neither the
Comintern nor the GPU had given any order or suggestion for the
dynamiting in Sofia. The Bulgarians had acted on their own.
Neither Kolarov nor Dimitrov, the two leaders of the Bulgarian

Communist Party, nor the GPU agents in Bulgaria, had sent in a report.

Then Zinoviev read aloud all orders he had sent out to Bulgaria in the last eighteen months. All ran more or less along the same lines: Overcome the opportunist policies which led to the serious defeats of June and September, 1923; construct an underground organization, establish a tie with the revolutionary peasants and their organizations, set up armed resistance against the extermination of the Bulgarian Communists by the police, and prepare the Party for the maturing new revolutionary situation that is inevitable.

Trilisser then took the floor and reported on the activity of his GPU agents in Bulgaria. It consisted chiefly in a struggle against the remnants of Wrangel's White Guards, who had received the right of asylum in Bulgaria and who were now being used by the government as civil-war guards against the Communists. He, too, declared categorically that the GPU had nothing whatever to do with the dynamiting.

There was no debate—no one knew what to say. A resolution was voted to await reports and the return of the Comintern agents, and then to state the attitude of the Executive Committee of the Comintern, in full publicity.

Bela Kun, head of the department for agitation and propaganda, was given the task of organizing a big propaganda campaign against Zankov, the Bulgarian prime minister.

Piatnitsky assumed responsibility for mobilizing all sections of the Comintern for assistance to the victims of the terror that followed upon the bombing.

* * * * *

The praesidium has not called a further session about the Bulgarian catastrophe. But now I understand what has happened in Sofia. Kolarov and Dimitrov escaped. The whole truth was not to be learned from their reports. Immediately on their arrival in Moscow they had gone to see Zinoviev, who as usual gave them their instructions.

But there were also some more lowly members of the Bulgarian Communist Party who arrived in Moscow after escaping from the blood purge visited upon the Bulgarian Communists by Zankov. They told me the truth.

The bombing had really originated in the heads of the two left wing leaders of the Bulgarian Communist Party, Jekov and Minkov; it had also been organized by their group. One of the wardens of the Cathedral of Sofia had helped the friends of Jekov and Minkov to place a bomb in the vaults of the Cathedral where it exploded without killing or even seriously wounding a single member of the Bulgarian government, all of whose ministers were assembled at the time in the Cathedral.

The Bulgarian Communists were in a desperate situation in the spring of 1925. In the fall of 1923, under the leadership of Kolarov and Dimitrov, they had committed a fatal blunder. They permitted the conservative Zankov to overthrow the government of the radical peasant leader, Stamboulinski, without calling out their powerful and influential party. They believed they could afford to sit on the fence and watch the two opposing factions—factions equally opposed, according to the prevailing viewpoint in the party, to the revolution—and reap the benefits of the struggle.

After Stamboulinski's downfall, however, Zankov immediately began a campaign of extermination against the Communists. Isolated from Stamboulinski's radical peasants, they tried to respond by insurrection but were quickly put down.

From then on the terror against the Communists intensified. The Party had to disappear underground.

Into this situation came Zinoviev's orders and suggestions to eliminate opportunist blunders and to prepare for a maturing revolutionary crisis which was absolutely inevitable. Dimitrov and Kolarov lost control of their party. As usual after a defeat, a radical left wing arose, accusing the two leaders of treason against the Bulgarian revolution.

Following his general political line, Zinoviev favored the Bulgarian leftists. But he overlooked completely that these were of a calibre different from the German leftists whom he had helped into power after the defeat of 1923, and who manifested their radicalism by the blowing of whistles and trumpets in the Reichstag.

Minkov and Jekov were revolutionaries of the type of the Russian

106

Narodniki, intellectuals and former officers of the Bulgarian army. Steeled by innumerable clashes with the police and Zankov's armed gangs, they entertained but one thought after 1923—revenge for their fallen comrades! Avenge their murders!

In Zinoviev's instructions they had read again and again about the new revolutionary tide that was coming. What would have been more natural than that the simultaneous death of the entire Bulgarian government would open the floodgates for the tidal wave to sweep in?

Zinoviev had been playing with fire, without giving a thought to the fact that it might burn the entire Bulgarian labor movement.

Minkov and Jekov could not be ordered to Moscow to be established there as scapegoats. They barricaded themselves with other members of their group in a house in Sofia, and defended themselves to the last bullet. They fell fighting.

Their friends who had been caught alive were hanged a few days later on Zankov's gallows.

The Bulgarian episode shattered Zinoviev's self-confidence. I posed the question to myself whether he really was convinced that after the defeat of 1923 a new revolutionary situation was ripening in Bulgaria when he gave out his directives. I am certain he was completely sincere and convinced. He is a fanatical, almost hysterical devotee of the revolution. Organically he is not capable of conceiving of any but revolutionary situations as long as the counter-revolution has not been definitely and conclusively victorious. He is not up to complicated situations, neither political nor psychological.

But this time neither motive played a role in his instructions to the Bulgarians. He wanted to demonstrate to the Russian party that the German defeat had been only a passing episode, that the Comintern was still able to wage a successful revolutionary war. His instructions to the Bulgarians were also a product of his factional fight against Stalin who keeps opposing Zinoviev's rule over the Comintern more and more—a tragic attempt to re-establish his prestige!

But all this was of no avail. At the Party Congress in December, Stalin openly turned his guns on Zinoviev. Neither the Bulgarian affair nor the Comintern were mentioned. Stalin destroyed Zinoviev with the weapons of factional intrigue of which the latter considered himself a master unsurpassed.

WORLD REVOLUTION IS DEAD IN RUSSIA
Spring, 1926

My personal position in the Executive Committee is strong. I have, so to speak, become part of the regular inventory of the building on the Machavaya. The Russian secretaries customarily refer all questions concerning France, Spain, and the Latin-American countries to me. Most of the representatives of these countries have no objection. I prepare the meetings and the resolutions. The tactical dots on the "i's" are made by the others.

In this way I avoid the fluctuations of the "line." Have I the right to interfere in the clash of the giants? Shouldn't I be grateful that these old Russian revolutionaries have forgotten my past and accepted me in their circle? Haven't I promised my comrades in Grenoble to serve the cause of the world revolution with everything at my command?

But am I still serving the cause of world revolution? It seems to me that there is very little revolutionary spirit in the building on the Machavaya. Life in there is more like the well-organized and smooth-functioning mechanism of the headquarters of a large industrial enterprise than of a revolutionary center.

All activity in the Machavaya building revolves around the secretariat of Piatnitsky. According to the constitution of the Executive Committee, it has only organizational and technical functions to fulfill. It should be only an administrative organ within the Comintern. Actually, however, its activity profoundly influences the political functions of the Executive Committee.

Piatnitsky personally is the head of the organizational and the financial divisions as well as of the OMS, the technical communications division. The divisions of information, news, publicity, agitation and propaganda, each with a member of the secretariat at its head, operate in close contact with Piatnitsky's secretariat.

The various secretariats for the different countries represent a second group of divisions. There are a German secretariat, one for

108

the Latin countries, for the Balkans, for Scandinavia, for the Anglo-Saxon countries, for Latin-America, and for China, and the Eastern secretariat for all of the colonial countries.

The delegates of the different Comintern sections and parties work in these national secretariats, but in their capacities as members of these secretariats they have only an advisory function. Only the Executive Committee and its Praesidium, the organ of which is represented by these secretariats, have the power of decision.

Two or three times a week the diplomatic couriers of the Narkomindel deliver the reports of the central committees of the various Comintern parties and sections. Every report or document arriving from abroad, even when it is addressed to one of the national representatives, first is routed through the secretariat. The same applies to every outgoing letter or report. It is difficult to imagine a more complete control than that exercised by the secretariat in regard to its members and collaborators.

Within the respective countries themselves this control is supplemented by special agents of the Executive Committee who exercise direct supervision over the central committees of the different countries. The Executive Committee has always followed the principle of selecting special agents for any specific sections from other sections. A German will never be a special agent for Germany, but for England or France; a Frenchman may work in Italy or Spain but not in France; an American in China or India but not in America. Only agents who are members of the Russian section may work in all Comintern parties. In this way the Russian monopoly in the Comintern is firmly anchored in its entire structure.

One day Piatnitsky asked me to give a talk on the international situation in his stead at a meeting of the workers of a big machine-tool plant. I was glad to do as he asked. Piatnitsky works so hard that everyone is always glad to help him out. I speak Russian well enough now to be able to give a prepared talk.

The meeting takes place after working hours in the large clubroom of the factory. I give the usual talk, strictly adhering to the thesis of the Executive: "The international situation is full of danger. All the imperialist conflicts are growing, particularly those between England and America. The danger of war against the Soviet Union

109

is becoming ever more threatening. The bourgeoisie has recovered from the postwar crisis but the stabilization of capitalism is still unsure and full of contradictions. It is certain that great new revolutionary developments will take place."

I talk for three-quarters of an hour without interruption by anyone. I feel that the assembly is bored, and I am happy when I finish.

The chairman thanks me profusely and opens the discussion. He waits a little while, but nobody wants to take the floor. The back rows of the meeting begin to disperse.

The chairman becomes nervous and uses his bell. An old worker sitting in one of the front rows asks for the floor. Immediately there is absolute quiet. I have the impression that most of the workers are surprised that one among them has something to say.

"Comrade X, it is very nice of you to come to us. Please do not take exception to my words. Because I want to tell you my opinion frankly and openly.

"You want the best for us Russian workers. Yet I advise you, return to France! I don't believe a word any more of the fairy tales of the Comintern. Since 1918 you've promised us the world revolution each year. Instead, there is defeat each year.

"Then we are told that we have to work harder than before to make good this defeat. . . . . Comrade X, go home! Do something useful there, to help your own workers. We, here in Russia, we will do our jobs by ourselves. You foreigners can't help us!"

Most of those present applaud his words. The chairman immediately comes back at the worker with a sharp attack, talking about dangerous deviations and hinting darkly at what will happen to him if he continues his vicious talk. He apologizes to me and offers me a chance to reply, but I refuse.

The car of the Red Director took me home. On the way he talked incessantly: "The old worker is a crank. I'll show him. There are black sheep everywhere."

I ignored his subservient remarks.

My thoughts turned back on myself. The few words the old worker had spoken called forth all the doubts that had crept into me since 1923. All the arguments I had invented to pacify the tor-

110

ment within me vanished into insignificance. There was nothing left in me but misery without end.

JEANNE IS HAPPY

At home Jeanne was waiting in the foyer of the hotel. On her lap she held two little Pioneer girls, who were listening to her tales with shining eyes.

Jeanne has become happy in Moscow. With great energy she has learned to talk Russian—more fluently than I. She is now the director of a children's home connected with a spinning mill. This work fills her entire life.

She is more than just a director—she is the goddess of the home, the adored of the children and the mothers. Two girls assist her, one a fourteen-year-old orphan, an intelligent girl with red cheeks and hair; the other a fifteen year old Circassian who was studying at the Eastern University, tall, slim, with serious sad eyes. Both of them feel duty-bound to read Jeanne the numerous principles proclaimed by the Communist Youth Organization for the training and education of the youngest generation of the Russian Revolution.

But Jeanne disposes of these strict orders with a smile. She has her own pedagogy.

When Jeanne was introduced to her new work by the leader of the Communist Youth Organization, she was given, in addition to many good wishes, a large house half in ruins. It had a neglected garden overgrown with weeds. It had formerly belonged to the owner of a factory. After the revolution it had served as a workers' club for some time, but had finally fallen into such dilapidation that it was deserted.

Jeanne never had heard of the Communist Saturdays. On these days, in the early years of the revolution, the Communist leaders and large sections of the population had voluntarily done many hours of overtime work to clear the streets and the cities of dirt and the debris of civil war. Now she was organizing her own Communist Saturdays for her children's home.

At the close of work in the spinning mill, she talked to the workers in her strange Russian and asked for voluntary assistance. She got all she wanted and more. Even from the factories in the vicinity.

111

There were building workers, carpenters, plumbers, cabinet makers, upholsterers—all came bringing their materials for repairs with them.

In a few weeks one could not recognize the house. New windows and doors had been set in. Everything was freshly painted. Several baths had even been installed with plumbing that really functioned, a rarity in Moscow! In the house was furniture fit for little children. In the garden weeds had been pulled out, fresh gravel strewn over newly made paths.

When Jeanne moved in with her twenty-five children, it was a day of festivity in the entire neighborhood.

Jeanne's children always looked clean as a whistle. Each child had two or three simple pinafores or suits, and a little red beret designed by Jeanne. These became the fashion for all the children's homes in Moscow.

Jeanne tried to accustom the children to light, easily digested food instead of the heavy Russian diet. Anything she needed and couldn't get from the authorities, she simply went out and requisitioned. She plundered all delegates mercilessly, and ran up debts in the cooperative stores that were rarely paid, and forgotten with pleasure.

She was proud that her children sang not only the "International," but also the "Carmagnole" and "Sur le Pont d'Avignon" in French. She had trained them for weeks, and now these little Russian children sang the favorite song of the children of her country with as much enjoyment as the children of Provence.

"Jeanne dear, I have an idea of handing in my resignation and returning to France."

"My God! Why that? We're so happy here now."

I told her of my experience in the machine-tool plant. All the bitterness accumulated during the years rose in me!

"I can't bear the hypocrisy of the Comintern people any longer. Some of them, like Manuilsky, are cynics. They make fun of everything and everybody. Others, like Piatnitsky, are like ants, indifferent to what they do. The Russian workers have no faith in the world revolution any longer, and they're right! What we're doing is just giving it a fresh coat of paint every year, in order to make the workers believe it's still alive."

Jeanne listened with great burning eyes. It was the first time I had ever expressed my doubts so openly.

"Do what you think is right, dear. I understand too little of the things you're telling me. But I'll weep if we leave. I love this country because it's making its children happy. My children's home means more to me than Communism. If their children stay happy, the Russians will win."

DECISION IN THE GENERAL STAFF

Summer, 1926

I did not hand in my resignation. For six long years I have devoted all my strength to Comintern work. I do not want to make a final break unless I consider everything completely lost.

In the Russian party a wild fight between Zinoviev and Stalin had developed, and spread excitement over the whole country. No one in the Comintern paid attention to the wishes of its president any longer. He was treated by everyone like a dead dog.

For some time I entertained the thought of writing to my friends in Grenoble, and asking them to decide whether I should stay in Moscow or not. The idea seemed too cowardly to me, though.

The crisis in the Comintern came to a climax in the summer of 1926, when *Pravda* reprinted on its first page a letter that Lenin had written just before the outbreak of the October Revolution in 1917, condemning Zinoviev and Kamenev for openly denouncing the insurrectionary plans of the party. That was the finish of Zinoviev.

In the preceding few months, Bukharin had become the object of all the attacks of the opposition, led by Zinoviev. Zinoviev dug in with his Leningrad workers and attacked the policy of Bukharin and Stalin:

"You are delivering the country up to the rich peasants. You are undermining the supremacy of the working class."

Stalin responded grimly at a stormy party conference:

"You are asking for the blood of Bukharin. We will not give it to you. Be sure of that!"

Bukharin received the presidency of the Comintern. I am not sure he regarded this as a victory. All the collaborators of the Comintern wrote long statements against Zinoviev. The most violent denunciations came from those who had been most subservient to him.

The same spectacle was repeated in the foreign Communist parties.

Beginning of 1927

Of the magnificent political teamwork of Lenin's circle, that so excited my admiration at the Third Congress, there is nothing left. In 1924, Zinoviev, Kamenev, and Bukharin united with Stalin to fight Trotsky. Nobody fought more violently against him than Zinoviev, who in 1925 demanded Trotsky's expulsion from the Party. At that time, Stalin refused to go along.

In 1926, the whole scene shifted. Now Zinoviev fought the coalition of Stalin and Bukharin, and concentrated his attack chiefly against the latter.

In 1927, another complete shift took place. Zinoviev combined with Trotsky against Stalin, with Bukharin in the background.

At the beginning of May, 1927, another session of the Praesidium took place, for which many delegates from abroad had been called. Trotsky, who was still a member of the Praesidium, had insisted on participating. Zinoviev had not. There was no way to keep Trotsky out.

The session took place in the small Red meeting hall of the Machavaya building. The hall was so crowded that it was nearly impossible to draw a breath. Everybody was nervous and tense. Everybody knew this would be Trotsky's last talk to the Comintern.

Stalin was not present. Bukharin gave the main talk. He was pale and exceedingly nervous. He did not look Trotsky in the eye.

Kuusinen was chairman, but he seemed to shrivel up when Trotsky mounted the small platform. I had the impression that he was afraid of Trotsky.

Some of the delegates expected Trotsky to talk about the fight in the Russian Party. They were disappointed. He still maintained strict party discipline and limited his speech to problems of the Comintern, asking for the immediate dissolution of the Anglo-Russian trade union committee and the withdrawal of the Chinese Communist Party from Chiang Kai Shek's Kuomintang.

In his bearing he was still the old Trotsky. But he talked into space. None of the delegates—and many of them admired him in their hearts—dared give a sign of agreement. Of the revolutionary

114

parliament of 1921 not a trace was left. Spiritual death was already hovering over the Comintern.

Trotsky's words cut like sharp knives. He was as brilliant as ever in his incomparable polemical oratory. When Bela Kun made a stupid and awkward interjection, Trotsky replied:

"I apologize to the Italian comrades for my misuse of the language of Dante: *La maniera della Bela non é bella maniera . . . . .*"

Bukharin's reply had even less vigor than his address. It was evident that he was very unhappy. When Trotsky left the hall, the meeting breathed easier, as if freed from a heavy weight. Again they were among themselves.

RADEK'S MISERY

After the German defeat of the fall of 1923, and his expulsion from the Comintern, Radek had gone with Trotsky. He had become president of the Sun Yat Sen University, where students from China and Japan studied Marx and Lenin. He submerged himself with passion in the study of Chinese languages and literature, and turned entirely to the East. People observed jokingly that Radek would soon have his famous beard clipped and would grow a pigtail.

To associate with Radek was frowned upon in the Comintern. Although he was a Russian and still had his quarters in the Kremlin, he belonged to the "impure."

His merciless wit pursued the new Comintern leaders. Notwithstanding the unwritten law not to talk with Radek, I saw him from time to time, and half an hour of conversation with him was more instructive than the longest meeting with Manuilsky, Kuusinen, or Bela Kun.

One morning I met Radek in the park adjoining the Kremlin walls, near the Comintern building. He was like a sleepwalker. When I gave him a friendly pat on the shoulder, he looked up as if jerked out of a deep sleep. I looked into a devastated face, into eyes stricken with grief.

"Larissa Reissner died during the night." And he ran away as if hounded by the Furies.

Larissa Reissner was the light that had entered Radek's life when his political star was sinking. Larissa was the most beautiful woman

I had ever met in Russia. It was sheer pleasure just to look at her. Wherever she went, she excited attention and admiration.

Larissa, daughter of a well-known Baltic jurist, had as a young girl participated in the civil war. A little book of her experiences had advanced her into the first rank of Red reporters.

Later she had married Raskolnikov, a leader of the rebellion in the Czarist navy, and had accompanied him to Afghanistan, where he had been the first Soviet ambassador. In Kabul, the capital, English and Russian interests in Asia met, and Larissa soon was in the center of all diplomatic intrigues at the court of the Emir. It was not long before she commanded even more confidence than Raskolnikov in the People's Commissariat of Foreign Affairs. Chicherin himself, who had little use for women, ventured the opinion that Larissa might cause him to forget his principle not to employ women in the diplomatic service.

In 1923 Larissa returned from Afghanistan. A new revolution in Germany appeared on the horizon, and she felt it impossible not to participate.

It was after her return that her romance with Radek began. For a few years he was happy.

"La Belle et la Bête!" Jeanne said about the uneven pair. Radek's ugliness was accentuated brutally in the company of this lovely woman. But Larissa loved him, and to Radek she was the greatest victory in his life. His political misfortune seemed of no consequence to him. He had more wit, more sparkle than ever.

It was the summer of 1927 when Larissa fell ill of typhoid fever. Within a few days she died.

I do not think Radek will recover from this blow.

STALIN TAKES OVER
Summer, 1927

Tremendous sensation in the Comintern building. At a meeting of the Secretariat, Piatnitsky announced that the next Congress, which had been postponed because of the conflict in the Russian party, would be held in the Trade Union building, former palace of the nobility, and not in the Kremlin. The Comintern was expelled from the Kremlin.

Bukharin was seen less than ever. He was working on the draft of a program for the Communist International, to be discussed by the coming Congress. The program was expected to be a comprehensive presentation of the principles of Communism, a sort of Communist Manifesto in modern dress. Yet again, just as at the time of Zinoviev's fall, rumors crept steadily through the halls. The atmosphere was no less poisonous.

Although Bukharin was drafting the program, nobody knew who would present it at the Congress. It was even whispered that Stalin, who can talk no foreign language, might make the programmatic speech.

Bukharin worked in a small country house near Moscow. One Sunday I decided to visit him, wanting to ask his advice. I was at the end of my moral resistance and could bear the suffocating atmosphere of the Comintern no longer.

I found Bukharin in the midst of his work, and asked him if he could spare me an hour. "You are the only man in Moscow in whom I still have confidence. I have to reach a decision that may change the course of my life. Please help me!"

I told him of all the doubts accumulated within me during the years, described the cynicism and the irresponsibility in the Executive Committee, and explained, finally, that I was fighting with myself whether to leave Moscow or to stay on longer. Bukharin, I felt, hesitated before he replied.

"Dear friend, I know what is happening in the Comintern. But that is without significance now. The bourgeois rule in Europe is secure for a long time, regardless of the policies we follow. We are not in a position to endanger it.

"The struggle for Communism is happening right here in Russia now. The decision will come soon, this year or next. Believe me, it is a life and death struggle!

"You have to listen every day to the bad jokes of Manuilsky. I have to listen every day to the crude words of Stalin. The intrigues in the Comintern are a storm in a teacup. It is the struggle in the leadership of our party that will decide the fate of the Soviet Union and the Comintern.

"Return to France if you cannot endure it here any longer. I envy you that you can leave. If Stalin is defeated, we will try to rebuild the International! If he wins out, there will be civil war in the Soviet Union, and the Comintern will go under!"

"But why don't we try now to mobilize the International against Stalin if, as you think, he is corrupting the Soviet Union and the Revolution?"

"Because by doing so, I put a weapon into the hands of Stalin against myself. He would simply say that I am attempting to mobilize the foreign workers against the Soviet Union. Believe me, there is no other way. For the time being we Russians have to bear the entire burden of the struggle."

I left Bukharin, determined to hand in my resignation at the first opportunity.

* * * * *

The Congress was a comedy worthy of the pen of Gogol. Bukharin acted as president and made the big programmatic speech. With the exception of a few insignificant incidents, everything went according to schedule.

But in the halls and corridors a flood of dirty rumors against Bukharin was spreading, such as I had never experienced in the Comintern. It was really in the halls and corridors that a change of regime was maneuvered while Bukharin himself was proclaiming the principles of Communism at the meetings.

Bukharin obeyed the rules of the game. He simply ignored what was happening in the corridors. In one of his speeches he reminded his listeners of one of Lenin's last warnings that it was preferable to have self-willed but talented men elected to the leadership of the Communist parties than to have obedient idiots.

Right after the close of the Congress the fight in the Russian Party in respect to the Five Year Plan came to a climax. The World Congress had unanimously approved the expulsion of Trotsky and his followers. The Russian leaders had assured the Comintern that after this, complete unanimity would be restored in their ranks. Yet not even all the delegates had departed when a new clash came out into the open.

Bukharin, Tomsky, and Rykov defended a plan of cautious industrialization of the country and a slow collectivization of agriculture

118

in order not to endanger the economic and social stability of the country. Stalin accepted a radical industrialization program developed by Trotsky in 1924, magnified it and demanded a merciless policy of collectivization in the agricultural districts in order to emancipate the cities from the sabotaging of grain deliveries by the peasants. The struggle in the Russian Party grew passionate and wild.

We in the Comintern are spectators to the fight, like children at a circus. Bukharin now becomes as invisible in the Comintern as Zinoviev had been two years ago. Everybody realizes he is finished.

AMERICAN INTERLUDE

Fall of 1928

The atmosphere on the Machavaya resembles that of a comic opera: lackeys with a knowledge of the bedchamber secrets of his majesty decide about politics. Our new general staff of the world revolution, solemnly and unanimously elected at the sessions of the Sixth World Congress, is as little informed as to Stalin's intentions as everybody else. Two young ambitious adventurers make the decision on the policies and destinies of entire Comintern sections. When I ask Piatnitsky what our intentions really are in the newest American party crisis, he answers ironically: "Why, don't ask me. Ask Heinz Neumann or Lominadze." Kuusinen, the responsible chief for American affairs, answers my question with a look of despair in his devoted dog's eyes.

I never participated in American party struggles as they were put on the Comintern stage. The Comintern habit of regarding oneself as an expert on any and every country because one happens to be a member of the committee for that particular country, I never made my own. To the wild and vague discussions of the U. S. A. committee I listened with indifference. They had absolutely no political substance and made the impression of boxing matches with the monopoly of party leadership as a prize. Not that the Communists were unaccustomed to factional struggles with a wild-west touch. Some people in the know remembered a session with the leadership of the Finnish Communists at which there had been dead and seriously wounded.

In the beginning I was inclined to regard the rudeness of some of the American Communists as an expression of their unbridled political temperaments. Once it looked as if one of them, purple in the face, would smother his adversary who had just called him by an unspeakable name. I jumped up to prevent a fist fight. My friend Lapinsky, the gentle Polish economist who had some understanding of America and Americans, motioned me back to my seat. "Remain calm. They do not bite. They are only trying to impress us in order to get one more vote for themselves. They'll do anything for that."

In the end the naive over-shrewdness of the leading American Communists led to their own downfall. They fell for all the traps set for them by Stalin's court intriguers, and at the same time lost Stalin's favor and their influence in the party.

Stalin had to move cautiously during and after the Sixth World Congress. His majority in the Politbureau was still uncertain. Kalinin and Voroshilov frequently voted against him. Bukharin and his friends Rykov and Tomsky had not yet been made ready for the kill.

Neumann and Lominadze were given the task of preparing things in the Comintern. From each delegation they selected a few who seemed to them worthy of confidence, and whispered in their ears: "Bukharin is finished. He is a dangerous opportunist. If he isn't eliminated soon from the Russian leadership, there will be famine in the cities. In the Comintern he works hand in glove with all the renegades."

Those particularly worthy of confidence were given a personal interview with Stalin. Among them was Bill Foster, the leader of the American minority. Originally Foster was not supposed to participate in the Congress, for he was the candidate of the American Communists for the presidential elections. When the list of delegates was made known, Kuusinen suggested having the American Communists withdraw Foster. This was unanimously decided upon, and certain observations not too flattering to the American party leadership were added to the decision. This was really a grotesque situation—a man supposed to be the candidate of a party attempting to expand its political influence in the United States to spend his time during the election campaign in Moscow. Yet that was what

120

actually happened. The resolution was never sent off to New York.

Heinz Neumann and Lominadze had personally decided to make Foster the leader of the American Communists at a time when he himself had to regard his chances as completely nil. For Foster was known as belonging to the "right" wing, and the entire drift in the Comintern was to the "left." By all the accepted rules of the Comintern, Lovestone had much greater chances of remaining leader than Foster of becoming leader.

Lovestone was tripped up with his friend Pepper-Pogany, at that time representative of the Comintern in the United States. Neumann and Lominadze had had a deadly hate for this ambitious and ruthless Hungarian since he had tried to counter them in China. This was the fact that decided the change in leadership in the American Communist party. In order to remain in power there was just one thing for Lovestone to do, to dissociate himself from Pepper. Naturally he did not and could not do it because the United States representative of the Comintern was his best support in his fight against Foster. So Foster became leader of the American Communists without knowing how and why.

Even when, with instructions from Neumann, he went to see Stalin, he was unaware of what really was happening. Stalin's English translator told me about the amusing interview. Foster had repeated the story invented by Heinz Neumann with telling effect. He told Stalin that Pepper had been whispering to everybody in New York that the Canton *putsch* of the Chinese Communists had been undertaken on Stalin's own initiation. As a finishing touch, Foster added, Lovestone was repeating Pepper's story wherever he had a chance.

Foster did not even have to present his criticism of Lovestone's policies in the United States. The interview with Stalin had taken less than ten minutes. Stalin was yellow with rage. Lovestone's fate was decided then and there. Not even when, back in the United States, Lovestone demanded the elimination of Bukharin from the Comintern, was it of any avail; nor that the overwhelming majority of the American Communists were on his side after the Sixth Congress. On the contrary, that was just one reason more for Neumann and Lominadze to wipe him out.

Finally Lovestone fell into their last trap. He returned to Moscow in May, 1929, where the American Commission of the Comintern decided the factional fight in favor of Foster. Lovestone was kept for months in Moscow, while in the meantime his majority in the United States was pulverized. When he got wise to the game it was too late. He left Moscow on his own, and before he arrived in New York he had been excommunicated from the Comintern.

In the secretariat, American affairs were no longer discussed during the period. The decisions came in sealed envelopes from Stalin's office and were transmitted directly to New York. Everybody was aware that they had been dictated by Lominadze. Nearly everybody was disgusted with these methods, but in the end what difference did it make whether Lovestone or Foster led the American Communists?

I myself was already completely indifferent. Without realizing it, I had already broken with the Comintern, and I was so tired that even a protest would have seemed a senseless effort.

FIRST PURGE IN THE COMINTERN
February, 1929

Nothing is left to keep me in Moscow. Not even the desire to see the result of the struggle in the party. I am determined to leave regardless of the outcome of this struggle. I no longer believe the Communist movement can be directed from Moscow.

There have been incidents that have destroyed the last trace of confidence in me. There has been an embezzlement in the German Communist Party. The Comintern had a very disagreeable surprise when it learned that the leader of the German Party, Thaelmann, had been aware of the embezzlement and had tried to cover it up.

The German Central Committee removed Thaelmann from office. But on order of Stalin the praesidium of the Comintern turned matters around, absolved Thaelmann of all guilt, and utilized the opportunity to remove the German opposition that had allied itself with Rykov, Tomsky, and Bukharin from the Party.

A short time afterwards, early in 1929, there was a purge in the Communist Party of the Soviet Union, and accordingly the same sort of purge was ordered for the members of the staff of the Comintern. The significance of such purges, as set forth in the statutes of the party, should have been to protect the organization from pernicious elements by examination of its members.

The secretary of the party organization in the Comintern building asked me surely to be present at the meeting. Strict orders had been given this time that everyone, regardless of position, would have to submit to the purge.

I arrived at the meeting late, after it had begun. The leader of the party organization in the Comintern, the Comintern "cell" as it was called, was an artisan employed in the building. Next to him sat Manuilsky and two other employees.

Standing was a German stenographer, a short woman who had worked for us for years. She was the daughter of a German Communist who had been sentenced to prison for a long term. She was slightly crippled, and shy. We all liked her very much. My seat was close enough for me to observe that she was trembling throughout her whole body and was suppressing her tears with effort.

"Why did you lie?" the chairman shouted at her.

"I didn't lie. I haven't seen Comrade Mueller for three months."

Comrade Mueller was one of the "impure" inhabiting a back room at the Hotel Lux. He had been there for years. I knew the stenographer was friendly with Mueller—there were no secrets at the Lux.

From the auditorium came a shrill voice.

"She's lying, impudently! Mueller visited her last night!" The voice belonged to another German stenographer.

Again the chairman shouted at the girl.

"If you don't tell the truth now, we will expel you immediately from the party."

By now she was weeping freely and admitted that Mueller had visited her the evening before. The chairman already was making a motion to have her expelled for three months because of lying to the purge committee, and to have the reasons for the expulsion entered in the party book.

I was aghast at the shamelessness of this procedure, and was ready to leave the hall when the voice of the chairman called me back.

"Comrade X, please stay here. The cell has decided to have your examination next."

Hundreds of eyes were staring at me. The purge of a high functionary apparently gave promise of being an interesting spectacle.

With courteous emphasis the chairman offered me a chair and turned to the meeting.

"Has anyone here any complaint against Comrade X?" At the same time he whispered confidentially, "You know, I have to preserve appearances."

A voice was heard from the auditorium. I recognized it as that of a translator whom I had had transferred a few months earlier because of incompetence, to a less well-paid job.

"Yes, I! I have seen Comrade X talking intimately to Radek. I do not understand how it is possible for a member of the Executive Committee to maintain relations with Radek."

The chairman turned to me. "Will you please answer, Comrade X?"

I looked at Manuilsky, who ostentatiously looked past me.

"Yes, surely I will. I talk to whom I please, and permit nobody to prescribe my associations."

Excited murmurs of "Incredible! Unbelievable!" were heard.

The chairman smiled pleasantly. "Certainly, Comrade X, we do not want to dictate your associations. But the cell has the right to inquire into the private affairs of every comrade. The real Communist has nothing to conceal. Please, can you tell me what you talked to Radek about?"

I had forgotten the content of our conversation, but I replied:

"What we talked about together is no concern of yours."

I noticed Manuilsky whispering something to the chairman, who took some document from a file.

"Comrade X, it seems necessary to ask you some further questions. What was your profession before you arrived in Moscow?"

I replied: "One year before my trip to Moscow I was a private instructor. Before that I was a minister in a church in a working class community of Grenoble."

There was suppressed laughter.

"You are married. I see from the files that your wife is not a party member. Why not?"

"That concerns only my wife."

Now the chairman again turned to the assemblage. "I do not want to impose my own opinion on you, comrades. Comrade X has worked for many years, to the complete satisfaction of the Executive Committee. Now he refuses to give information to his party organization about his 'private affairs' as he calls them.

"He has been a member of the party for nine years, and his wife has not joined. Possibly the Communist Party has been too quick in giving Comrade X its confidence! We ought to think of Lenin's words: 'Do not look at the lips of the Communists, but at their hands.'

"Now," again turning to me, "wasn't your father also a minister?"

At this everybody laughed aloud. I jumped up and shouted at him:

"Do not dare to take the name of my father into your dirty mouth!"

I ran out of the hall into my office, and began packing my things feverishly. Then I called up Jeanne and asked her to get ready for our departure. Over the telephone I felt her breathless terror.

Two days later we left. None of the colleagues with whom I had worked all these years took leave of me.

At the station were Jeanne's two little assistants. One had Jeanne's favorite child, Marussya, a three-year-old with light gold hair, on her arm.

The train pulled out of the station. Jeanne wept as if her heart would break!

CHAPTER VI

Financial Agent of the Comintern (Cont.)

(From the Memoirs of Comrade Y)

March, 1927

SINCE 1926 I HAD BEEN ENTRUSTED BY PIATNITSKY WITH THE direction of all financial affairs in Western Europe. At that time I took over the reins that had fallen from Comrade T's hands. But I was strictly accountable only to headquarters under Piatnitsky. The business affairs of the German party were very favorable now. Their printing establishments were so prosperous they could pay their earnings over to the party. Their newspapers had gained more than a hundred thousand readers in one year; they made big profits by favorable contracts with paper manufacturers; they no longer needed subsidies from Moscow for their normal budget.

This was all very well, but we could not derive real pleasure and satisfaction from it. We had all accustomed ourselves to the atmosphere of stability and comfort. The fever of former years was gone. In the morning one trotted off to the office in the huge Karl Liebknecht building which we had bought when our old house became too small for us. We were eating at regular hours, at noon and in the evening. Government officials could not have lived a more routined life. Sometimes I was overcome with despair and rage, and I would get drunk and sigh for the good old times. But the daily routine quickly disposed of these moods. The next morning one went to the office and again dictated business letters and examined the accounts.

Only from time to time did I visit the Prussian Diet of which I was a deputy, or speak at mass meetings. I became completely occupied with business matters. One conference after another. With our attorneys I had to discuss the complicated legal affairs resulting from our vast real estate holdings. Mortgages and bank credits had to be arranged for. The Communist party in Germany had become a good and acceptable credit risk for the banks. The paper manufacturers handled our orders with the greatest care. We had become one of their best clients and paid our bills on the dot.

Party salaries were raised. Many hundreds of comrades were employed in the numerous business agencies of the Soviet Union in Germany. Never did we have as many party employees as at that time. Nevertheless Moscow sent one slogan for "Bolshevization of the party" after another, and called for preparation for revolutionary action.

Were we Bolshevized? Nobody knew. And nobody really cared.

STALIN TAKES A HAND

October, 1928

In the fall of 1928, the German Communist party experienced a palace revolution, tearing down the entire old structure and laying it waste. I was involved as an instrument in this change, without knowing it and without wanting it. . . . .

For months there had been rumors in Hamburg of irregularities of a financial nature in the leading cadres of the party district. The Control Committee of the district had examined the books, but nothing could be discovered. Explanatory statements were published in the party press. But they could not squelch the rumors. Talk about embezzling of funds became more and more insistent, and it was impossible to discover its source. Finally the matter popped up in all the newspapers of Hamburg. Some of them asked insulting questions. The situation was becoming intolerable.

The party found itself in a very unpleasant position. Two years earlier a popular referendum of ours had brought a sweeping success to the party. The imperial family and the other ruling houses of the various German states demanded huge contributions from the public treasury as compensation for the loss of their thrones. We had opposed this. We had succeeded in drawing the Social Democrats and the Democratic party into the movement and in rallying more than fourteen million votes around our slogan "No compensation to the Kaiser!" This success induced us to launch a second referendum on whether to build the first German battle cruiser after Versailles, for the construction of which the Reichstag had already voted the money. But the popular interest was small. We had to expect failure, although we were utilizing all means of propaganda as well as considerable financial resources.

In this situation the scandalous rumors in Hamburg were even less tolerable. Our Central Committee decided to look into the matter and sent me, together with another member of the Central Control Commission, to Hamburg for a complete and sweeping investigation.

For many reasons the trip was not entirely to my liking. I was immersed in difficult and engrossing business negotiations and didn't want to lose the time. I did not like the party atmosphere in Hamburg. This city was the home district of the party chief, Ernst Thaelmann. He had belonged to the left wing of the Independent Socialist party and was not very much liked by the former members of the Spartacus group in Hamburg. Yet it was impossible to refuse the job. The Central Committee insisted and Thaelmann himself, who at that time was in Moscow, had asked for the investigation by wire.

So neither my colleague nor I were in the best of spirits when we boarded the train for Hamburg. Without too much zest we examined all the records and account books of the party district, and at the end of the third day we decided to wind up our checking process. We wrote a sharply worded statement, to be published in the newspapers, in which we said that we personally would vouch for the honesty and correctness of the financial behavior of the Hamburg district and its leading functionaries. We expected to squelch the disagreeable rumors once and for all.

We were saying goodbye to the comrades in Hamburg, ready to take the train for Berlin in a few minutes. Suddenly someone said I was wanted on the telephone. The person insisted it was something of the utmost urgency and importance for the entire party. I took up the receiver.

"Who's talking?"

"I can't tell you my name. But listen carefully to what I'm

going to tell you now. The Secretary of the Hamburg party, Wittorf, has embezzled two thousand marks!"

I called into the telephone: "If there is nothing else you want to tell me, you might as well save your breath. If you can't tell me your name, I will hang up!" Yet I did not do as I said. The anonymous voice sounded firm and impressive. "Yes, I know you examined the books for three days and you found nothing irregular. Quite natural. For the two thousand marks were never entered in the books."

My colleague urged me: "Hurry up, we'll miss the train." I motioned him to keep quiet, because now I wanted to listen to the end.

"Wittorf received two thousand marks from the Soviet Russian Consul General in Hamburg as a subsidy for the spring elections. He spent them on the race tracks. Two members of the Control Commission, Presche and Riess, as well as the organizational secretary, Schehr, know about the whole business."

I couldn't answer. The anonymous caller had hung up.

I asked the Hamburg comrades to leave the room and repeated the telephone conversation to my colleague. We were sure that I had been in touch with the source of the anonymous rumors.

After a few hours of hurried conferences, all the participants in the affair had admitted their wrongdoings. I had told them directly that I knew the whole story. It did not take me long to find out that the unknown person had told me the truth over the telephone.

Late at night I called a meeting of the Hamburg district leadership. I informed them of the result of my investigation and suggested expelling the thief and his helpers from the party, Wittorf permanently, the other three for two years.

No sooner had I finished my presentation when an old worker, a personal friend of Thaelmann's, rose amidst the embarrassed silence of the district leaders and said:

"Oh no, Comrade Y, that is not the way this affair will end. Wittorf has embezzled money—he has to get out of the party. With Presche, Schehr, and Riess it's a different matter. These three are good and honest comrades. They have covered the embezzlement only under the compulsion of party discipline. Teddy gave them the order. It took a long time for him to convince them. We will not drop them. If they are guilty, then Teddy is more guilty!"

I had difficulty staying on my feet. Teddy was the party chief, Ernst Thaelmann. He had been elected a few weeks before as Acting President of the Comintern. Now it was not just an affair involving these four poor sinners—it involved the entire party and even the International!

I took a car and sped with my colleague through the mists of an early morning towards Berlin.

At the Hamburg district meeting, I had imposed absolute silence upon all members. Nevertheless on the following day the enemy press in Hamburg was asking: Is Thaelmann an embezzler? The scandal was out in the open. More was lost than our battle-cruiser campaign. The very cause the party stood for was in danger. The mists of corruption that arose in Hamburg were clouding the vision of our followers.

The Central Committee in Berlin called a plenary session for the twenty-sixth of September and had sent a wire to Moscow asking Thaelmann to return immediately. On his return trip he visited Hamburg first, before coming to Berlin. There he tried to rally his friends, but without success. His authority seemed destroyed. When the meeting of the Central Committee was called to order, Thaelmann was sitting in his usual place, a broken man.

Now it appeared that his career had come to an end. He sensed it himself and was ready to accept the decision. I explained to the Central Committee what had happened in Hamburg and spent much time on the confessions of Presche, Schehr, and Riess, who had covered Wittorf's embezzlement.

They had stated that when Wittorf told them of the embezzlement of two thousand marks, Thaelmann had ordered them to keep absolutely silent. "If it should become known that the Secretary of my own home district has embezzled money," he had said, "it will throw a bad light on me. Since I am the chief of the party, the party will be disgraced. Under no circumstances should we do such a service to the bourgeoisie and the Social Democrats! And there is another reason: The opposition within the party will surely benefit from this—maybe even gain a majority and defeat us, the

130

revolutionary wing of the movement. So you'd better keep quiet about it. Wittorf will go to a different district and soon the whole thing will be forgotten."

Things developed quite differently. The opposition against Thaelmann at the session of the Central Committee of the party was determined and sharp, but it was surpassed by his own group which condemned its leader in unmistakable terms and with utter sincerity. There was no solution other than the complete divorce of Thaelmann from the party leadership. In the German labor movement it was unthinkable that a man who had covered an embezzlement could continue to play a leading role. A unanimous resolution with Thaelmann himself subscribing was passed. It read:

"The Central Committee sharply disapproves, as a severe political blunder, the attempt on the part of Comrade Thaelmann to keep the events in Hamburg secret from the proper authorities within the party. On his own initiative the affair is referred to the Executive Committee of the Comintern. He is removed from all party functions until a decision by the Executive Committee has been reached."

The full text of the resolution was wired to Moscow and published the following morning in the party papers.

A few days later we received a telegram asking us to appear in Moscow immediately. The phrasing of the wire did not look like a good omen. Yet what we found in Moscow exceeded even the worst expectations of the blackest pessimists. There we were told that not the Central Committee but Thaelmann had behaved in the right way. In the course of a few hours a whole world of ideas about the proper relationships between policies and ethics crashed down over my head.

Only Piatnitsky, Kuusinen, and Molotov were present on the day of our arrival in Moscow. The other members of the Praesidium, including Stalin, were on their summer vacations in the Caucasus and the Crimea. When Piatnitsky informed them of the resolution passed by the German Central Committee, Manuilsky, Bela Kun, and Humbert Droz returned immediately to Moscow. They were all enthusiastic about the German resolution, with the exception of Molotov and Kuusinen, who kept their own counsels. But the general enthusiasm did not last long! A short wire from Stalin, sent from

Sochi where he was spending his vacation, put an abrupt end to it. The wire read: "Thaelmann is to be confirmed in all his functions, the opposition to be excluded from the Central Committee."

I too belonged to this very opposition. This opposition group had maintained ties with the opposition group of Bukharin, Rykov, and Tomsky in the Russian party.

At the meeting of the Praesidium every vote except one was cast in favor of Stalin's decision. This was confirmation that Stalin had become the absolute dictator not only of the Soviet Union, but of the Communist International as well. Except for the Swiss Humbert Droz, not a single member of the "High Command of the World Revolution" had the personal courage to vote against Stalin's decision.

Thaelmann was again on top. Unwittingly he had behaved entirely in the new spirit of the International. In disregarding the most elementary principles of the labor movement, he had acted in accord with the new motto: "The end justifies the means." Stalin reproached him behind locked doors for his awkwardness; then he returned triumphantly to Germany.

The end was more a comedy than a tragedy. A resolution was passed accusing the opposition of a devilish conspiracy against Thaelmann. It was stated that Thaelmann had committed a "serious blunder," but that the Central Committee by publishing its resolution of September 26 had seriously endangered the party. Furthermore, the Praesidium expressed its full political confidence in Thaelmann.

What had at first seemed a petty financial scandal in Hamburg became a major turning point. The moral backbone of a great working class party had been broken.

TROUBLE-SHOOTER OF THE COMINTERN

1931

The Wittorf affair had completely changed my way of life. I was relieved of all responsibilities concerning the German party and was ordered not to interfere further in its financial affairs. My financial tasks and discretionary powers in all the other European parties, however, had multiplied. Piatnitsky could not prevent the friends of Thaelmann from administering the German budget of the Comintern, but he would not permit them to get their fingers into the finan-

132

cial affairs of the International itself. The high command was agreed that they could not find a better financial trouble-shooter than I. But I was given strict orders not to interfere in any way in political affairs from then on. That was all right with me—I had lost all such desire.

So I began my travels throughout Europe: Prague, Vienna, Zurich, Paris, Brussels, Amsterdam, London, Copenhagen, Stockholm—two or three times a year. Everywhere I found the same story: empty party cash boxes, newspapers with decreasing circulations which would have had to close down but for the subsidies from Moscow, nearly everywhere hopeless indifference of the party employees, not the slightest trace of any initiative, no interest other than that in a miserly salary. The very day that the subsidies from Moscow ceased, they would turn their backs on the party. Things were worse than in Germany.

In France I had to solve a problem of a special nature. When the Socialist party had split in 1920, the Communists had gained possession of the paper *L'Humanité* by good fortune only. Jean Jaurès, the great Socialist leader who had been shot at the outbreak of war, had left the controlling block of shares of the newspaper in the hands of a friend, who transferred it to the Communists at the time of the split. The paper represented the greatest political asset the party possessed in France.

As the party affairs were very unsettled, I demanded that the shares be deposited as guaranty with the Comintern. The French Central Committee agreed after considerable hesitation.

Before the First World War, whenever the old imperial Russian government had wished to float a loan with the investing public in France, rubles from the Czar's treasuries would roll in to many of the large metropolitan newspapers in Paris, like *Le Temps*. The Socialist papers had aroused great public indignation over this, and so the sources of newspaper funds were always under very close scrutiny. That was the real reason why Moscow could not allow its rubles to roll directly into *L'Humanité*.

What I did was to set up an advertising agency placing advertisements for various business concerns. When the Galleries Lafayette, for instance, wanted to run an ad in *L'Humanité*, they paid our

133

agency ten thousand francs for the ad, while we, the agency, paid out fifty thousand to the newspaper. Nobody in Paris suspected us.

L'Humanité was the only daily newspaper of the French Communists. It consumed an annual subsidy of between two and three million francs. To my utter surprise I did not find any account books there, and not even data to permit the establishment of a budget. To attempt to bring order into this situation appeared hopeless.

Nevertheless I asked two experienced newspaper administrators from Germany to come over and organize a clean administration of the paper. This met with great opposition from the French comrades. In the editorial offices of *L'Humanité* at that time were approximately seventy editors, more than three times the number of those in the *Rote Fahne,* central organ of the German Communist party. Most of their time was spent in the cafés of the district. Checking up on them we found that some of them were not even members of the party, which was inadmissible according to the statutes of the International! I fired about a third of the editors and reduced the budget to about half its former size. Had I doubled it, the unfavorable position of the French party would not have been changed. It was their ridiculous policies, not the budget, that were wrong.

From 1929 to 1933 the Comintern spent approximately one million dollars annually for European purposes. Frequently when I went to Moscow I observed to Piatnitsky that our entire European "enterprise" was not worth even fifty thousand dollars. Piatnitsky only shrugged his shoulders.

I became a different man. I turned into a drinker. The generous travelling expenses permitted me to lead a life I would have regarded with contempt and disgust a few years earlier. I was constantly torn between self-contempt and a hopeless "there-is-nothing-to-do-about-it."

* * * * *

In 1930 I went to China on a special mission for Piatnitsky, to investigate the machinery of the Comintern in that country. Piatnitsky knew how to size up his men. It rarely happened that one of them betrayed his confidence. But in China it had happened.

Piatnitsky's machine, known as OMS (the Russian initials for International Liaison Section) encircled the globe. It was an excellent organization. The OMS fulfilled technical tasks that were of the greatest importance for the work of the Communist International. Among them was the underground courier service; the smuggling of propaganda material; of men, money, and arms, from one country into another; the preparation of false passports which were as necessary to the Comintern as oxygen for breathing. The Central Passport Office of the Comintern operated in the top story of the building on the Machavaya, and was always guarded by GPU men. Nobody was allowed to enter these rooms without the personal permission of Piatnitsky. This central passport organization had its subsidiaries in all the capitals of Europe and Asia. It was so ably staffed that it could equip a man nearly anywhere in the world with documents from birth to death. This was surely the most accomplished organization of this nature that ever existed.

In European countries, the OMS agents were unassuming young men who accomplished their work and were not too ambitious for a career.

It was different in China where the OMS organization disposed independently of great sums of money and employed many agents to keep up connections with the underground Communist party in that tremendous country. The chief of the Chinese OMS organization, Comrade L, was a Finnish Communist. He had organized an import business in Pekin and Shanghai as a facade for his activities. He imported German and French wines, perfumes, expensive leather goods, and similar luxury wares. In the course of time, the OMS import business had developed into a flourishing enterprise with substantial profits. At the same time, however, it accomplished its tasks for the purposes of the Comintern with the greatest success. As Comrade L never gave Piatnitsky an accounting of his profits, my mission was to take this matter up with him.

L received me with great amiability. He prepared a princely reception for me—a house with twelve Chinese servants was at my disposal. A new American car, equipped with a chauffeur in uniform, was at my door. All this baffled me, but I was told that

135

without such ostentation the OMS organization would long ago have become a victim of the police.

I checked L's books without great care, knowing that my job was to trace not a deficit but a surplus. The books showed an annual surplus of more than one hundred thousand dollars. When I asked what he expected to do with this surplus, L explained briefly and determinedly:

"The net profit is my personal affair. True, I have built up the enterprise with capital that Piatnitsky put at my disposal. But, see for yourself, the capital is there intact. I am paying interest at 10 per cent on it. The expenses of the OMS agents, who act at the same time as my traveling salesmen, are charged half on OMS and half on the business account. This is completely loyal and right."

I was not prepared for such an answer. This was altogether foreign to my previous experience. I had L trailed and watched for weeks. Nothing unfavorable was brought to light. He was as efficient an OMS agent as a businessman. I wired Piatnitsky and asked for new orders, but received the reply, "Do as you think best!"

During these weeks I had come into closer personal contact with L. One evening when we were drinking together on the terrace of his house, I had the feeling this was the moment to reach a decision. I approached the subject with a few sentimental phrases about not continuing a game of this sort with the Communist International. A Communist should not behave as he did, and so on.

L looked at me for some minutes with fixed eyes, emptied his glass and with one gesture tore open the thin Chinese shirt that covered his body. I drew back. In the mild moonlight that traced black shadows on the dimly lit terrace, his torso looked as if it had been ripped open by the sharp teeth of a rake! Dozens of scars covered it. Deep cuts crossed from his chest to his back. In his shoulders and arms were deep black holes.

"Do you know where these come from?" he asked with a soft voice. "These are my memories of Esthonia. You recall the uprising in 1924? I was the last man on the roof of the barracks. They got me only when my last bullet had been shot. I was caught

136

with twelve shots in my body. Then the White officers gave me a treatment of many hours with their whips. I stood up to that. My eyes and my mouth were full of blood. I drank it so as not to suffocate. They didn't succeed in finishing me off. Later I broke out of the jail in Reval and escaped to Moscow. After that I was a Comintern agent for three years in India. That is something different from Europe, or even from lousy China, where one can buy any cop for a few dollars. From the moment of my arrival in Bombay I was hunted by the British Intelligence Service like a dog. I ran hundreds of miles through India, with bleeding feet and a parched tongue. Eight long months I hid among rebellious inhabitants of the Northern mountains of India. When I ran out of money they kicked and beat me. I trembled lest they might learn that there was a price on my head, dead or alive, of one thousand pounds. . . . ."

Without raising his voice he went on. "I tell you, I'd be willing to start everything anew, I'd be willing to feel the pain of each beating again, to go through these tortures again—if the Communist International still existed! It is no more. The Comintern is dead. Everything was in vain. The revolution is dead. I will never return to Moscow."

I could not answer. Everything in me cried "You're right, brother!" But I kept still.

L continued: "I regard the people in Moscow as business partners. I will not betray them. I wouldn't lower myself." There was a cynical smile on his face. "It isn't even worth while. If the police could look behind the façade of our wonderful organization, they wouldn't care to bother. I will not put any obstacles in your way. If you decide to take over the OMS, I will return all the money to you that Piatnitsky has sent me. I will keep the import business for myself, however. I have built it up with my own strength and intelligence. Maybe some day I will use it for other purposes than Piatnitsky does his OMS show! Anyhow you would not know what to do with it. To do business in China, you need more than the experience of a European."

The next day we began to segregate the OMS activities from

L's import business. We finished the job in a few weeks. To my regret, many agents did not wish to part from L.

Piatnitsky never asked me why L had left our employ, nor did I tell him the story. My task had been accomplished. Piatnitsky's money was secure and the OMS in China out of L's hands.

AS IF IT HAD NEVER BEEN . . .

1933

The night of the Reichstag fire my phone rang. I was sleeping heavily after a long night of drinking. I answered the phone two or three times but couldn't understand a word. So I slept.

Early the next morning I was arrested in my apartment—luckily not by storm troopers but by civilian police from police headquarters. Among them was a Social Democrat police officer whom I knew well. Thanks to him, I was not taken to headquarters as I expected, but only to the next local police station. In a little while I just walked out and nobody tried to prevent my "escape."

My friends told me later I had had better luck than I deserved. They had tried and tried that night to warn me over the telephone, to make me leave my apartment at once!

I stayed on underground for several weeks and tried to dissolve the affairs of my offices. This was no easy job. The newly organized Gestapo was always trying to catch me and had dozens of agents on my tracks. One of my assistants whom I loved like a son was beaten to death when they arrested him!

There were files of an incriminating nature to dispose of. I had to get hundreds of thousands of dollars of the International's money out of the country. A difficult job. But finally I succeeded without incurring great losses.

In Prague new orders awaited me. Piatnitsky wanted me to supervise the printing of the underground propaganda literature and its despatch into Germany. Really this should have been the task of the German Central Committee of which I was no longer a member. But in those early days of the Hitler regime, the German Central Committee remained in Germany since they regarded anyone who left the country as a coward.

I engaged upon my new work with some of the old enthusiasm

138

and abandon. There was action again at last, and the intoxication of fighting a dangerous enemy—like during the First World War in the days of the Spartacus group. In the course of a few weeks, with the help of a small circle of friends and assistants, I organized underground "trenches" along the entire German border from Czechoslovakia to Austria to Switzerland to Alsace and into the Saar. Our "trenches" had to remain underground in both directions—for Germany and for the democratic border countries whose governments did not wish to have any unnecessary friction with the Third Reich.

The party presses in Czechoslovakia, Austria, and Switzerland printed huge editions of propaganda literature—leaflets, newspapers, periodicals, brochures—enough to distribute to the whole German population down to the tiniest infant. Piatnitsky had instructed me not to save money.

In the Bohemian woods, on the banks of the Rhine, in sleepy Alsatian villages, sentries were placed on duty for our "trenches," to guard the movement of our anti-Hitler propaganda into Germany. Hundreds of courageous Communist inhabitants of border districts helped us enthusiastically. In many cases we had to work together with professional smugglers who took our material at the existing rates across the border.

We went on this way up to the autumn. Then the proud new organization collapsed completely because the Gestapo was far better organized than we. The greater part of our underground shipments was intercepted right at the border, and hundreds of comrades were arrested, dozens killed! In Germany many of our best friends refused to accept our literature. They did not share the illusion that the downfall of Hitler was just around the corner.

From all sides I was the target of reproaches. Some accused me of too much audacity; others of too much caution. The Communist party groups of the border countries, which suffered considerable losses, began to regard the German Communists as a disagreeable burden. Confusion was everywhere. It became unbearable.

Piatnitsky had not lost his confidence in me. He knew such crises from his own experience. But my strength and my courage broke down. Alcohol became my only solace. I drank more and more.

Externally, my life did not change much. I continued to travel from country to country, organizing, checking, acting as strong man, ordering party comrades, assistants, and friends around like a Prussian sergeant. All this work—the whole thing—was a farce!

In Zurich I was spending a night in a small hotel on the Limat-quai. Suddenly I was torn out of my sleep by cries that went on and on! Someone was screaming in unspeakable anguish. My body broke out in cold perspiration. The cries continued: "Help! Help! They are coming. Help! They're killing me!" People ran into the halls. The door was forced open. A man in his nightgown was hiding under the bed yelling "Help! Help! The Gestapo!" The man had gone insane. He was a Communist who had escaped a few days earlier into Switzerland.

I lost my sleep completely. I sank into utter despair and was unable to live without alcohol. Sometimes I suffered from crying spasms which shook my entire body.

Now I knew our defeat was final, inescapable. L was right: everything had been in vain, everything was lost, everything! . . . . As if it had never been!

*　　*　　*　　*　　*

In 1936, Comrade Y was arrested in Strasbourg, France. In his possession were found compromising documents and big sums of money. A large section of the French newspapers called insistently for his severe punishment as an agent of Moscow. At that time, however, Y had had no dealings that concerned France directly, having been chiefly occupied with shipping Communist underground material into Germany. For that reason the German government asked the Foreign Committee of the French Chamber for his extradition. Finally a compromise was arranged, and Comrade Y was returned to the Soviet Union. A year later he disappeared there in the whirlpool of the purges . . . . without leaving a trace. . . . .

Part II

PROFESSIONAL REVOLUTIONARIES

CHAPTER VII

Boris Savinkov: The Curse of the Precursors

MEETING AT THE CROSSROADS

IN APRIL, 1925, BORIS SAVINKOV, THE RUSSIAN SOCIAL REVOlutionary and terrorist, was led into the secret courtroom of the GPU prison in Moscow. In the few rows of closely packed chairs sat the Bolshevist revolutionaries, Savinkov's former comrades in the revolution of 1905, now his judges. Here the past of the Russian revolution met its present and its future.

In the small room were seated many of the leaders of the victorious Bolshevist party and of the Comintern. Facing them stood as defendant the last living heir of the tradition of the terrorist precursors of the revolution. The praesidium of the court was in the hands of Ulrich, of the same Soviet judge who many years later was to pronounce sentence of death on most of the participants in this secret trial of Savinkov.

Since the October Revolution Savinkov had waged war, cruel and merciless war, against the Bolsheviki. He had become one of their most hated and respected foes. Nevertheless neither the state attorney nor the judges gave vent to a feeling of personal hatred in word or gesture. Frequently the court proceedings became a passionate and moving discussion between the Bolshevists and the terrorist professional revolutionary who had now become a professional counter-revolutionary.

Between Savinkov and his judges, above all the bitter enmity, existed a bond. Savinkov had spent his life in accord with the heritage of the Russian terrorist revolutionaries of the nineteenth century, of men who knew that when they joined the revolutionary organization sacrificial death would mean the accomplishment of the task and aim of their lives. In the early youth of their movement the Bolshevist professional revolutionaries had given up the political philosophy of these terrorists, but morally they had remained loyal to the ideal of their predecessors.

143

An awesome silence pervaded the courtroom when Savinkov, a bald man of about forty-five, entered, bowing briefly to the court and the auditorium. He did not come as a captured enemy: he came as a defeated man who had voluntarily delivered himself into the hands of those against whom he had fought. When he crossed the Russian frontier coming from Czechoslovakia, the GPU knew of his intentions and his trip, because it had been arranged between him and them.

The Bolshevik leaders returned the greeting of the man who had caused infinite harm to the Soviet Republic, who had been the revolutionary comrade of their youth, who had fought against them and their entire political philosophy, and who had now capitulated. This capitulation was to them a bow of the immortal precursors of their revolution to its ultimate victors.

There was not a trace of skepticism in the faces and eyes of his listeners when Savinkov, in a low voice, sad as death itself, declared:

"I am a revolutionary. That means not only that I accept all weapons of combat up to terrorist action, but that I fight to the end, to the last moment, when I am either destroyed or convinced of my error."

As a young man and son of a high Russian government official in Warsaw, he had been expelled from the University of St. Petersburg in 1902 for having participated in Marxist student groups that Lenin was then organizing. He was sent to Siberia, but fled from there to Switzerland. Here old Breshkovskaya, "grandmother of the Russian Revolution," won him away from the Marxist Social Democrats to the terrorist Social Revolutionaries. The war of these terrorist revolutionaries against the rule of the Czars had already been going on for fifty years. Each successful assassination had been followed by a wave of executions of terrorists. No terrorist had ever asked for mercy. To deviate from this path of sacrifice was inconceivable; to vacillate from this path, once chosen, was punishable by death. The famous terrorist Nechayev had killed his best friend only because the latter seemed to weaken in his revolutionary determination. The gallows of the executed terrorists became the altars for the succeeding revolutionary generation.

Boris Savinkov had stepped into the tradition of these professional revolutionaries. He became the last of the great terrorists.

On the eve of the Russian Revolution of 1905 he had organized the two attacks on the Minister of the Interior, Plehve, and on Prince Sergius. When he revived the story of these attacks before the court, tears covered his face as he told how he had kissed the dead eyes of his friends Sasonov and Kalayev, whose bodies had been mutilated by the very bombs they had thrown.

A short time after this, a tremendous calamity had befallen the revolutionary terrorists. Savinkov had organized an attempt to kill the last Russian Czar, Nicholas II, on his luxurious yacht. Asev, one of his best friends and one of the most trusted members of the innermost terrorist group, had turned out to be a traitor. He had transmitted an unloaded bomb to the sailor who was to throw it. Asev had all along been the leader of the terrorist group of the Social Revolutionaries and an agent for the Ochrana, the Czarist secret police.

His treason had given a mortal blow to the terrorist organization. The unconditional confidence that had tied one member of it to all the others had vanished. After that no major attack had been successful, and hundreds of terrorists had been arrested. That was the end!

Savinkov had been arrested in Sevastopol, but the cadet who guarded his prison cell had been a Social Revolutionary too, so he escaped in a little fishing boat across the Black Sea. Years of bitter spiritual misery and despair had followed. Everything that the professional revolutionaries in the terrorist organization had lived for seemed to have died. Their innumerable sacrifices for Russian freedom and liberty appeared to have been in vain.

During these years, Savinkov had written some novels, among them *As If It Had Never Been,* a long necrology for a world of fraternity, love and sacrificial death gone under. Here the terrorist had described the life and philosophy of a professional revolutionary who had been defeated in the revolution of 1905. It was the individualist Slavic morality that had found a final and exaggerated expression in the life of the Russian professional revolutionary: when you throw the bomb you are liberating not only holy Mother

Russia, but also yourself; when you hurl your dead body at the autocracy you do more than destroy its sinister morality—you free the individual from the last obstacles that block his entrance into the realm of freedom and fraternity.

When the February, 1917, revolution destroyed the autocracy of the Czar, a new realm of individual freedom and self-expression appeared to be opening up before the eyes of Savinkov and his friends. Their dreams seemed realized: a Social and Democratic republic that made the liberation of the individual its final goal had been born.

Yet, just as it stepped into its new world, a new enemy had arisen: Bolshevism. To democratic parliamentarianism, which Savinkov regarded as an expression of self-rule for the Russian people, Lenin opposed the Soviet State, the dictatorship of a class, suppression of all the individual liberties that Savinkov had fought for over so many years.

With the same passion that had guided his struggle against the autocracy, he had taken up the fight against the rising new dictatorial powers. As Acting Secretary of War in the Kerensky government, he had supported all its steps against the looming second revolution. But soon he realized that Kerensky was not Lenin's equal. He therefore did not hesitate to ally himself with the monarchist general, Kornilov, in order to overthrow Kerensky, convinced that after the destruction of the Bolshevists he, and not Kornilov, would become the heir to power. Yet Lenin had proved stronger than Savinkov, Kornilov, and Kerensky together.

After the Bolshevist victory in October, 1917, Savinkov had made himself one of the driving forces of the civil war against the revolution. He had organized many bloody revolts. In Siberia he had formed White armies and had planned the assassination of Lenin and Trotsky. When the Bolshevists again had proved stronger he had transferred his headquarters to Poland from where, in agreement with Pilsudski, he had sent armed gangs into the Ukraine.

He had become the most efficient of all the conspirators against the Soviet Republic, for the Bolshevik revolution had rendered his life's work worthless. It had desecrated the sacrificial blood shed

146

by his friends. To extirpate it from the face of the earth appeared to him his holy duty to the hanged martyrs.

The sighs of the terrorist prisoners in the Peter and Paul Fortress, whose bodies were rotting away in its damp cells, had become the eternal torture of Savinkov's sleepless nights during his long years of exile, and had driven him on from Prague to Paris, from Paris to London, to marshal and organize the forces of revenge. This memory drove him on in his fight against the Bolsheviks whom he accused of having betrayed the "immortal victims." But his search for revenge had brought him only further painful defeats. His face twitched with impotent rage when he described his negotiations with Foch, Lloyd George, and Winston Churchill, then Secretary of War. These negotiations had finally made him realize, as he said, that Russia was lost if her deliverance depended on the help of foreign countries. This was why the old-time professional revolutionary, turned counter-revolutionary during these years, finally had been convinced of his error.

"See, this is my army," he reported Churchill to have said, pointing with his hand to a spot on the map of Southern Ukraine where Denikin was fighting with his soldiers against the Bolsheviks.

"All that I have done since 1917 has been wrong!" Savinkov cried out. "Worse, I have covered myself with the dirt of the enemies of my Russian people. That is why I am here. I want to take the punishment for what I have done."

Turning to the court and his listeners, Savinkov concluded: "I anticipate your sentence. I place no value on my life and am not afraid to die. My sin is involuntary, and I have never sought personal objectives nor personal advantages. I have had but one guide—overwhelming love for my people!"

The court sentenced Savinkov to die but recommended clemency "as Savinkov has renounced his counter-revolutionary allegiance and is prepared to repair his crimes against the toiling masses of the Soviet Union by sincere and honest services on their behalf."

Kalinin commuted Savinkov's sentence to ten years of imprisonment. "The revolutionary people is not seeking revenge. It does not need his death."

The generosity of the Soviet government towards Savinkov did not last long. The logic of the GPU was stronger than all the ties to the childhood of the Revolution. The GPU, although still under the leadership of the fanatic ascetic Felix Dzierzynski, was already changing into an institution similar to the Czarist Ochrana rather than to the Committees of Public Security of the French Revolution on which the Wecheka had originally been modelled.

Some months later *Pravda* announced that Savinkov had committed suicide by jumping out of the window of his prison cell. The truth was different. Savinkov had disclosed all the conspiracies inimical to the Soviet Union abroad but had refused to betray a single former comrade still operating in Russia. The GPU believed that after the commutation of sentence he would take this step too. Yet he remained adamant.

"I am Savinkov, not Asev. I am no agent provocateur!"

While he was sitting in his prison cell the terrorist movement that he had once led showed some signs of revival. It was nearly impossible for him to have had any direct influence upon it, but the GPU considered nothing impossible to Savinkov.

Again his fate became a matter of debate in the leading party group. The decision by the Central Committee involving the commutation of Savinkov's sentence was changed. His "suicide" was not voluntary.

BOW TO THE SOVIET

The Bolshevik professional revolutionaries were of the same flesh as the Social Revolutionaries, but of a different spirit. Lenin had always expressed the greatest respect for the terrorists, particularly for the Narodnaya Volya, predecessor of the terrorist Social Revolutionaries. He himself had decided to become a professional revolutionary when his beloved older brother Alexander had been hanged for participating in a terrorist attack.

But he did not accept the terrorist philosophy of the Social Revolutionaries. The Bolshevik professional revolutionaries were orthodox unyielding Marxists. They not only refused to accept individual terror as a weapon in the fight against Czarism, but they rejected the entire individualist philosophy of the Social Revolutionaries. They did not regard themselves as aristocrats of the revolution, as

148

saviors of the people, but as the driving force of an inevitable development that would necessarily lead to a revolt of the entire suppressed people.

Yet since a mass movement of the people towards Socialism did not exist, particularly in the early years of the century, they had to rely and live on their faith, a faith that burned as high in them as it did in the terrorists, so that every means of getting closer to their goal appeared justified to them. They too, like the terrorist professional revolutionaries, were compelled to organize themselves in small conspiratorial circles with iron discipline. They too had to lead the dull life of conspiracy. For them too their professions as civil members of society were only blinds for their real profession as revolutionaries.

The moral satisfaction at Savinkov's confession had been for them more than joy at the repentance of a dangerous and defeated enemy. The confession seemed a historical testimony to the correctness of the Bolshevik road, of its principles and its entire doctrine. The Bolshevik professional revolutionaries saw in the defeat of the terrorist Savinkov a vindication of their own moral doctrines over those of their predecessors. For them, individual morality as such did not exist. It was but hypocrisy if it was not tied to the morality of the revolutionary class. In their view the individual was separated from revolutionary morality: You may lie and betray if your reason indicates that it is necessary. If by such lie and betrayal you serve the revolutionary class, your so doing is not only permissible but justified. You will walk through the mire a pure and untouched man if you act in the interests of the revolution. You need no personal protection from degeneration.

Do not seek standards of morality within yourself, but in the critique of the mass that creates the revolution and the critique of history of which you represent only an instrument. Vanish as an individual from the realm of good and evil; dissolve your being into the party that is the ultimate repository of truth.

None of the old Bolsheviki in 1925 saw any tie between Savinkov's fate and their own but that of a common past. None of them suspected that Savinkov's trial was the precursor of their own trials, just as the terrorism of the Narodnaya Volya had been the precursor of their own movement. The mighty of 1925 could not suspect that Savinkov's destiny only anticipated their own; that they themselves would be accused before the same Judge Ullrich of the same crimes that Savinkov had actually committed.

Nor could they suspect that in 1936-38 they would bow to the same power to which Savinkov had attributed his defeat in his final words: "If you are Russian, if you love your country, then bow before the power of the Soviet. Recognize it without reserve."

Savinkov's confession had been a true description of his life. His judges of 1925 were to lose even the privilege of a truthful description of their lives. Their confessions in 1936-38 were dictated by the counter-revolution that had arisen out of their own victorious revolution. The counter-revolution of 1937 did not know the gesture of generosity. It cut the umbilical cord to the common revolutionary past and prevented its victims from dying as martyrs or even as sinners in good faith.

In the Stalinite counter-revolution that grew out of the revolution of the terrorists and out of that of the Marxists, both the terrorist and the Marxist doctrine of morality are present, but both have been turned upside down. The individual is no longer in need of self-renunciation in the service of an ideal. For the state has lifted from his shoulders all care and concern for his fellowmen. Stalin proclaimed ultimate victory, the classless society, at the very moment when Soviet citizens had lost all rights except to work and to die. The production of sacrificial bodies is no more in the hands of the individual. The state becomes the collective terrorist for the entire people. The Bolshevist professional revolutionaries caused the individual to disappear into the party. The counter-revolution needs neither the party nor the purified individual.

The era of Stalin leads to so complete a divorce of the individual from revolutionary morality that the individual becomes Public Enemy Number One. The prerogatives of party and individual merge into a collective individual who proclaims himself the measure of all things. The last surviving professional revolutionary evolves into a professional counter-revolutionary. He becomes The Leader!

The Comintern professional revolutionaries were caricatures of the Russian professional revolutionaries. The Westerners who had become professional revolutionaries after the founding of the Comintern had no Narodnaya Volya as precursors. Only rarely did they feel the burning revolutionary hatred which led the Russian professional revolutionary to a complete denial of his own self. The underground and the conspiracy were not the rules of their existence. They were being carried away by a revolutionary current, but they were not themselves the source from which the current sprang.

They always remained apprentices of the Russian professional revolutionaries. They could never rid themselves of the faults that originated in a democratic labor movement, nor of their cultural and educational ties to the West.

They attempted to receive and to accept with devotion the doctrine of revolutionary morality of the Russians, but they all failed. Many tried to escape, but they escaped only to the refuge of isolation. Some tried to create a Western type of professional revolutionary. But they became sectarians of a revolutionary faith.

Untold hundreds had to pay for their attempt to become professional revolutionaries on the Russian pattern with their lives. Only few knew why they were dying. They avowed their innocence up to the last moment. They had always been only apprentices. They had never really understood the magicians of the revolution.

Some of the surviving Western professional revolutionaries are serving the counter-revolution that arose from the revolution of the professional revolutionaries. But they are not its apprentices: they are its slaves.

While the history of the Russian professional revolutionaries represents a terrible tragedy, the history of its European and American counterparts frequently bears the character of a horrible banality. In the West the mystique of the conspiratorial call did not flourish. It created at one and the same time both heroes and fools, victims and traitors, desperate adventurers and petty Philistines.

Russian professional revolutionaries, even in Lenin's days, could say to their Western followers:

"You resemble the spirit you comprehend, not me."

CHAPTER VIII

Georg Lukacz: Sorcerer's Apprentice

PHILOSOPHER'S TRIP INTO THE REVOLUTION

SEVERAL YEARS BEFORE THE OUTBREAK OF THE FIRST WORLD War a young Hungarian scholar was studying at the University of Heidelberg in Germany. His highly original talents excited the admiration of his teachers. His many literary essays revealed a sovereign knowledge of classical and modern philosophy, a mastery of language, and a penetrating mind. If Georg von Lukacz had chosen to continue his academic career, there is little doubt that he would have become renowned in the philosophic world of postwar Europe.

He came of a wealthy bourgeois family that had been elevated to the nobility. His world was the world of ideas. The actual world he lived and moved in was of small interest to him.

A man of small stature and unhealthy pallor, his tired eyes bore witness to long working nights. For him life could bring fulfillment only in libraries and on the lecturer's platform.

But the war came and Georg Lukacz, to the surprise of his family and friends, joined his fate with that of the revolution. He returned to Budapest from Germany, preceded by his reputation as a philosopher, to become one of the champions of the revolutionary Socialist movement.

When Bela Kun came into power he gave Lukacz the Ministry of Popular Education. As People's Commissar he drew up a sweeping program of popular education in the spirit of Marxist materialism. When the Rumanian armies of intervention invaded Hungarian Soviet territory, he left his comfortable desk in the Ministry of Education and became a political commissar at the front.

After the political and military debacle of the Hungarian Soviet republic he did not immediately attempt to escape and seek protection in Vienna as did most of the other People's Commissars. He concentrated all his efforts on holding together the remains of his defeated party. Thus he demonstrated his personal courage and unswerving devotion to his revolutionary ideal.

For most Hungarian revolutionaries the sudden collapse of their revolution was a terrible blow, leaving them confused and bewildered. Not so for Lukacz. For most revolutionaries revolution is civil war, destruction, blood, insurrection, hope, and faith in a future. For the philosopher from Heidelberg all this was only the setting. It meant the start of a journey of discovery into unknown countries of the human mind, into the mysterious and winding paths of human thought. It meant the opportunity to confront philosophy with reality, even to impose philosophy upon reality.

So Lukacz from the philosophic ivory tower he built for himself within the Comintern began to guide the Communists of the West in their searchings. Entangled in the factional fights of the Hungarian and German Communists, he nevertheless maintained an aristocratic distance from their plebeian quarrels. For what mattered to him was not their actual doings but the hidden significance in them. His objective was to create and guide a school of professional revolutionaries in the West.

The Hungarian revolution had been defeated and the German had not been successful, although millions of people had been willing to support it, thousands had been ready to die for it, and the Soviet Republic had backed it with all its moral and political power.

In despair, the German Communists sought to discover the causes for their failures. Many of the leading German Communists came from the intellectual school of Rosa Luxemburg, who believed that revolution is a spontaneous uprising by the people, a power that moves the minds and convictions of men before it causes their action. It is not, as the Bolsheviks had it, a conviction carried to the people by a revolutionary group or party.

"We refuse to accept political power only because the bourgeoisie and the Social Democrats are bankrupt!" Rosa Luxemburg had declared at the founding Congress of the German Communist Party. "The quest for power by the Communists is identical with the conscious quest for power by the people themselves."

Although the great masses of the German workers had been radicalized by the experiences of the war and their political passions had been awakened, only a minority entertained conscious Socialist beliefs.

But from Russia had come the call: Emulate us! All the conditions for Socialist success are there. Seize power!

The German professional revolutionaries swung back and forth between the opposing views. Into this conflict—psychological as well as political—the philosopher from Heidelberg injected himself. Now or never the moment was at hand to utilize the teachings of philosophy for an active change of history.

Why does the revolution fail, asked Lukacz, although the ruling class is unable to maintain its old social order and to give the people the life of stability and security that was formerly theirs? The reason is, he answered his own question, that the masses of people cannot tear themselves loose from the beliefs that tie them to the capitalist order. There is among them, as Rosa Luxemburg maintained, a nascent Socialist belief and a rising revolutionary faith. But this is not sufficient in itself. In order to free this belief from its fetters, an elite, a revolutionary *"avant guard"* is necessary that will by its action remove the obstacles and free the spontaneous will of the people that is now kept back by the old ties.

This elite is an embodiment of its own insight into the laws of motion of human society. It will cut the ideological inhibitions of the working classes.

In his theories Lukacz presented the ideal figure of a revolutionary reborn through his immersion in Communism, secured against all temptations of the hostile world surrounding him, treading his revolutionary path with foreknowledge. Lukacz warned against the romantic conspiratorial philosophy of the East, as represented in Savinkov's philosophy up to 1917. In the West the sun of rational knowledge, freed of all emotions, will enlighten the road of the ideal Communist who will maintain an attitude of complete indifference towards the law and order of the capitalist state. Once he has accomplished this attitude, he will have freed himself from all the moral and ideological ties that connect the individual with the bourgeois world, and his revolutionary action will become second nature.

Such a revolutionary, with others, will form an elite, an *"avant guard,"* to move the masses to their destiny. The audacity of this

154

elite, its scientific insight, its high morality, its discipline, its sacrifice, and its example will fertilize the fallow mind of the masses and give it a new form.

At the same time as Lukacz, another young intellectual in southern Italy subordinated his fate to that of the revolution. He too had studied classical philosophy and his background too was that of a wealthy bourgeois family. His talents had marked him for an important role in bourgeois Italy. Yet Ignazio Silone became a professional revolutionary.

For him, however, the revolution was not a philosophic speculation as it was for Lukacz. It represented solidarity with the hungry and the suffering, and the hope that Communism would lead his poor Italian people to a brighter day. An earthquake had robbed him in a single day of his father and five brothers. Such catastrophe opens men's souls to the sufferings of their fellows.

Silone had not the time to ponder the interrelationship of philosophy and revolution. As a Communist editor in pre-Fascist Italy he worked day and night in small and stuffy editorial offices and in the narrow suffocating meeting halls of the Italian workers.

As a professional revolutionary in Fascist Italy, Silone gave to the revolutionary movement all that he possessed in physical strength. He remained strong, passionate, and unbroken. The sufferings of the Italian workers and peasants redoubled his revolutionary energies.

He belonged to those of whom the celebrated Russian terrorist Nechayev had written in 1877: "The true revolutionary must regard himself as consecrated. He must have no personal interests, no personal affairs, no emotions, no relationships, no property, not even a name of his own. Everything in him should be absorbed by one exclusive interest, by one single idea, by one passion—the revolution!"

Silone seemed to be as ideal a member of a community of intellectual professional revolutionaries as Lukacz' philosophic speculation could envisage.

According to Lukacz' doctrine, the greatest impediment to the development of such a community of professional revolutionaries is to be found in the will of the individual to achieve his own individual freedom. For the capitalist world always tempts the professional revolutionary back into its fold. The requirements of his material

155

existence as well as the intellectual and spiritual ties that bind him to the existing world threaten to make him deviate from the path of his revolutionary calling. It is only in the eternal struggle within and against himself that the professional revolutionary can assert his revolutionary existence.

Lukacz had some disappointing initial experiences with his theory. He tried to create his elite among the Hungarian emigrés in Vienna. Being himself a pure and self-sacrificing man, he attracted the best and most loyal elements among the Hungarian professional revolutionaries. His circle developed into a political faction which he regarded as a preliminary to the real elite of his theory.

This, however, brought on the personal enmity of Bela Kun, the fallen Hungarian dictator. He considered the Hungarian elite as his own private monopoly.

Actually there was no fundamental difference between the conceptions of the two men. Yet for the moral aspects of Lukacz' theory Kun had the gay contempt of the man of the world towards the asceticism of the monk. Bela Kun looked upon Lukacz' claim to the leadership of the Hungarian elite as an excess of the latter's individual will to liberty and self-expression.

The resulting clash between Kun and Lukacz was a malodorous one. In a pamphlet bearing the challenging title: "The Hungarian Pest in Moscow," a follower of Lukacz wrote of Bela Kun's wing of the Hungarian professional revolutionaries in colors that might have been taken from Zola's portrait of the corruption in the Third French Empire.

The fact that Lukacz himself acted on a high ethical plane did not do him much good. His unmoral adversaries drew practical inferences from his idealistic theory. The factional fight among the Hungarians was a practical illustration of the fact that in western Europe his theory of professional revolutionaries leads to corruption, careerism, and demoralization.

Yet Lukacz remained unconvinced. The Hungarian factional struggle appeared to him as one of the practical difficulties to be met in applying his theory. That the behavior of Bela Kun's professional revolutionaries was unmoral and corrupt was nothing but a little detour on the road to creating an elite of real professional revolutionaries.

156

In Germany Lukacz found many followers. In the spring of 1921 the powerful German Communist Party even attempted to act according to his prescription by audaciously creating the longed-for revolutionary situation.

At the Third World Congress in Moscow in 1921, Lukacz found to his disappointment that Lenin and Trotsky, the two personifications of his theory of professional revolutionaries, were hostile to his principles and rejected his theories.

The World Congress emphasized as the main line of approach the maintenance of immediate touch and contact with the masses; it condemned independent revolutionary action. Frightened, the Heidelberg philosopher retired into his ivory tower.

In a few years, Bela Kun and he became reconciled. Later Lukacz withdrew from factional politics and immersed himself in the development of a Marxist literary critique and aesthetics.

PHILOSOPHER'S PURGATORY

More years went by. All revolutionary hopes seemed lost, and the ideological inhibitions in the working class appeared to have won supremacy. The savior role of the revolutionary elite had disappeared.

Yet Lukacz' philosophy could enjoy a triumph never foreseen by its author. First his principle of an all-powerful *"avant guard"* won out in the form of an almighty central committee of the party, initially in the Soviet Union, later in all parties of the Comintern. These central committees very prosaically did not attach much importance to morality or to any form of philosophy. But they put into practice Lukacz' demand to exclude the will of the individual for freedom and liberty in the party. In so doing, they destroyed entire cadres of professional revolutionaries from whom Lukacz had been expecting the revolutionary act of emancipation.

By 1932, the last of these professional revolutionaries had disappeared from the Comintern. There was no longer place for apostles and fanatics of the revolutionary faith. Socialism as a purpose of the revolutionary movement was banished from the halls of the Comintern. The place of the professional revolutionary was taken by the revolutionary bureaucrat whose morality was determined by the political requirements of the Soviet Union, and whose philosophy was regulated by the military commands of his respective central committee. . . . .

The Italian professional revolutionary, Ignazio Silone, silent and shaken, retired from the Comintern. He belonged to those who tried to escape to a lonely isle. A dramatic adieu to the party to which he had given his best fifteen years and his health seemed absurd to him.

In the loneliness of peaceful Switzerland he began to ponder the deeper causes of the defeat of Socialist idealism within the ranks of the Comintern. The results were not formed into political pamphlets but into thoughtful novels about the lives of the peasants at home in Calabria. There they had developed a Socialism with the religious faith that has no connection with Marxist doctrine, but seeks to establish the eternal verities in the life of man. His revolutionary heroes are not political men, but revolutionaries of the everyday, whose moral example becomes a terror to the barbarism of the ruling class, and at the same time the ideal of the future for the poor and the suffering.

In these novels he preaches an ethical concept of Socialism superior as he believed to the Communism of the Comintern—a Socialism that will survive Fascism, National Socialism, and Bolshevism, because human life cannot be lived on this planet without freedom and love. Man never will cease fighting until he has reached this goal! The gray mass of the people whose call comes from its own life and sufferings takes the place in his philosophy of the *avant guard* mobilized by the call of the professional revolutionary.

While Silone was writing his novels, things in the Soviet Union were taking a new turn. The individual will to freedom had finally been eradicated and in its stead an iron discipline had been established in the *avant guard* of the party. This *avant guard* gave birth to a leader who laid claim to all the qualities that Lukacz demanded of and for his revolutionary elite. He was becoming omniscient and irreplaceable. Philosophy thereby lost its purpose and thinking had become superfluous. From now on the leader thought for the entire *avant guard*.

Lukacz had good fortune: he survived Stalin's purges. For a

Hungarian professional revolutionary in Russia this was amazing. Very few Hungarian Communists survived. Of all who had been members of the Hungarian Soviet government in 1919, only Matthias Rakoczi, who in 1937 was still in a Hungarian jail, and Eugen Varga are known to be still alive.

Varga, a Hungarian professor of economics, throughout his career as a professional revolutionary, had never delivered himself of an independent political thought. Trotsky had characterized the Hungarian economist as the theoretical Polonius of the Comintern who, as he said, "is always ready to prove theoretically that the clouds in the sky look like a camel's back, but if you prefer they resemble a fish, and if the Prince desires it, they bear witness to 'Socialism in one country.' "

Varga for long years had been the economic weather prophet of the Comintern, always cautious enough to forecast the weather only after assuring himself directly from the executive committee whether it was rain or snow that was desired. His statistics and economic analyses always corresponded precisely to the last political resolutions of the high command. Nobody in Russia or in the Comintern ever has accused Varga of even a secret rebellious idea.

But Lukacz had to tremble for his life even long after the purges. He therefore conducted a trial by himself against himself. He wrote an unending essay full of sharp self-criticism proving the undeniably counter-revolutionary nature of his former writings. Then, in the grand style of the trials, he condemned himself to an ideological death, but soon commuted his sentence to life imprisonment in the torture cell of the purged but ever tormented individual: the *avant guard* of the anti-Fascist fight is eternally chained to the rock of Prometheus while the vultures of the various reactionary ideologies and prejudices claw at his living flesh.

Lukacz' adversary, Bela Kun, contemptuous of ascetic morality, the man who had indulged in intrigues and the rough enjoyment of life, died in a prison of the GPU. He refused to play along with the witch trials of Stalin and remained steadfast up to death.

CHAPTER IX

Ernst Thaelmann, or the Debacle of German Communism

A GAME OF BOLSHEVIK POKER—SECOND PART

JANUARY 21, 1933: A NASTY DAY IN BERLIN, COLD AND DAMP. The city was filled with terror, with the vague horror of things to come. On the preceding day the National Socialists had staged a big demonstration on the great square in front of the Communist Karl Liebknecht building.

Now the Communist as well as the Social Democratic workers of Berlin were answering the Nazi demonstration. Hours and hours on end, hundreds of thousands of workers marched across the square with grim faces, determined to stem the swelling Nazi tide with their own bodies.

In an office high above the square sat Ernst Thaelmann, "leader of the German working class," listening to the shouts of the marchers: You give us the word; we are ready to fight!

Thaelmann had become a party leader without knowing why or how. Nothing had marked him for the leadership of a party with more than one hundred and fifty thousand members and three and a half million voters. A poor speaker, unable to pronounce one coherent sentence, he made up for this deficiency by a voice that could silence a siren. In the port of Hamburg he had led the hard life of a seaman and stevedore. His political training was below the average of the ordinary party member. He knew of the classical Marxist and Communist literature not even by hearsay, but he had a flaring revolutionary temperament and considerable physical courage. He was shrewd, tough, and enduring. He was always at the head of any group to break up the meetings of enemies.

While in 1923 the German Communists in general capitulated to the Reichswehr without giving battle, three hundred Communists under Thaelmann's personal leadership fought twenty thousand police and soldiers for three days. At that time Thael-

160

mann's name got to be known all over Germany. He became the symbol of a revolutionary who does not give a hang for the tactical fine points and objections of soft bureaucrats. When the old Sparta- cus leadership was dethroned in 1924, the new leader group which came to the front made Thaelmann their showpiece. He was elected deputy to the Reichstag. When the President of the Reich, Ebert, died, the party put up Thaelmann as their presidential candidate against Hindenburg. Although everyone in the party laughed at his election speeches, he had acquired a certain popularity. Zino- viev glorified him as the "gold of the German working class." When the group of revolutionary literati with whom Thaelmann had come to the fore disappeared, he remained on the scene as victor. Finally he had become the chief of the party.

Thaelmann was not the man to shy away from a fight. Now the hour of decision was there, and it was he who was to decide for millions.

But he had always been a loyal servant to the master in the Kremlin. So what could one do but wait for orders to come from Moscow. They never came. Stalin did not answer any of the appeals made to him during these January days.

On the night of January 30, Hitler was made Chancellor of the Reich. On February 27, the Reichstag burned.

There were many reasons why the Kremlin remained wrapped in silence during these weeks of crisis. One of the most important was that Stalin believed he could rely on the pro-Russian attitude of the Reichswehr generals. Both the Russians and the German generals had been very well satisfied with the fruits of the secret treaty that had existed between the Red Army and the Reichswehr since 1921. In the Russian embassy on Unter den Linden, Kres- tinsky, one of the oldest friends of Lenin and Trotsky, continued for ten long years to hold in his hands all the threads that connected the Red Army with the Reichswehr. He had become the inheritor of the assets left from the poker game of Chicherin, Brockdorff-Rant- zau, and Radek. Like most Russian observers, his successor, Chin- chuk, did not believe the future would belong to Hitler. He expected General Schleicher and the Reichswehr generals to carry the day.

Stalin shared this opinion. He feared an alliance between Germany and England more than the Nazis. To him the group in Germany that involved the greatest threat in this direction was the Social Democracy, traditionally the party of friendship with the West. He did not forget that in 1926 the Social Democrats had attempted to destroy the secret German-Russian pact by exposing the Russian shipments of bombs to the German army. He had also not failed to take notice of Goebbels' statement made in the best tradition of Count Reventlow: "In domestic affairs Bolshevism is the main enemy; in foreign affairs the capitalism of the West."

Therefore Stalin declared the Social Democracy to be the main enemy: "Is it not clear, comrades," he said, "that Social Democracy and Fascism are twins? It seems to me this is decidedly clear."

Russian policy in German affairs had been entirely guided by these conceptions. The Communist debacle of 1933 leads back to the entanglements of the "Free German Committee" of 1931.

After the success of Hitler and his Brown cohorts in the September 1930 elections, when the National Socialists had in one great leap become the second largest party in the German Reichstag, the German Communists were feverishly seeking ways and means of damming the rush of the incoming Nazi tide. The decision what to do and what dams to erect, however, was entirely in the hands of Stalin. Thaelmann and his lieutenants, who at that time were in command of the German Communist Party, looked up to him as to a god.

Stalin's answer to the swelling Nazi tide appeared in a manifesto published in the Communist press under the heading "For the National and Social Liberation of the German People." In this manifesto the National Socialists were represented as agents of big industry and the banks allied with the finance capital of the West. The Germans were told that only the Communists would be able to free them from the chains of the Treaty of Versailles and the reparation payments. Only by looking towards the Soviet Union would they find an escape from the misery of the depression and the national humiliation.

Stalin now revived the maneuver that Radek had attempted in 1923, with new nuances. The place of the "brave soldier of the counter-revolution" in 1923, Schlageter, was taken by Lieutenant

162

Schehringer who had been dismissed by the Reichswehr and had joined the Communists after a short association with Hitler's National Socialists. In the spring of 1931 the National Socialists had been agitating for a plebiscite to oust the Prussian government at that time in the hands of the Social Democrats. Just before the plebiscite was to come to a final vote, Stalin issued an order to the German Communists to participate and vote for the ouster of the Social Democrats. Without hesitating, the high command in Moscow had transmitted this order to Berlin. There a panic had ensued.

For many weeks the German Communists had been conducting a campaign of their own against the plebiscite of the National Socialists. There had been severe encounters between the two hostile groups with many killed on both sides. Thaelmann begged the Comintern in January for a change of decision, to no avail.

Notwithstanding the Communist participation side by side with the National Socialists, the plebiscite had been a failure. The Social Democratic government remained in power. Stalin's "Free German Committee" of 1931 ended in the same failure as had Radek's "wanderer into nothingness" of 1923.

Nevertheless Hitler became the victor of the day. For between the Communists and the Social Democratic workers, together numbering more than twelve million people, an abyss had been opened which was one of the prerequisites for Hitler's victory.

The Kremlin had continued the same line of policy throughout 1932. In July of that year the Social Democrats had been ousted from the Prussian government by a quick coup d'état of von Papen. Many of the Communists, loyal to the party and the prescriptions of the Kremlin, had enjoyed the downfall of their "Social Fascist" enemies. The millions of Communist followers in the country remained inactive and passive during these months, waiting for the orders that they expected from their higher-ups. Actually a large majority of them had already been demoralized by the terror of the Nazis, the unemployment continuing for many years, and the policy of the Communist leadership that remained a bitter mystery to them. A similar state of affairs prevailed among the seven or eight million followers of the Social Democrats who were convinced that their experienced leaders would be able to master the situation without

163

civil war. The impotence of these leaders played into Hitler's hands as much as the miscalculations resulting from the German-Russian poker game.

In the late fall of 1932 the crisis that had been impending became an actuality. Thaelmann and his lieutenants did not know what to do. Above their heads dangled Stalin's sword of Damocles: The main enemy is the Social Democracy. Under their feet the ground was giving way.

The Russian agents of the Comintern in Berlin were panic-stricken, fearing the National Socialists might actually cause Schleicher to fall and seize power themselves. Although they were all loyal followers of Stalin and did not permit themselves a doubt in the doctrines enunciated by the leader, they nevertheless had reported their fears again and again to Moscow.

In the beginning of November, 1932, a session of the Politbureau was called in Moscow to discuss the situation in Germany. The Comintern leadership, particularly Manuilsky and also many German Communists, hoped for a decision on the part of Stalin that would enable them to offer the Social Democrats an alliance against Hitler. But Stalin remained adamant: "The National Socialists will not attain power! They already lost many hundreds of thousands of votes in the last elections while the Communists were still gaining. The National Socialists cannot seize power against the will of the army. General Schleicher, the new chancellor, is their determined enemy. Don't permit yourselves to become confused by the panic-makers. The main enemy is and remains the Social Democracy."

Stalin derived his assurance from contacts his Berlin representatives were maintaining with General von Schleicher and other Reichswehr generals.

Again a campaign prepared by the Communists against the National Socialists had to be called off, a substitute campaign against the Social Democracy organized, and functionaries of the Party who, together with Democratic organizations had formed committees against the National Socialists, had to be called to order publicly.

At the end of January, 1933, the tension in Germany had reached a climax. General Schleicher had lost the support of President Hindenburg. He had turned to the leaders of the German Federation of Labor, asking them to proclaim a general strike which would enable him to declare martial law and dissolve the National Socialist Party of Hitler. But they had refused.

When the news that Hitler had taken power in the Reich reached Moscow it caused a paralysis. The first wire that arrived was believed to be a hoax. The newspapers did not dare publish any comments on the event. Stalin had been wrong in his appraisal of the German generals.

When the Praesidium of the Communist International convened, it announced to an amazed world its solemn interpretation of the events: "The conquest of power by Hitler does not signify a defeat for the Communist Party and the working class. The revolutionary upsurge has been temporarily interrupted."

Stalin maintained his prestige. But among the many thousands who paid for it was his German knight, Ernst Thaelmann, who refused to flee after the Reichstag fire, deciding to stay with his men, the workers of Berlin and Germany, in their defeat.

AFTERMATH

"We are not beaten," cried those German Communists who still loyally followed the lead of the Comintern. "We are temporarily retreating. We will rise to power soon. Hitler is just a steppingstone for the Communist revolution in Germany."

Such thoughts delivered Thaelmann into the hands of the Gestapo. He could not hide himself. Millions of people had seen his pictures posted for years in all German cities. Hundreds of thousands were familiar with his huge bulky figure. Friends jokingly referred to his bow legs as the "widest working class circles."

Thaelmann felt safe in the working class districts of Berlin. Yet it was there he was arrested and his entire staff was trapped.

In his entourage were two intimate collaborators, Alfred Kattner and Werner Hirsch. Kattner was a young Berlin Communist, an associate of the organizer of the Communist Party Secretariat, Leo Flieg. He held the unlimited confidence of Ernst Thaelmann, and knew all the party secrets.

The Gestapo had easy dealings with him. He told them all he knew and entered their service. This was a terrific blow for the underground Communist Party. Kattner knew of all the underground communications. He knew, too, all the leading Communists of the last ten years, face to face. As soon as a Communist was arrested under a false name, he was confronted with Kattner. Kattner led the Gestapo to the very tracks of the underground organizations, accompanying Gestapo agents through the busiest thoroughfares of Berlin in order to pick up Communists. Soon his victims were numbered by the dozen.

In 1934 he succeeded in dealing a vicious blow: he delivered Thaelmann's best friend, the leader of the underground German Central Committee, Johnny Schehr, into the hands of the Gestapo. This was his last blow.

A few days later, in the early morning hours, somebody knocked at Kattner's door. His wife opened the door. An insignificant-looking young man stood there.

Kattner was still in bed.....A few shots ended his life. The avenger of the Communist Party descended the staircase, took his bicycle from out in front where he had left it standing, and rode off.

Goering was head of the Gestapo at that time. He had Johnny Schehr and two other leading Communists shot the next day.

Schehr had been tortured for weeks, as few men before him, in the Columbia House, torture chamber of the Berlin Gestapo. The nails had been torn from his fingers and his toes, water driven into his testicles and his body pressed down onto a red hot iron chair. The Gestapo had not gotten a single word out of Schehr.

Werner Hirsch, chief editor of *Die Rote Fahne*, who had become Thaelmann's adviser, also kept silent. When after many months' stay at the Columbia House he was delivered into the concentration camp of Oranienburg, none of the other prisoners who saw him believed he could survive the next few days. Yet he did. He not only stayed alive: he was dismissed from the concentration camp three years after, a real and true miracle of the Third Reich.

The miracle that saved Werner Hirsch was his mother. She came from a well-known Protestant family of Berlin and as a young girl had known many aristocratic officers' families, among them the family of von Hammerstein, later to become the commanding general of the Reichswehr. Even after she had married her Jewish husband, the family relationship with von Hammerstein continued.

Her son Werner, who had become a revolutionary, converted the two daughters of the commanding general of the Reichswehr to Communism. The two girls to whom their father was lovingly devoted were quick to grasp Hirsch's teachings. According to him, the revolutionary front on which it was their duty to fight was the writing desk of their father.

For years they had been stealing and photographing the documents they found on the desk of their father. They had listened to all the conversations that went on in their father's house, and reported loyally to their teacher. They were among the best agents of the Communist secret service in the German army.

In 1934, General von Hammerstein had been dismissed from his post, but his influence was still strong enough to save the head of the only son of his friend. Werner Hirsch was released from the concentration camp the following year. He managed to flee the country.

Some time later he arrived in Moscow and was welcomed as a hero. He had deserved the honors shown him. A man who had passed through the Columbia House and the concentration camp of Oranienburg as a Jew and a Communist, and had come out alive without having committed treason to his party, could entertain the hope of having withstood all tests that life might impose upon a professional revolutionary. But Werner Hirsch had still to face the most difficult task and test of his life.

In 1936 Hans Kippenberger, another intimate friend of Ernst Thaelmann's, arrived in Moscow. He had been the leader of the secret information service of the German Communist Party. On his arrival in Moscow he was arrested by the GPU and accused of having been an agent of the Reichswehr for years.

Kippenberger had been one of the experts on insurrection of the German Communist Party. As a young student, in 1923, he had participated in the insurrection of Hamburg, and since that time had remained in the underground organization of the Communist Party, that occupied itself with the disintegration and the espionage in the German army.

In 1928 Kippenberger had become a deputy to the Reichstag and a member of the military committee of parliament. The generals with whom he now came into contact were aware of his functions. But they were not very much troubled by the Communist attempts at disintegration in the army. Some of them wanted to maintain the relationship with Kippenberger, particularly because in his hands lay also the communication with the Red Army's secret service, and he was an important instrument for carrying out their secret pact with the Red Army. For many years he had been in close contact with the military attaché of Soviet Russia in Berlin, General Putna, who had collaborated with General von Bredow, Schleicher's expert on Russia.

On June 30, 1934, Hitler had Schleicher, his most dangerous enemy in the army, murdered. Some of his friends managed to escape to Switzerland. Kippenberger immediately resumed relations with them there.

In 1937 General Putna was arrested by the GPU and accused of espionage in favor of Germany, just as were Tukhachevsky and the majority of the other commanding generals of the Red Army later on. Since Kippenberger had worked closely with Putna, Putna's fate became Kippenberger's fate, and also that of Kippenberger's collaborator, Werner Hirsch.

All Werner Hirsch's achievements now became material for accusation against him. His relationship with the daughters of General von Hammerstein was one of the main points of accusation. Having been saved from the concentration camp with the help of the General was another valid proof against him.

The same happened with the long and arduous work of Kippenberger. Both were shot. Werner Hirsch's mother had saved him only for the revolvers of the GPU.

During all these years Ernst Thaelmann was kept in a Nazi prison. For much of this time the Comintern had kept his name and his memory alive all over Europe. But the campaign for his liberation slowly died down until finally his name no longer was mentioned by the High Command of the World Revolution.

In the spring of 1944 Nazi papers reported that during a severe air raid Thaelmann had broken out of his prison cell. After the German collapse the truth became known. The SS had murdered Thaelmann in the concentration camp of Buchenwald.

168

CHAPTER X

Max Hoelz: Free Lance of the Revolution

COMMUNIST ROBIN HOOD

MAX HOELZ WAS ONE OF THE STRANGEST ACTORS EVER TO TAKE part in the Comintern drama. He was of the flesh and blood of those peasant rebels who at the end of the Middle Ages had sought a road to freedom in bloody battles against noblemen and townships. A romantic seeker after justice and truth on earth, he lost his way into the Comintern only because he happened to grow up at a time when the East was attracting, together with the hardboiled realists of the revolution, its dreamers.

He was a rebel who refused to bow to the realities of politics. Of middle height, with big strong shoulders and a dark head with piercing, penetrating eyes, he carried himself like a born leader.

Max Hoelz was born in the poorest part of Germany, the Vogtland. Between the foothills of Saxony and Czechoslovakia live the weavers of this countryside. They know little but hunger and misery. Working hard for a piece of bread, they do not complain: they wait for the day the Savior will come and deliver them from their misery.

There Max Hoelz grew up, the son of a day-laborer whom he later described as a typical non-class-conscious worker, and of a deeply religious mother who took her six children to mass and never permitted them to eat or go to sleep without first saying their prayers.

A family so poor could afford no schooling for the boy. He had to work for his food. At sixteen he ran off to England. There too he starved, but at least he could study. Once he fainted from hunger in the street. In the daytime he worked as a car washer in a garage; evenings he studied technical questions, preparing himself to become an engineer.

He was happy. This was different from Germany. Nobody in England asked who his father was: he was judged by his own deeds and accomplishments.

At twenty-one he had to return to Germany for military service.

Eager to become an officer in the army, he worked day and night to acquire the necessary education and schooling. Too many hours of work and undernourishment caused a breakdown, so he was rejected by the army.

When war broke out he enlisted as a volunteer, an enthusiastic patriot. But the horror of war soon destroyed his youthful enthusiasm for the fatherland. He learned to hate Prussian military bureaucracy.

Talking in friendly fashion with British prisoners, he was suspected of being a spy. He refused to be hospitalized when he suffered a concussion of the brain. He had seen how Prussian military physicians treated his comrades. After an attempted suicide he was sent back from the front to an institution for nervous cases.

When the war ended Max Hoelz returned home to the Vogtland. The war had killed his faith in God, social justice, and humanity. He had come to hate everything that made men as miserable as he himself had become.

He settled down in Falkenstein, a village of about fifteen thousand inhabitants, of whom six thousand were unemployed. Six thousand had given up hope. Hoelz became their leader. He spread a new doctrine through the countryside:

"Take away from where there is, and give where there is not!"

At the head of a small group of armed men, he would go to the market places, confiscate food and distribute it among the families of the unemployed. He would take over the handling of the dole, confiscating the treasuries of the various small municipalities of that section and distributing their funds among the poor.

He became the uncrowned king of the Vogtland. In the hungry valleys, the legend spread: The Savior has arrived!

Dozens of times he was arrested, and dozens of times his followers liberated him. His audaciousness knew no bounds.

To seven gendarmes who tried to arrest him in a train compartment, he exhibited a hand grenade, asking them whether they wished to accompany him on a trip into the Great Beyond.

The Communist Party publicly disassociated itself from Max Hoelz. It had tried to impose its discipline upon him, but he would not submit. He did not give a hoot for its orders, nor did he observe its counsels. His only guide was his hatred for the wealthy and his

170

pity for the poor and the wretched. He was not a politician. He was the avenger of the proletariat.

In the year 1920, the year of the reactionary Kapp putsch, Hoelz began to wage war on his own account. With his military bands he occupied many small villages in the Vogtland. The native middle classes thought the end of the world had come.

The Reichswehr surrounded the area held by Hoelz. He took hostages and set fire to a few big houses, just to show that he meant business. Finally, as resistance became more and more impossible, he escaped into Czechoslovakia, where as a political refugee he received the right of asylum.

After a short while he returned illegally to Germany and began to ignite the flames of rebellion, this time in Central Germany. A high price was set on his head. But Hoelz found hiding places and allies everywhere. His glory had spread from the Vogtland over the entire central part of Germany. He knew how to enhance it.

To a state attorney who, in a public notice, described his long black hair as a special characteristic that would lead to his seizure, he wrote a letter: "Here is some of the long black hair that is to betray Hoelz. Go and look for the owner."

In March, 1921, his great hour arrived. The Communist Party seemed finally to have accepted what he had always believed, that direct action was the only way to arrive at your goal. Hoelz immediately started to wage war in Central Germany, where the struggle was at its hottest, against army and police. Just as in 1920 he had become the terror of the Vogtland, now he was the terror of Central Germany. When one of the Central German towns heard the news that Hoelz was on the march, the well-to-do citizens fled and the poor rejoiced.

After a few months, he was arrested in Berlin. His trial was a spectacular show. A large part of public opinion urged the death sentence for him. The judges seemed unable to handle him. The newspapers demanded the dissolution of a court that was scorned by the defendant and did not know how to deal with him.

He compared the court to a theater of marionettes, the judges to puppets manipulated by the bourgeoisie. He addressed the State's Attorney always as the "defendant" and thanked him for a trial

171

that was more beneficial to the revolution than all his own previous deeds.

"Should you acquit me," he exclaimed to the court, "you would be condemning yourselves as well as me to commit suicide! You judges would have to string yourselves up the next day, because you would be ashamed before your own class. And I would kill myself because I would not be able to endure the contempt of the revolutionary proletariat. Should you condemn me to ten years in prison, you would be giving me a failing mark; fifteen years would be better. Life imprisonment would be excellent. If you condemn me to death, that would be the best mark you could possibly give me."

He was sentenced to life imprisonment. Throughout Germany his name became a symbol of struggle. Mass meetings and petitions called for his release. Many democratic intellectuals joined the Communists in these demands. In 1927 after five years of imprisonment he was set free, released in a general political amnesty.

On his return from prison he was greeted in Berlin by more than half a million people. He cried for joy. His sufferings had not been in vain. The workers had not forgotten him.

He spoke to the masses, his mighty voice ringing out over the big square: "I have stayed the same, and when the hour strikes again you can be sure I will again do my duty!"

DEATH ON THE VOLGA

This was the pinnacle of his life. Yet at this very moment his descent had already begun. The Central Committee of the Communist Party was consulting about his fate.

Nobody doubted that he was far more popular than any of the Communist leaders, including Ernst Thaelmann, but nobody wanted him in the Communist leadership. They were afraid of his incalculability. He had lost nothing of his wild and uncontrollable temperament in prison. In a situation similar to that of 1920 or 1921, he would probably again act as leader of the rebellion and upset all well-laid political plans for the Communist Party. But weightier than all these considerations was the knowledge that he would surpass them all in popularity.

After a few months of triumphant travelling through Germany, he was finally persuaded to go to Moscow, for he wanted to become a revolutionary leader measuring up to all the standards of the Communist International. He thought in Moscow he would acquire the theoretical training he lacked, and then return to Germany.

In Moscow, too, he was received by enthusiastic crowds as triumphantly as in Germany. Assigned to propaganda work for the International Red Aid, he travelled throughout Russia. Hundreds of plants had adopted his name. He became honorary commander of a Red regiment. There was little time for theoretical study, for now he was immersed in the happy life of the emancipated working class. So the first two years of his Russian stay went by.

Finally he began to long for his homeland and asked to be permitted to return. In the Comintern he was advised that his studies had not yet been completed. In reality the German Communist leaders had decided never to have Hoelz return to Germany.

In 1930 a new chapter opened in his life, the last one. Thousands of German workers had emigrated into the Soviet Union to participate there in the Socialist reconstruction of the country. Many of them could not adjust themselves to conditions of life so different from those they were accustomed to, and came into conflict with their colleagues, the plant administrations, and police.

For two years Max Hoelz had attempted to become a disciplined Communist leader, submitting to all the requirements of high policy in the Comintern. Now the old rebel, the leader of the unemployed, came to the fore again. Again Max Hoelz wanted to help those who had come into conflict with authority. He ran from pillar to post demanding justice. He kicked open all doors, even those that led into the highest places.

All his efforts were in vain. Everywhere, and particularly in the Comintern building, he uttered wild imprecations against everybody. Soon he became the terror of Moscow officials. He was no longer seen at mass meetings. He was forsaken and became a lonely man.

Meanwhile Fascism was growing by leaps and bounds in Germany. The idea of living in a hotel room in Moscow while workers were preparing for great battles in his homeland was unendurable to Hoelz. But the Comintern rejected his demand to return with even greater determination than before. Hoelz realized he had become a prisoner.

In November, 1932, he took matters into his own hands. With the same blind rebellious instinct of old he went right into the German Embassy, demanding a passport. The official, thinking Hoelz was threatening him with murder, became frightened and ran for help. Hoelz in helpless rage grew panicky and fled so quickly from the Embassy building that the GPU officers waiting for him on the street could not arrest him.

He barricaded himself in his room in the Hotel Metropole. To all intermediaries he had the same answer:

"I've got sixty bullets ready—fifty-nine for the GPU and one for myself!" This went on for three days.

Finally some comrades convinced him that nobody wanted to do him any harm, and that his appeal to the German Embassy would not be held against him.

Actually, Hoelz was a dead man from the day he crossed the threshold of the German Embassy. To appeal to one's own government was a crime not forgiven any foreign Communist in the Soviet Union. But it was decided to handle the matter without much noise. Hoelz' name was too well known, his popularity too great, to risk a public step.

When the news about Hitler's victory came through, and the representative of the German Communist Party in Moscow, Fritz Heckert, publicly announced that the German Communists had not suffered defeat, Hoelz went mad with fury. He stormed into the Machavaya building and beat up Heckert.

After the incident, Hoelz was persuaded that he was suffering from nerves, that he needed a rest, and should go to different surroundings for a while. He was offered a stay on a Soviet farm in the vicinity of Nizhny Novgorod to restore his strength.

A short time later, a notice appeared in *Pravda* that Max Hoelz was drowned while bathing in the Oka River. He was a good swimmer and at the place he was drowned the river was only a few feet deep.

His body was found between the connecting posts of a wooden bridge. There were many wounds in his head.

Hoelz was given a funeral befitting a revolutionary of his rank.

André Marty and Fritz Heckert were his pallbearers. Funeral orators eulogized his life and his heroic revolutionary deeds.

"The courage that Max Hoelz showed, regardless of the peril to his own life, whenever revolutionary action demanded it," Fritz Heckert said at his grave, "remained with him to his last hour!"

Many workers' delegations carried their Red flags behind his coffin, and deputies of the regiment whose honorary commander he was fired a salute over his grave.

CHAPTER XI

Bohumir Smeral: Victim of an Oath

FROM THE HAPSBURGS TO LENIN

ONE OF THE MOST PEACEFUL COUNTRIES IN EUROPE BEFORE THE
First World War was the Kingdom of Bohemia. Its capital city
was Prague—the Czechs proudly called it "Golden Prague!"—
the most peaceful of all capitals in Europe. Prague was the residence
of the most peaceful party of the Second International, the Czech
Social Democracy. Its most peaceful leader was Bohumir Smeral.

The Czechoslovakian Social Democrats frequently battled their
Austrian comrades in Vienna on matters of Czech concern—but
always in words only. They never dreamed of revolutionary action,
either against the bourgeoisie in general, or the monarchy of the
Hapsburgs in particular.

They fought for labor reforms and registered modest success. They
conducted animated election campaigns, with big talk and bigger
consumption of good Czechoslovakian beer! With great relish they
took the train to Vienna to attend meetings of the Austro-Hungarian
parliament, where they threatened the imperial bureaucracy in long
speeches. Satisfied, they returned to their Golden Prague and sat
hoping for the best, on shady beer terraces at the Moldava, watching
the river slowly meandering through the luxuriant country.

Bohumir Smeral loved his Prague, the workers, and the entire
world! A large round belly proclaimed his appreciation of Pilsener
beer, the best in the world; a good slice of Prague ham, the most
delicious of all hams in the world; and a substantial piece of tasty
Czech bread.

His philosophy was to live and let live. In a self-satisfied country
like Bohemia, one could conduct even a Socialist-like policy on this
principle.

The Czechoslovakian workers to whom Smeral had dedicated
his life did not like ascetic-looking agitators. Their ideal was a man
like Smeral whose powerful figure exuded a mighty self-assurance,

whose genial sky-blue eyes looked with benevolence at the world, whose speech was flavored with the friendly peasant humor of the Slavs.

For the Czech Social Democrats, and particularly for Bohumir Smeral, the outbreak of the war was a disturbing event. With bands playing, the Czech regiments at the front went over to the Czarist armies. The longer the unpopular war lasted, the stronger became the national revolutionary tension all over the country. Nationalist intellectuals started secret organizations conspiring with the Allies. Abroad Masaryk and Benes formed a national committee of liberation.

But Bohumir Smeral remained true to his emperor. He did not wish to entangle the working class organizations entrusted to him in revolutionary adventures. One never knew how they might end. He sent telegrams of congratulations to victorious Austrian generals and even appeared, after the death of the old Kaiser Franz Joseph, before his successor to assure him of his loyalty.

In October, 1918, the Austro-Hungarian monarchy collapsed, the Czechoslovakian republic was born, and the Bolshevist revolution was consolidating its victory. For thirty years Smeral had fought to better this world. Now it had suddenly gone under.

To enter the new government of the young republic would not have been difficult for a man with his influence on the masses. The new leaders were of a pacific inclination of mind, and would gladly have forgiven Smeral his sins during the war had he been willing to put his great political talents at the service of the new state. But Smeral took the most surprising and incomprehensible turn of his life!

Immediately after the revolution he disappeared from Prague and retired for several months to Switzerland. On his return he explained that he had given up opportunism for the rest of his life and that, from then on, he would tread the path of Lenin. The reappearance of the Golem right in the center of Prague could not have created a greater sensation.

Bolshevism at that time was in great disfavor in Czechoslovakia. The Czech legions that had been formed in Russia waged war in Siberia against the Bolsheviks. When they returned home via Vladivostok, they brought with them a great part of the Russian gold treasures they had taken from Admiral Kolchak. The Czechoslovaks

177

were among Moscow's most-hated counter-revolutionary nations, and Czechoslovakia reciprocated with similar feelings: it did not recognize the Soviet government until 1934.

The first Bolshevik agitators, former Czechoslovakian prisoners of war returning from Russia, were beaten up. They found no response among Czech labor. Yet Smeral, the most peaceful and most bourgeois of all Social Democrats in Czechoslovakia, became a Bolshevik.

Many of his friends did not take this step seriously, nor did his enemies. But Smeral was in dead earnest! He broke with all friends of his thirty-year-old brilliant career, and went to Moscow. Humbly he appeared before Lenin and Trotsky, whom he had known in former years at Congress sessions of the Second International.

And now the second miracle happened. Lenin, who hated nothing in the world more than the social patriotic leaders of the Second International, gave the repentant sinner his confidence. Smeral won over not only Lenin and Trotsky, but Zinoviev too. When the latter was asked why he placed more confidence in Smeral than in Serrati, he answered smilingly:

"Really I don't know myself. The man smells of fresh earth. It's simply impossible not to believe in him."

The trust that the Bolshevik leaders placed in Smeral, however, had other aspects as well. Lenin was afraid Prague might become a rallying center for a Pan-Slavic bloc against the Soviet Union and coordinate the forces of the Little Entente with the remnants of the Pan-Slavic movement of old and with all the Russians who had fled from Russia to fight Bolshevism. Before the war Prague had been one of the centers of the Pan-Slavic movement, at that time a vehicle for the imperialism of the Czar. The leader of the Czechoslovakian National Democrats, Kramarcz, had been one of its Western heads and the tradition of this movement was still strong in Prague, Belgrade, and other centers of Western and Southern Slavs. Lenin expected Smeral to defeat such a potential threat and to outmaneuver such an anti-Bolshevist bloc.

The confidence that Lenin and Zinoviev had in Smeral was not misplaced. He solved his task in such sovereign fashion as to keep friends and enemies breathless.

After his return from Moscow he began a campaign for the Soviet

Union and the Communist International, conducting it usually in the market places. These meetings turned out to be a real *"levée en masse."* Whenever he talked from the steps of Prague's municipal building the streets surrounding the square were jammed.

No one gave a thought now to the telegrams of congratulations sent to the Austrian generals, and when Smeral's enemies tried to remind the people of his sins during the World War, they were shouted down.

Smeral translated the message of the East into the daily language of the Czechoslovakian workers. He simplified the main ideas of Bolshevism so that even the most primitive could understand them. To Pan-Slavic nationalism he opposed the fraternity that Jan Huss, the great popular reformer, had preached to the Slavs of his day.

He conquered the hearts of the Czech workers for the Russian revolution. The peaceful parliamentarian and reformer of the Hapsburg days had turned into a revolutionary strategist and people's tribune.

With his success Smeral's ambition grew. He intended to take into the Communist International not only a powerful Communist Party but the entire labor movement of Czechoslovakia. "It will be necessary," he said, "to separate from the reformists and all those who do not want to go along with Lenin and Trotsky. Communism will grow within the labor party. If the reformers cannot live within such a party, it will be just too bad for them!"

In September, 1920, he organized a left wing in the Social Democracy. The masses were on his side. He did not give up the Social Democratic name nor the Social Democratic properties because this party had been the organizing center for the Czech workers for more than forty years. His slogan was: A Social Democrat who does not become a follower of the Communist International is a traitor to Social Democracy!

In Moscow they didn't know whether to laugh or cry over this; yet the Czech workers took the slogan seriously.

In December, 1920, the first conflict between Smeral and the young Czechoslovak state occurred. Smeral and his followers had appropriated not only the Social Democratic name but also the properties of the party. They were in physical possession of the

179

People's Building, a huge structure erected from the small savings of the working people, but the legal title to the building was contested by the minority Social Democrats in whose personal names the building happened to be registered. The latter were therefore able to compel a legal surrender of the building through the courts and they were supported in their proceedings by the government that was largely in their hands.

For the first time in his life Smeral resisted force. The police had to carry him out of the building. There was great excitement in the working districts. In Prague a general strike was proclaimed that quickly spread through the entire country. Attempts were made to storm parliament in Prague. In some cities Soviet republics were proclaimed.

ETERNAL REFUGEE

Smeral's first battle against the republic was also his last. In May of the following year he founded the Czechoslovakian Communist Party that united within its ranks the great majority of the Czech and Slovak Social Democratic workers. A short time later the Czechoslovakian Communist Party merged with the German Communists from the Sudeten areas.

Up to that point Smeral had been treading his own paths. In the years that followed each and every gesture of independence immediately led to a clash with Moscow. Smeral tried to adjust himself to the spirit of Zinoviev, but he soon realized this was something he could not do. He was a popular tribune but not a professional revolutionary.

When Zinoviev introduced his great change of leadership after the German defeat of October, 1923, Smeral resigned without giving battle. Had he chosen to fight, the followers of Zinoviev in Czechoslovakia would have remained a small sect. Smeral's personal influence on the masses was unbreakable. But he had decided not to fight against the Bolsheviki. "I have given Lenin my word. I will keep it as long as I live. I will never come out against Moscow!"

The Czech popular tribune now began his years of learning and travelling in the Comintern. In Moscow he belonged to the "impure" first class. He was permitted to sit in the galleries of the High Command of the world revolution, and from time to time to repre-

180

sent the Comintern at meetings abroad where great revolutionary speeches mattered less than political cunning and revolutionary diplomacy.

In Soviet Mongolia, on one of his missions, he participated in conferences with the Korean Communists. On his return he reported with horror that at the banquet he had been offered a live louse as dessert. He said it was considered a delicacy and an honor to the guest. He would have preferred a glass of his beloved Pilsener which he now could get only on rare occasions.

Sometimes he travelled to Paris, sometimes to Berlin—always a loyal officer of Moscow. Whenever he returned to Prague the Communist workers there cheered him as they always had, although Moscow's lieutenants were busy denouncing him as an incorrigible opportunist. Usually Smeral fled from Prague after a few days, not wanting to create any difficulties for the professional revolutionaries who had been installed in Prague by Moscow.

For a long time he lived in dark and dreary Berlin where the beer was even more sour than his life there as head of the League against Imperialism. He was forced to occupy himself with problems that held no interest for him and with men whom he did not understand.

Smeral anticipated the German catastrophe of 1933 for many years. But he kept his silence and travelled sadly from country to country, a loyal yet unbelieving missionary of the Comintern.

Smeral's political life ended in a caricature. When the Second World War broke out he began to preach to the French and British workers, in dutiful obeisance to the prescription of the High Command of the world revolution, the anti-war defeatism of Lenin. But he did not exhort the workers of Germany whose troops had occupied his beloved Prague to rise against their masters and defeat the imperialism of their own country, for there was a pact between Hitler and Stalin!

Shortly afterward, Smeral died a natural death in Moscow.

CHAPTER XII

Heinz Neumann and Besso Lominadze—
Stalin's Fair-Haired Sons

"YOU OUGHT TO BE SHOT . . . . ."

YOU OUGHT TO BE SHOT FOR WHAT YOU DID IN CANTON!"
The man who shouted these words, trembling with rage, at a
secret session of the praesidium of the Executive Committee of
the Comintern, was Bukharin. The man at whom they were aimed
was Heinz Neumann, one of the agents of the Comintern during the
putsch in Canton, on December 11, 1927.

Heinz Neumann lowered his eyes like a schoolboy being scolded
by his teacher. But immediately afterward an arrogant knowing
smile passed quickly over his features.

"Say what you will. I know what I know."

"Ah, too bad my couriers failed to reach you when you fled from
Canton to Hongkong!" Yeh-Ting, the military commander of the
insurrection, said quietly, "Probably you would not have succeeded
in getting away alive."

In Yeh-Ting's eyes burned scorching fire. This time Heinz Neumann trembled. He knew the Chinese revolutionaries were deadly
serious.

The young man whom Bukharin was calling to task was about
twenty-six. A college boy who had reached maturity too early, he
seemed. Chalk white face that knew of many vices, big watery-blue
eyes that never fixed on anything, hands always nervously clasped,
awkward movements.

With his colleague Besso Lominadze, another agent of the Comintern in Canton, Neumann had succeeded in starting an armed insurrection there. It lasted exactly fifty hours and cost the lives of between
six and ten thousand workers, the flower of the Communist Party in
Southern China. Heinz Neumann, who had been the *enfant terrible*
of the Comintern, had become the "butcher of Canton."

In the year 1919, this nineteen-year-old son of a wealthy grain merchant in Berlin dived head first into the currents of the revolution. Why? Nobody could answer that question precisely. Not even he, who had an answer for everything.

In the streets of Berlin there were shootings at that time. At night all lights were extinguished. The police had unwound spools of barbed wire along the streets to block them. The government of the Reich had put up large posters on the walls. It was fun to knock over the barbed wire spools, to tear down the posters, and to run for one's life afterwards. There was a revolution on, and one had to do something about it.

Heinz Neumann had always been an enterprising child. The first time he ran away from home he was not quite thirteen. Yet he got as far as Genoa, Italy. Right after the war he paid Paris and London a visit. His dad always called to get his darling son back again. If, on his return, the old man gave his son a thrashing, Heinz would again disappear for a few days, and wait in hiding somewhere until he saw the customary advertisement in the newspaper:

"Return home. Everything forgiven."

In 1920 he did not return home. He had become a professional revolutionary.

Everything he did he accomplished in a flash. As a youngster he learned to speak French, English, and Italian fluently. He learned Dutch and Hungarian just for the fun of it. Once he vanished from a courtroom where he was about to be sentenced.

He was just past twenty when he became associate editor of the Berlin party organ, *Die Rote Fahne*.

It was natural that he belonged to the most revolutionary wing of his party. He regarded the fact that the party leadership had not yet changed Germany into a Soviet republic as a sort of treason committed against himself personally.

"If only they had my courage and cunning!"

THE RABBIT THAT DID NOT DIE

In the summer of 1923 a "revolutionary situation" had arisen in Germany. Heinz Neumann was still too young to be acceptable for one of the military staffs that were engaged in preparation of an insurrection. This made him despondent. Nobody wanted to recognize the excellence of his revolutionary talents.

When the "revolutionary situation" had passed and the party leadership again had failed to show what he deemed the proper courage and cunning, Heinz Neumann conceived an audacious scheme. Once and for all he would achieve a deed to inscribe his name on the scroll of the immortals. He would kill General von Seeckt whose army had destroyed the insurrection plans of the Communists in Saxony.

This time he found a companion of like mind, a former employee of the Reichsbank whom fate had placed in a responsible post within the insurrectionary organization of the Communists. By chance he was a namesake of Heinz Neumann, by the name of Felix Neumann.

Heinz and Felix decided to do away with von Seeckt according to the time-honored prescription of the Borgias—poison. Felix first procured at the cost of large sums of money a dose of cyanide of potassium.

"But," the sinister conspirators declared, "we have to make absolutely sure. The scoundrel von Seeckt shall not escape his fate. We have to test out the poison first."

So they bought a rabbit. With great care they sprinkled the poison over the greens for the rabbit. Heinz and Felix awaited results: The rabbit ate up his salad and showed no signs of departing this world. For a whole week they kept repeating the experiment; the rabbit grew fatter and happier.

This was too much for Heinz. He decided on direct action. He purchased a revolver. Now Seeckt was to be shot on one of his daily morning rides through the Berlin Tiergarten.

Felix explored the terrain. For days he went beating around in the Tiergarten to establish what paths von Seeckt frequented on his rides.

Heinz practiced with his revolver in front of the mirror, in his rented room. He had never yet in his life fired a shot. Naturally he couldn't actually shoot off the pistol in his room, but it sufficed, for him, to practice by bringing the revolver with a movement of his right arm in line with the tip of his nose, palely reflected in the mirror.

Thus fully prepared, Heinz went out to the Tiergarten each morning at an early hour. His cap pulled down over his eyes, his fist thrust deep into his pocket where the instrument of murder reposed, he stalked his victim through the wet grass.

But fate did not mean well by Heinz. Seeckt no longer went on his morning rides. Perhaps he had received word of a conspiracy afoot. In any case Heinz did not get him within range of his revolver.

He put all the blame on Felix, charging him with poor exploratory work. The latter accused Heinz of losing his nerve. The conspirators separated in cold hostility.

Heinz had caught a terrific cold, to boot, out in the damp grass. He lay in bed with fever. Von Seeckt lived on for many years in good health.

This was not Heinz Neumann's only accident. He tripped up politically as well.

TRIP INTO POWER

After the passing of the "revolutionary situation" in 1923, the miracle boy failed to watch his step. He bet on the wrong horse and allied himself with a group that was rejected by the Communist International as opportunist. For this reason Heinz Neumann felt that Berlin had become too small for him—it was better to change his field of activity.

He put in an appearance in Moscow, not suspecting that the trip to Moscow was a trip into the big career of his life.

His first months there were hard and bitter. He had neither function nor occupation. Had it not been for the numerous stenographers of the Comintern who took pity on the poor deserted boy, he might have gone under. So desperate was he that he volunteered for the Red Army. His services were rejected because he was too weak to carry a gun.

Heinz Neumann would not have been the man he was if he had not succeeded within a few months in edging his way into the machinery of the Executive Committee of the Comintern. It did not take him long to learn Russian fluently and perfectly—most Germans and other foreigners never learned more than a few everyday words, even after years of residence in Moscow.

In the Machavaya building he had access to all offices and often was asked to collaborate. Knowing all the languages spoken there, he became the irreplaceable translator at all confidential conferences.

The Russian secretaries found the miracle boy to their liking. They took him under their wings like a child of whose talents one expects much in the future.

Heinz Neumann was shrewd. He accepted the protection of the "grown-ups" for the time being, but with fists clenched: "You wait! I'll show you!"

Often he would play the clown for the Comintern secretaries, imitating both them and the high and mighty of the Comintern. He had a gift for caricature. But more than that, weeks after he had heard a speech, he could impersonate the speaker and repeat the speech, word for word, in any language. In this way he wormed himself into the drinking parties of his superiors, amusing them and at the same time gaining the personal confidence of those who happened to be most important in the movement, in their moments of relaxation.

He tiptoed into the confidence of the Comintern like a thief in the night.

After that, he began to send unauthorized reports on the secret affairs of the Russian party to his comrades in Germany. So he acquired a unique value for his German comrades, for it was impossible to be a Communist politician in Germany without knowing exactly what was going on in Russia. Heinz Neumann always knew.

In Moscow he had learned to bet on the right horse. In 1926 he had already graduated from the *enfant terrible* into a politician in his own right. Now he began to conduct his own political affairs.

He had mastered the art of intrigue like a pigmy Machiavelli. He knew how to separate himself at exactly the right moment from a particular group, and to ally himself with the next one that was rising to power. Everyone said of him: "This young man was born without a character!"

In fact, to be without moral inhibitions was his real nature. Sometimes he was asked whether he had no pricks of remorse after playing one of his scoundrel's tricks. He would laugh in great amusement. For Heinz Neumann these were only the infantile prejudices of hopeless Philistines who could not understand that all moral proscriptions were but petty bourgeois prejudice.

186

His great years began after the fall of Zinoviev, when the *"clair-obscur"* of the Bukharin-Stalin leadership commenced to set over the Comintern. Heinz Neumann had become the intimate friend of Besso Lominadze, who had followed the Yugoslav Vujovic as president of the Communist Youth International. Lominadze had introduced Heinz Neumann into the personal circle of Stalin. Neumann had made a big hit—he had become the white-haired boy of the strong man from Georgia!

He reported with pride, at the end of 1926: "I have addressed Stalin as 'Koba.'" (This was Stalin's pseudonym during the period of Czarist illegality.) "And he was very friendly with me!"

Lominadze was in every respect the opposite of Heinz Neumann, a tremendous clumsy Georgian with the strength of a bear and nerves of steel. He was a dangerous man to challenge. At seventeen he had bragged at a drinking bout in Petrograd that he was able to bathe in the Neva at any temperature. His drinking companions ridiculed him. The temperature was then fifty degrees below zero. Lominadze immediately took his whole group of drunken students over to the river, where they hacked a hole in the ice, and he crawled in. He paid for this joke with the loss of one kidney. But he never was sorry.

Stalin loved Lominadze. In this man he found all the wildness of his Caucasian mountains. This was no effeminate intellectual like those in the circle of Red professors Bukharin had assembled around himself. This was a real man from head to toe, a lad able to drink the heavy Katechinic wine from nightfall to dawn and between drinks to extinguish the electric light bulbs with shots from his pistol, not missing a single shot.

Lominadze possessed a quality that was of inestimable value to Stalin at this time. In addition to having a fiery revolutionary temperament, he was also a serious student of Marxism. Among the incoming Communist generation he was regarded as one of the most original theoretical talents. Most of the young men of that sort grouped themselves around Bukharin. Lominadze organized an elite of young theoreticians around Stalin, as a counterweight to the school of professors of Bukharin. In 1926, young Lominadze was looked upon by everyone as Stalin's crown prince.

ADVENTURE IN WORLD POLITICS

Lominadze and Heinz Neumann had become an inseparable pair. Together they moved up in the Comintern, step by step, to the very top; and together, ten years later, they sank into a common grave.

It was in July, 1927, that they received their first great mission from Stalin, their adored master. The two apprentices of the revolution were to become master artisans, and even more. They were to avenge an insult to Stalin's self-love.

Never had two agents of the Comintern taken their seats in the Vladivostok express with such high hopes as these two friends. Heinz Neumann at this time was twenty-six years old, Lominadze three years his senior.

Stalin had suffered his first great defeat on the battlefield of the Comintern, for which he had been personally responsible, in April, 1927. This defeat had been as decisive for the Far East as had been the German defeat of the Comintern in 1923 for the West.

The struggle between Stalin and Bukharin on the one side, and the opposition front of Trotsky and Zinoviev on the other, had centered since 1926 on the Chinese question. The problem was whether to break with Chiang Kai Shek or not. In 1922 the Chinese Communist Party had allied itself, under the direction of the Comintern which was then still in the hands of Trotsky and Zinoviev, with the Kuomintang, the ruling party of the Chinese struggle for national liberation. The Chinese Communist Party had given the Kuomintang the working class support in the big cities which was so essential to its success.

In March, 1926, Chiang Kai Shek had become the master of the Chinese South with the help of the Soviet Union and the Communist Party of China, and at the same time had acquired the undisputed leadership of the Kuomintang. But as soon as Chiang, supported by the Communists, had consolidated his power in Canton, he immediately started taking more and more measures hostile to the Communists. He began to liquidate the trade unions, and had Communists shot in rows.

Now Trotsky and Zinoviev demanded a change in tactics. They urged the Chinese Communists to leave the Kuomintang and to organize the Chinese workers and peasants into Soviets, according to the Russian scheme. But Stalin and Bukharin categorically refused to change their policy.

On April 11, a long discussion took place in the Trade Union building in Moscow. Radek spoke for the opposition and warned, in impressive words, that a coup d'état by Chiang Kai Shek was impending. Stalin and Bukharin defended the alliance with Chiang, and charged the opposition with leading the Chinese revolution to suicide with their policy.

The very next morning Radek's predictions came true. Chiang Kai Shek moved into Shanghai and instituted the greatest blood bath of the Chinese civil war among the workers of that unfortunate city. The Communists of Shanghai were absolutely unprepared for this assault. In two bloody insurrections they had overthrown the rule of its governor whom they believed to be a mortal enemy of Chiang Kai Shek. After their victory, Chiang's troops were able to march into Shanghai and were received with triumphant joy.

Most of the Communists had buried their arms on order of Moscow and of their leaders to avoid all possibility of conflict with the soldiers of Chiang Kai Shek. The staggering blow dealt them by Chiang Kai Shek found them unarmed. Thousands of them were beheaded. Their trade unions were disbanded, their clubs and homes burned down. Only a few leaders escaped.

Chiang Kai Shek, who had received and accepted millions of dollars from Moscow, among whose advisers were several brilliant military instructors from Russia like General Galen-Bluecher, whose entire army had been equipped through Moscow—Chiang Kai Shek betrayed his Russian protectors with all the arts of Chinese political cunning.

Stalin does not like to be taken for a sucker! Those April days of 1927 were among the worst of his life. He fumed with rage. . . . .

Lominadze and Heinz Neumann were charged with showing Chiang Kai Shek that one cannot make a sucker out of Stalin with impunity.

Their first job was simple. On the eleventh of August they dismissed the whole Chinese Central Committee, which had frequently executed Stalin's and Bukharin's policies against its own better judgment, and

189

organized a new one of their own making. In Li-Li-San, a young intellectual whom they made the new leader of the Communist Party, they found a kindred soul. He too was thirsting for action.

Heinz Neumann and Lominadze were no idiots. They realized that from a military standpoint the situation in Canton held out no hope for them. Chiang Kai Shek's army of fifty thousand men was well equipped with English and Russian weapons. On their own side they counted twelve hundred student officers and approximately three thousand workers, but few arms. But only people worm-eaten by opportunism permit themselves to be impressed by such figures. Professional revolutionaries like Heinz Neumann and Lominadze give their attention, not to relationships of strength and power like these, but to imponderables.

If the insurrectionists were to be joined by tens of thousands of coolies and by the peasants around Canton, then a victory could happen. A risky game certainly. But what is the risk against the prize of victory!

To conquer Canton and take revenge for the defeat of Shanghai and the insult to Stalin, then to take the big jump into the High Command of the world revolution whose instrument one had been up to then—with such a prize in sight, all risk seems small.

Yet the hurdle into this adventure was not so easy. Lominadze and Heinz Neumann possessed Stalin's confidence, but no mandate from the Comintern to start an armed insurrection. Bukharin, president of the Communist International, had ordered them to institute a new leadership to organize propaganda for Soviets, to observe and to report.

From Peikin, John Pepper (Pogany)—Bela Kun's comrade during the days of the Hungarian Soviet republic in 1918 and the German insurrection in March, 1921, and in later years representative of the Comintern in the United States—was following their activities with suspicious eyes. The Chinese Central Committee had not arrived at a decision in favor of an insurrection.

Heinz Neumann overcame Lominadze's doubts. "Who knows whether ever again in life we will have such a chance?"

He knew how to handle adversaries and enemies within the party. He sent the members of the Chinese Central Committee to various parts of the provinces. Only loyal Li-Li-San was permitted to remain in Canton. Yeh-Ting, military commander in Canton, was informed that the Comintern had ordered an insurrection.

The third representative of the Comintern, John Pepper, was put into refrigeration: he was given no information whatever.

In the early morning hours of December 12, the insurrection began according to all the rules of the game that they had taken from the instructions of the Comintern for armed insurrections. On December 13, thousands and thousands of dead workers covered the streets of Canton, and Heinz Neumann and Lominadze took an American steamer in Hongkong for Kobe, from where they embarked for Vladivostok.

They had no reason to tremble for their careers when Bukharin, who had learned about the Canton insurrection only from the wires published in the newspapers, was shouting at them during the secret session of the Comintern in Moscow. In back of them stood a mightier man who gave the two bad boys a thorough scolding but did not permit any harm to come to them.

A year later Bukharin was finished in the Comintern and a new leadership instituted. Heinz Neumann returned to Germany, became a deputy in the German Reichstag, and one of the mighty in the German Communist Party. By then he was twenty-seven years old. Lominadze, a little later, was made general secretary of the Trans-Caucasian party, one of the most important posts in Stalin's hands. The insurrection in Canton had borne its fruit.

For three years Heinz Neumann played at party leadership in Germany. He made incendiary speeches in the Reichstag and at mass meetings, and groomed himself to become dictator in Germany. But in order to accomplish this objective, the official leader of the Communist Party, Ernest Thaelmann, had to be removed.

In August, 1931, Heinz Neumann thought he was strong enough, but this time he miscalculated. With a gesture of his hand, Stalin destroyed the career of the presumptive dictator, and sent him to Spain. As representative of the Executive Committee of the Comintern there, Heinz Neumann had to lead a drab and colorless existence. From Madrid he attempted to organize a faction against his old enemy Manuilsky and to cooperate with Willi Muenzenberg in Paris

191

and Herrmann Remmele, the representative of the German Communist Party in Moscow, to this end. The High Command, however, ordered him to leave Spain and go to Switzerland to await orders. But the Swiss authorities arrested him. The German government demanded that the Swiss government extradite him as a criminal because of an alleged participation in the shooting of two Prussian police officers in 1931. Once more he believed his star was to rise again. The Comintern organized an intensive campaign to save Heinz Neumann. Finally the Swiss government expelled him to Russia.

At the same time his friend Lominadze was tripped up in the collectivization of agriculture in the Caucasus. Being involved in the activities of the Zinoviev and Kamenev faction, he too was dismissed from Stalin's table.

In 1934 the two met again in Moscow. Heinz Neumann's lucky star had gone down forever. Embittered about his fall, he had been rash enough to criticize the policy of the Comintern during the days of Hitler's victory, well aware that the policy of the Comintern at that time was the policy of Stalin. Enraged, he had exclaimed, in the summer of 1933: "Stalin is a semi-Fascist!"

In Moscow he began again to intrigue, to lie, to calumniate, to flatter. He wrote dozens of personal letters to Stalin asking his forgiveness. But in vain. He remained among the unfortunate "impure" in the Hotel Lux. Stalin does not forgive.

Lominadze had been more fortunate. After his fall in the Caucasus he had become the organizer of one of the newly developed gigantic industrial plants. He worked with such devotion that Stalin permitted him to become a member of the Central Committee again and made him party boss of the greatest industrial combination in the Soviet Union at Magnitogorsk. His devotion, his charming personality, soon made him the real leader of the hundred thousand workers who, at great sacrifice, were constructing the most important war plant of the Soviet Union.

In 1937 destiny overtook him. Stalin's great purge had begun. Lominadze, during the short period of his fall from grace, had kept up a close relationship with Ryutin, a secretary of the Moscow party organization. In the earlier years Ryutin had belonged to the intellectual elite Lominadze had organized for Stalin. Since then he had become one of Stalin's most bitter enemies, like Sten, another intimate friend of Lominadze.

Ryutin was one of the first Russian oppositionists to be shot. The GPU boss Yezhov, who had succeeded Yagoda, had an orderly system for his arrests. He always used a complete list, taken from his thorough files. On Ryutin's list was also the name of Lominadze.

One day Lominadze was invited to visit the local GPU boss in Magnitogorsk. On his way there he shot himself.

The day after, Heinz Neumann was arrested. He cried for mercy even to the GPU men. He shouted for help. His screams shrilled through the corridors of the Hotel Lux.

He was shot the same day in the GPU prison in Moscow.

CHAPTER XIII

Willi Muenzenberg: Hearst of the Comintern

COMMUNIST YOUTH INTERNATIONAL

IN THE LATE FALL OF 1940 THE HALF-DECAYED BODY OF A MAN about fifty years old was found near a village in Central France. The cause of death could no longer be determined.

Papers discovered on the body identified the dead man as Willi Muenzenberg. From these documents the authorities learned that their owner had been a German refugee interned in a camp for enemy aliens.

Several weeks later the news of his death was published in a small paper of a town in the vicinity. What significance could there be in the death of a German refugee? In those days a whole land—happy smiling France—had died.

Willi Muenzenberg had dreamed in his younger years of dying as a hero on a barricade. In later years he had given little thought to death, for he had become the most efficient propagandist of the revolutionary movement of the postwar period, the Hearst of the Comintern. Life had brought glory, popularity, power and money to this poor shoemaker's apprentice who had grown up in a small city of Central Germany and, with a few pennies in his pocket, had left his home town a few years before the great war, for Switzerland.

In friendly and hospitable Switzerland Muenzenberg, by nature gay, genial, active, and a good speaker, rose quickly to a position of leadership among the young Socialist workers.

During the war he met Lenin in Zurich and became a fiery apostle of Lenin's revolutionary ideas among the Socialist youth. At the time of Germany's defeat, the activities of this temperamental young radical became too much for the Swiss authorities. First he was interned, then pushed across the border. He transferred his Youth Secretariat to Berlin, and there, with the support of Russian friends, began the struggle against the youth associations of the Second International.

194

He and his friends from Switzerland, France, Czechoslovakia, Austria, and Yugoslavia soon founded the Communist Youth International, which staged its first World Congress in May, 1920, in Moscow. Muenzenberg became its first president.

He was then a little over thirty, a "professional youth" as he was ironically called. But the praesidium of an organization that counted several hundred thousand members could not be left in the hands of one of its members, who were all under twenty.

The Communist Youth International was a miniature Comintern with praesidium and secretariat, representatives abroad, papers, factions, and intrigues. With all these imitations of the adults, the Youth International was not easy to direct.

At its Third World Congress which took place at the same time as the Third World Congress of the Comintern, Muenzenberg suddenly retired. He was given a new office, the organization of the International Workers Aid.

The culmination point of the terrible famine devastating Russia had already passed, but the wave of solidarity and sympathy with the Soviet Union that had touched the working masses in other countries had not yet receded. Muenzenberg accepted the task of organizing this solidarity.

With great enthusiasm and fiery imagination he explained his plans to Lenin, depicting how he would help the Soviet Union. Smiling, Lenin asked: "How much will your help cost the Soviet Union?"

Whatever the cost of Muenzenberg's Workers Aid, it paid good dividends. In short order he produced the first non-party mass organization of the Communists which penetrated deeply into the non-Communist groups of workers and intellectuals, an example for all organizations of this sort founded later on by the Communists in all countries of the world.

BIG BUSINESS COMMUNISM

The International Workers Aid was just a beginning, a modest one. Before the German Communists and the Comintern could turn around, Willi Muenzenberg had organized a huge propaganda trust centering about his own person. Naturally he was subject to the discipline of the German Communist Party and of the Comintern.

But in the course of the years, the real power of Muenzenberg increased to such an extent that the discipline had become a formality only.

He was a decidedly gifted businessman. To him, propaganda was a commodity like any other. To bring it to the buyer one must serve it up in a fashion fitting his tastes.

The popular press of the German Communists did not have a wide circulation. Their newspapers came out only in small editions because the majority of the workers simply could not digest the party language in which they were written.

That was where Muenzenberg came in. He published two dailies that soon reached a circulation many times that of the open Communist press in Berlin. He saw that an illustrated rotogravure weekly had the largest circulation of any periodical in German, so he immediately imitated it with an edition for workers, which shortly ran up a circulation of close to a million copies.

Workers in republican Germany were joiners: one worker would often join as many as ten different groups or clubs. Muenzenberg quickly exploited the boom in photography and radio clubs by publishing several periodicals for them.

The Communist Party maintained several publishing firms that sent out their own literature. Muenzenberg organized his own publishing firm to issue fiction and illustrated editions for gift purposes. To make sure of his sales, he also organized a book club of his own.

One of the first Russian films shown in Germany was Eisenstein's picture of the cruiser "Potemkin," a silent movie about the famous rebellion of the sailors aboard the "Potemkin" in 1905. The film had tremendous success. Before the German movie companies could rub their eyes, Muenzenberg had acquired a monopoly on all Russian pictures to be shown in Germany and had founded a company for the purpose.

The Russian branch of the Muenzenberg trust consisted of a building in Moscow, a big estate in Kazan, tremendous woods, cooperatives, and many movie houses.

Muenzenberg had become a party within the Party. He directed his affairs by sound business methods and principles. He enjoyed a great advantage over his competitors: from the ranks of the Communist Party and from his own organizations, he had thousands and tens of thousands of volunteer helpers. The products of his publishing ventures were sold by newsstands, bookstores, the Communist Party organization, and its subsidiaries.

Muenzenberg's talents as organizer and propagandist were matched by his financial ability. The generosity of the Comintern was at his disposal, and he knew how to utilize it. Piatnitsky said jokingly about him: "He hates everybody in whose pockets he suspects there still remains a single dollar."

His financial ambition, however, reached beyond the Comintern. He attempted to become a financial power independent of the Kremlin.

"It isn't difficult to accept money from Moscow and publish newspapers with it," he would say. "Any idiot can do that. But it's a hard job to get Communist propaganda financed by the bourgeoisie. And that I am doing."

Soon he had learned to finance his enterprises with credit instead of investing money of his own or that of the Comintern. In the beginning, the terms were murderous, but later on he received terms befitting the size of his enterprises.

He never invested capital in buildings and printing establishments. He favored movable capital that he could dispose of at a moment's notice.

Events proved his foresight. When Hitler came to power and Muenzenberg had to flee, his capital moved out of the country with him. In Berlin he left only a huge portfolio of promissory notes.

All conflicts within the Party had passed without touching Muenzenberg. He always belonged to the faction that happened to be in power. But at the same time he never lost touch with the others. A good friend to everybody, he was liked by everybody. He knew how to keep friendships. Even the most radical of Communists likes to stretch his limbs once in a while in a civilized home, likes to be carried about in a big luxurious limousine or to dine at a fine little restaurant such as Muenzenberg, turned gourmet during the course of the years, knew how to select.

At the pinnacle of his power, the director of the Communist trust had lost nothing of his youthfulness nor of his oratorical gifts. He was as brilliant in the debates of the Reichstag as he was masterful in the salons of the Berlin intellectuals, where his many-sided interests lay.

FELLOW TRAVELLER SPECIALIST

Muenzenberg's trust, long before Hitler's victory, anticipated the popular front strategy of the Comintern that came into favor after 1935. In his trust, Communists, Social Democrats, Liberals, and faithful Catholics worked peacefully side by side. He was the discoverer of the "fellow traveller"! With his fine instinct he could always ferret out intellectuals, first in Germany and later on in France and England, who had fallen into despair over the failure of democracy, and who admired the achievements of the Soviet Union without having become Communists.

He organized the fellow travellers without their knowing it. He gave them space in his newspapers and books which the bourgeois publishing houses would not concede them. He offered them an opportunity to develop their ideas in mass meetings: otherwise they would have had to be satisfied with a round table in a coffee house. He offered them pleasure trips to the Soviet Union: otherwise they would have had to be content with canoe trips on their local rivers.

When in 1935 the Comintern evolved its policy of cooperation among all anti-Fascists, Muenzenberg could already point with pride to his tremendous circle of fellow travellers:

"Cooperation is already here. Please be served."

By then he was not in Germany any longer, but in France, eating the bitter bread of emigration. In reality, the bread was not so bitter for Willi Muenzenberg: he had taken his capital with him. After a few weeks his trust was already functioning in France, although on a reduced scale. A new publishing house was founded that issued a series of books against Hitler's regime of terror. They created a sensation throughout the world.

In these books military experts disclosed the secret rearmament of the German army. Brochures and pamphlets explained to the French and English workers the dangers of Fascism. In very short time Muenzenberg had made himself the center of anti-Nazi propaganda in western Europe.

His break with the Comintern at the end of 1937 came like a shot! Muenzenberg, in emigration, had remained a true partisan of the Comintern. Only among intimate friends had he expressed his skepticism about Stalin's policy. In 1933 he had become indignant at the cynicism of the Comintern.

"But what shall I do? I can't fight a sixth of the earth's surface!"

At the Stalin-Laval pact he exclaimed: "First Stalin sacrificed the German workers. Now he is preparing to sacrifice the French!"

But as far as the public was concerned, he glorified Stalin and Dimitrov, the new president of the Communist International. Out of the celebrated Reichstag fire he created a legend that had no end. It came to life again and again in a thousand variations, immortalizing the glory of the great Bulgarian.

Even the intrigues of the German Central Committee in Paris against Muenzenberg did not play an important role. France had now become the great testing ground for the policies of the Comintern. The French Communists had become the leading party in the Comintern, as the Germans had been for fifteen years.

The German Communists had attempted to organize a popular front among the emigrés, a caricature of the popular front in France. It caused commotion only in the back rooms of the Parisian cafes and hotels.

The entire Central Committee of the German Communist Party in Paris had less influence and authority than Muenzenberg. Its representatives in Moscow began to complain, accusing him of conspiracy. His intimate friendship with Heinz Neumann, a Comintern outcast of those days, was called to mind. Yet all this would not have caused Muenzenberg's downfall, for Dimitrov needed him.

But in 1936 he committed a serious blunder. After the Zinoviev trial he told his old friend Fritz Brupbacher in Zurich that he did not believe a word of the accusation or the confession of Zinoviev. Brupbacher indiscreetly published Muenzenberg's statement. Muenzenberg received a friendly invitation to visit Moscow. For many months he remained undecided. Couriers and messages came through frequently. Finally he decided to refuse the invitation, as pleasantly and courteously as it had been given.

In Moscow the terror of Yezhov, the new boss of the GPU, was raging. Muenzenberg knew that he would be as helpless in Moscow as any other German Communist. All the guarantees Dimitrov was offering him in his personal letters seemed insufficient. He did not need the financial support of the Comintern.

He did not go to Moscow, and was expelled.

But even after his expulsion from the Comintern, nobody knew whether he had actually broken with Stalin. Maybe that was the cause of his undoing.

To the Comintern commissar Smeral, who came from Moscow, Muenzenberg handed over his affairs in good order. He gave him the furniture of his publishing house, the supplies of unsold books, and a few francs. His behavior was beyond reproach.

CERCLE DES NATIONS

After some time he founded his own periodical and began to build the foundation of his own organization, in which he brought together Communists, Social Democrats, Liberals and Christians. He created a party after the pattern of the popular front, with this difference: that nobody knew the purpose nor for what shores it was embarking. The truth was that Muenzenberg himself did not know. He shoved off and drifted with the current, waiting. In the course of his career, he had turned too cynical to believe a party needed principles.

He established his headquarters at the Cercle des Nations, an elegant political club. He did not retire to the Montmartre or the Quartier Latin, where the poor German refugees conspired desperately against Hitler. He did not have to. A short time after his break with the Comintern, he succeeded in penetrating into the demi-monde of French politics.

Since he couldn't speak French, he had to take an interpreter along to every meeting with French politicians. Yet he found support among many French statesmen who were dissatisfied with the official French policy in regard to Germany. In his periodical, in addition to the German refugee contributors of all political descriptions, Paul Boncour, Pierre Cot, even the chief of propaganda of the French Right Kerillis, a decided opponent of Leon Blum's pacificist and Laval's and Bonnet's defeatist policy, were included.

He negotiated with the German industrialist Thyssen, who had escaped from Germany. He had his finger in all political pies.

But rumors soon began to circulate concerning secret relations between the revolutionary refugee and the French police. As things in Europe turned more and more chaotic, Muenzenberg displayed more and more opportunism.

In the beginning of 1939 he was convinced he would be able to gather around himself the majority of German refugees and, after the rapid downfall of Hitler—which he had always expected and prophesied, with or without war, for the following spring—return to Germany with a claim to power.

His agents were busy all over France, and in England as well, where they spread the glory of a man who not only had opposed Moscow, but was a target of Nazi hatred. The newspapers printed stories about Muenzenberg's huge underground organization that caused the more sophisticated to smile but that found credence in many circles.

When the German-Russian pact was concluded, Muenzenberg gloated: his luck had not betrayed him. In breaking with the Comintern, he had bet on the right horse.

He came out unreservedly for the defense of France, always wore a little tricolor in his buttonhole, founded a French patriotic club among the German refugees, and agitated for the admission of German refugees into the French Foreign Legion, the only military organization available for foreigners in France.

Yet he had bet on the wrong horse after all.

When, in the middle of May, 1940, the military situation of France became critical, the French Minister of the Interior, Mandel, had him interned, like all other German refugees. His good connections did not help. All his demonstrations of loyalty had been in vain.

At this juncture, one part of the French police took him for a Russian agent, another for a German. He was neither the one nor the other. He was a gambler spoiled by too much luck, who had played in France with a currency that he took for gold but which was really counterfeit money.

The German troops were within a few miles of the internment camp where Muenzenberg was being held. He became panicky, not without reason. Were he to fall into the hands of the Germans, his life would not be worth much. He could not depend on the protection of the French authorities. And so one night, in the company of two young comrades, he fled from the camp.

From that moment on, all trace of Muenzenberg is lost. Even the most intense investigations by his friends did not avail to reconstruct his end. His two companions have not been found.

CHAPTER XIV

Christian Rakovsky: Revolutionary from the Balkans

GRAND SEIGNEUR AS REBEL

I N THE SPRING OF 1922, RAKOVSKY, THE FIRST PRESIDENT OF THE Ukrainian Soviet Republic, went as Russian delegate to the international conference in Genoa. When he arrived at one of the luxurious hotels provided for the Russian delegation, the manager of the hotel approached him, bowing reverently.

"My lord, you are at the wrong place. The English delegation is not staying at my hotel."

In London and Paris, where Rakovsky later represented the Soviet Union as ambassador, he became an insoluble puzzle to the diplomatic elite. Could it be that this elegant and spirited gentleman, this many-tongued and charming conversationalist, and favorite of society, was a dangerous Bolshevik revolutionary? How could this aesthete, at home in French language and French literature, be a leader of uncultured and uncivilized masses? How did Bolshevik asceticism, with its will to level off the differences between all people, fit in with the sophisticated tastes of this gourmand, whose knowledge and experience in matters of cuisine was a marvel even to French experts?

Christian Rakovsky was highly amused at the amazement with which he was regarded in London and Paris. The aristocratic atmosphere of his surroundings always gave rise to pleasantries, but he knew very well how to utilize his attractiveness in diplomatic circles to further his political purposes. The beauties and satisfactions of life were a source of pleasure to him, but only the revolution fulfilled his personality.

Rakovsky came from the heart of the Bulgarian Dobrudja, the center of the struggle for liberation by the Balkan peoples against the empire of the Osman Turks which, until the beginning of the century, stretched right up to the Adriatic Sea. Rakovsky's grandfather belonged to the Bulgarian Komitatchi, who fought a war of their own against the Turkish Sultan. He had been hanged in Constantinople.

The father of Rakovsky owned huge tracts of land in the very heart of the Dobrudja.

This wealthy landowner's son was a wild and untrammeled boy. None of his French governesses could keep him in check. He went to France, as a young man, was graduated as a doctor of medicine, and became a revolutionary Socialist.

At the death of his father, Rakovsky, the revolutionary Socialist, became the owner of vast landed estates. In consequence, peasant revolts occurred more frequently there than in other parts of the Dobrudja.

In later years Rakovsky loved to tell the story of how his peasants had sent a delegation to see him. They were in conflict with their consciences—whether or not to burn down one of his farmhouses. Rakovsky assured them he would not be angry at them for such doings. The peasants bowed respectfully as they went out, and burned the building.

Rakovsky's reputation as a revolutionary landlord who was handing out Socialist propaganda among his workers and who paid wages many times greater than the customary ones paid on the surrounding estates, penetrated throughout Rumania, which had received the Dobrudja as part of her own territory after the war of 1906-07. He was deported from Rumania. The Rumanian Socialist party that he had founded made the fight for his return one of the main points of their platform.

He returned triumphantly to Rumania in 1912. In this country of Boyar rule, corruption was a holy national institution. Even the postmaster selling a stamp expected his rightful payment of an Oriental *bakshish*. A higher administrative post without bribes was unthinkable.

In this atmosphere the wealthy landlord who used his income to finance a Socialist Party and a Socialist newspaper looked like a fool.

But the "fool" was popular among workers and peasants. He was a member of the Executive Committee of the Second International and known throughout Europe. He had many contacts abroad, particularly in Paris, the dream city of every Rumanian citizen. He was a fool dangerous to Rumanian rule.

When war broke out, the Rumanian government had to flee from the approaching German troops. It was so afraid of Rakovsky and his influence that it decided to take him along to Jassy, together with the entire court of the crown and the gold hoard of the state bank.

Unwittingly, they thus did Rakovsky a good turn. The Russians occupied Jassy, and after the victorious October Revolution in 1917, revolutionary soldiers liberated Rakovsky from his prison. He deserted his estates and, indeed, the entire Balkans, and went to Russia. There he was received with open arms by his friend, Leon Trotsky.

Between the two there had existed for years a profound and intimate friendship. Rakovsky was one of the few men whom Trotsky admired. He became one of the select few who founded the Communist International.

RED AMBASSADOR

The great field of activity that offered him a chance to use all his talents and gifts was the Ukraine. During the negotiations in Brest-Litovsk, the German forces of occupation in the Ukraine had supported a Ukrainian Council or Rada, which, as far as the Germans were concerned, was serving their purposes while pursuing the goal of Ukrainian independence. The Bolsheviks were without power in most parts of the Ukraine, and their followers were being brutally persecuted.

After Brest-Litovsk, the Soviet government had to negotiate with the Ukrainian Rada. Technically the questions under discussion concerned boundary lines, trade relationships, and the elimination of the Ukraine from the Russian political structure. In reality, Rakovsky, through his procedures of negotiation, created a screen behind which preparations for the reoccupation of the Ukraine by the Bolsheviks were going on. When Rakovsky was later asked where he had acquired his diplomatic skill, he replied in the negotiations "with the Ukrainian bandits!" He negotiated until the German breakdown occurred and the Bolshevik revolution in the Ukraine was able to remove the Rada with no more than a gesture.

Among all the Bolsheviks, Lenin knew of no better president for the Ukrainian Soviet Republic than the Bulgarian-Rumanian-French Rakovsky. But after Lenin's death, when Trotsky's star was sinking,

Rakovsky had to leave his Ukrainian field of activity. The Triumvirate —Stalin, Zinoviev, Kamenev—could not tolerate that the highest post of the second largest of the federated Soviet Republics was filled by Leon Trotsky's most intimate friend. So Rakovsky began his brilliant diplomatic career in London and Paris.

In England the Labor Party under the leadership of MacDonald was heading a British government for the first time in its history. To take up friendly relations with the Soviet Republic had been one of the main objectives of its foreign policy while it was still in opposition. When Rakovsky arrived as Soviet ambassador in London, he found a wide field for his diplomatic activity.

But in those years a Soviet ambassador abroad did not lead an easy life. Each morning in the newspapers, he was served for breakfast quotations from the revolutionary pronouncements of the Comintern that called for destruction of the British Empire. Rakovsky had only one stereotyped formula to oppose to the protests of the British Foreign Office that came in with disquieting regularity: Mr. Zinoviev is not a member of the Soviet government. My government is not responsible for the activity of the Comintern. That organization enjoys only the hospitality of the Soviet government just as the Second International temporarily enjoyed yours here in London.

Yet it never occurred to Rakovsky to disassociate himself and his work from the aims of the Third International, for he regarded his diplomatic activity as reconnaissance within the territory of its most determined enemy.

British conservatives did not differ very much in their appraisal of the activity of the Russian ambassador. They were still of the opinion that eventually the Soviet government would fall by its own weight. In order to contribute something to this fall and at the same time sweep out the Labor government of MacDonald, which they despised, they conceived of a plan to use the Russian ambassador for this purpose. The fall elections of 1925 were impending and the Conservatives were in need of an effective election campaign slogan.

The British Intelligence Service procured a letter from Zinoviev to the British Communists. In this letter Zinoviev outlined in great detail steps to be taken to insure the Bolshevization of the British army and the organization of a revolution in India. The letter was manifestly false, as MacDonald later admitted, although it contained nothing that the Foreign Office could not have read in the open publications of the Comintern.

The *Daily Mail* published the letter fourteen days after it had come into the hands of the Foreign Office, giving the Conservatives the sensational election issue they needed. The result accorded with the expectations. The Conservatives won an overwhelming majority in the "Zinoviev election." Rakovsky had to leave London and transfer his diplomatic activities to Paris.

But his work in the ranks of the Labor Party and the trade unions was bearing fruit. A British-Russian Trade Union Committee was formed in 1926. When the miners struck and a general strike, the greatest in English history, was proclaimed in their support, the Conservatives blamed the Bolshevist influence in the British trade unions. This was a considerable exaggeration. Rakovsky had only given the sympathies of broad sections of British labor a solid foundation. However, the Conservatives decided to wipe the slate clean: In the beginning of February, 1927, the Russian trading company Arcos in London was searched by the police, new Comintern documents of a compromising nature were published, and finally British-Russian relationships were completely severed.

In France the government had expected to persuade Rakovsky to have his government pay up the old debts of the Czar. The Soviet government at this time was ready to recognize the Czarist debts, but it demanded as compensation immediate credits in an amount at least equal to the old debts. These demands were unacceptable in Paris, and so the hopes of the financial and banking world for a settlement of the debt problem were again frustrated.

The popularity of the Soviet ambassador in the financial world was therefore negligible. But his conquests in the world of politics, art, and literature made the halls of the Soviet embassy in the Rue de Grenelle the center of all radical democratic France. Only the officers of the general staff and the directors of the big banks were missing at Rakovsky's receptions.

When Great Britain severed relations with Russia, France also thought it time to act. Looking for a pretext to get rid of Rakovsky, it finally found one in a manifesto published by the Trotsky opposition in Russian and signed by Rakovsky. The French government insisted that this manifesto was an interference in the domestic affairs of France, for in it the Trotsky opposition had attacked not only the domestic policy of the Soviets but the international policies of the Comintern in France and in other countries. In vain did the Soviet government explain that Rakovsky's signature to the manifesto represented his policy as a member of the Russian Central Committee and not his action as Soviet ambassador.

SUBMISSION TO STALIN

Rakovsky was happy to shed the ambassador's frock, to return to the Soviet Union, and to participate there in the struggles of the Russian Party for the realization of Socialism.

With his return to Russia his tragedy began. The man who had made innumerable friends for the Soviet Republic in Europe became a pariah in the country of his election.

When Rakovsky returned to Moscow Trotsky and his opposition had already lost out in their fight against Stalin in the Russian Party as well as in the Comintern. Rakovsky, nevertheless, remained loyal to his friend Trotsky who, at the end of 1927, was banished to Alma Ata at the Chinese-Turkestan border. He himself was sent to Siberia. The reactionary French press was triumphant: this man was too dangerous even for the Soviet government!

During a sojourn of many years in Siberia, where his once huge and powerful figure wasted away, Rakovsky experienced all the tortures of conscience of the Russian professional revolutionary: What is higher, revolutionary conscience or Soviet patriotism? Submit to whom: the all powerful Party, or the opposition of Trotsky embodying the old beliefs of world revolution? Is Stalin's path a detour to Socialism or the road to counter-revolution?

In hundreds of letters to friends, in endless memoranda, the imprisoned professional revolutionary sought a way out of the most difficult dilemma of his life. The only way out that he found was to break with Trotsky.

Stalin accepted Rakovsky's capitulation in May, 1934, as a victory of special significance. This was no journalist like Radek to be broken down, nor a Zinoviev who regarded statements of capitulation as weapons in political fights. Here a professional revolutionary out of a world foreign to Stalin's had broken down. This was the grandson of the Komitatchi hanged in Constantinople, the man of the world who would sacrifice everything to save the revolution, the proud European.

But Rakovsky failed to find the peace he sought; he was given a small post in one of the government departments and sent on a diplomatic mission to Tokyo. This mission became one of the points of his undoing when in 1938 he was among the defendants in the Bukharin trial.

The Christian Rakovsky who was led into the courtroom was a broken old man. Nothing was left in him of his former powers of resistance and rebellion. He did not bother to defend himself against the accusation of the prosecution that he was a British and Japanese spy. He explained to the court in a low monotonous voice his motive for turning into a spy. In 1924, when he had been Soviet Russia's proud ambassador to London, a petty British agent had taken him into the British secret service. In 1934 he had become a Japanese spy for the same reason; in 1935, during Laval's mission to Moscow, he had attempted to prevent the conclusion of a French-Russian pact. All these activities were on the order of Leon Trotsky who in 1918 had entered the service of the British as a spy.

At the same time Rakovsky confirmed that Trotsky and his adherents had always represented a foreign body in the Bolshevik party. He described them as insane men who regarded themselves as superior to ordinary human beings but sent by fate to direct their destinies.

In his concluding words Rakovsky went down on his knees before Stalin asking for mercy, for dear life. He confessed to a feeling of deep shame for his former participation in the opposition. He demanded that "no mercy" be shown his former comrades and called for "the shooting of the murderers."

Rakovsky's moral collapse was the most dreadful blow Stalin could have dealt Trotsky. Rakovsky had loved Trotsky. With no one had Trotsky maintained so many and intimate personal ties. On no one else except Lenin had Trotsky bestowed his admiration. Now Stalin spread before him his friend's demoralization: Rakovsky alone among the defendants was compelled to talk about Trotsky with bitter hatred.

209

His words were a message to Trotsky that Stalin's revenge would pursue him inevitably: "It is true that even beyond the Mexican meridian Trotsky will not escape the complete and final ignominy that we are all undergoing here."

Two years later the prophetic forecast came true. A pickaxe crushed the skull of this greatest of Stalin's adversaries.

Rakovsky was one of the defendants in the Bukharin trial whose sentence was commuted and to whom clemency was shown: at the age of sixty he was sentenced to twenty-five years in prison. For the other Red ambassador who was with Rakovsky among the defendants, Stalin showed no mercy: Krestinsky was executed.

CHAPTER XV

Jacques Doriot: Renegade of the Revolution

KARL LIEBKNECHT'S DISCIPLE IN FRANCE

IT IS FALL 1943. THROUGH THE SPACIOUS INNER COURTYARD OF the old Ecole Militaire in Paris where the troops of Napoleon I paraded more than one hundred years earlier, music of Prussian military marches intermingles with tunes from the French Revolution. Prussian generals stand at attention as French troops in German uniform march by.

Among the group of German officers is a Frenchman in the uniform of a German lieutenant. Jacques Doriot carries his great, somewhat bulky figure nearly as stiffly erect as his German military colleagues in their splendid uniforms.

After the parade Jacques Doriot, founder of the French anti-Bolshevist legion, ready to depart for the Russian front, addresses his soldiers briefly, exhorting them to save France by fighting the Bolsheviks side by side with the Germans. Then a German general steps out of the group of officers and decorates Jacques Doriot with the Iron Cross, saying: "In the name of the Fuehrer I have the honor of conferring upon you, Lieutenant Doriot, the Iron Cross . . . . for the courage of which you have given proof. . . . . You were a volunteer in the Legion in the first lines on the Eastern front. Before Moscow, in the course of the difficult winter of 1941-42 you were the only one among the political founders of the Legion to take part personally in the struggle of the German army against our common enemy, Bolshevism. . . . ."

Ten years earlier Jacques Doriot had been the most popular Communist leader in France, one of the great hopes of the High Command of the world revolution.

He had become a Communist in 1919, not because, traditionally, the most leftist of all parties exerted the greatest attraction among the young generation of politicians, but because he believed he understood the Communism of Moscow and was completely devoted to it.

Doriot had been a "professional youth" like Muenzenberg in Germany, and like Muenzenberg he spent his apprentice years as professional revolutionary in the Communist Youth International. But whereas Muenzenberg changed into a Communist trust magnate, Doriot throughout his revolutionary career remained closely attached to the working masses.

Karl Liebknecht, the leader of the German revolutionary movement, the fighter against war and militarism, the rebel who, almost alone, had opposed the war efforts of his own country, was the hero and the saint of the Communist Youth International. He had also been the hero and the saint of young Doriot.

When Poincaré occupied the Ruhr district in 1923, Doriot emerged in the army of occupation as an agitator. He and his young comrades visited the military barracks and addressed the soldiers there with flaming words, inciting them to disobedience of military orders and to fraternization with the German workers. His work there was so effective that the French command had to withdraw several regiments and send them back to France.

The Communist Youth International was full of the glory of Doriot, the indefatigable fighter against militarism.

Still a young man, he was elected to the French parliament. Even there where brilliant oratory was a commonplace, his first speech was an event. Aristide Briand, the French Foreign Minister, expressed his appreciation directly to Doriot who had attacked the policies of his government: "My friend, you'll go far in the world." Maybe he was thinking of his own career that had also begun with revolutionary anti-militarist propaganda.

But Doriot was not seeking a parliamentary career. From the Palais Bourbon he went to meetings of French workers and disclosed the ructions and scandals of French Parliament. At every encounter between the Paris police and Communist demonstrators, Doriot marched at their head. He was always to be found where danger was greatest.

MISSION TO ABD-EL-KRIM

The Comintern sent him to Abd-El-Krim, the rebellious sheik of the Moroccan mountains, whose insurrection had been keeping the French army of occupation on the move for months. Abd-El-Krim

212

was neither a Chiang Kai Shek nor an Enver Pasha. He was the last of those heroic Saracens who once had subjected Spain and then, when driven back, had retired into the wilderness of the Atlas Mountains of Morocco brooding revenge against the infidels. But even under Abd-El-Krim's leadership the mutually hostile and suspicious Arabian sheiks were not able to wage more than a guerrilla war against the French army of occupation.

The Comintern utilized the opportunity of the Abd-El-Krim insurrection to demonstrate its unceasing opposition to colonial imperialism and to increase the difficulties of France, still the main enemy of the Soviet Union. Incidentally it was not only the Comintern that supported Abd-El-Krim. The British Intelligence Service, at that time the most decided opponent of France in the Arabian world, also sent arms and weapons.

Doriot crossed the Mediterranean secretly in a small fishing boat. It took him weeks to penetrate through the wild mountains of the Atlas region to the headquarters of Abd-El-Krim.

The French military authorities organized an armed hunt to intercept him. They put a price on his head. In Morocco, parliamentary immunity would not have protected Doriot. A military tribunal would have decided his fate.

But he saw his mission through, gave Abd-El-Krim several hundred thousand francs, assured him of the sympathies of the Comintern, and put him in touch with several munitions agents in Algiers and Casablanca who were working there for the account of the Comintern.

After his return to France, Doriot made a sensational speech in the Chamber, denouncing the inhumanity of the war waged by the French colonial authorities against the Arabs. Public opinion regarded him as a traitor, but he remained the pride of the Comintern. This was in 1925.

In 1929 the Comintern decided on a new line of policy for the French Communists. Under the slogan "class against class" a political strategy was introduced that turned the French Communist Party into a small sectarian group. Under this slogan the French Communists were prohibited from cooperating in elections with liberal or Socialist groups which meant, on the basis of the existing electoral system in France, not only parliamentary self-liquidation of the Communists but effective support of the reactionary candidate.

Doriot opposed this policy sharply from the beginning and retired from active participation in the leadership of Communist party affairs. Instead he began to fortify his position as deputy mayor of St. Denis.

St. Denis was a fort in the Red fortifications encircling Paris and the position of deputy mayor was among the most influential in the Third Republic. The deputy mayor through his municipality maintained direct and immediate relations with the governing authorities in Paris that made his power independent of his position in his party and his parliamentary group. He could therefore afford to shape his political strategy according to his own judgment without consulting his party or his constituency.

Doriot was a good deputy mayor. With the same intensity he had formerly employed in his destructive work in the army, he now turned to constructive work in his municipal duties. His budget was always so well balanced that even the suspicious investigating committees of the Ministry of the Interior could find no fault. He did away with the traditional French corruption in municipal affairs and built parks, schools, sport centers, and crèches. He became a social reformer in the best sense of the world.

But his relations with the Communist Party became strained. After the defeat of the German Communist Party through Hitler, he emerged from his reserve demanding a change of policy, a united front with the Socialist Party and the trade unions influenced by it. However, the order for a change in policy had not yet arrived from Moscow. The party leadership attacked him bitterly, and relations seemed to drift towards a rupture.

The opposition Communists of all countries, even Trotsky, concentrated their attention on Doriot, expecting him to turn St. Denis into a fortress of Communist opposition. But they figured without Stalin and without Doriot. In the winter of 1934, a personal emissary of the Executive Committee of the Comintern arrived in Paris and immediately went to St. Denis. He offered Doriot the leadership of the Communist Party and said that the Comintern was now ready to accept the program for which Doriot had fought in vain during the last two years. He brought Doriot a very flattering invitation to Moscow where his authority as the recognized leader of the French

214

Communist Party would be established. Stalin had chosen the oppositionist Doriot for the execution of his grand turn in France.

Stalin did not believe that his contemplated change of policy in France—a change more fundamental than anything the Comintern had attempted in its long history of grand turns—could be accomplished by any man associated with the old leadership. He had no confidence in Marcel Cachin, the former Social Democrat, nor in Thorez or Duclos, the organizational secretaries of the party, for this purpose.

The Comintern representative was flabbergasted at Doriot's refusal to accept his offer. Such a thing was unknown in the Comintern up to that time. Many foreign Communists had been turned out of their offices by the Comintern, but never yet had anyone refused a proffered leadership. Moscow believed this could only be due to a misunderstanding.

More couriers arrived and offered Doriot a degree of power never yet possessed by any Communist leader in the West. They hinted that the composition of the new leadership would be entirely in line with his own wishes and that he was at liberty to recommend some of his adversaries in the party for a longer sojourn in Moscow. Thorez and Duclos trembled for their political existence.

HITLER'S APPRENTICE

But it had not been just a misunderstanding. At the end of 1934 Doriot had definitely broken with the Comintern. He had decided to travel along paths of which Stalin's negotiators had not even dreamed.

A political figure of Doriot's stature could choose, after his break with the Comintern, among any and all careers in the Third Republic. In the Socialist Party Doriot could have taken over the leadership of the rapidly increasing left wing which was in opposition to the weak policy of Leon Blum. As an Independent Radical he could have embarked on a career similar to that of Aristide Briand or Laval.

At this point Doriot was in the front rank of candidates for minister in the French government. But the change that Doriot was making was more profound than anything his friends had foreseen.

He broke not only with the Comintern but with all shades of Socialism. The defeat of the German workers led him to conclude

215

that the era of Marxist Socialism had definitely passed; the corruption and weakness of the Third Republic led him to infer that French democracy also had arrived at the end.

Doriot became Fascist. He decided to tread the path of Mussolini and Hitler in France.

He founded his French Popular Party accompanied by the benedictions of the entire French reaction. In France they were accustomed to quick swings from extreme left to extreme right. Millerand; Briand; Froissard, the French delegate to Moscow in 1920; and Laval had withdrawn from immediate contact with the movement of the masses and had emerged in the halls and corridors of parliament and the political salons.

But Doriot was the first Red who fought Socialism within the masses, and who set himself the task of fashioning a Fascist movement out of the ranks of the Socialist and Communist masses themselves.

He seemed made for the task. This man of the people, who talked their language, who knew their miseries, and who in St. Denis possessed a point of support in the very heart of the Red circle around Paris, became the white hope of French reaction.

As a springboard to power, he had envisaged a break between France and the Soviet Union, and the establishment of a block between Germany, Italy, and France against Russia. He was tireless in his efforts to convince public opinion that the significance of Stalin's French policy lay in setting the scene for a German-French war, and that the French-Soviet pact of 1935 would make France a slave state of Moscow.

He was certain that after the desired break with Russia he would be able to deal with the French Communists quickly, either in the Italian or in the German fashion.

Yet Doriot was unsuccessful in climbing up even the first rungs of the dictatorship ladder. Both government and working masses ignored him. The latter accepted Stalin's slogan of a popular front against Fascism with such enthusiasm as to suffocate Doriot's propaganda completely. The government vacillated between a coalition with Stalin and one with Hitler. The risks that arose from the tremendous armament efforts of the Third Reich were too great to permit of a firm decision in one or the other direction.

The Third Republic was weak and corrupt, but none of the reactionary parties or conspiratory cliques had the strength for a coup d'etat. Doriot's attempts to undermine the parliamentary system by a mass movement against it failed from the beginning. Wherever his terrorist gangs, organized according to German and Italian example, put in an appearance, they were beaten up and their parades drowned in the ridicule of the streets. France was no soil for the growth of Fascism!

The man of revolutionary mass action had become a back room conspirator in French politics.

For some years Doriot maintained himself in St. Denis, but finally he was unseated by his Communist opponents. Now he could no longer look for success among the masses but had to move in the *chambres séparées* of the Café de Paris where French industrialists spent their money in the hope of finding men willing to organize raiding gangs against their striking workers.

Doriot became a Pinkerton of French industry, like the Cagoulards and the Croix de Feu. He depended more and more on Abetz, the French emissary of Hitler, who was distributing huge funds among French politicians.

His great figure had grown fat and flabby from his too frequent visits to luxurious Parisian restaurants. His oratory that had carried away thousands now sounded hollow and creaky. His erstwhile bright shining eyes now looked out into the world with defiance and hate.

Before the outbreak of war, Doriot was defeated and lost. Then came the German-Russian pact, and Doriot's star rose anew. The Communists were stricken dumb and in despair. Doriot's treasure chests overflowed with new millions.

This time his agents could talk in the working class suburbs without hindrance. Nobody shouted them down when they praised Doriot, arch enemy of Bolshevism, who had predicted Stalin's policy. Nobody had faith in the Communist leaders who in painful embarrassment described the Stalin-Hitler pact as an act of peace.

Doriot's organization grew in great strides. He himself volunteered to make people forget his former intimate connection with Hitler. Friendly officers promoted him quickly and secured for him the Croix de Guerre. His party gave large and loud publicity to its hero

217

leader! But the quick military collapse put an end to Doriot's patriotic career.

When the Germans occupied Paris he was the first to jump on the victory band wagon and to proclaim that the collapse of France was due to the French Socialists and Democrats. As the main enemy, he now selected England which, according to him, was responsible for the alliance with the Bolsheviks.

This time Doriot was right. His main enemy really was England. Had there been a quick peace between Germany and England after the French collapse, there might have been no obstacle to Doriot's career as Gauleiter for France. But England continued to fight and Hitler selected as his partners Laval and Pétain, who could command more solid support than Doriot.

Again Doriot was left adrift.

His organization remained under the protection of the German occupation. His French Popular Party became a department of the Gestapo. At his meetings he was surrounded by a triple cordon of guards. The Germans knew that Doriot had even less influence on the people than Pétain and Laval.

He had succeeded in drawing to his side some former Communist leaders. The most important of them, Marcel Gitton, was shot by the Communists in his apartment.

When the German armies retreated from France, Doriot went with them, to become minister in their French puppet government. Finally he was killed by an Allied bomb.

CHAPTER XVI

André Marty: Underground General

MEN OF THE FIRST HOUR

THE HIGH COMMAND OF THE WORLD REVOLUTION WAS A HUNGRY Moloch. It consumed hundreds and hundreds of revolutionary leaders from all countries of the world. Many disappeared without a trace, some retired into an embittered private life, others returned to the Social Democratic parties. A few formed a Fourth International with Leon Trotsky.

Of the Russian founders of the Communist International, no one is alive. Of the foreigners, the men of the "first hour" who remained loyal to Moscow regardless of all changes, only a few are still living. Among them the Frenchman, André Marty, is one of the most outstanding figures.

André Marty's revolutionary career began on the Black Sea in 1918. There did not yet exist in France at that time a Communist party. French battleships were threatening Odessa, the Black Sea port held by the Bolsheviks, and André Marty was a sailor on one of them. It was on his initiative that the sailors and marines of the French fleet got together in revolt and presented to the commanding admiral this ultimatum:

"Either the fleet returns immediately to France and gives up the attempt to suppress the revolution in the south of Russia, or we sailors will take the command of these battleships into our own hands, and sail the ships home ourselves!"

Probably he did not believe in the possibility of success. But André Marty was one of those genuine rebels whose strong unconscious personal power carries others along with it. The fleet was withdrawn from the Black Sea.

Marty, however, was sentenced to twenty years in prison. After the sentence was pronounced he wrote to his brother: "I will not weaken. You take revenge for me."

He spent four and a half years in the military prison of the Third

Republic. When he was released he wrote about his experiences and the brutality of the military prison system in a small volume that caused an uproar among the Socialists and Liberals of France.

Poincaré did not release Marty of his own free will. The French Communist masses won him as one wins a battle. For four and a half years the name of Marty was the battle cry of the French revolutionary workers. Numerous municipalities elected him to their councils, and he was even elected several times to the French Chamber.

He was the last of the rebels of Odessa to be released. He came out of prison unbroken. The rebellious sailor had become a professional revolutionary.

Marty had regained his liberty only to immerse himself immediately in activities that meant bitter conflict with the French military and civil authorities. Whenever the French Communists organized a dangerous campaign, they put André Marty at its head. Together with Jacques Doriot, he took charge of the fight against the French Moroccan expedition of 1925 as well as of the rebellion against the French colonial administration in Syria.

The police hounded him throughout the country. He had to keep on the move. Frequently there were bills posted on the very doors of the houses where he concealed himself, public announcements by the authorities putting a price on his head.

In easygoing, carefree France he was a strange figure. No Frenchman, not even the most ardent revolutionary, can bear the burden of being looked upon as a traitor. Marty bore up under the cross that public opinion pressed down on him as if it had been the crown of a victor.

"Traitor? I agree. But traitor only to an order of society that rests on exploitation and war. Never have I betrayed the workers, soldiers, and peasants who have given me their confidence. Never have I betrayed the proletarian revolution!"

But he could not get along with the leaders of the French Communist Party, Thorez and Duclos. The rebel of Odessa could not yet stomach the patriotic policy of the Popular Front, glorifying the tricolor. During these years he was happy to live in Russia instead of in France, for there his name and his deeds were kept alive among the masses. Thousands of public squares and factories were named after him.

SPANISH EXECUTIONER

When the Spanish Civil War broke out in 1936, Marty was sent by Moscow to organize the International Brigades in Spain. Such a task was to his liking.

Tens of thousands of volunteers flowed into Spain from all countries of the world. In Albacete, Marty's headquarters, they were organized into brigades and received military training, and they were sent from there to the front. In some of the International Brigades there were party Communists accustomed to semi-military discipline. But a greater part were workers who had come to Spain following their own revolutionary convictions without knowing what the Communists meant when they talked about revolutionary discipline.

It was André Marty into whose hands the enforcement of military discipline in the International Brigades was placed. Hundreds of revolutionary soldiers who had committed a breach of Communist discipline were sentenced by his military tribunal and shot.

Marty reasoned that a rigidly organized Republican army required such hardness. How otherwise would it be possible to instill into an international army of volunteers the military obedience of a national army?

Yet it was not only military discipline that mattered. Marty demanded political discipline as well; or better, complete unthinking submission to the political conception of the Communist International. Political rebellion was punished even more mercilessly than military disobedience.

Shortly after the outbreak of the Civil War, Moscow ordered all Trotskyites in Spain to be treated as spies and agents provocateurs— a fifth column of France. Marty became the executioner of Moscow's order. The slightest suspicion of sympathy with Trotsky's ideas, or doubt that the man fighting desperately at your side was a traitor when Moscow said so, was sufficient to incur death.

The Spanish newspapers hostile to the Communists branded André Marty the "butcher of Albacete." The Communists themselves were more afraid of Marty than devoted to him.

221

What an incomprehensible change in the heart of a professional revolutionary. An order from Moscow sufficed to transfigure the rebel of Odessa into the executioner of Albacete.

Marty knew the traps of military discipline from personal experience. He had seen its victims in the French prisons. He himself had been chained and brutally beaten. Yet without hesitation he condemned hundreds of soldiers of the International Brigade to death.

He knew that these soldiers were revolutionaries as he himself had been in his youth. But he had as little mercy with them as the military tribunal in Galatz had had with him in 1919.

The transformation of Marty leads into the mystery of those few professional revolutionaries who have remained in the Comintern since Stalin's ascendancy. A French Communist who had worked for some time with Marty in Albacete, said of him:

"He is so merciless because he envies his victims their revolutionary convictions!"

Maybe the former Italian professional revolutionary, Ignazio Silone, analyzed Marty's strange psychological state better when he wrote:

"We know the story of the hermit who, in order to give himself wholly to God and renounce his earthly desires, castrated himself with his own hand. He was, it is true, delivered from certain inner conflicts; but at the same time he lost the energy of his love for God, and he was forever more incapable of returning to normal life.

"The case is the same with many Communist bureaucrats who have lost their faith in the always changing party line and who, as a result of their spiritual self-mutilation, can never return to normal humanity."

When Marty returned to France after Franco's victory, he looked more than ten years older.

After the French defeat, he escaped to London. When Hitler commenced his attacks on the Soviet Union, he again moved into the foreground. He became one of the organizers of the Partisans in France. He was selected chief of the semi-military forces that the Communists were gathering together in their struggle against the German occupation.

André Marty is one of those Communist leaders who will remain in the midst of action as long as he is alive.

222

Part III

DECLINE OF WORLD REVOLUTION
THE END OF THE COMINTERN

CHAPTER XVII

Espionage Embroglio in the Comintern

POLISH PRELUDE

THE RUSSIAN RED ARMY ADVANCING IN THE SUMMER OF 1920 towards the gates of Warsaw was accompanied by a Polish-Communist Party delegation. Its leader, Felix Dzierzynski, was closely associated with the general staff of the Red Army. These Polish Communists regarded themselves as the nucleus of a coming Polish Soviet government mobilizing Soviets in all conquered territories, proclaiming the distribution of land and the nationalization of industry.

The Polish Communist leaders including Dzierzynski, Warski, Kosczewa, who had called a conference of Polish Communists in Russia before the beginning of the campaign, were entirely of like mind with the Bolshevists. None of them feared that the national independence of Poland might be threatened by the Kremlin. In their eyes Pilsudski, who was opposing the Red Army and cooperating with the French general, Weygand, was a traitor to Poland.

When the Red Army was forced to withdraw from Poland, thousands of Polish Communists escaped to the safety of Soviet Russia. Even after the official peace of Riga between Russia and Poland, these Polish Communists did not put down their arms. From behind the protection of the Russian border they maintained innumerable communications with the underground organization in Poland. Frequently they penetrated with small armed detachments into Poland proper and assisted rebellious peasants.

On the other side of the border the Poles maintained a status of underground warfare against the Soviets. Warsaw became the headquarters of the White Russian leader, Bulak Bulakovitch. His gangs butchered Soviet Russian border patrols, penetrated deep into Russian territory, kidnapped Polish as well as Russian Communists, and burned down many Russian establishments. Many years after the official conclusion of peace, a bitter war was still being waged between Poland and Russia.

Even though diplomatic relationships between Moscow and Warsaw had been firmly established, their mutual hatred did not diminish. The first Soviet Russian ambassador to Warsaw, Voikov, was shot by a Russian emigré. The Soviet government accused the secret Polish police of having lent a hand in this assassination.

Obviously there was truth in this accusation. The Polish government replied with an accusation that the Soviet embassy in Warsaw was a center for the underground movement. Obviously there was truth in this too!

Pilsudski was a pathological hater of the Bolshevists. This "Socialist Bonaparte," as Lloyd George had called him, flew into violent fits of rage when anyone around him so much as mentioned the names of Lenin and Trotsky. The Bolshevist hatred for Pilsudski was as great as his for them. It was nourished by disappointment, for when Pilsudski engineered his coup d'état of May 19, 1926, which gave him dictatorial power in Poland, the Polish Socialists as well as most of the Communists aided him by proclaiming a general strike against the reactionary peasant government of Witos, then in power. Their move was based on the hope that Pilsudski would be more conciliatory to labor if his rise to power were furthered by the labor movement. They failed to realize that Pilsudski's aim was the inauguration of a dictatorial regime.

In compensation for their support, he persecuted the Polish Communists with a cruelty unequalled in the Europe of the twenties. The office of his General Staff became one of the chief centers of the European espionage directed against the Soviet Union.

In the course of the years, the guerrilla warfare at the borders was extinguished and diplomatic relationships were more firmly established. Yet the feeling between Moscow and Warsaw remained hostile. Every Pole not registered with the Comintern was regarded as a spy in Moscow.

THE AFFAIR OF SOCHATZKI

The Polish embassy in Moscow and the Polish consular offices in other Russian cities were carefully watched by a special division of the GPU. Nobody who maintained any sort of connection with anyone in the Polish embassy or consular offices could take a single step without being shadowed by the GPU. The technique of shadowing people had been developed to a finer art by the GPU than by any other secret police in the world.

In the winter of 1931-1932 a special agent of the GPU, in the course of his routine supervision of Polish activities, was shadowing a member of the Polish embassy in Moscow. The Pole walked slowly through the streets of Moscow. He went into different streets, made some purchases, stopped for refreshments in a restaurant—in a word, he acted like any ordinary person passing a few leisurely hours. Yet the attention of the GPU officer did not lessen for an instant.

Finally the Pole stopped in front of a newspaper stand around which a crowd was milling. He bought a paper, glanced at the headline, and turned to go on.

At this moment he bumped into another man who had also just bought a newspaper. The Pole raised his hat politely and continued on his way.

The suspicion of the GPU agent was immediately aroused. People in Moscow are usually very courteous, but raising one's hat to a stranger at such a moment is unusual. Who could the stranger be?

For hours the GPU agent followed him from one street to another. At last the man took a cab and drove to a railway station. There he stayed a while in the waiting room among the travellers. Then he boarded a streetcar and returned to the center of town. He next went to a movie, leaving it in the middle of the performance.

Finally he walked down Tverskaya Street and disappeared at the entrance of the Hotel Lux. A few seconds later the GPU agent entered the hall and asked his colleague at the door for the man's name.

When the GPU agent reported to the chief of the counter-espionage, Trilisser, he received the ironic reply:

"This time you have spent your efforts for nothing. Do you know whom you have been following? My own friend Sochatzki, a member of the Central Committee of the Polish Communist Party. If he is a spy so am I!"

However, the suspicion aroused was too strong. The encounter

227

with the Polish diplomat might have been accidental. Yet why had Sochatzki spent hours after the encounter in the cold wintry streets of Moscow? Why had he acted like a trained conspirator who always after a secret meeting will make several detours to get home, even when he knows he is not being followed?

Trilisser conferred with his friend Piatnitsky. The latter, too, shook his head doubtfully. Sochatzki was above suspicion.

Yet since grounds for suspicion existed in the case of Sochatzki, his innocence had to be proven. Routine also required an investigation. The GPU was given a free hand in its surveillance, and used its best men for the purpose. He was shadowed for months, but nothing out of the ordinary came to light. Sochatzki led the life of all the foreign Communists in Moscow. Personally he was always gay and friendly. He exhibited no sign of nervousness nor did he have any other encounters out of the ordinary.

Several times he was given missions outside of Moscow. During his absences from the city, his room at the Hotel Lux was searched, but without result.

Finally to conclude the surveillance, Trilisser laid a trap for him. On one of his frequent visits he placed into Sochatzki's hands the name of a fictitious GPU agent in Warsaw, who in reality was a harmless citizen. After a short time one of the GPU agents who worked in the Polish secret police reported that the Polish police had taken up the surveillance of the fictitious GPU agent in Warsaw. No one in Moscow except Sochatzki had ever heard the name of this man. Here was the proof. Sochatzki was in the service of the Polish secret police.

Word of his arrest hit high party circles in Moscow like a bomb. The comment of Karl Radek was: "If Sochatzki is an agent provocateur, anything is possible! If tomorrow morning the comrades in the black leather coats come to me and say 'Comrade Radek, we arrest you. We have proof you are a spy,' I would reply: 'Comrades, I know nothing about this. But if you say so, it must be the truth!'"

Radek little knew at that time how good a prophet he was.

Panic seized the Comintern and many officers of the GPU. Sochatzki-Bratkovski had been a member of the inner circle of the Polish Communist Party since his entry into it in 1921, when he had left the Polish Socialists. He knew the party secrets. He knew the underground names of the Polish Communists and the underground organization in Poland as well as abroad.

Even though his intimate association with the leadership of the Polish Communist Party had forced Sochatzki to proceed with utmost caution, there could be no doubt that the Polish Communist Party had been operating for ten years under the close surveillance of the Polish secret police.

For the inner circle of the leadership of the Polish Communists in Moscow, Sochatzki's treason was the worst disaster that could have happened to them. This man had been their trusted comrade for ten years. For ten years they had lived together like members of one family. They knew every trait of his character as their own faces in a mirror.

He had been one of the best, respected and beloved by all. He had shared their joy when their work bore fruit and had wept with them when news came of comrades murdered in Polish prisons. And this man had been betraying them all these ten years. They could not comprehend.

One of Sochatzki's most intimate friends went into a state of deep melancholia, repeating over and over: "If Sochatzki was a traitor, then no comrade can be trusted! Maybe I am suspect too."

His comrades, themselves in deep despair, tried to console him. Piatnitsky assured him a hundred times that nobody was in doubt about him. As proof of the confidence placed in him, they offered him an important post abroad.

But it was all in vain: he committed suicide, leaving a farewell message to his comrades: "Forgive me! I cannot endure life any longer after this treason!"

Although the GPU had succeeded in unmasking Sochatzki, it was nevertheless a heavy blow. Certain of its departments from the times of Felix Dzierzynski had been completely in Polish hands. Dzierzynski had entrusted many responsible posts in the GPU to his Polish comrades. His successor Menzhinsky, as well as the acting chief Unschlicht, were Poles.

Intimate personal relationships and close political cooperation had existed between the Polish functionaries in the GPU and the leading members of the Polish Communist Party since the days of the Polish-Russian war. No party in the Comintern had ever been on as intimate terms with the innermost circles of the Soviet government as had the Polish Communists. A man like Sochatzki, in his capacity as member of the Polish Politbureau, knew many of the important secrets of the Soviet government and the Red Army.

Sochatzki-Bratkovski was a close friend and fanatic follower of Pilsudski. At Pilsudski's order he had joined the Communist Party in 1921. Shortly before his execution he told the judge:

"I have always hated you Bolsheviks as one hates a pestilence. I shall die proud and happy for my leader, Pilsudski."

In the course of time the GPU and the Comintern were able to compensate for the consequences of Sochatzki's treason. They made it public only in the fall of 1933, and confused the Polish secret police by this delay.

But the psychological mystery of the treason they could not solve. How had it been possible that such an enemy of the revolution could play his double role for ten years without arousing suspicion anywhere? There was no rational answer to this question.

Like poison, the case of Sochatzki ate its way into the body of the Comintern. Piatnitsky's exaggeration became a principle: Everybody who has not proved his innocence is a spy!

Sochatzki was able to operate for ten years as an agent of the Polish General Staff and secret service in Russia because during the entire period he never maintained direct contacts with his superiors. He was aware of the close scrutiny of the GPU and knew that any direct contact could cause his quick destruction. He reported his observations only from abroad on his numerous trips to Germany and Danzig, from where communications with the underground Polish Communist organization in Western Poland were maintained.

The examining judge, with the natural admiration of one expert for another, especially for one who had performed his espionage work under the judge's own nose, asked why he had committed the blunder of meeting another Polish agent in Moscow.

"Because I was convinced that the Soviet was finished anyway!"

230

AFTERMATH IN THE COMINTERN

In the beginning of 1932 the idea that the Soviet was finished had been not only the opinion of Sochatzki and many foreign observers in Moscow but also the belief of many Russian Communists. The crisis of the first Five Year Plan was at a culmination point. In many parts of the Soviet Union civil war again was raging.

Millions of peasants were being chased from their holdings. In the cities there was a famine as severe as in the worst days of the revolution. Stalin had gained a monopoly of party leadership, but the famine was undermining the confidence of even a party that had been purged of all opposition.

After the breaking off of relationships with England and Nanking in 1927, the Soviet government was living in continuous fear of war, a state of mind heightened by the Japanese invasion of Manchuria. Stalin had used this fear to call forth from the masses of the working people those superhuman efforts essential for the building up of Russia's new industries.

In the fall of 1931 the Ramzin trial had been staged. Professor Ramzin, an internationally known industrial physicist, was accused of having organized an "industry party" with the help of the Second International in order to involve Russia in a war with the West.

That Ramzin was not guilty of high treason was tacitly admitted by Stalin himself, first when he commuted his sentence to ten years' imprisonment and then in 1943 when he decorated him with the Lenin medal and granted him a bonus of one hundred thousand rubles as recognition for his important patriotic services in the field of industrial electricity.

The Ramzin trial in 1931, as well as others that preceded it, permitted the dictatorship to explain its regime of terror as a protective measure against hostile activities from abroad.

The entire country was thrown into a paroxysm of persecution— foreign spies everywhere, in every Soviet plant, in every Soviet shop, in every Soviet office. The stories in circulation were always highly characteristic of the atmosphere in Russia.

At that time the following was making the rounds: Two friends meet on a wide open meadow. X expresses his pleasure at seeing Y. Y puts his finger to his mouth.

"Speak softly, for God's sake! There might be a foreign spy some-where around, listening in!"

X looks around. Far and wide no one is in sight.

"What nonsense are you talking? There's nobody around."

Y: "How can you say there is nobody around? Are we two no-body?"

Everyone was afraid of his own shadow. Everyone was assisting the GPU in uncovering foreign spies, hoping thereby to stay outside the area of GPU suspicion.

It was unavoidable that this atmosphere would penetrate into the Comintern too. Thousands of ties bound it to all the other countries to which suspicion attached. The affair of Sochatzki had demon-strated that even the trusted cannot be trusted.

In former years there had been cases in which foreign Communist leaders had been under suspicion. In 1929 the well-known Indian Communist Manabendranath Roy, whom Lenin had looked upon as the hope of the Communist movement in the Far East and who had been the representative of the Comintern at the side of Michael Borodin during the years of the civil war in China and a member of the Executive Committee of the praesidium of the Comintern, was expelled from the organization because of a disagreement with Stalin in matters of Chinese policies. In 1931 the Comintern officially and positively affirmed that Roy, whom the British secret service was chasing from one country to the next, had been a British agent.

Roy succeeded in returning on his own to India, evading the nets of the British secret service, and in developing independent political activity in that country. He was soon arrested there and sentenced by a British court to long years of imprisonment.

But even such proofs of innocence were now no longer acceptable to the GPU. It claimed this might be a sophisticated trick of the foreign espionage system.

Sometimes in its search for spies the GPU received accidental aid. One day the head of the British department of the Comintern, Petrovsky-Bennet, was stopped on the street in Moscow by an old workman.

"Didn't we meet in Kiev?" the old man asked.

Petrovsky paled and continued on his way. The old man went

232

after him. "Why don't you answer me, comrade? Have you something to hide?"

"Don't molest me! I have more urgent business to attend to than talking to you!"

, The worker grabbed him by the collar. "You scoundrel! You hooligan! You murderer!"

A policeman appeared on the scene. Petrovsky identified himself with the help of his Comintern documents. The worker was arrested and taken to the police station. He insisted that Petrovsky had been a follower of the Ukrainian leader Petliura, and had been responsible in 1918 for the arrest of many Bolshevik workers. He himself had been thrown into prison on Petrovsky's order. Petrovsky's face, with its huge nose and big projecting ears, was unforgettable.

The police made the usual report to the GPU. During Petrovsky's cross-examination it was found that the worker was right. The Petrovsky of Petliura and the Petrovsky representing the Comintern all these years in England were one and the same man.

* * * * *

For ten years Bela Kun had tried again and again to create an underground Communist organization in Hungary. Again and again he had sent daring comrades, willing to sacrifice their lives, to Hungary. Again and again they had been arrested shortly after their arrival. But Bela Kun did not give up.

In 1925 he had sent his best friend, Matthias Rakoczi, to Budapest. He too had been arrested. Bela Kun himself, in all his untiring efforts to create a new basis for Communism in Hungary, had been arrested once in Vienna; a second time he had managed to extricate himself at the last instant. In 1929 the unceasing efforts of Bela Kun and his friends appeared to bear the first fruits. Arrests had been fewer. In some of the big plants and factories of Hungary secret Communist cells had been formed. The Hungarian Communists began to participate under various names in the elections. In 1932 Bela Kun and the Hungarian Central Committee decided to convoke a conference of the Hungarian underground organization in Moscow in order to impart new impetus to the movement in Hungary.

About twenty young underground workers had arrived from Hungary and made a great impression in the Comintern. After its disastrous defeat following the fall of the Hungarian Soviet Republic, Communism in Hungary seemed again to have pushed its roots deep into Hungarian soil. Kun was overjoyed. The conference lasted about two weeks and was regarded as a great success by everybody. A brotherly atmosphere prevailed. All resolutions were passed unanimously. The factional fight that had disrupted and poisoned the Hungarian party for many years was submerged. A new Central Committee was elected, giving heavy representation to the Hungarian underground groups.

As soon as the conference closed, the GPU moved like lightning. All the representatives from Hungary had been under strict surveillance since the very moment of setting foot on Russian soil. One of them had aroused suspicion. He did not put any great obstacles in the way of the GPU investigation, but quickly admitted being a Hungarian police officer.

Not only he but more than half the delegates from Hungary turned out to be police officers. Of these the majority had been elected to the new Central Committee and two into the highest body of the Hungarian Party, the Politbureau.

It developed that the Hungarian police had cooperated industriously with Bela Kun in the building up of his new organization.

The GPU had given a new demonstration that without its check-up the Comintern would become a helpless victim of the foreign espionage system.

THE GPU GROWS SPIES

In the summer of 1932 the GPU quietly took possession of the Comintern building in Moscow. It had its guards not only at the entrance gate of the building on the Machavaya and on the top floor where the OMS offices were located, but on every floor. It was impossible to go from one floor to another without passing the GPU guard.

Entry into the OMS division was permitted only with a special pass signed by the GPU Commissar and Piatnitsky. All talk in the halls and corridors was strictly prohibited. Nobody could take a file out of the building. Brief cases were not allowed. But even without a brief case, a person working for the Comintern had to be prepared at any time for physical inspection by the GPU. Everybody was constantly suspect.

The chief of the counter-espionage division of the GPU, Trilisser, concealed under the name of Moskvin, was placed in the praesidium of the Executive Committee of the Comintern. Stalin had confidence in Manuilsky, Piatnitsky, and Molotov, but the fight against spies could be waged by experts only. The GPU officially took upon itself the protection of the Comintern. In reality, they took over the Comintern.

Trilisser transformed the organization division into a so-called cadre division to collect the *curricula vitae* of all Communists playing leading roles in the various parties or in some of the auxiliary organizations. These *curricula vitae* began with birth and described all major and minor incidents in the life of that person and of his relatives and friends. The slightest omission of detail was punishable with expulsion from the Comintern.

The X-rays of Communist lives led to the discovery that many Communists before their entry into the Communist movement had been members of bourgeois or Social Democratic parties and had either not disclosed, or actually concealed, these facts in their applications for admission.

Not only the political, but also the social background became a criterion of the person's reliability. The unhappy Polish revolutionaries of the older generation, with rare exceptions, came from bourgeois families. Most of them were sons of wealthy businessmen or of big landowners. Hundreds of them got hopelessly enmeshed in the machinery of the cadre division and were banished to Siberia.

The Central Committees in Berlin, Paris, London, Prague, and New York were ordered to organize similar cadre divisions and to send copies of their files to the central cadre division in Moscow.

The Germans, as usual, performed their work most methodically. They extended their cadre records beyond the leading members and functionaries of the party to a great part of the membership itself. When the Gestapo occupied the Karl Liebknecht building in Berlin, after the Reichstag fire in February 1933, they did not find at the headquarters of the German Communists bombs and leaflets inciting to armed insurrection against the government, as they had led the German public to expect. What they found were the names and addresses of most of the Communist Party membership. These files of the cadre division proved a disaster to the underground organization for years to come.

Along with the files and organization of the Comintern, the GPU took charge of its thinking as well. Whatever happened in the Comintern parties that did not completely fit the Comintern's decisions of policy was interpreted as the work of the capitalist secret police. If a Central Committee in one country failed in its job, such failure could be due only to the work of agents provocateurs. If a strike was lost, saboteurs were to blame. If a current of opinion frowned upon by Moscow began to circulate, it was quickly traced back to the work and wish of the secret police of that country. If a Communist leader was found pursuing one of Moscow's policies so energetically that he had neglected to observe that Moscow had in the meantime switched to a different one, it was obvious he was an agent provocateur.

Discussions of Communist theory had long since became taboo in the Comintern. Now they were all branded with one label: Espionage!

In 1932 the Comintern decided to hold the Central Committees of France and Esthonia responsible for the failures of their respective parties. The GPU immediately took upon itself to prove that these failures were traceable to the work of the French and Esthonian secret police. The GPU became a *"deus ex machina"* inside and outside of Russia. Its success in the Sochatzki case and that of the Hungarian Communist Party had given its opinions and judgments the character of infallibility.

Overnight the leading groups of the French and Esthonian parties were revealed to a surprised world as agents of the intelligence service. The explanations did not ring entirely true, yet European Communists were seized with horror when they read them.

In Esthonia a common criminal had won the confidence of some Communists during their imprisonment. They had been so impressed by his capability that they accepted him into the party after his release, and made him the leader of the transport workers union. The police had employed the services of this individual at the same

236

time, using him to ruin the transport workers union. Through him they also organized a complete net of secret police in the ranks of the Esthonian Communist Party. Among these agents were two deputies in the Esthonian parliament as well as some editors of trade union papers.

France had no genuine spy of her own. Therefore a similar discovery had to be made in France. There an entire group of party leaders, among them Barbé and Célor, were shown to be agents of the French secret service. The reasons given sounded somewhat fantastic in France:

"The decision of the Central Committee to exclude Célor will certainly be a surprise to many. Nothing is more intelligible. Célor left the party in ignorance of his dark past, hid his betrayal behind a model simplicity and modesty, always created the impression of being absorbed in his work to the exclusion of every other interest, did not allow himself a holiday in spite of his illness, was always full of activity and zeal. This man was not a common traitor. No, he was a master of hypocrisy which he used with quite exceptional cleverness. This explains how this agent of the bourgeoisie could abuse the confidence and the sympathies of many comrades and thus could become a leading figure of the party."

A Communist Party without a master spy was no longer a genuine Communist Party! The French Communists were not able to produce master spies, so the GPU delivered one.

The discovery of spies became a hobby in the Communist parties of the world after their respective purges by the GPU. The mass work against espionage demanded by the resolutions of the Comintern was transformed into a spy hunt within the Communist parties themselves. In 1931 Stalin had solemnly labelled the Trotskyites the "scum of humanity" and the "advance guard of the bourgeois counter-revolution."

Anyone failing to find favor in the eyes of the Comintern qualified: a Communist who had left the Comintern, a Social Democrat who denied having participated in a conspiracy against the Soviet Union, a bourgeois intellectual returning from a trip to the Soviet Union and making unfavorable comments.

And Trotskyism was identical with espionage. In the spy fiction of the Comintern tens of thousands of spies were busy day and night in all countries of the world, plotting the downfall of the Soviet Union.

Abroad, the spy scare of the Comintern was frequently a subject for amusement. In Moscow, however, it was a very serious matter. One hasty word might bring upon a foreign Communist in Moscow suspicion of deviating from the line of policy enunciated by the almighty General Secretary—suspicion therefore of Trotskyism, suspicion therefore of espionage.

Actually there were few Communists who in former years had not in some way deviated, for all had participated in discussions of theory. All these now were duly registered in the files of the cadre division. At any instant past sins might lead to present catastrophe. A leading foreign Communist who spent these years in Moscow could verily say of himself that he had suffered all the tortures of hell.

From 1930 to 1935 punishment by the GPU meant anything from exclusion from the party to banishment to Siberia; after 1935 it might mean execution.

THE HARVEST IS GATHERED

In the summer of 1936 the Gestapo dealt the underground organization of the Berlin Communists a deadly blow. In the course of a few days hundreds of the leading party workers were arrested and the backbone of the organization was broken.

Those who were not arrested had the choice of crossing the border into Czechoslovakia, France, or Scandinavia, or leaving their residences and acquiring new identities and other shelter till the storm had passed. But the storm did not pass. When the wave of arrests stopped, the psychological attack of the Gestapo against the remnants of the underground organization began.

After 1934 the Berlin Communists had constructed a smooth and efficiently functioning mechanism of an underground organization. They had had several thousand paying members and many hundred active ones. Secret cells had been set up in many factories. Many well-concealed multigraphing machines supplied the underground organization with propaganda leaflets and material. At all frontiers secret crossings were available to smuggle men and literature in and out. The underground now felt so strong that it no longer concerned itself with the causes of defeat at Hitler's hands in 1933, but already envisaged a mass movement against Fascism. The German Central Committee abroad, as well as the Comintern, did nothing to disturb this illusion. On the contrary, they strengthened it. This weakened the underground's alertness against the Gestapo and made them overlook the fact that, with the increase in their own numbers, the surveillance of the Gestapo over them had intensified.

Against every active Communist the Gestapo set several of its own special agents. They studied the methods of the underground Communist work with the same care and industry as did the Communists themselves. They knew the different ideological groupings, the personal rivalries that were the unavoidable result of the continuous terror practiced against the Communists, the theoretical literature of the conspiratorial work. The Gestapo organized lectures and courses for its agents to study all the turns and intricacies of Comintern policy. It was only natural that these agents, now experts, were able to discover quickly the weak spots of the underground work. When one Communist was arrested, two had always been ready to take his place. When the Gestapo succeeded in destroying one underground organization, there had always developed a new one to take its place. When one Communist was executed, hundreds had sworn to avenge him. Even many years after Hitler's victory, the fanatic devotion of German workers to Communism represented a reservoir of strength for the underground work of the Communists. Terror alone could not break them. Only moral disintegration could lead to their defeat.

After each wave of arrests, the tormenting question arose: How had it been possible?

The Communists worked in small split-up units. Only in rare instances did one unit's members know the members of another. Only seldom had it been possible after such arrests to discover what link of their underground chain had given way. On the other hand, continuation of the underground work following such arrests, without a prior reply to this question, was next to impossible. It was essential to know who of the arrested had held out and who had weakened. It was vital to appraise who had been compromised by a statement made during the Gestapo examination and who was carrying the normal risk.

Now the Gestapo decided to answer these questions. On the morning after an arrest, rumors would spread: X is a traitor. He has been working for months with the Gestapo. He has only been arrested for appearance's sake. Y exposed everything and everybody at his examination. Z's wife has betrayed us out of jealousy. A trusted woman comrade has a love affair with an SS man. Another woman comrade wears luxurious clothes—where does the money come from?

The espionage campaign of the Comintern had prepared the soil well for the psychological attack of the Gestapo.

After the blow dealt in the summer of 1936, the Gestapo spread the rumor in Berlin that the leader of the biggest underground division had been in its service for years. This very rumor in itself impelled many active Communists who had not been arrested to remove themselves from the scene. To lend more credibility to the rumor, a woman friend of the arrested man who had been arrested with him was released and even permitted to flee the country. Outside of Germany, the Communist organization also accepted the rumor, and treated the girl as an emissary of the Gestapo. Many months later when the rumor had performed its work, the man who had heroically withstood all the tortures to which the Gestapo had subjected him was sentenced to life imprisonment. His revolutionary honor was restored to him, but the revolutionary organization had been destroyed.

In the summer of 1935, the Central Committee of the German Communist Party sent one of its best men from abroad into Germany to take over the direction of the underground work. This man was an old and experienced Communist and had not been in Germany for several years. After years of Comintern work in South America he had, in fact, been forgotten in Germany. He arrived in Berlin with an Argentinean passport. As he checked into the hotel, before he had even been in touch with anyone, he was arrested. Only three people outside of Germany knew about this trip. All three of them had been beyond suspicion. Had one of them been a traitor, the Gestapo would no longer have required agents of its own.

Efforts to clarify the causes of the arrests were never successful. But soon rumors began to circulate: One of those three was the traitor. X is the betrayer—Y is the betrayer—Z is the betrayer. X, Y, and Z belonged to the most enthusiastic spy hunters in the Comintern. Now the spy hunt was on them.

END OF THE POLISH COMMUNISTS

Opposition in the Comintern had become an unmistakable sign of espionage work. This was now one of the axioms of Comintern policy. From here to the physical extermination during the time of the great purges of everybody suspected of any connection with the espionage organizations was not a far step. The first victim to fall under the blows of the purgatorial spy hunt was the Polish Communist Party.

In 1936 Yezhov, the "Iron" People's Commissar, took over the task of purging Soviet Russia of all foreign spies, of all those who had disagreed with Stalin in the past or had shown an inclination to disagree.

Stalin ordered the dissolution of the entire Polish Communist Party and entrusted to Yezhov the execution of most of those Poles in Russia who had ever entertained any connection with the Polish Communist Party.

This step also expressed completely the logic of the GPU, at that time the supreme law of the Soviet Republic. For the Polish Communists had been an integral part of the machinery of government in Russia. And finally Moscow had not forgotten that its neighbor Poland was by tradition its treacherous and contemptible arch enemy.

The first to be delivered to the firing squad were the survivors of the old revolutionary generation of Rosa Luxemburg and Felix Dzierzynski. Warski, Kosczewa, Pruchnjak, Krayevsky, Bronski, Doletski, and Domski came from the Social Democratic Party that had been founded in 1893 by Rosa Luxemburg within the territory of Russian Poland. From its inception this party had opposed the national revolutionary group of Pilsudski. Its leaders had been fiery idealists, men and women who knew of no life outside of or beyond the revolutionary movement.

This was the only group of professional revolutionists in Europe comparable to Lenin's group in intellectual and moral strength. Out of this group, in 1918, had emerged the Polish Communist Party under the leadership of Dzierzynski. After the victory of the October Revolution, Dzierzynski had become the chief of the all-powerful Russian Cheka. As long as he lived, Polish Communists held posts of high political and military importance in the Sovet Union as well as in the Comintern. Dzierzynski had been a bitter opponent of Trotsky, and the Polish Communists had formed the first faction within the Communist International to support Stalin against the old leadership.

Unschlicht, the acting chief of the GPU after Dzierzynski's death in 1927, like his predecessor, was a powerful friend to Polish Communists in the Soviet Union. Yet when finally the hour of danger struck, Unschlicht could not even save his own skin, much less that of his Polish friends.

Along with Trilisser, chief of the counter-espionage, and many other Poles in GPU service, he became a victim of the terrific purge visited upon them. The group of Warski and Koszczewa were shot as agents of Pilsudski and spies of Trotsky. Ten years earlier they had been among those who wavered between a policy of support for Pilsudski and one for the peasant government of Witos. Now the GPU regarded their vacillation as proof of espionage work in the service of Pilsudski and Trotsky.

The Domski group belonged to Zinoviev's faction. They were destroyed along with Zinoviev. Domski had been the chief of the Polish Communists in Warsaw in 1920. He had not succeeded at that time, during the advance of the Red Army towards Warsaw, in organizing an armed insurrection in the Polish capital. Sixteen years later this was shown to be irrefutable proof that back in 1920 he had been a Polish spy.

In 1921, after the split in the Polish Socialist Party, many Polish intellectuals had joined the Communist Party. Lapinski, Valetski, Sochatzki, and many others were among them. The fact that Lapinski and Valetski had joined the Comintern at the same time as Sochatzki in 1921 proved in 1936 that they too were spies. They met the same fate.

The next party of the Comintern to be hit by the full blows of the purge was the Communist Party of Germany. The executions were performed with the help of the cadre division's files. Hundreds of German Communists who had lived in the Soviet Union for many years and had become Soviet citizens, holding high posts in industry, were wiped out indiscriminately. Refugees from the Germany of 1933 were treated similarly.

Only a few hundred German Communists fleeing from Hitler's terrorism had been admitted to the Soviet Union, after having been put through a most careful investigation. Nevertheless they were liquidated and the Soviet Union, for fear of foreign spies, cancelled the right of asylum for members of foreign Communist parties. Yezhov's purgatorial paroxysm knew no bounds.

All those who had been suspected of even an inclination towards opposition in the last ten years were put on the executioner's lists.

The Hotel Lux became a purgatory. All the ties of friendship and of common conviction that formerly had united men became knots of friction. The terror made primitive savages out of "pure" and "impure" alike. They fought for dear life, friend denouncing friend, husband his wife, wife her husband, father his son and son his father.

Arrests usually took place during the early morning hours. In the tragic days of 1937 the inhabitants of the Lux waited each morning fully clothed and bags packed. Arrests were made quietly in most cases. Only the heavy steps of the GPU officers and banging doors announced that death had again snatched a victim. When the cranking of the GPU cars was heard, those left behind knew that another life would be wiped out within twenty-four hours.

One morning in 1937 the entire hotel was aroused in panic. The GPU officers were meeting resistance! They had knocked at a door: "Open! GPU!"

There was no answer. They knocked and shouted louder. No sound came from the room. Then they forced open the door.

In the middle of the room stood an old man in his nightgown. A long unkempt gray beard covered his hollow face. His shaggy hair fell over his eyes.

As a GPU man approached him, the old man pounced on him like a wild animal: "Murderer! Scoundrel! Traitor!" His cries resounded through the narrow corridors of the Lux, but no door opened.

The old man put up a desperate fight. He threw himself on the floor and struggled ferociously. The two men dragged him by his hands and feet from the room. On the stairs, one of them hit him over the head with the butt of his revolver. Like a lifeless sack he was thrown into the GPU car.

Thus was Herrmann Remmele, for many years a member of the praesidium of the Comintern and one of the most popular leaders of the German Communists, arrested.

Remmele came from the easy-going southwest of Germany. He was born in a family indoctrinating its children with Socialism from their earliest years. His father was a respected Social Democrat, and his older brother became premier of one of the southwestern states of Germany after the revolution. He himself was one of the few popular mass speakers of the German Communists. His broad humor and his mighty voice always insured enthusiastic applause for the Communist Party at his meetings.

Remmele did not take politics too tragically. He was a handsome man—loved a glass of wine and a good-looking girl more than endless debates about revolutionary strategy. As a member of the Reichstag, he made a few speeches and all in all paid as little attention as possible to politics. During the last years before the rise of Fascism, Remmele had been only rarely in Germany. He lived in Moscow as emissary of the German Communist Party. Here, too, he pursued his merry life, free of all cares. Crimean wines weren't bad, and among the stenographers were many who, in spite of his more than fifty years, were more than glad to have Herrmann Remmele court them.

Hitler's victory hit Remmele a heavy blow. In a few weeks his *joie de vivre* was gone, and he became a gray old man. He was among the few German Communists in Moscow who could not get over the breakdown of the labor movement. A blinding bitterness against the Comintern and Stalin took possession of him.

Pretty soon people began avoiding him, because in his talks he kept trying to prove that Stalin had acted as a traitor. In the end, everyone withdrew from him, and he became a ghost in the Lux.

Most of his time he spent in his hotel room, leaving it only for meals. He saw no one, not even his son Helmuth, a leader of the Communist Youth Organization living in the same building.

Helmuth accepted the defeat with the nonchalance of youth.

244

One day he too was tripped up by the GPU. The naive boy confirmed his innocence as best he could, swearing a thousand oaths that he had nothing in common with his father. The examining magistrate easily secured from Helmuth many of the former statements of his father about Stalin, and just as easily got his signature to a confession according to which the old man had been implicated in a plot against Stalin. The young man believed he had saved his own life at the cost of his father's.

Herrmann Remmele was shot soon after his arrest, along with many German Communists whose friend he had been in former years.

A similar fate befell the Austrian Protective Guards, Social Democratic workers who had fought heroically in March, 1934, against the rising wave of Fascism in Vienna and who had been solemnly invited to become the honored guests of the Soviet government.

* * * * *

The annals of the Comintern report the purges of the terror years in a few sparse words. Manuilsky in his speech to the Eighteenth Party Congress in March, 1939, made the following statement:

"Most contaminated by hostile elements was the Communist Party of Poland where agents of Polish Fascism managed to gain positions of leadership. These scoundrels tried to get the Party to support Pilsudski's Fascist coup in May, 1926. When this failed they feigned repentance of their 'May' error, made a show of self-criticism and deceived the Comintern just as Lovestone and the police 'factionalists' of the Hungarian and Yugoslav parties had once done. And it was the fault of the Comintern workers that they allowed themselves to be deceived by the class enemy, failed to detect his maneuvers in time, and were late in taking measures against the contamination of the Communist parties by enemy elements. . . . .

"The Communist parties have investigated their leading workers and removed those whose political honesty was questionable. They have dissolved illegal organizations which were particularly contaminated, and have begun to form new ones in their place. . . . ."

CHAPTER XVIII

The Strange Career of Georg Dimitrov

CAREER BEGINS IN A BERLIN CAFE

THREE MEN SITTING IN A CORNER OF A BAVARIAN RESTAURANT IN Berlin, on an early March day in 1933, were whispering under their breaths to each other. They had good reason to be circumspect.

A few days before their meeting, the Reichstag had gone up in flames. Throughout Germany, Democrats, Socialists, and Communists were outside the law. In the cellars of the SA, bones were being broken and skulls crushed. Hitler's murder gangs were enjoying the free rein given them these days.

Headlines announced the arrest of the Chairman of the Communist parliamentary faction, Torgler, and of a Dutch vagabond, Van Der Lubbe, as incendiaries of the Reichstag. Further arrests were promised. The Reichstag fire was described as the signal for a Bolshevist revolution in Germany.

The three men in the restaurant were Georg Dimitrov, secretary of the Communist Balkan Federation, and his two friends, Vasilyi Tanev and Blagoye Popoff. They were discussing, in whispers, their departure to Moscow.

Dimitrov had iron nerves. But this time he was angry and nervous. He would already have been on his way several days ago had not Popoff and Tanev arrived in Berlin. Neither knew a word of German, and it was their first visit to Berlin. Dimitrov had to take personal charge of them because the Comintern organization in Berlin was in complete disorder due to innumerable arrests.

He stressed the absolute necessity of exercising caution until their departure, urged them to remain in their hotel rooms up to the last hour, then gave them their passports and tickets.

He had just paid his check and was getting up from the table, when detectives entered the restaurant. They came in at all the doors. Escape was impossible.

The waiter who was serving the three Bulgarians had heard a few words of their whispered conversation. The foreign language sounded like Russian to him. Surely suspicious characters! These foreigners were just the sort of men, in the imagination of an excited Berlin waiter, to have burned the Reichstag—big black fellows with wavy hair and burning eyes. He phoned the police. Dimitrov and his friends were under arrest.

A few hours later the headlines announced: The Comintern has burned the Reichstag. Dimitrov is the leader of the incendiary gang.

The Bulgarian revolutionary had mounted the first step of the ladder to his world reputation.

Dimitrov knew from personal experience the significance of a victorious counter-revolution. He was not one of those Communist leaders to adopt resolutions on the world revolution at a comfortable desk. He had been one of the leaders of the unhappy September insurrection of 1923 in Bulgaria. As a leader of the only real Bolshevik group in the Balkans, he knew how to handle a gun as well as the teachings of Marx and Engels.

After the defeated September insurrection, Dimitrov had continued the fight with thousands of his comrades. He gave furious battle to the gendarmes of Tsankov before he retired with his small army to Yugoslav territory.

In Dimitrov's mind at his arrest in 1933 lived the thousands of Bulgarian Communists who had been hanged or shot. The Communist Party had been his home; its members his family. From his sixteenth year on, the young printer had lived in this family. It had made a man of him, had given him knowledge, and had put him at its head. In 1913 it had elected him a deputy to the Bulgarian parliament. For it he had suffered imprisonment in 1917. For it he had twice been sentenced to death in absentia.

He had not been one of those Communists who had minimized the National Socialist danger. He had been bitter about those verbal magicians who knew beyond any doubt that the Nazis could not seize power in Germany as had the Fascists in Italy and who were equally sure that a National Socialist Germany would only serve as a springboard for the Communists to seize power in the country.

In 1932 Dimitrov had feared that the Communist Party of Germany would share the fate of its Bulgarian sister party. He had attended mass meetings and had listened to the revolutionary bragging of the leaders as well as the pitiful proclamations of the Social Democrats who were relying completely on constitutional promises.

The experienced eye of the civil war veteran observed the well-trained battalions of the SA led by professional soldiers, opposed by willing but untrained Communists and Social Democratic organizations. He felt the pressure of the rising National Socialist power on the weakening democratic state machinery. The revolutionary from the Balkans saw through the intricacies of the game played by politicians in the entourage of the senile president of the Reich, by generals who thought they were all-powerful, by shrewd industrialists, by tricky intriguers behind the curtains, and by the power-hungry adventurer Hitler, better than most of the experienced German politicians.

Dimitrov was a member of the Communist International Executive Committee and wielded considerable influence in its Balkan policies. In Germany, however, he was powerless, not belonging to the intimate circle of Comintern leadership. After the Bulgarian defeat, he had been in the background for many years. The German Communist leaders regarded him as a vacillating opportunist.

In the fall of 1932, Dimitrov had written a memorandum to the praesidium of the Comintern Executive Committee, criticizing the policy of the German Communists severely and prophesying a victory for Hitler unless a swift change in their policies was inaugurated. Moscow's reply was in his possession when he was arrested: a cold rejection of his criticism and of his suggestions, as well as an order for his immediate return to Moscow.

Dimitrov knew what that meant. He was prepared for a long exile among the "impure" of the Hotel Lux, and he was indifferent. The victory of German Fascism had killed all revolutionary hope in him.

DIMITROV-GOERING DUET

Why the Nazis implicated Dimitrov in the Reichstag trial has remained a mystery. They knew from the pre-examination that Dimitrov had an ironclad alibi for the night of the twenty-seventh to the twenty-eighth of February, the night the Reichstag was burning. He had been in Munich, at a very unpolitical rendezvous with a beautiful lady who knew him under an entirely different name but who had sworn to the identity of the man who had spent that night with her as that of the supposed Reichstag incendiary.

Probably the Nazis had counted on the docility of the German Supreme Court in Leipzig. The judges and state attorneys of this highest republican tribunal belonged to the gravediggers of the Weimar Republic. They had sentenced thousands of Democrats, Social Democrats, and Communists to long years of imprisonment, even at the mere suspicion of high treason, and had set hundreds of nationalist insurrectionists free even when their crimes had been proved beyond doubt.

Yet this time the question did not concern the usual preparation for high treason. The task of the state attorney this time was to prove that Dimitrov, together with his two Bulgarian friends, Torgler and the Dutch idiot Van der Lubbe, had committed arson.

Hitler, Goering, and Goebbels had presented the German Supreme Court with an insoluble task. The trial developed into an indescribable defeat for the new German dictatorship.

Goebbels dramatized the trial to the world as if the fate of the Nazi dictatorship depended on its outcome. The Nazis, blinded by their recent victory, believed they would be able to convince the world that the Communists, not they, had laid fire to the Reichstag. They accomplished exactly the opposite.

Dimitrov, at his arrest, did not believe that his life was still worth a cent. He expected to be slaughtered in an SA cellar. The most favorable possibility appeared to him to be an extradition to Bulgaria, where the gallows awaited him.

When he was told that he was to be given a public trial, he recognized his great chance.

Entering the courtroom and seeing its galleries crowded with journalists from all over the world, he realized his game was half won.

The Nazis staged the trial in Leipzig as a proof of their willingness and ability to rid the world of Bolshevism. Goebbels acted as an informed expert on the mysteries of Bolshevism. In fact, however, the trial demonstrated that he knew little about the psychology of a professional revolutionary.

The Nazis delivered into the hands of Dimitrov the one and only weapon with which he could hope to defeat them, the forum of public opinion. They simply could not conceive that the moral power of one single individual might equal and even surpass the political power of their entire state in the eyes of the world.

In his defense Dimitrov did not have his personal fate in the forefront of his mind. In Bulgaria he had risked his life many times for less important purposes. He conducted his defense for the purpose of shielding the reputation of the Communist International and of the Soviet Union.

The Court had refused to allow him the Communist attorneys he had asked for. He himself did not wish to use the official attorneys that the Court was willing to offer him for his defense. He therefore conducted his own defense personally. In his prison cell he studied the administrative code of German criminal law. He utilized his newly acquired juridical knowledge to the frequent embarrassment of the Court. Although he was no master of the German language, he remained the oratorical center of the proceedings throughout the trial.

Hundreds of thousands in Germany listened in on the radio to these proceedings. Dimitrov rapidly became the most popular figure among the anti-Fascists in the country. The conservative and Catholic adversaries of the Nazis welcomed the Nazi defeats at the hands of Dimitrov. His reputation spread over the world.

In a last effort to save his trial for their purposes, the Nazis hit upon an idea that clinched Dimitrov's triumph. They confronted him with the powerful Prussian president Goering. With the superiority of a revolutionary dialectician and the shrewdness of a Bulgarian Komitatchi, Dimitrov began to drive his questions into the fat and bulbous Goering. Without offending a single paragraph of the Supreme Court code, he entangled the witness in such a maze as to make the Prussian president fly off in a rage.

"You're a scoundrel! A scoundrel! You ought to hang on the gallows!" bellowed the Prussian president and omnipotent chief of the Gestapo. He had no other arguments to use.

250

Dimitrov bowed ironically. "I am very well satisfied with the reply of the witness."

By this time, Goering had completely forgotten he was in a court-room. Paying no attention to the presiding judge, he ordered the defendant dragged from the Court by the attending guards. This was the final touch to Dimitrov's triumph.

"You seem afraid of my questions," the indefatigable Bulgarian exclaimed.

"You'll fall into my hands yet—when you get out of this court-room," Goering screamed back at him.

TRIUMPH IN MOSCOW

But Dimitrov was not given up to Goering. The Court had to acquit him, and with him his two Bulgarian friends as well as Torgler. Only the poor idiot, Van der Lubbe, remained in the hands of the Nazis.

But even after his acquittal Dimitrov was still not released from prison by the Nazi authorities. As the weeks went by, protests from all over the world swarmed in. The Soviet Government had made Dimitrov and his two Bulgarian friends Soviet citizens and demanded their release.

Hitler at that time was still much concerned about his reputation abroad, and also did not wish to embitter relations with the Soviet Union. So he set Dimitrov and his two friends free.

A special plane took Dimitrov to Moscow. The first few days there he did not realize what was happening to him. Certainly he had done his duty in Leipzig. He had made his trial into a triumph for the Communist International. Yet at no time had a foreign Communist been received in Moscow as he was. All the people and all the newspapers sang his praises; and more important, Stalin, already the "great" Stalin, received him personally and expressed his warmest congratulations and admiration.

His opportunist sins were forgotten. The Leipzig trial had raised Dimitrov to the most important figure in the Comintern.

Stalin immediately seized the opportunity that the Leipzig trial presented to him. His Comintern had been as badly hit by the Fascist victory in Germany as had the Second International.

Dimitrov jumped into the gap that had opened around the Comintern after the German defeat. His audacity and agility had fascinated the world. For the first time in its history, there was in its ranks a leader whose words carried weight outside the sphere of convinced Communists.

For Stalin he was a gift from heaven, a man who fitted exactly into his new conception of world policies. He made him his leading man in the Comintern, and Dimitrov quickly proved himself a worthy disciple of his master.

The intelligent Bulgarian prepared himself for his new office with great care and industry. Responsibility for the defeats he left to his predecessors. He waited more than a year before permitting his induction into his new office. In the interim he established himself at the headquarters of the High Command of the world revolution. It took the revolutionary from the Balkans only a few weeks to change over into the dictator of the Comintern.

First he cleaned up the staff of the High Command, ousting all those who had opposed him in the past. His revenge was merciless. Old Piatnitsky who had served the Comintern for fifteen years loyally, as a good dog his master, and who could not put up with the new sweeping dictatorial methods, was dismissed from his political posts without a word. Another Russian secretary of the Comintern, Knorin, refusing to go along with Dimitrov, was fired. Friends who supported him abroad and to whom he appealed against Dimitrov's methods were ordered to come to Moscow, then were banished to some distant Russian province.

Bela Kun, who had opposed Dimitrov in many conflicts within the Balkan federation, was also banished. Dimitrov had nothing to fear from Kuusinen. Only Manuilsky remained. He adjusted himself as quickly to Stalin's new man as he had previously to the various Comintern presidents.

The Bulgarian Central Committee that had refused to support him during the Reichstag trial because it had seen in him an inveterate opportunist was dissolved. Popoff and Tanev were publicly denounced for their "un-Bolshevist behavior" during the trial. Neither of them knew German nor had either of them had an interpreter during the trial. Actually, therefore, they had not been able to take part at all. But Dimitrov wanted to make certain. He did not wish to share the glory of Leipzig with anyone. The propaganda departments of the Comintern were given the task of keeping the Leipzig trial in the limelight of public attention and singing its praises to all the world. In the building on the Machavaya new offices were equipped for the new General Secretary. Dimitrov did not reside any longer in the Hotel Lux. A spacious home was built for him in the suburbs of Moscow. Everything was done to surround the office of the dictator of the Comintern with the glory of the "happy Socialist life" that, according to Stalin, was just beginning to make its bow in Soviet Russia.

Public acclaim was as generous to Dimitrov as Stalin's benevolence. When he finished his long speech at the Seventh World Congress of the Comintern in the summer of 1935, he was greeted with an ovation beyond anything ever accorded Lenin and Trotsky or Zinoviev and Bukharin. The minutes of the Congress record the following:

"At the last words of Dimitrov the entire Congress rises to its feet. A tidal wave of enthusiasm resounds through the hall. Cries and exclamations from all the delegations intermingle. Even the visitors in the galleries follow suit. The manifestations merge into the singing of the International. After further outbursts, the delegations sing the Carmagnole and after that revolutionary songs in dozens of different languages. Manuilsky shouts: 'Long live the loyal and tried comrade-in-arms of the great Stalin, the captain of the Communist International!' Now the enthusiasm rises to a new climax. Everybody cheers Dimitrov!"

CHAPTER XIX

Trojan Horse of the Comintern

STALIN A RAISON!

ACCORDING TO THE STATUTES OF THE COMINTERN, WORLD CONgresses were to be called every two years. Zinoviev abided by this rule. During Bukharin's presidency, four years had elapsed between the Fifth and Sixth World Congresses. After Bukharin's dismissal, it took seven years for Stalin to give permission for the Seventh World Congress to take place.

In the building on the Machavaya, the High Command had grown accustomed to directing the work without World Congresses. Small intimate conferences were substituted.

Hitler's victory had completely changed the world situation; the Communist parties were in great confusion and a new definition of Communist policy was inescapable. A World Congress had to be called. All preparations were made and the different parties were advised that the meetings were to take place in the spring of 1935.

Yet orders from Stalin caused the opening date to be postponed again and again. No one knew why. Even the new favorite, Georg Dimitrov, was at a loss to understand the reasons.

Who would connect the arrival of the French Foreign Minister Laval in April, 1935, with the continued delay in setting the opening date of the World Congress? The Narkomindel had long since been closed as a source of information for the Machavaya. Not even Manuilsky and Piatnitsky, who were members of the Russian Central Committee, knew that Laval had insisted upon a repudiation of the Comintern by the Soviet government as a prerequisite to the conclusion of a French-Russian pact. For this reason the opening of the Congress was postponed from day to day.

No diplomat of the capitalist countries had ever succeeded with such a demand. When Chicherin once recommended a minor compromise in this direction, Lenin proposed a rest cure or him. During the conference of Genoa in 1922 Rakovsky had refused even to discuss the problem of the Comintern although the Bolsheviki at that time were ready to pay any other price for economic cooperation with England. For more than ten years the Soviet government had consistently denied any responsibility for the Communist International, insisting that this institution represented an international body under its own jurisdiction, enjoying merely the hospitality of Soviet Russia. All states maintaining diplomatic relations with the Soviet government recognized this contention de facto by the very maintenance of their diplomatic relations. Now, where Lloyd George, Poincaré, Churchill, Stresemann and Barthou had failed, the mayor of Aubervillers, who had become head of the Quai d'Orsay, succeeded.

Pravda published a communique about the Laval-Stalin talk: "Stalin approves absolutely the policy of French national defense and the maintenance of its armed forces at the level required for her security."

Laval had not gotten everything he had asked for from Stalin. Stalin did not repudiate the Comintern or the French Communists. He simply annulled the first of the Ten Communist Commandments: Thou shalt not vote for war credits in a capitalist country.

Laval's success was due less to his personality and ability as a negotiator than to Adolf Hitler. Stalin was urgently in need of a pact with France after the stabilization of the anti-Bolshevik regime in Germany.

The High Command of the world revolution did not know what to say for several days after the publication of Stalin's statement. By now it was realized why the opening date of the World Congress had been continuously postponed. A *fait accompli* had been neatly deposited at the open gates of the Congress. With one stroke of the pen the entire policy of the Comintern had been changed without prior notice to its leadership.

A critical discussion of Stalin's statements was beyond the realm of possibility. As a member of the Russian Central Committee, Manuilsky could risk a critical attitude towards the almighty Stalin only at the threat of political death. Kuusinen, the small attorney from Finland, as usual did not utter a superfluous word. He lived up to the characterization Manuilsky had given of him: "Before

255

Kuusinen expresses a thought he first examines all possible objections. Then he goes to sleep. Next morning after further examination, if he can discover no possible objection to the thought—he falls into a deep silence!" The Italian Ercoli had been suspected of secret sympathies with Bukharin and had already been deeply embarrassed by the defection of his intimate friend Ignazio Silone.

The German Pieck regarded the mere thought of opposition to Stalin as an unpardonable sin. The Czechoslovak Gottwald was aware that the Czechoslovakian Foreign Minister was expected in Moscow and that after his visit the Czechoslovakian party would be squeezed into the same position as was the French.

The Americans, English, Austrians, and others did not even count. In the High Command, the representatives of the small parties had but one privilege: to maintain their silence and to vote "Yea" whenever resolutions were presented. Therefore complete unanimity reigned.

Unanimity, however, was not enough. Each statement of Stalin had to be received as an event of historic significance and acclaimed with such enthusiasm as to call forth the popular echo that it merited. Here Dimitrov injected himself and showed that he could execute Stalin's policies in the spirit of his master.

The French Central Committee in Paris had been as taken by surprise by the Stalin-Laval statement as had the Executive Committee in Moscow. It received the information through the official French news agency.

For two days Cachin, Thorez, and Vaillant-Couturier, the former captain in the French Army and delegate to the Third World Congress, did not know what to say. France was still the greatest military power in Europe. The fight against militarism had been the *raison d'etre* of the French Communist Party. Even the French Socialists had voted for many years against the war budgets.

Confusion vanished when Dimitrov's clear and strict orders came through. Their effect could be seen a few days later when Parisians stared curiously at huge yellow and red placards covering the billboards of the great boulevards and working class suburbs. They bore tremendous letters announcing: *Stalin a Raison!*

The placards quoted the announcement made by Stalin concerning French national defense. They stayed posted for months. When wind and weather tore them down, they were immediately renewed. Passersby in Paris and all the cities of France were being constantly reminded that Stalin was right.

And Stalin was right! At a small movie theatre in a working-class suburb of Paris, a newsreel portrayed Hitler with wide-open mouth, eyes popping out of their sockets, body trembling with rage, bellowing as if to burst his lungs. A little Parisian woman covered her face with her hands, crying: *"Mon Dieu!* What a horror!" Then Stalin appeared on the screen, reviewing his Red Army on the Red Square. Quiet and motionless, he greeted the marching columns. The theatre exploded in a frenzy of enthusiasm. Here was the force that would save them from Fascism—this quiet and serious man; these fine soldiers with iron faces and eyes alight!

The masses in Western Europe stared with horror at the German tragedy, with only one thought in mind: Anything but that! The Jacobin tradition in France was still alive. Robespierre, Marat, and Danton, who had sent the armies of the Revolution out against the Prussian and Austrian Junkers, were still a living force in the minds of the nation. The Communist Party of France lowered the Red Flag and raised the Tricolor of the *sans culottes.* The chief editor of *L'Humanité,* Vaillant-Couturier, appeared at mass meetings decorated with all his medals for heroism won during the First World War.

Stalin was right: Lenin's International was dead in Europe.

ENTER YE: HERE LIVE THE GODS (SECOND EDITION)

In July of 1935 Communist delegates from all four corners of the earth again poured into Moscow. Again at the frontiers of the Soviet Union huge banners greeted the arrivals: Workers of the world, unite!

But these delegates to the Seventh World Congress were not welcomed at the borders by crudely erected arches of triumph made of flimsy wood, as were those to the Second and Third Congresses in 1920 and 1921. Here were arches of solid concrete and steel construction. Nor were the flags ragged and torn like those of fifteen years earlier: they were proud and luxurious banners.

Moscow breathed the air of the victorious First Five Year Plan. New buildings were rising everywhere, main streets were paved in solid concrete, huge industrial establishments stood where once had been suburban slums. The first lines of the new subway had been completed.

To the few delegates who remembered Moscow from former years the city was scarcely recognizable. To those who had never seen the city it offered fulfillment of everything Comintern propaganda had led them to expect. Moscow had become the symbol of Stalin's policy of industrialization.

Even the German delegates were lost in admiration. Most of them had not come directly from Germany, but were refugees coming from Prague, Zurich, Paris, and Stockholm. Because they had lost their own homes, their home of election became even dearer to them.

The Kremlin was closed to the delegates. They could only walk along its great walls and peer cautiously, like the natives of Moscow themselves, through the great gates guarded by powerful GPU soldiers.

Lenin's mausoleum was open to visitors. The delegates, like millions before them, passed reverently by the glass coffin to regard with respectful eyes the mummy of the great man.

The citizens of Moscow paid scant attention to the delegates. Nobody asked, as in former times: When will we finally achieve the world revolution? The citizens knew only too well that these poor devils from abroad needed sympathy, pity, and help, themselves.

When one of them in an address to a Moscow regiment reverted to the old theme of world revolution, the commanding officer replied: "The Soviet Union does not await the assistance of a world revolution. We will soon be strong enough to carry Socialism to you." Then he gave the delegate the uniform of an honorary corporal of the Red Army. In former years foreign delegates had been made honorary colonels.

The Congress did not meet in the golden coronation hall of the Kremlin. The cold marble of the House of Nobles, outside of the gates of the Kremlin, was a more fitting place for its meetings than the Byzantine luxury of the Andreyevsky Palace. And the acoustics were far better in the House of Nobles than in the rather long coronation hall of the Kremlin. Against its high walls, the mass chants of the Congress echoed as in a well-constructed music hall. This was important—because the delegates from Europe, America, and Asia had little to say, and therefore much to sing.

Whenever the name of Stalin was mentioned or whenever Dimitrov addressed them, they responded with songs in all languages. The French were the main party of this Congress and their Carmagnole drowned out all other national songs.

There had been considerable embarrassment before the opening of the Congress. Somebody had to give the customary report on the activities of the Comintern between the years of the Sixth and Seventh World Congresses. Dimitrov had refused to burden himself with the tale of these last hungry seven years. Molotov, who had succeeded Bukharin, had long ago returned to the praesidium of the Council of People's Commissars. Even Manuilsky and Kuusinen hesitated.

So the task was dumped into the unhappy lap of the German Wilhelm Pieck who had been in Moscow only rarely during these last seven years, who had never participated in the work of the Executive Committee, and who had not the slightest idea about the backstage developments of this Congress. To ease the task for him, a Russian assistant by the name of Krugliyansky, who had worked for several years in Germany under the name of Fritz David, was given him. (Just one year after this Congress, in the trial of Zinoviev, this same man was to be accused of having planned the assassination of Stalin.)

Pieck was not pleased with his task. He had to deal in his report with the defeat of the Comintern in Germany and blame it on the old leadership. But he could not shirk his assignment for he was aware that the new General Secretary was a hard man to deal with.

Zinoviev and Bukharin had been the presidents of their Executive Committees and had ruled the Comintern by the authority of their personalities. Under them secretaries had sufficient freedom of movement. Dimitrov, the first General Secretary of the Comintern, was the executive arm of Stalin. Under him there was no freedom of movement for anybody. No longer were any votes taken in the praesidium of the Comintern. The General Secretary had become the first and last authority.

The Seventh Congress developed into a comedy in the grand manner. Manuilsky, a new Columbus, took the delegates on a trip of discovery through the new world: Socialism, having accomplished a definitive and permanent victory on one-sixth of the world's surface, has completely changed the situation for the other five-sixths of the world. The defeat of the German workers is a terrible thing, but measured against the success in Russia, it is a mere bagatelle. Only one task now remains for the workers in all other lands, to follow enthusiastically and obediently the course charted by the Soviet Union. Then some fine day they, too, will arrive in their own countries at the open gates of their own Socialist paradise.

Manuilsky's magic formula was supplemented in Dimitrov's grand address. Here the answer was supplied to the question why the Communists were going along with Stalin's ersatz Communism as blindly as the children followed the Pied Piper of Hamelin.

Upon their arrival in Moscow, the delegates had already become aware of the imminence of a great turn in Comintern policies. Yet nobody realized how far this turn would go. Dimitrov's address was a surprise even to the intimate circles of Comintern leadership. For seven years Comintern policies had conducted the various parties through the labyrinthian paths of ultra-revolutionary sectarianism. For a long time after the victory of German Fascism, a Communist loyal to the Moscow line had to insist that not the Fascists but the Social Democrats were the chief enemy, those same Social Democrats who were sharing the concentration camps with the Communists. The French Communists had followed a similar sectarian line well into the year 1934, when they had participated in a demonstration of French reactionaries and Fascists against Daladier in front of the Palais Bourbon.

With a sovereign nonchalance, Dimitrov dumped overboard the entire sectarian philosophy of the last seven years. No longer was the Social Democracy the main enemy. No longer were the Social Democrats Social Fascists. And no longer was the fight against the Social Democracy the main task of every loyal Communist.

Dimitrov in his speech cast out sectarianism, inviting Communists

260

to join with all other sections of the labor movement in a spirit of brotherly love and harmony. His slogan was unity and cooperation at all costs: Merge the conflicting wings of the various trade union movements of Europe and America; yes, and even eliminate the political split existing in the Socialist movement since the days of the First World War when the Communist International was founded to struggle against the treason of the Second International.

During the last sixteen years, the Communists had been defeated again and again. Now Dimitrov pointed out to them a new road to success, victory, and power—to unite with Socialists, radical Democrats, liberals, Catholics, in a popular front supported by extraparliamentary organs of democracy like shop councils and trade union organizations. In this way Communists, together with their friends of the popular front, would march along the royal road to power and form a popular front government.

No wonder the French Communists cheered Dimitrov: For years and years they had stood hungrily by at the dinner table of French parliamentarianism, unable to sit down for a good feast. Dimitrov's formula satisfied their political appetites as much as it appeased their revolutionary conscience. The unhappy choice between reformist gradualism and revolutionary radicalism disappeared.

Dimitrov's address removed another great weight from their souls. The Communist masses in France were no less afraid of war than the rest of humanity. The French Communists, like all the other Communist parties of the world, had always had to preach the Communist dogma to the masses: that in a capitalist world imperialist wars are inevitable. Now at last Dimitrov's speech relieved French Communists from the annoying task of fighting militarism and imperialism. The glorious new world that Dimitrov painted permitted them to forget that Hitler had just torn up the Treaty of Versailles and was building a new powerful army which was ready to move into the officially demilitarized Rhineland zone.

There was even something for the German Communists in what Dimitrov said. For nearly three years they had been attempting to undermine the Fascist dictatorship at terrific sacrifice. Dimitrov pointed out a new path for them to take:

"Comrades, you recall the old legend of the conquest of Troy. The city had protected itself against the attack of the enemy by an unassailable wall. The attacking army which had suffered great losses was unable to break into this wall until at last it found a way of penetrating into the city, into the heart of the enemy, with the help of the Trojan horse.

"It seems to me that we revolutionaries should use the same strategy against the living wall that our enemy Fascism is using to protect itself against the people."

The poor defeated Germans were overjoyed—Dimitrov had led them, too, to the philosopher's stone. Now the Nazis were doomed.

The hero of Leipzig had become the prophet of the Comintern. The Seventh Congress departed in a happy delirium.

Nobody had thought it possible that the masses would again respond after the devastating defeat in Germany. But again, as in 1920, the Comintern called out to the world: "Enter ye! Here live the gods!" and again a flood tide of enthusiasm arose. The gods who called this time were not the gods of world revolution. Yet they promised unity and fraternity among the workers, peace among the peoples, and the destruction of Fascist barbarism.

The masses in Western Europe responded to Stalin and Dimitrov in 1935 as they had to Lenin and Zinoviev in the spring of 1920.

LE FILS DU PEUPLE

Dimitrov's slogans had an immediate success in France. The Communist Party there grew with the speed of an avalanche. Within a few months the membership increased from forty to two hundred thousand. The now united reformist and Communist trade unions could not register the new members who applied for admission as fast as they enrolled. In place of twelve Communist deputies, seventy were elected to the French Parliament in the May elections of 1936.

After these elections, the government had to resign. But even before the first Popular Front government under the leadership of Léon Blum had been formed, the avalanche threatened to burst the dams of all the old political institutions.

In the first days of May, the workers in various factories in Paris had struck for higher wages. The strike soon spread throughout Paris and large sections of the French provinces. No one from the outside had urged the workers to strike—not the Socialists nor the Communists nor the trade unions. The strike had erupted like a volcano.

It was no normal general strike. The workers did not leave their places of employment but remained in the shops and hoisted red flags on the factory buildings.

The bourgeois world was horrified: Was this a dress rehearsal for the Bolshevik revolution, or was it perhaps the revolution itself? The gendarmes usually employed in the case of mass strikes remained in their barracks. At factory gates traffic police were posted with orders to disperse all street gatherings.

In the factories the workers had become the masters. They took charge of the managerial offices and the storerooms, seeing to it that the machinery was kept in good order.

The yards looked like country fairs. Meals were cooked in great open pots. Meetings were held, card games played. People laughed, danced, and made merry.

The Communists were as surprised at the vehemence of this movement as were the Socialists. Like all Communist parties they had called for general strikes hundreds of times without response from the workers. Now there was a general strike, the pre-condition for a revolution, such as many of them had dreamed of for years. But the Popular Front policy had made the old Bolshevik conception of civil war and revolution inapplicable. For the first time during a strike, Communist leaders took over the mission of angels of peace.

In the interim there were nervous negotiations in Parliament to bring the strike to an end. For years France had belonged to the backward countries of Europe in matters of social legislation. Now Parliament voted unanimously the most generous social legislation that France had ever enjoyed. Most important, it provided for a paid two weeks vacation for every French worker. A considerable increase in wage scales accompanied these social reforms.

But certain groups wanted more. It was clearly discernible that below the surface of the strike lurked dangerous possibilities.

At this point the general secretary of the Communist Party, Maurice Thorez, took a hand. When Parliament had passed its measures of social reform, he had declared: "It is necessary to know how to bring a strike to an end!" Moscow did not like to see mass strikes in a country with which it hoped to conclude a military alliance.

The workers returned home, the red flags came down from the factory buildings, and in July the first paid vacations were enjoyed. Hundreds of thousands for the first time in their lives trooped down to the sunny south of France. The Riviera swarmed with Parisian workers. The Popular Front had given the masses their small place in the sun.

Bastille Day, July 14th, was celebrated as never before. Rarely had the Carmagnole been sung with such abandon and victorious expectation. On the square where one hundred and fifty years before the Bastille had been stormed, Daladier, leader of the French Radical Socialists, Léon Blum, and Thorez, arm in arm, swore undying allegiance to the Republic and its people. Skeptical spectators wondered whether the tired Third Republic would really be able to recover the lost power of her youth.

"A HAPPY FRANCE, FREE AND STRONG . . . . ."

Of this, Maurice Thorez had no doubts. He was full of the zest of life and overflowing with optimism. His fresh and rosy cheeks, and blue eyes bespoke neither troubles nor doubts. There was courage and power in this big blond man from the North of France. The masses had more confidence in Thorez than in any previous Communist leader.

They were accustomed to being led by intellectuals, attorneys, and professors. The great Jean Jaurès had been a university professor, Léon Blum was a lawyer. The Communist leaders too had for the most part been intellectuals.

For the first time a real worker, *le fils du peuple* as Thorez called himself, became a leader of the Communist Party. Thorez did not have to acquaint himself with the miseries of the working classes from books. He knew them from his own experience. As a thirteen-year-old this miner's boy had gone into the mines. Often when unemployed he would work by the day on farms. In 1919 he joined the Communist Party, and five years later he became a member of its Central Committee. He belonged to the "gold" of the working class discovered by Zinoviev when he forced the first generation of Communist leaders to resign to serve him as scapegoats.

Thorez was modest, a good speaker, and a good organizer. He stayed in the background of the Central Committee until 1934. Then Dimitrov, after the break with Doriot, called him to become general secretary of the party. Dimitrov showed the same good sense in selecting the leaders for the reorganized Communist parties as had Stalin in making him, Dimitrov, general secretary of the Comintern.

The masses who were now pouring into the French Communist Party, as well as those even more numerous who were in sympathy with its political aims, had little or no Socialist and revolutionary tradition. In their enthusiasm they did not expect a quick trip into Utopia, but a steadfast defense of their living standards and a merciless struggle against their deadly enemy, Fascism.

The former miner, Thorez, who led the Communist Party, together with the former baker Duclos and the former mechanic Gitton, understood these masses better than all the revolutionary dialecticians who, in other years, had been the Parisian lieutenants of the Moscow High Command. They themselves were free of all inhibitions of a Marxist or revolutionary nature. Nor were they afraid of difficulties with Moscow when issuing slogans that would have made the most backward social reformer blush with shame.

They were shrewd and knew how to flatter the masses. Thorez did not lower his eyes when he explained at a mass meeting that he expected every loyal party Communist to accompany his wife to the movies at least once a week. He made an instantaneous hit with the women. When the *midinettes,* the dressmakers of Paris, went out on strike and marched down the boulevards demonstrating, gallant and charming Maurice joined them immediately. The hearts of the ladies of Paris were his.

The proletarian leaders of the Communists led all other parties in affirming the joys and pleasures of life. For them as for the masses in Russia, the "happy Socialist life" had begun. Around this Central Committee gathered a circle of young workers who overnight had changed from shop counsels into deputies, and whose incomes had therefore doubled and trebled. "To live and let live" had become the principle of the Communist Party in France.

The Comintern had become generous and considerate with its devoted adherents. The material well-being that spread among the functionaries of the French party did not arouse any objections as would have been the case in the past. At least these people did not attempt to enrich themselves. They did not participate in the usual parliamentary corruption that had permitted Pierre Laval, for instance, to rise within a few years from a poor provincial attorney to a millionaire. These party functionaries and deputies merely deported themselves like well-to-do bourgeois with well-secured incomes. They all had small savings accounts. They moved from cramped furnished rooms into comfortable residences. They began to acquire a taste for the best French cuisine.

It was well known in French party circles that several of their leaders were maintaining mistresses as well as wives. But nobody minded. In this respect France knew no class morals.

Around the Communist leadership grew up a coterie of functionaries employed by the municipalities and provincial administrations. France was always ruled according to the principle that one good turn deserves another. The Communist functionaries in the provinces were apt disciples of their masters in Paris. They stayed aloof from the corruption and scandals of the French provinces. But they shared the hundred little advantages that every municipal or provincial deputy in France enjoyed: a cheap apartment in a new municipal building, coal at the low municipal cost price, municipal farms at low rentals, free passes on railroads and bus lines, and free room and board in municipal hospitals and sanatoriums.

These were the agreeable consequences of Popular Front policy and were amply provided.

The Communist Party had become a profitable business enterprise. The party paper, L'Humanité, increased its circulation to half a million and became one of the biggest dailies in France. A huge net of circulation and advertising agencies employing hundreds of people spread out. The bank accounts of the party and those of the trade unions dominated largely by the French Communists expanded rapidly.

Big plans were drawn up for cooperatives and building associations. The French Communists showed all signs of developing into a party similar in its economic structure to that of the German Social Democracy or the British Labor Party.

The masses supporting the French Communists had acquired not only higher wages and paid vacations but also an increased sense of power. They had seen bourgeois France tremble for an entire week— an experience not quickly to be forgotten.

To the government and the upper class they had become less calculable than ever. To Moscow and its French lieutenants they did not represent a problem because these masses had full confidence in those who had led them from one success to another. They believed in Thorez' slogan of a "strong, free, and happy France."

SPANISH INTERLUDE

The Spanish Civil War had not been anticipated or included in Dimitrov's Popular Front policy. His aim was the creation of a peaceable popular movement and the constitution of an English-French-Russian block against Germany. The outbreak of the Spanish Civil War had been highly unwelcome in Moscow, for it had intensified Chamberlain's policy of appeasement, and at the same time had sharpened the conflict in France between the friends and enemies of the policy of collective security.

Stalin had been sure that the Spanish war could last only a few weeks. He did not concede the Republican side a real chance. Stalin's thinking, like that of other men, moves in terms of his own past experience. Bolshevism had always emphasized the overwhelming role of organization in history, and according to one of the chief Bolshevik tenets, a Socialist revolution as well as the civil war that leads up to it is impossible without the prior existence of an organized and powerful revolutionary party.

Up to 1935 the Communist Party of Spain had been an insignificant group. Not even during the first years of the revolution in Russia had there been any real life in the small Communist groupings in

267

Spain. Consequently Stalin inferred that Franco's opponents in the civil war had practically no chance of success.

The Russian papers were ordered to place news about the Spanish civil war on the back page in the column headed "News From Abroad." The Russian diplomatic representatives in Paris and London were given strict orders to hold themselves aloof.

Dimitrov was aware that such aloofness meant risking the newly won confidence of the working masses in Europe. But as general secretary of the Communist International he knew how to deport himself according to the rules of discipline.

The Communist Party press had just published various articles explaining in discreet and diplomatic language why the present policy was in accord with the real interests of the Spanish revolution and of the struggle against Fascism when Stalin suddenly changed his mind.

After two months it had become evident that the civil war would be an extended one. The rebellions of the army in Madrid and Barcelona had been put down. Hitler and Mussolini were supporting Franco in full public view. Continuation of the initial Spanish policy would necessarily shake the confidence of the masses in Europe and turn the idea of collective security against the aggressor nation into a meaningless gesture.

Stalin therefore made the cause of the Spanish Republic the "cause of progressive humanity."

On the Rue Lafayette in Paris, where the French Communist headquarters were now located in a luxurious modern building, the Central Committee was faced with a curious dilemma. Léon Blum, the French premier, was very much in favor of equipping some Communists with ministerial powers. Thorez, and particularly the ambitious Duclos, evidenced a great longing to occupy ministerial posts. The masses of their supporters, however, were in violent opposition to the Spanish nonintervention policy of the French government. Another obstacle also intervened between the desire of Blum and the longings of the Communist leaders. It was the harsh condition laid down by Stalin to any entry of the popular Communist leaders into the ranks of the French government: No Communist

268

participation in the French government without an expansion of the French-Russian pact into a full military alliance.

However, Blum was closely tied to the policies of the British government as well as to the French General Staff who still thought in terms of a war of intervention against Russia. Laval had adorned the French-Russian pact with so many provisions open to various interpretations that every French Foreign Minister could do with it what he pleased. Blum's everlasting hesitations robbed the pact of all value for the Russians.

As a consequence of Blum's policy, the French Communists developed into a party simultaneously supporting and opposing the government. In Parliament they voted the Popular Front government of Blum into existence. Outside of Parliament they made its functioning difficult by opposing its nonintervention policy in Spain.

Between the directions from Moscow, the convulsions of the French Popular Front government and the storms passing through the masses of France, the French Communist leaders learned all the tricks in the game of high politics.

When a deputation of German refugees congratulated Jacques Duclos on the success of the Popular Front policy, the latter replied: "We will avenge you against Hitler by learning his tricks."

Actually they were learning Hitler's tricks. Just as the latter had risen to power by promising Socialism to the workers, security of property to the capitalists, maintenance of its privileges to the big landed estates, and reforms at the cost of these privileges to the peasants, so the French Communists now promised to all sections of France whatever their hearts desired. Only to the enemies of the Soviet Union they promised death and destruction.

Hostility to the open foes and the wavering friends of the Soviet Union became the only effective principle for the French Communists. All other traditional principles of Communist or Socialist policy were interpreted into nonexistence.

Maurice Thorez, for instance, disposed of the anticlerical principles without hesitation or inhibition when he proclaimed the policy of the "main tendue." The struggle against the influence of the Catholic Church had been a tradition of the French labor movement and an inheritance that the French Communists had taken over. Thorez explained in *L'Humanité* that the Communists, as followers of the materialist interpretation of history, did not believe in the Biblical stories of creation, but that this did not prevent their working harmoniously with ministers of the faith. He referred to the papal encyclical *Quadragesimo Anno*. Had not the Pope expressed there the same opinion about monopolies as did the Communists? The encyclical *De Rerum Novarum,* according to Thorez, had condemned human misery and poverty in terms similar to those of the Communist Manifesto of Karl Marx. "Unite, the Pope wants you to" became a Communist slogan.

The real objective of the Communist leader had been to win over French Catholics for a military alliance with Russia. For this purpose he had sacrificed another of the traditional principles of French Communism and of the French labor movement.

Dimitrov's Trojan horse strategy, aimed at the Fascist countries, had its real success in the democracies. Particularly in France the strength and logic of Soviet foreign policy, the insufficiency of French statesmanship, the successes of the Popular Front, the delusions and hopes of the masses, the metamorphosis of the Communist leaders, turned the Communist Party into a real Trojan cavalry "in the heart of the enemy."

Dimitrov had really expected to push his Trojan horse into both Germany and Italy. But in these countries his Trojan horse became a trap for the underground organizations of the Communists. Their attempts to penetrate into the Fascist mass organizations were frustrated, while Hitler and Mussolini were piling up success upon success. The underground Italian and German Communists paid for the policy of the Trojan horse with the loss of their last underground cadres.

The German and Italian Communists developed into the Don Quixotes of the Front Populaire. Their ambition to emulate the great French party knew no bounds. Their central committees in exile abroad issued proclamations for unity and peace at home. In the manifesto of the Italian party it said: "We are well aware that there are many Fascists who have not forgotten their demands of 1919: general suffrage, creation of a Senate, a secure minimum income, nationalization of the armament industries, progressive taxa-

270

tion of wealth, confiscation of church property and of war profits. We are telling these Fascists that we are ready to fight side by side with them in order to realize the demands of this program. The entire Italian nation must be mobilized for these demands. Long live the reconciliation and the fraternization with all Fascists who are willing to stand up for their own program!"

With the success of the Popular Front policies in the democracies and the failure of the Trojan horse strategy in the Fascist countries, the Comintern organizations had not only become superfluous but even a burden on Soviet foreign policy. The dissolution of the Comintern might have taken place in 1938 had Munich not caused Stalin to call it back on the stage of history for a short farewell performance.

CHAPTER XX

Fellow Travellers, French Style

FRENCH HONEYMOON

THE POPULAR FRONT INVADED THE INTELLECTUAL WORLD AND emerged there as a new institution: the fellow travellers.

Beyond the Rhine the Teutonic hordes were again singing their barbaric battle-hymns and a triumphant radio was blaring into the ears of everybody in France who wished to listen that the ideas of the French Revolution—Liberty, Equality, Fraternity—were senile beliefs of a century long dead. The Fuehrer had cleansed the German nation of the last remnants of these beliefs. The chains that had tied the Germans to the humanism of the West had been broken by his action. Today Germany is ours—tomorrow the world! threatened the Brown Battalions from beyond the Rhine.

Horrified and trembling, French intellectuals were scanning the horizon for protection against the Teutonic plague. Although the Maginot Line appeared secure and invincible and France was still the strongest military power in Europe, they were pervaded by a sense of weakness and insecurity. Even steel walls many feet in depth and forests of bayonets were not a safe dam against the tide of ideas that rolled in from the Rhine.

Little comfort or strength could be derived from London. Cool detachment towards the rising French restlessness marked the attitude of the Allies on the other side of the Channel. The might of the British crown still sheltered the ideals of humanism, but only on the banks of the Thames.

The Russians, however, understood the unhappy restlessness on the Seine. They had just sacrificed hundreds of thousands of human lives to emancipate their country from its industrial backwardness. Now they presented to the outside world the fruits of their labor and their sufferings: "Man finally liberated by Socialism."

All seekers after new ideals might admire the magic works of the Five Year Plan—health centers built by the country for its Socialist youth, innumerable creches and children's homes where happy and healthy youngsters were being raised, a huge network of up-to-date scientific laboratories, heroes winging their way across the North Pole, great musicians, great writers!

Moscow said to Europe: Here I stand, the final accomplishment of human happiness. The new Russian constitution promises full Socialist democracy, the ultimate realization of France's revolutionary goals: Liberty, Equality, Fraternity. The literary salons of Paris recognized the dawning glory of the new Russian humanism on the eastern horizon. A new faith was born.

The French were aware that the Moscow paradise was more a promise for the future than a present accomplishment. But they were in need of a promise to protect them from the threats of the Brown barbarism. They saw themselves in such complete isolation and their humanistic ideals so defenseless that even the promise of a new idea with the strength to instill confidence was welcome. All Europe's intelligentsia shared this feeling of insulation and loneliness with the French—the Germans who had been chased out of their country by Hitler as well as the others who saw the philosophy of race and revenge as a terrible threat to the existence of their own small nations.

The new creed of fellow travellership became the Maginot Line of the Radical French intelligentsia. The French intellectuals choosing the Communism of the new Russia as a protection against the rising wave of Fascism, as a shelter against the loneliness that had engulfed their ideals of humanism, were never further from real Communism. But to "fellow travel" gave their lives a sense of optimism and joy necessary to overcome the despair that was threatening them from beyond the Rhine. It was the start of a honeymoon, and, as a honeymoon should, it overflowed with optimism and joy. It promised a long and happy marriage. The French fellow travellers were marrying their illusions about Communism sent to them in the bridal dress of Soviet propaganda from Moscow.

Their Russian marital partners entered this French marriage without illusion. They had just dumped overboard the heritage of the French Revolution and the ideals of Lenin's October Revolution. They were neither fearful nor obsessed with a feeling of loneliness.

They came as the representatives of a self-seeking state that had out-grown the ideals of its origin. To play with the ideas of the West was a mere technique for this new state. The fact that some of Russia's literary elite still cherished a secret longing for the ideals of the French Revolution only made the affair more confusing to the French.

"I am a Frenchman and an internationalist," exclaimed André Gide, one of the greatest among the great French writers. "I am an individualist and a Communist at the same time."

"Very good indeed," a many-voiced choir from the Soviet Union responded. "The essential feature of Communism is its concern with man. Stalin is most deeply concerned with the Socialist development of the individual. Your internationalism is genuine, for France is a revolutionary nation. We Bolsheviki are the inheritors of your glorious Jacobin tradition."

"Nothing is further from the truth than the contention that the Soviet Union levels down and standardizes the individual," continued André Gide.

"Yes, you are right," replied Johannes R. Becher, a German poet at the court of Stalin. "Above all strikes and martyrs' cells, above all the storms of insurrection and the struggles of the Red Army, hovers the picture of man, the dream picture of emancipated man."

The French fellow travellers were essentially literary men. They became a real power, for in the France before 1939 literature was still an essential ingredient of civil society.

The International Writers' Congress that assembled in Paris in July, 1935, was an event of significance far beyond the literary—a beautiful orchestration of the tunes sung by the Russian diplomacy in Geneva, a masterpiece of organization of the International of intellectual and literary fellow travellers. The most illustrious names of world literature were present.

Some disagreeable incidents occurred at the Congress. A group of delegates called for the release of the French-Russian writer, Victor Serge, who because of Trotskyite inclinations had been sent to a Siberian concentration camp. They wanted the Congress to deliver a practical demonstration of its willingness to serve the ideals of humanism.

André Gide arose and declared: "The success of the Soviet Union has more importance for us than anything else. It should be understood in this case that our confidence is the best proof of our love." The Russians took notice. The honeymoon was not yet over. They did not disappoint André Gide: Victor Serge was released. The dark shadows of the Siberian concentration camps had defaced the sunny picture of the Soviet Union that the new humanist Communists had painted for themselves. Now they were lifted.

The literary friends of the Soviet Union of 1935 were the ideal type of fellow traveller. As a dowry they brought their own national brands of ideology. They presented their own illusions about Communism as a philosophy, encompassing a militant rebirth of the humanism of the Revolution supported by "the brotherly alliance with the country where fraternity has been made the foundation of the state."

The French fellow travellers possessed real faith in their mission. For this reason their propaganda for the Soviet Republic was often more effective than even that of Moscow. And Moscow, sensing this, was grateful. It allowed them to pose as Communists with equal birthright, yet did not demand of them acceptance of the essential feature of Communism: the social revolution. Moscow asked of its fellow travellers neither sacrifices nor party discipline. It pacified their torn humanistic conscience and in return demanded only recognition of Stalin as the savior of traditional humanism. The fellow traveller, to save himself, had merely to become a fellow savior of the Soviet Union. Salvation of the other sections of humanity could then be achieved in the realms of literature.

Criticism of capitalist society without cost and without risk became in turn a blind adoration of the light from the East. Moscow declared the French writers to be the enlightenment of the twentieth century. Thus fellow travellership raised French literature to a new dignity. Without Voltaire, Robespierre would have been but a loquacious agitator. The struggle for a new life, for a new order of life, consists in the protest against convention, against the rottenness of bourgeois society, declared the Congress of the literary humanists. The fellow travellers delivered the protest; the Russians the Socialist illusion without which the protest would have been impossible.

The Russians had entered the alliance for a definite purpose. To

275

the French fellow travellers it became a theory of life. The great French writer, Romain Rolland, wrote a pamphlet against the slanderers of the Soviet Republic. In it he attacked the individualists who did not wish to see happiness imposed on men against their will. In a world held in dark and sinister ignorance by a small minority of exploiters, the millions of suffering men and women were robbed of the strength and the vision to tread the road to their own happiness. In the Soviet Union, he contended, such a question as that raised by the individualists who wished to see everybody take his own individual happiness to his own heart in his own way, would be met only with scorn.

"People must be led to their own happiness against their own will. This is a difficult task. At all times the simple minds will bitterly oppose those who are attempting to save them."

In addition to Romain Rolland, many other literary descendants of the French Revolution, struggling for the maintenance of their humanistic inheritance and traditions, finally found themselves on exactly the opposite side of the philosophic barricade against which they had been fighting their entire lives.

"People must be led to their own happiness against their own wills." Enlightenment comes from above. To achieve salvation man becomes the slave of his own enlighteners.

To transform the philosophic heritage of the French Revolution into its very opposite was not just a matter of kowtowing before the Kremlin, which prescribes as a condition of Socialist victory the suffocation of all spontaneous democratic inclinations in the masses of men. It meant neither more nor less than, in the end, the *cul-de-sac* of fellow travellership, an ideological suicide or an escape.

THE ADVENTURES OF ANDRÉ GIDE

One year after the World Peace Congress arranged by the Comintern and celebrated by its fellow travellers, André Gide arrived in the Soviet Union and bowed his head in grief at the bier of Maxim Gorki. There he shared their sorrow with the hundreds of thousands of men and women who walked past the dead poet with tears in their eyes.

At the grave of Gorki, Gide spoke with high admiration of the

276

Soviet Republic which had emancipated not only man but the creative artist as well. In his words was nothing to indicate that his ideas, in their meeting with Russian reality on the very day of his arrival in Leningrad, had suffered a first great shock.

In response to a request by the writers of Leningrad who had asked him to formulate the articles of his artistic faith, he had drafted the following sentences: "At the very moment when the revolution triumphs, and installs and establishes itself, art courts a terrible danger, a danger that is nearly as great as that presented by the worst Fascist oppression. It is the danger of orthodoxy. Art that submits to orthodoxy, be it even the most healthy of doctrines, is lost. It goes to sleep in conforming. What the triumphant revolution can and ought to offer to the artist is above all freedom. Without that, art loses significance and value."

His Russian friends had read the draft in an embarrassed silence. They had urged him not to deliver it to the public. Gide had given in.

In Leningrad he was hailed as had been the heroes of the revolution in the early years, with red flags, delegations from the factories and universities, groups of jubilant enthusiastic youth. The heart of the great humanist from the West beat in tune with the heart of the great Russian people.

In his speech in Moscow the doubts of his undelivered address seemed to have vanished, the disquieting problems to have been solved: "Today in the Soviet Union for the first time the problem is posed in a very different way. In becoming a revolutionary the writer ceases to be an oppositionist. On the contrary, he responds to the will of the great majority of the entire people and, what is most admirable, to that of its leaders. In this way the problem vanishes; or better, is changed so completely that the mind, in facing it, is at first disconcerted."

The Russians, masters at organizing humanistic congresses abroad, committed fatal blunders in their treatment of foreigners at home. They completely misjudged André Gide, believing that an exhibition of luxury and comfort equalling and surpassing that to which he was accustomed in France would dissolve the last doubts that might linger in the mind of the humanist from the West. They provided the finest

277

limousines, special de luxe trains with private cars, elaborate banquets, everything that had caused André Gide to doubt and despise the civilization of the West.

This was not a foolish blunder committed accidentally by his Russian guides. It was a spontaneous if unconscious expression of their own order of values by the new Russian elite whom Gide had taken for pioneers of humanism. They were offering him on his journey of discovery the very things they themselves longed for. They were measuring him by their own standards.

Gide overflowed with anger and bitterness: "And now look what is happening in the USSR: The new bourgeoisie that is developing has all the faults of our own. Immediately after having itself risen out of poverty it despises the poor. It is intent on all the comforts that it was so long deprived of, and it knows well how to behave to acquire and maintain them. 'Are these really the people who made the revolution?' No, these are the ones who have profited by it . . . . Well they may be registered members of the Party. But they have nothing Communist in their hearts!"

André Gide's disappointment after his first meeting with Russian reality and his bitterness against the guides of his Russian itinerary only intensified his desire to unriddle the Russian mystery and to arrive at the whole truth in regard to the Soviet experiment. The eyes of the humanist from the West were not focused on the grandiose industrial construction schemes and works of the Five Year Plan, on the gigantic new industrial enterprises, the waterworks, the electrical plants, the dams, that Soviet hospitality was inviting him to inspect. His eyes were not even focused on the beauty of nature in Russia and the pastoral attractions of the Russian countryside. They were trying to fathom man in Russia, whom he had believed liberated and emancipated.

But in vain did he seek the creative spirit that would merge Marxist philosophy with the French humanist enlightenment of the eighteenth century. Instead he found a complete depersonalization and a rigid standardization of thought, the physical and mental behavior of slaves: "Spirit has lost the consciousness of its own slavery."

Poor Gide! Had he arrived in the Soviet Republic fifteen years earlier, he would not have found the newly erected plants nor the huge industrial enterprises, but the creative critical spirit that he was seeking. In its youth the revolution was overflowing with the spirit of critical Jacobinism and of rebellion against all orthodoxies.

But fifteen years earlier the Bolshevik revolution was not building bridges for despairing Western humanists nor was it seeking support in the illusions of its fellow travellers. The Bolshevist Jacobins had been as proud as their French predecessors. They asked the world squarely to face their reality: *Hic Rhodos, hic salta!* Here is the revolution, here let you dance!

When Gide discovered the Russian revolution it was already in its death agonies. He had mistaken a corpse in the undertaker's parlor for living life.

The disillusioning experiences during his travels through Russia also had their comical side. In Paris he had frequently read Lenin's speeches to Russian youth: "If we do not acquire all the cultural heritage of the bourgeois period we will be lost." Yet now in his own meetings with Russian youth he found a primitive complex of superiority towards everything non-Russian. "Foreign countries have nothing to teach us." Children smiled incredulously when Gide told them there was a subway in Paris. Adults were incredulous at Gide's statement that children were not beaten in French schools. Nor was he believed when he told them that in Paris films of the Russian revolution had been successful. When he voiced a cautious doubt about whether Russians were well-informed about foreign countries, a young naval officer had exclaimed: "There is not sufficient paper in the world to report everything new and beautiful within the Soviet Union!"

Gide saw that the picture of the Western world which had arisen behind the Chinese wall of Stalin's dictatorship in the mind of Russia had become a new factor in its life. Russian youth no longer was dreaming about the world revolution. It was fanatically patriotic.

Gide's journey of exploration into the Soviet Union represented disastrous failure for those who had undertaken the responsibility of guiding the fellow travellers. Gide did not succumb as did some others to the temptations of money. On the contrary he exposed the financial weaknesses of other fellow travellers who permitted their public statements about the Soviet Union to be influenced by the literary fees and privileges that Moscow was offering to its knights errant.

This exposure changed Gide into a "counter-revolutionary." In Russia his name was no longer mentioned. In France, however, Communists and fellow travellers covered his name with shame and calumny. André Gide gave up his Russian fees and his Eastern illusions. He retired into the dream world of his poetic humanism.

Others more chained to their ideals and illusions than Gide continued to cling to their dream of the true Socialist life in the lands of the Soviet. The futility and emptiness of the Western world, the horror arising from the dust of the collapse in Germany, created the demand for a new philosophy of life, be it a mere ersatz ideology.

In becoming a fellow traveller one says goodbye to common sense, one must look down upon logic and eliminate all genuine thinking within oneself. But in exchange one receives something bordering on the miraculous. One can live in opposition to the world and its terrors without incurring the risks of opposition. In a world in collapse, engaged in reappraising all its values, one can go to sleep in the bed of opposition dreaming oneself to be a hero. One becomes an emissary of the Socialist empire in the clouds. One can carry the inflammatory power of the revolution in one's pocket like a box of matches. One can save the world and be saved oneself. One can go to sleep in peace in a world at war with itself.

CHAPTER XXI

Death Without End

LULL BEFORE THE STORM

WITHIN THE SOVIET UNION THE COMMUNIST INTERNATIONAL went down to final destruction in the convulsions of the great trials of Zinoviev, Radek, and Bukharin, its leaders from Lenin's days. In the raging storms of the general purge thousands who once had been the faithful of the world revolution perished, and hundreds of thousands lost their liberty.

The year that preceded this tempest was a quiet one. Many members of the former opposition had been permitted to return from their places of exile to Moscow. There was talk that Kirov, one of Stalin's closest friends and general secretary of the party organization in Leningrad, was advocating an open reconciliation between Stalin and the former opposition. The mission abroad that Stalin entrusted to Bukharin in the fall of 1934 confirmed these rumors.

When Bukharin arrived in Paris he told his friends that all differences with Stalin had been settled. In his last personal interview Stalin had given him full discretion for his foreign mission and had expressed a feeling of personal friendship for him and a hope that a real reconciliation with the former opposition would be accomplished.

After his removal from the Presidency of the Comintern in 1928 and from the Politbureau of the Russian party, Bukharin had ceased to participate actively in politics. His only political activity was his work as a member of the committee for the technological reconstruction of the country. In the early thirties he had become chief editor of *Izvestia,* the official government daily. But even this function did not prevent him from concentrating all his energies on his scientific work. This work had always been closest to his heart. The theoretical problems of Marxism had absorbed his thought since his early student days. In 1915 while the First World War was raging, he had begun to work out a theoretical system of his own, an application of Marxism to the economic and political structure of world capitalism as it was developing in the twentieth century.

Even in those years of political retirement he had never lost the affection and admiration of everybody in Moscow. People flocked to the few lectures he gave, though his subjects were theoretic and highly abstract.

In Paris Bukharin won many friends among France's intellectual leaders. University professors of radical leanings to whom he explained Soviet problems and with whom he discussed theoretical problems in the fields of physics and mathematics were enchanted with him. French writers to whom he suggested calling a writers' congress were impressed by his knowledge in the field of literature and art.

But even in intimate conversations with political friends of former times, he always maintained a cautious reserve. He had made his political peace with Stalin, and he would not permit himself to do or say anything that might disturb it. Only once did Bukharin break through this reserve. An old friend was describing the struggles of the defeated German Communists, hopeless and despairing, and accused Stalin of the disaster that had befallen the revolutionary movement in Germany.

"Some fine day he will hang us all," Bukharin sighed, his face reflecting the despondency of his words. He seemed to sense the gathering storm clouds. The peace that he had achieved with Stalin was insecure and might be shattered any day.

Sad and resigned, he rejected all suggestions to stay in France where he would enjoy freedom to continue his scientific work. That would be desertion, he said, but no way out. "You can free yourself from force and coercion but not from yourself. The generation that has made the revolution in Russia has to go its road to the end, whatever that end may be."

One day in December, 1934, Bukharin received a wire from Moscow. Kirov had been murdered. Stalin requested Bukharin's immediate return.

Bukharin stood aghast as he read. The following day he took the train back to Moscow.

ZINOVIEV'S END

A few days after Kirov's murder, Zinoviev, who had been living in a cottage on the outskirts of Moscow under continuous strict GPU surveillance, was arrested. The curtain had risen on the first act in the tragedy of the old leaders of the Comintern.

Stalin had received the news of the murder of his intimate friend Kirov with the quiet reserve that rarely deserts him, but Zinoviev had been seized with panic. His nerves were already worn thin, his hands trembled, and at the least excitement has face would become contorted.

Kirov had been killed by Nikolayev, the husband of his personal secretary. Zinoviev had never heard of the man. The few friends who had remained loyal to him all this time were equally unaware of Nikolayev's existence.

It was not in Zinoviev's nature to use terroristic means, even in the struggle against Stalin. The last serious attempt on the part of Zinoviev to fight Stalin had been his bloc with Trotsky in 1926 after his own fall as president of the Communist International. Since then he had indulged only in empty threats which always ended quickly in submission.

But he realized immediately the personal danger in which this assassination might involve him. He saw that Stalin might pin the responsibility on him, for he had once been the uncrowned king of Leningrad. When he had joined forces with the opposition against Stalin, Leningrad with its entire pivotal party organization had followed him. Now Stalin might seize this chance to wipe out the remnants of his influence in Leningrad.

Zinoviev, therefore, wrote a eulogy of Kirov with the idea of protecting himself. At a later date his accusers claimed he had only tried to cover up his traces.

His efforts were in vain. Arrested with thousands of others from Leningrad, he was sent to the jail of Verkhne Uralsk in Siberia. Later he was brought back to Moscow for a secret trial. At this trial he admitted only that there might possibly have been an indirect connection between his opposition and the crime. He was sentenced to five years' imprisonment and sent back to Verkhne Uralsk.

"The trial in Moscow was not so bad!" he shouted to a comrade through the bars of his cell. He was not dissatisfied with his sentence to five years in prison for a crime with which he had as little to do as the judges.

In his jail Zinoviev led the life of a common prisoner, delivered up like everyone else to the chicaneries of a harsh prison administration. In the spring of 1936 he again was taken from Verkhne Uralsk to the GPU prison on the Lyubyanka in Moscow. This time the prison gates closed on a man at the end of his physical and moral powers of resistance.

In August of that year he was subjected to a second trial for the murder of Kirov, and to this accusation was added the charge of having subsequently attempted to murder Stalin and many others as well. This trial rolled on to its grim end. The personal tragedy of Zinoviev was woven on the same loom as the general tragedy of the Comintern.

There was only one weapon that Zinoviev might have used to defeat the rising power of Stalinism after Lenin's death. An appeal to the world revolutionary mission of the Soviet Union might have rallied around him all those forces and groups hostile to the incipient nationalist developments in Russia. For Zinoviev as first president of the Comintern symbolized the internationalist message of Lenin's days. However, he had blunted this weapon in the vast and intricate entanglements of his inner party maneuvers against Stalin.

When Lenin died, Zinoviev had joined forces with Stalin against Trotsky, believing that he would gather to himself the power that Lenin had commanded but forgetting the Comintern during those first years of struggle within the Russian party. After losing out there, he found he had also lost his control of the Comintern and could no longer use the International as a rallying point against his former associate Stalin, who had now become his bitter opponent. In 1926 during his bloc with Trotsky against Stalin, he had admitted freely and cynically that his ideological and political struggles against Trotsky in 1924-1925 had been only a screen for the conspiracy of power that he and Stalin together had been plotting. Fundamentally, he had used the same weapons in his battle against Trotsky as Stalin had been employing since then for his own destruction.

284

In 1930 foreign friends had suggested that he emigrate from Russia and carry on the fight against Stalin from abroad. Like Bukharin, he had rejected the suggestion, thus signing his own death warrant.

Finally there remained in his hands only a few weapons from the attic of the revolutionary past: to conspire, to mislead the enemy, and to conduct a whispering campaign. But in the use of these weapons Stalin was his superior. To employ them against Stalin could only destroy Zinoviev completely, morally as well as politically.

By 1935 Zinoviev was a defeated man, physically and spiritually. He was able neither to wage a political struggle nor to protest in an individualist fashion by suicide, as Joffe, Tomsky, Skrypnik, and other adversaries of Stalin had done. Suicide was an individualist solution rejected by Bolshevik theory as decidedly as terrorist action. Zinoviev never could transcend the fetters of an ideology that was identical with his own thinking. Perhaps, too, his lack of personal courage made him cling to the old precepts at a time when their entire foundation was weakening. The court as well as the prosecution could be sure that Zinoviev would play the role assigned him to the end. They did not have to fear that he might attempt at some point in the trial to act as a martyr of the world revolution.

Zinoviev understood world revolution and Socialism exclusively in terms of struggle for power. In 1935 Stalin was power in the Soviet Union; in Germany, Hitler. Between these two poles there was no room for him. He had been a fanatic of revolution, but revolution was impossible either within or without Russia.

His confession at the trial was a logical consequence of the last ten years of his life, of his entire psychology, of his bankruptcy. His confession to the innumerable crimes with which he was charged was an expression of utter resignation. The revolutionary past was dead and buried; there was no future for the Comintern nor for himself.

Maybe his last hysterical gesture of self-accusation: "I am a Fascist dog!" contained an ultimate protest against Stalin, against the man who in putting him to death was annulling the content and significance of his whole life.

285

"SOCIALISM IN ONE COUNTRY"

After the execution of Zinoviev, a statement was published in the Soviet press to the effect that the investigation of the circumstances surrounding the Kirov murder had absolved Bukharin of any involvement. This statement was interpreted as an indication that the trial of Zinoviev had accomplished its purpose: to give a warning to all who had ever belonged to the opposition, as well as to those who might harbor thoughts of future opposition.

A few months after the publication of this statement, the general purge began.

The trial of Radek and Piatakov in January, 1937, showed that the aim was the final destruction of all that still remained of Lenin's party.

Many explanations have been offered for the Saint Bartholomew's massacre that Stalin directed during the next two years, and there is truth in many of them.

The defeated opposition in itself did not represent a great danger in Stalin's eyes. He knew that it possessed no organization, that it was not bound together by a common ideology, and that most of its former adherents were men physically, mentally, and morally broken. He had seen to that.

Yet he was aware that a war would test all the weak points of his regime. He must have recalled vividly how the tiny insignificant Bolshevik groups during the First World War had ridden to victory on the sudden military and political collapse of the Czar's empire.

All members of the former opposition with the exception of Trotsky, who was living as an exile in Mexico, had submitted to his leadership. Yet Stalin knew that all but Karl Radek hated him with a deadly hate. Only recently he had received what seemed to him conclusive evidence of such hate. During the Zinoviev trial many hundreds of old Bolsheviki had pleaded with him to show mercy to the defendant, quoting Lenin's last will: "Do not permit blood to come between members of our party."

All great wars bring about serious social and political repercussions. Between 1936 and 1937 Stalin had become convinced that a new world war was fast approaching. Though it did not seem

286

probable that the now isolated generation of the October revolution could become a menace to his regime, yet he did not exclude the possibility. He wanted to eliminate all risk.

Further, between 1929 and 1937 the Soviet Union had undergone the greatest change in its history. Millions of young men and women, eager for political and economic activity, were pushing to the fore. This new generation needed new ideas to guide and direct it: The October Revolution, writing in bold strokes across the sky its message of the world revolutionary call of Soviet Russia, no longer had any vital significance. Stalin offered the idea of "Socialism in one country." With the October Revolution it had in common only the nationalization of industry, of the banks, and of the big landed estates.

"Socialism in one country" was Stalin's theory, not Lenin's. But it was essential to the monopolization of power in Stalin's hands that this new generation should view the figures of Lenin and Stalin as one. Only then could Stalin become the omnipotent lord of all the Russias—of souls as well as of bodies. Only when all the survivors of Lenin's time had been spiritually disgraced and physically wiped out, and when the history of the October Revolution had been rewritten, could Stalin's own person in the eyes of this new generation symbolize both the present and the past glories of the revolution. Therefore all those who symbolized the past had to vanish in shame and ignominy, for only then would the light of Stalin shine out of the past as a beacon into the future for the new generation.

Perhaps the shooting of Tukhachevsky and his generals in the summer of 1937 was part of this pattern. Perhaps there really had been plottings among them with intent to depose Stalin. There are no proofs in either direction. Probably outside of Stalin only two or three persons living know the truth. The members of the military court that heard the evidence against these generals and pronounced sentence of death soon met the same death themselves.

In 1936, during the trial of Zinoviev, there was still doubt and hesitation: Might not the extermination of the revolutionary past and its personalities arouse the masses in the West who had recently bowed to the new gods of the Comintern against Stalin and the policies that his new state was pursuing abroad? The reaction to the

287

Zinoviev trial and to the execution of the first president of the Comintern gave a conclusive answer to this question. Stalin had nothing to fear from these quarters.

RADEK PLAYS HIS LAST ROLE

During the trial of Zinoviev the candidates for the next trial were already raising their hands.

Karl Radek, in one of his articles denouncing the crimes of Zinoviev and his group, wrote: "The proletarian court will pronounce sentence on this gang of murderers they have deserved a hundred times. . . . ."

Piatakov, one of the most brilliant economists of the Soviet Union and a former follower and friend of Trotsky, was also calling for blood: "These contemptible murderers and traitors have to be destroyed without mercy!"

A few months after these denouncements both of them confessed to the same crimes, with a series of new crimes thrown in.

When the struggle broke out between Stalin and Zinoviev on the one side and Trotsky on the other, Karl Radek had joined forces with Trotsky, after some hesitation. In 1927 he had been exiled. He was the first among Trotsky's followers who broke with their leader.

In 1930 he was permitted to return to Moscow. The Comintern however, remained prohibited territory for him. Stalin made him his leading Russian propagandist for the capitalist countries. Again as in the early days of his career, he began to write article after article praising the gigantic and heroic deeds of industrial reconstruction in Russia. The industrial plants that were mushrooming forth all over the country, the millions of illiterate peasants transforming themselves overnight into skilled workers, the grand and cruel shift of a peasant country into an industrialized nation, captured his imagination.

It was natural that Stalin, pursuing his aims and never shying away from the brutal consequences they entailed, should fascinate a man like Radek who had always admired and adored the Caesars of history, those who had wielded power without limit.

Stalin in turn had taken Radek into his personal confidence. He needed somebody who could quickly inform him about foreign countries and who would spare him the reading of the tedious reports of his own Narkomindel. Radek became the chief of his personal foreign information bureau. Whenever Stalin could not sleep at night, in these years of upheaval, Radek was at his beck and call. Frequently the two could be seen walking together for hours on end in the courtyards of the Kremlin. Stalin would be listening in silence while Radek, gesticulating excitedly, overflowed with stories and news items.

After he had parted company with Trotsky and had joined Stalin, Radek had permitted his loyalty to his new chief only one moment of failure, if so slight a weakness could be called that. It was in the winter of 1931-32. The sufferings of that winter were brutal. Even the Comintern building frequently went unheated for want of coal or wood. It was known that Stalin in the discussions of the Politbureau had lost his majority several times, and that even Kalinin and Voroshilov, two of his most steadfast adherents, had refused to follow his lead.

Questions like these were being asked: What will happen if Stalin falls and what will the opposition do if its turn to wield power arrives? What will happen if Hitler takes power and, together with Japan, uses this hour of distress to attack the country? Many followers of the opposition had replied that the only possible response would be a repetition of Lenin's Brest-Litovsk policy. Radek's well-known formula from those days was again circulated: to trade space for time.

Radek had participated in some of the discussions of the opposition that winter for the simple reason that he could never resist an opportunity to participate in any discussion. In 1937, this contributed to his destruction.

From such discussions the prosecution in 1937 worked up its list of accusations. The very conversations were claimed to have been assignments by the German and Japanese general staffs. Members of the opposition were accused of having acted as German and Japanese agents, preparing to deliver the Ukraine and Vladivostok into the enemies' hands.

According to his own testimony at the trial, Radek had first held out and refused for three months to play the role of a repentant sinner, but finally accepted it and threw himself into it with full enthusiasm. It was really he and not the prosecution who conducted his own trial. He injected the proper cues. He formulated the political significance of his crimes in much more eloquent terms than the unimaginative prosecutor, Vischinsky, who lacked his oratorical and dramatic gifts.

Without ever having himself been a jurist, Radek knew the technical procedures of such show trials better than the prosecuting attorney. In 1925 he had directed such a trial by order of the Russian Central Committee. At the end of 1923 the military leader of the planned insurrection in Germany, the Russian general Gorev-Skoblevsky, had been arrested and sentenced to death. To extricate Skoblevsky the GPU had tricked three harmless German students into a pleasure trip to Soviet Russia and arrested them upon their arrival. They were charged with plotting against the lives of Soviet leaders. Some flimsy evidence was served up for the purpose of the trial which was conducted according to all the rules of Soviet criminal procedure.

The director behind the scenes, pulling the strings and making the marionettes move according to the requirements of the play, had been Radek. The three defendants were sentenced to death, and a few months later two of them were exchanged for Gorev Skoblevsky, thus accomplishing the purpose of the trial.

Now, in 1937, Radek used the experience of 1925 against himself and did so with the virtuosity of an accomplished prosecuting attorney. He made his exit from life a satire on the life story of his own aspirations.

Stalin commuted the sentence to ten years' imprisonment. Maybe this was in compensation for his having served as his own prosecutor. Since that day nothing has been heard of Radek. Rumor had it that in 1941, he was shot by a prison guard.

THE MYSTERY OF NICOLAI BUKHARIN

The trial of Nicolai Bukharin and his codefendants in 1938 was the climax of the purges that were visited upon Russia from 1936 to 1938. It was the revolutionary past of the Soviet Union that was to be buried in the avalanche of accusations that were brought against Bukharin and his codefendants.

Bukharin was charged by the prosecution with having organized an attempt against Lenin's life twenty years earlier. He and his codefendants, Rykov, Krestinsky, Rakovsky, and Yagoda, former chief of the GPU who had supplied the proof of Zinoviev's guilt, were accused of having been German and Japanese spies from the very moment of their first participation in the revolution. Everyone familiar with the course of the Russian revolution and the history of the Communist International was aghast at the long list of crimes charged against Bukharin and the others. From simple thievery and arson through first degree murder—everything was included. Even Gorki's death was laid at Bukharin's feet.

Although the inference of these charges was not drawn directly during the trials, it was evident to the vast public audience in Russia for which the trial had been staged: the world revolutionary mission of the October Revolution had been an unhappy venture for the Russian people, the work of spies who had deliberately used the revolution to weaken the Russian people.

Bukharin was not as easy to deal with as most of his codefendants nor as Zinoviev and Radek had been before him. He was in full command of his moral and intellectual faculties and did not during the entire trial lose his self-control. His health had not been seriously undermined by the twelve months he had spent in the GPU prison.

Many explanations have been given of Bukharin's defense and confession. But his tragedy needs neither mystification nor glorification. He went his way to the end in the manner he had foretold in 1934 in Paris. The essential difference between Bukharin and the other accused of the great trials consisted in the fact that his capitulation and self-humiliation were the outcome of a theoretical conviction developed over many years. His own theory called for him to take his place at the side of Stalin whom he hated bitterly. In the contradiction between his theoretical and moral-emotional self lies the mystery of his behavior and conduct during the trial.

His strategy through the trial consisted in this: he admitted having opposed Stalin in the past. He accepted the terminology of the prosecution that identified such opposition with "counter-revolution" and "terrorism." He accepted political responsibility for all the crimes laid at the doorstep of the opposition. But he denied categorically any personal participation. He did not grant the slightest concession to the prosecution in their accusations of plotting the death of Lenin, taking part in the murder of Gorki, spying for Germany or Japan, or participating personally in the alleged terrorist acts of the opposition. The witnesses of the prosecuting attorney who attempted to prove such participation he denounced as agents provocateurs.

In his speeches before the court Bukharin employed the so-called "slave language." The expression had been coined by Lenin during the reactionary period following the revolution of 1905. Bolshevist propaganda at that time was conducted in two different ways: there were publications printed for underground circulation in which the Bolshevist position was expressed in clear and unmistakable language; there were also publications legally permitted to the Bolshevists, that expressed their position in veiled fashion in academic and scientific terms. These Lenin called the "slave language." Bukharin used this language during his trial, particularly in his summing-up speech in which he attempted to explain the reasons for his conduct to all those who knew and could decipher the Bolshevist slave language.

For three months Bukharin had refused to become a party to the trial. In his concluding words he said: "Then I began to testify. Why? Because while in prison I had made a revaluation of my entire past. And when I asked myself: If you must die, what are you dying for? an absolutely black vacuity suddenly rose before me with startling vividness. There was nothing to die for if one wanted to die unrepentant! . . . ."

"There was nothing to die for." These were the words of a man who had fought in 1918 to carry the Russian revolution in one quick leap to the borders of the Rhine, who after Lenin's death had become the last great Communist theoretician and who had drafted the program of the Communist International.

"An absolutely black vacuity suddenly rose before me." This could mean only that he realized that the ideas of world revolution that had shaped his life were in their death agonies. Bukharin had never envisaged the nature and the power of world revolution in the same

292

way as had Lenin and the old revolutionary leadership. He had always appraised the recuperative powers inherent in the capitalist system as much stronger than had the other Bolshevik theoreticians, including Lenin. In the early days of the revolution he had already rejected what seemed to him the too simple alternative of Communist policy: a speedy dash of the world revolution to victory or the recovery of the capitalist system in the various countries to its old accustomed forms. Even at that time he had formulated in his writings a third possibility that had been violently debated in Bolshevist circles, a fundamental change in the structure of capitalist society. He envisaged the replacement of the system of private capitalism by a system of huge state capitalist trusts that would eliminate the democratic forms of organization possible to private capitalism and, through newly developed organs of terror, would suppress all spontaneous movements of revolution.

These ideas had once led him into the left wing of the Communist Party. In 1918 he had demanded a revolutionary war against Germany for, according to his theory, it was imperative to utilize this deepest and most profound crisis of European capitalism. To pass this opportunity by, might endanger the future course of the world revolution and permit the powerful state capitalist trusts to take matters into their hands. Although his efforts failed, he continued to advocate this policy. In 1921 he supported the German Communists in their strategy of attack. In 1922 he went along with Karl Radek in his attempt to carry the revolution to the West via a French-German conflict. In 1923 he finally became convinced that the forces of capitalist recovery had won ascendancy, and that it was now necessary to adjust Communist policy and strategy to the new situation.

The German Communists had been defeated in October, 1923. This defeat marked the turning point for Bukharin. It cleared the path, from his viewpoint, for the forces of state capitalism and monopolistic trusts to gain supremacy in Germany and thereby to render the ideas of revolution as conceived by the Communist International during its first years of existence an anachronism. He therefore joined the right wing of the Communist Party, wishing to make over the Communist parties, in close alliance with the democratic trade unions, into mass parties and to fortify them against the coming assaults of the state capitalist trusts and their organs of terror.

As far as the Soviet Union was concerned, he saw only one way, a cautious policy in regard to the peasants who represented more than 80 per cent of the entire population. A slow and gradual transformation of the huge peasant country in the direction of Socialism appeared to him the only possibility. He did not believe in coercing the peasant masses into cooperation, but in winning their voluntary assistance for Socialism. Only in this fashion could the inner harmony within the Soviet Republic be maintained and the dangers from the outside averted.

Such were Bukharin's conceptions of political strategy that made him ally himself with Stalin from 1924 to 1927. In 1927 Stalin abandoned this strategy, substituting for it a hurried industrialization accompanied by and purchased at the cost of unspeakable misery among the masses of the people. Bukharin regarded this shift as the opening of an abyss into which both the Soviet Union and the Comintern were bound to fall to their destruction!

Stalin's slogan of the time, to "pass and surpass" the production of the capitalist countries, he treated with the contempt of the trained economist familiar with the tremendous productive powers of the capitalist countries of Europe and America. To try to hypnotize foreign countries into believing in an impending Communist revolution, as Stalin wanted, by the profuse use of revolutionary phrases and an incessant show of activity, he considered folly.

Bukharin's personality was made up of conflicting elements. In his thinking and his theoretical convictions he was uncompromising. He thought through an issue to the end and could never be deflected from his conclusions. As a practical politician he was soft, willing to concede a point to his adversary. In his personal nature he was generous, gentle, and without the power or strength of authority that his theory called for. This contradiction between his unflinching theoretical thought and his personal political ambivalence dominated his entire life.

Hitler's victory and the consequent destruction of the German Communist Party as well as of the entire German labor movement appeared to him as a last historical confirmation of his theory. It

294

showed that the monopolization of economic and social power by the trusts led to their acquisition of political power, and that the National Socialist regime in Germany meant the merger of the economic bureaucracy of the trusts with that of the state. The workers, therefore, were becoming slaves of the state.

With developments like those in Germany and those he foresaw as potential in other countries, the very foundations of the Communist International were being destroyed. The possibility of preventing the rise of state capitalist monopoly power by the rebellion of the masses, in line with the old plans, was gone.

Contrary to his expectations, however, the Soviet Union survived its great crisis. The assaults by the state capitalist powers of the West and the Far East did not occur. Although it did not "pass and surpass" the capitalist countries abroad, the Soviet Union nevertheless laid the foundations for the development of heavy industry. The Russian countryside did not turn Socialist. The Russian State had become almighty, and the people its slaves.

What Bukharin had foreseen as the outcome of political developments in the West occurred in the Soviet Union as well. Only in Russia the last remnant of private property, even on a small scale, had been extinguished. In the West and in the land of the revolution itself the ideas of world revolution had come to an end. In the West and in the Soviet Union a new social and political structure had arisen.

It was now necessary to chart a new course, and Bukharin set out on the journey. Yet scientific insight into the new trends of development is one thing, the spiritual casting out of the old hopes another. It involves a long hard struggle against oneself, a chain of painful attempts, ever repeated and ever failing, to adjust oneself to the standards of the new order. The life and aspirations of the old revolutionary faith keep calling.

It had been only a few years before this trial that Bukharin had given expression to Communist idealism in somewhat over-enthusiastic words: "We, the USSR," he had exclaimed, "are the watchtower of the whole world, the skeleton army of future mankind. . . . . Our vision extends over thousands of years. . . . . We are not living an existence on paper, in a manifesto, nor in the dreamlands of great minds and hearts. . . . . We are the glorious vanguard of the workers who are changing the world, a grim army getting ready for fresh battles. We are the triumphant driving force of world history. On the topmost ranges of human will and action we build and struggle, suffer and triumph. Our responsibility before history is tremendous. . . . ."

In former years Bukharin had rarely exhibited such poetic enthusiasm; his words had been colder and his thoughts more restrained. Maybe he was now anticipating the shocks and tribulations that were sending the country into the convulsions of the trials?

The ultimate consequences of the new scientific conviction is moral self-destruction, a *conditio sine qua non* of the principle of the new order. Expressed by Bukharin in the slave language at the trial, it reads: All the positive glistening accomplishments in the Soviet Union "acquire new dimensions in a man's mind. These in the end disarmed me completely."

Then he continued: "It seems probable to me that every one of us sitting here in the dock suffered from a peculiar duality of mind, an incomplete faith in his counter-revolutionary cause. I will not say that the consciousness of this was absent, but it was incomplete. Hence a certain semi-paralysis of the will. . . . . And this was due not to the absence of constant thought but to the objective grandeur of Socialist construction. The contradiction that arose between the acceleration of our degeneration and this paralysis of the will expressed the position of a counter-revolutionary, or a developing counter-revolutionary, under the conditions of developing Socialist construction. A dual psychology arose. Each one of us can discern this in his own soul!"

Translated from slave language into the ideas that Bukharin wished to express, this could only mean: "peculiar duality of mind," "dual psychology" were the academic "slave words" for the inability of Bukharin and his friends to accept and adjust themselves to the ethical code of the Stalin regime. "Semi-paralysis of the will" and "our degeneration" conceal the inner struggle between the theoretical conviction that leads to a political capitulation before Stalin and the moral consequences of such capitulation. "A counter-revolutionary, or a developing counter-revolutionary, under the conditions of

296

developing Socialist construction" is the old Bolshevik professional revolutionary whose heart yearns for the idealistic dreams of world revolution of the past while his mind tells him there is no alternative: subordinate yourself to the cruel, brutal, barbaric Socialism that despises our humanism yet lifts the life of the masses to a plane that, historically speaking, is higher than the "anarchy of private capitalism."

Bukharin concluded his defense with the words: "May this trial be the last severe lesson and may the great might of the USSR become clear to all. Let it be clear to all that our thesis that Socialism limited to one country, the USSR, will destroy itself, is counter-revolutionary and has no validity in the new world surrounding us!" This meant for all who were able to understand the language and interpret it: The world revolution is dead; the old ideas of Lenin on revolution are dead; yet in the Soviet Union a new social form foreign to the alternative of these days—capitalism or Socialism—has arisen, a collective state capitalism that opposes itself in the arena of world history to the state capitalist systems of the West which are rising on the social basis of private property. Whether I am for or against this new form, whether I am for or against Stalin, is irrelevant. But I must choose between Russia and the West. There is no other possibility. I have chosen!

The new social form imposed in the Soviet Union of Stalin, Bukharin told his listeners in the last speech, cannot and will not move towards the West through revolutionary eruptions, as Lenin's scheme provided. The decision between this new principle of Stalin and those holding sway in the West will take place in the form of wars. Russia and the West will meet not in the arena of world revolution, as envisaged by Lenin, but in armed clashes of their state capitalist systems that are girding for battle. I warn all Socialists and Communists: There is no way out. . . . .

Bukharin in this trial turned to those intellectuals of Europe who saw in the confessions an outpouring and self-expression of the Slavic soul, a sort of mystic insanity arising from the urge to sacrifice oneself for the world, like the idiot of Dostoevsky: "Beat me, beat me, ye faithful! I am a sinner." The Slavic soul, said Bukharin, is a

297

matter of the Russian past. Now it is to be found elsewhere in Europe, not in the new Russia.

Bukharin who embodied in his own person all the refinements of European civilization and science could not feel the Slavic soul as a motive force within himself. Yet this trial as well as the team play between the victims and their executioners could have taken place only in Russia. Perhaps it was not just an accident that Savinkov, the last of the great terrorists who had died in a state of blessed paroxysm, had said his adieu to life in words not unlike those of Bukharin.

Surely Stalin understood the significance of Bukharin's "confessions." But they did not stay his judgment. The die was cast. The new principle required the blood of Bukharin and of the old apostles of world revolution. There was no bridge between "Socialism in one country" and world revolution.

CHIPS FROM THE POKER GAME

The former ambassador of the Soviet Union in Berlin, Nikolai Krestinsky, had a political task to fulfill at this trial different from that of his codefendants. His function was to bring to an end the German-Russian poker game that Radek and Chicherin had started in 1921 and that he himself had continued. At the same time he was to deal out a few new cards for the game just beginning.

Early in 1938 Stalin had begun to build his first bridges to Berlin. He felt sure at the time that Chamberlain's policy of directing Hitler's expansion towards the East had secured complete ascendancy in the Western countries. He knew that the British conservatives were not going to resist the occupation of Austria by Hitler.

He began to take precautionary measures by personally initiating negotiations with Hitler. For the latter the secret negotiations with Stalin at that time were not much more than a means of pressure on the West as well as an assurance for the future. At the same time they represented a weapon in his hands in his struggle for supremacy in the German army.

On the thirtieth of June, 1934, Hitler had had General von Schleicher executed as a traitor to Germany. The Reichswehr generals had later forced him to make a speech retracting the charge and redeeming the honor of the murdered general.

When Krestinsky was accused of having been a spy of the German Reichswehr since 1921, Stalin did not have a German denial to fear. Krestinsky's chief partners, General von Seeckt and General von Schleicher, were dead. Hitler could have no objections if Stalin were to discredit the old relationships between the German and Russian armies. On the contrary, this would fit his own purposes perfectly.

Krestinsky could therefore testify that he had been receiving sixty thousand dollars a year from Seeckt, personally, to organize a net of spies throughout Russia. Payments actually made by Seeckt on the account of some of the secret German munitions factories in Russia were represented as contributions for the organization of a net of Trotskyite spies.

Between Vishinsky, prosecuting attorney, and Krestinsky the following dialogue occurred:

Vishinsky: "Did you transmit espionage information?"

Krestinsky: "I would say not I but we, the Russian Trotskyites."

Vishinsky: "In what year did the negotiations with von Seeckt begin?"

Krestinsky: "It was in the spring and summer of 1922. In the indictment it says 1921. This is of no great consequence, but this first meeting of an official nature which Trotsky suggested that I take advantage of occurred in the winter of 1921-22."

In further questionings Krestinsky insisted obstinately that his espionage work had begun not in 1921 but in 1922. He had already confessed to innumerable crimes, but in regard to this one apparently insignificant detail he remained adamant.

The reason was simple: Although there actually had been negotiations between the Red Army and the Reichswehr in the winter of 1921-22, these were only preparatory to the Treaty of Rapallo and had not gone beyond the stage of plan and blueprint. Only after the Treaty of Rapallo was concluded a few months later did the secret pact between the Red Army and the Reichswehr come into being and the preparatory negotiations translated from their blueprints into actual munitions and aviation factories in Russia, for which Krestinsky had received payments from the Germans. What the prosecution presented as the espionage activity had really been the deliberate policy of the Soviet government and its Red Army. Krestinsky expected by his insistence on the precise sequence of events to throw out a hint to the initiate among his listeners into what role he had been forced.

It was no lie when he said that these negotiations had been started on Trotsky's order, for nobody else could have given the order at the time. Trotsky had been chief of the Red Army.

GHOSTS OF THE COMINTERN

"In the house of the hanged, one does not discuss the merits of rope!" The Comintern was not mentioned during these trials.

Only two men connected primarily with the Comintern passed over the stage of the court. One was Bela Kun, the other Mirov.

Bukharin put some questions to one of Vishinsky's witnesses who was represented as an accomplice in the plot against Lenin. The witness, a well-known Social Revolutionary, had been engaged in active military struggle against the Soviet Union up to 1920. Bukharin asked this witness whether he recalled that Bela Kun had fought in 1920 against an insurrectionary attempt of the Social Revolutionaries in Moscow.

Bukharin knew that the prosecution was trying to involve Bela Kun as well in the plot against Lenin's life. His question was designed to ward off this attempt of the prosecution.

Mirov-Abramov, the second Comintern figure that passed over the Vishinsky stage, had been Piatnitsky's closest associate and the third secretary of the Soviet embassy in Berlin under Krestinsky. From 1926 to 1930 he had been the chief of the OMS for Europe. Through his hands went all the technical threads of the conspiratorial work of the Comintern. At the same time he was the chief of the industrial information service of the Soviet Union in Europe.

With the assistance and the cooperation of the various European Communist parties, particularly the German, he had secured many technical and industrial secrets for Soviet use without cost. The Soviet government was indebted to the loyal efforts of Mirov and his collaborators to the extent of many millions of gold rubles that the pur-

300

chase and acquisition of patents and processes, particularly in the fields of chemistry, machine tools, and aviation, would have cost.

Mirov had had his office in the second back yard of the Berlin Soviet embassy. Few people had access to it.

He was a small, amiable man. He looked like a bank teller who had made good. He was a good psychologist and a loyal comrade. Not a single Communist who left the party ever betrayed him or his secrets.

In Berlin, Mirov had met a young Russian Jewess who had emigrated from Russia with her parents in 1917. Vera had become, as had many of the Russian emigré youth, an enthusiastic Soviet patriot. She married Mirov and became an important figure in the Soviet embassy. The wife of the ambassador Krestinsky, a physician who preferred to spend her time in the hospitals rather than at diplomatic receptions, frequently found in Vera a talented substitute.

In 1927 Mirov had been recalled to Moscow and became the acting assistant to Ossip Piatnitsky. Since 1933 his functions had included the direction of a special school in a suburb of Moscow where foreign Communists were trained as specialists in the fight against the Gestapo. Mirov made Vera, his wife, the financial director of this secret school.

In 1936 Piatnitsky was deposed, and all his assistants, including Mirov, were arrested. Vera "confessed" that she had married Mirov only for the purpose of getting into the Soviet Union as a German spy and that Mirov had sent thirty thousand dollars to Trotsky which he had received from the Trotsky opposition in Russia. Mirov, like most of his codefendants, was felled by the bullets of the GPU executioner.

Ossip Piatnitsky, chief organizer of the Comintern, who had first served Zinoviev and Bukharin and later Stalin with the same unquestioning devotion, vanished in the night of the purges.

THE SCALES ARE BALANCED

At the Eighteenth Congress of the Communist Party of the Soviet Union, Stalin struck a balance sheet. That was in March, 1939. The years of terror were past. All traces that Moscow had once been the capital city of the world revolution had been erased.

301

The huge building of the Comintern at the gates of the Kremlin on the Machavaya street was empty. What was left of the Comintern was located in an obscure suburb of Moscow.

From all Russian libraries the works of Trotsky, Zinoviev, Radek, Bukharin, and their adherents had been removed and burned. The history of the Russian Revolution and of the Comintern had been written anew, first in the bloody letters of the trials, then in two standard works describing the role of the Comintern leaders in the words of Vishinsky.

In one of these standard works, a short biography of Stalin, the revised description of the days of the October Revolution omitted all mention of Trotsky's name. The revolution of 1917 had become exclusively the work of Lenin and Stalin.

These two standard histories were circulated by the million. They presented the only official and permissible historical source of the Russian Revolution. The aim had been accomplished: In the minds of the new generation, Lenin and Stalin were fused into one person.

The Comintern was mentioned in the official biography of Stalin in only one sentence: "In January, 1918, on the instructions of the Central Committee, Stalin arranged a conference of representatives of the revolutionary wings of various Socialist parties of Europe and America, which was an important step towards the formation of the Third Communist International."

The official history did not indicate that the Third International founded by Stalin had been an instrument in the hands of foreign spies from its inception. This discovery was announced by Stalin at the Eighteenth Party Congress when he struck his final balance sheet:

"Is it not surprising that we learned about the espionage and conspiratorial activities of the Trotskyite and Bukharinite leaders only quite recently in 1937 and 1938 although, as the evidence shows, these gentry were in the service of foreign espionage organizations and carried on conspiratorial activities from the very first days of the October Revolution?"

The new history of the Russian Revolution had already become a matter of common acceptance. A touch from Gogol was injected

302

into the somber deliberations of the Eighteenth Party Congress when one of the speakers jokingly told how a provincial party secretary had divided all party members into three categories: "The first type is the fellow who shows a lot of activity. That means he is worth checking up. You may be certain the trail will lead to the enemy. The second type is the fellow with a "past," the fellow with a lot on his mind. He is bound to lag—the load will tell. Keep an eye on him. Check him up. This trail will also most likely lead to the enemy. And the third type is the man who works because he has got to. There too you can't go wrong—he is an enemy!"

The speaker quoted this only as an example to deter would-be imitators. Yet the naive secretary from the provinces had formulated the dominant spirit of the purgatorial years that established Stalin's monopolization of power, simply and superbly.

BIRTH OF THE FIFTH COLUMN

Throughout August, 1939, and even up to the very day of the German-Russian pact, the Communist press of the world unanimously branded rumors about an impending agreement between Hitler and Stalin as one of the worst slanders ever invented by the fifth column of Hitler and Trotsky.

The various central committees of the Communist parties had received denials from the High Command that a pact was in preparation. They were acting in good faith on the basis of their orders when they continued to call for war on Hitler and Fascism and competed with each other in declarations of willingness to wage war on the Nazis. But they were misleading themselves as well as the masses of their followers, and only intensifying the fog that Moscow was spreading around the impending pact with Hitler.

In France the mystification was nearly complete. The French Foreign Minister Bonnet on the night of August 29 awoke the French Premier Daladier by telephone to inform him of the announcement that the pact had just been concluded. Daladier told him to go back to bed and not let himself be taken in by such rumors.

The following day the masses were just as unbelieving as Daladier had been. But that evening the Moscow communiques were published in the newspapers. They printed pictures of Stalin with a broad smile standing next to Ribbentrop who said: "The Fuehrer and Stalin have become friends!"

The Communist leaders declared that the pact was intended only to preserve peace. But the blow to the masses dreaming of a strong and happy France with Russia as its faithful ally, was devastating. In front of the Communist Party quarters in France were mountains of membership books torn up. Copies of *L'Humanité* were slapped into the faces of the newsdealers. In the red suburbs of Paris functionaries of the Communist Party were beaten up.

At party headquarters in the Rue Lafayette the Central Committee was in complete confusion. The radio station of the Comintern was silent. The Comintern representatives remained invisible. The Soviet Russian embassy would answer no questions and issued no guiding orders.

In London the British Communist leader, Harry Pollit, stated: "We are supporting all national measures to secure the victory of democracy over Fascism."

Thorez breathed easier, believing that Moscow even after the conclusion of the German-Russian pact was permitting a continuation of the patriotic Popular Front policy. He called the Communist deputies together, and they published the following communiqué: "The Communist parliamentary group met today under the presidency of Maurice Thorez in the Chamber of Deputies. After an exposé of the situation by Jacques Duclos, the group unanimously reaffirmed its will to exert all efforts in order to assure the defense of the country against the Fascist aggressors of the Third Reich." Immediately after the outbreak of war, Thorez volunteered.

In Moscow the change of scenery was accomplished with much less noise. The Executive Committee of the Comintern maintained a stubborn silence. The German Communists who had survived the great purge vanished from the city. Courtesy demanded that the hundreds of Nazis arriving in Moscow for negotiations be relieved of the sight of Communist refugees banished from the Third Reich. So most of them were sent into obscurity in the Russian provinces. The same happened to the Czechs and to the other nationals from Germany's new lebensraum.

It took two weeks for Stalin to give the Comintern High Command now located in a small building on the outskirts of Moscow their new slogan: The chief enemy is England. The war of England and France against Germany is not a war against Fascism. It is a war between imperialist rivals. The blame for this war is entirely on the side of the Allies: it is undeniable that they and not Germany started this war.

Pravda began to publish articles calling for rebellion in the British and French colonies and threatening insurrections in India, Egypt, and Syria. The Communist parties of the countries warring against Hitler were charged with the task of bringing the war to an end as expeditiously as possible.

The Comintern now stepped on to the stage of European history for a last performance. The patriots who had solemnly sworn during the last five years to die fighting for their fatherlands were now prepared to denounce their fatherlands as arch enemies of mankind.

Maurice Thorez undertook the role of a French Karl Liebknecht. He deserted from the army and began to live underground. In the meantime, André Marty was organizing defeatist action from Belgium. In France the Communists circularized their first leaflets: Down with the imperialist war! Long live the struggle of the masses for peace, liberty, and bread.

Harry Pollit was disowned, and the British Communists declared that the chief enemy was in their own country. It was a hard test for the entire staff of Communist leaders. For they had not only to repeat the revolutionary phrases of Lenin's days but at the same time to cooperate with the victorious Nazis in the occupied countries.

The Norwegian Communists, immediately after the occupation of the country by the Germans, declared that not the Nazis but England and the Norwegian government in exile were the enemy.

After some time a few German Communists were permitted to make a reappearance in Moscow, but were prohibited from participating in the "Leninist" defeatist propaganda. Theirs was the most difficult task—to defend the Russian-German pact in the name of the German people. They solved their problems heroically. Their leader, Walter Ulbricht, wrote: "Whoever intrigues against the friendship of the German and the Soviet people is an enemy of the German people and so exposes himself as an agent of British imperialism." He called all his followers in Germany as well as all other Germans who believed in the friendship between the German and Russian nations to uncover the enemies of the Soviet-German pact without mercy and to expose their leaders, particularly the Thyssen clique, the traitors in the ranks of the Social Democracy, and the Catholic labor movement to the public contempt they so amply deserved. What his call really amounted to was a challenge to have all enemies of Moscow and all anti-Fascists denounced to the Gestapo.

Erich Weinert at that time wrote flaming protests against the English-French imperialist attack on Germany—from Moscow.

In the German concentration camps were thousands of Communists, many of whom had been there for long years. They had to take the ridicule of their SA guards who told them: Now *we* are Stalin's allies and not you.

After the outbreak of the Polish-German war, one of the former Communist Reichstag deputies wrote from the concentration camp to some friends abroad: We Communists in the concentration camps have been buried alive. Forget about us.

They were buried alive. Moscow did not make the slightest attempt during the entire period of the pact with Germany to ease the life of Communists in the German concentration camps and prisons, to say nothing of rescuing them.

The Communist masses in Europe disappeared from the political calculations of the Kremlin with the conclusion of the German-Russian pact. Thereafter only the fifth column was still of relevance. The term "fifth column" had originated during the Spanish civil war. The Communist leaders had contributed in large share to the popularity of this new political term. All of their enemies were so branded. Their own turn towards defeatism in the Allied countries demonstrated that they themselves had become a fifth column, if ever the word had any meaning.

They had been separated from the masses. They had lost their family ties, their homes, and their countries. They were ready to accept all persecution and peril, not on the dictate of their own conscience or their own convictions, but to obey orders emanating from Moscow.

They had stepped out of the Trojan horse of Dimitrov as a real fifth column of the Soviet Republic in the Allied countries.

THE "DRÔLE DE GUERRE" AS SAVIOR OF FRENCH COMMUNISM

In their efforts to recover from the shock of the German-Russian pact the French Communists received assistance from an unexpected quarter. Daladier, the French Premier, in his bitter and unthinking rage over the pact, immediately had the Communist newspaper *L'Humanité* suppressed, and thereby helped the Communists to extricate themselves from the public accounting that otherwise would have been unavoidable.

Daladier usually hit hard at the wrong time and the wrong place. Had he not made it impossible for the Communists to state their policy and opinions publicly, their difficulties would have resulted without fail in complete disintegration. *L'Humanité* would have died a natural death.

Yet Daladier confined his suppression of the press to the Communist paper and permitted other periodicals presenting notorious Nazi propaganda to appear unmolested, thus enabling them to change into patriotic garb.

Daladier went even further. He made the members of the Communist parliamentary group personally responsible for the German-Russian pact. Some deputies of the group condemned the pact, others vacillated. Daladier made a vacillation impossible. He openly violated the constitution that gave immunity to deputies, threw the Communists out of parliament, brought arbitrary indictments for high treason against many of them, and locked up the majority of them in a concentration camp. He liquidated the Communist trade unions, cooperatives, and even the creches that were maintained by the Communist Party, and dissolved the Communist municipal administrations. Thus he smoothed the way for hundreds of thousands of workers to whom the Moscow pact was a terrific blow to become irreconcilable foes to his own regime.

Many Communist deputies had been very popular with their constituents. Unsophisticated French workers did not hold their own deputies or mayors responsible for a pact signed in Moscow. Daladier made martyrs out of them and reunited them with the fifth column of Thorez-Duclos-Marty.

In the concentration camp there was no room for vacillation. Prisoners soon became real defeatists.

The greatest help Daladier extended to the Communists was his method of waging war, the *"drôle de guerre,"* as it was termed in popular parlance. After a few exchanges, complete quiet reigned on the Western Front. From time to time there were air raid alarms, but no German bomb was dropped on French soil nor was any French bomb dropped on German soil.

All France had gone into the war with great reluctance. The *drôle de guerre* only intensified this feeling.

The pitiable way in which the families of the men who had been mobilized were cared for also contributed to this. Shortly after the beginning of the war, soldiers were begging on the streets. Many of them on furlough returned to their old jobs because there was nothing to eat at home. In such soil the defeatism of the Communists found plenty of nourishment.

When the Finnish-Russian war began in December, the papers of the Right increased their campaign against the Soviet Union. Frequently it seemed that the war against Germany was altogether forgotten. A British-French expedition that was to fight on the side of Finland against Russia was being set up. In Syria a substantial army under Weygand, the old enemy of Bolshevism, was being assembled. There were hints that this army was destined to conquer the Caucasus, but on the German battlefront there still remained complete quiet.

Stalin's fifth column immediately seized the opportunity and began a subterranean campaign. Large editions of leaflets were circularized throughout the country: Was not Stalin right? Where is the war against Fascism? Daladier is preparing war against the Soviet Union! *Vous êtes vendus*—you've been sold out!

This propaganda had its effects. It crawled into factories, homes, barracks, trenches, where the soldiers were listening almost daily to the German loud-speakers: Hitler does not want to fight France.

He does not want anything from you. Go home to your families who have nothing to eat.

The Comintern radio stations had only one theme: England and Churchill want to immerse the entire world in a bloody war and to involve all the neutral countries in the slaughter, just to prevent the loss of the British Empire.

The Nazi radio stations echoed those of the Comintern, the leader of the German Labor Front, Robert Ley, exhorting: "Proletarians of all countries, unite against British capitalism!"

Moscow must have been convinced of the success of this defeatist propaganda for without such conviction the adventures of O. W. Kuusinen would be incomprehensible. At the beginning of the war against Finland Stalin had made him head of a Finnish people's government and had concluded a solemn treaty of peace with him. Kuusinen established the seat of his government in a little Finnish village close to the Russian border that had been occupied by Russian troops. Stalin was certain that the Finnish masses would welcome the Red Army as liberators. But the Finnish workers fought just as bravely and courageously as did the Russian soldiers.

The longer the campaign lasted, the less was heard of Kuusinen's people's government. Finally the war ended with a compromise, Stalin recognizing the Finnish government in Helsingfors and poor O. W. Kuusinen vanishing into the dark to reappear only at the dissolution of the Comintern.

In England, also, the defeatist propaganda of the Comintern had been without the slightest effect on the masses. Only in France did it succeed. When Hitler began his offensive against the West on May 10, 1940, France had been eaten by all the worms of defeatism. For six weeks there was no propaganda of any kind. There were only German bombers demolishing French cities and German tank columns dispersing French armies. After the catastrophe, the entire country cried out in pain: *On nous a vendu*—they've sold us out! And nobody cried with more indignation than the Communists. Had not Stalin been right in advising the French to extricate themselves quickly from the unhappy war? Had not they been right in warning against Chamberlain and Churchill who had deserted France and who were willing to fight to the last Frenchman?

The Communists were the first to recover from the debacle. They had no masses that followed them; but, in compensation, the organization of the other French parties had been destroyed, and, even more, their moral foundations had been shattered. The Communists, however, had an underground apparatus of some hundreds of men and women which expanded quickly. Theirs was the only party in France that had the slightest conception of how to run an underground organization or how to get leaflets and pamphlets printed in underground printing establishments.

The Communists were faced by another great advantage: The overwhelming majority of the demoralized French people immediately after the defeat rallied behind the new national government of Pétain and with them the shells of the former political parties. The Communists were "protected" by the political illegality in which they found themselves. They did not commit the "error" of their party comrades in Norway who had tried to establish friendly relationships with the German forces of occupation. With the exception of an attempt by a small group to get permission from the German occupation authorities to publish *L'Humanité,* they maintained a hostile attitude towards the Nazis.

Between them and the other patriotic groups up to the summer of 1941 stood the figure of General de Gaulle, who had become the symbol of anti-German resistance. Moscow had prohibited any cooperation with de Gaulle, Churchill's protégé, because as far as Moscow was concerned Churchill and England were the chief enemies.

The Communists organized their campaign around the question of the blame for the collapse and the means to combat the misery that was spreading ever further. This gave them a chance to work unremittingly at the expansion of their underground organization. On June 22, 1941, they recovered their complete liberty of action. Now France had to be defended. Now England was a heroic paladin of democracy. Now Stalin's fifth column gave enthusiastic support to the Allies. Now the war became a democratic crusade against Fascist barbarism. . . . .

Two years later the Third or Communist International was dissolved by a decree from the hand of Stalin. During the two years that followed the dissolution a new international organization arose from the ashes of the second World War and the military victory of Russia.

The Comintern, dissolved in 1943, was the international aspect of the Communist equalitarian experiments initiated by the October revolution. The successor organization—the Stalintern—arises together with the new Russian Empire, from the totalitarian liquidation of the October revolution.

Part IV

STALINTERN

CHAPTER XXII

The Victor

MYSTERY OF THE STALINTERN

WHEN LENIN FOUNDED THE COMMUNIST INTERNATIONAL HE stated his motives and objectives clearly and unequivocally. The founding documents reflected the acts that brought it into being—the doctrine of world revolution.

Stalin dissolved the Communist International in an atmosphere of vagueness and ambiguity. In the dissolution decree one will seek in vain for an unequivocal definition or a clear doctrine. The document is veiled and obscure.

The successor organization of the Comintern tiptoed from the dissolution decree into the arena of world politics as it behooves this illegitimate child of the totalitarian transformation of the Russian Revolution.

During the twenty-five years that had passed since its birth the Revolution had outgrown its Marxist and equalitarian origin and transformed itself into a totalitarian autocracy. Totalitarian transformations usually have no program of their own. Fundamentally they are but processes of disintegration, dissolving all order of society. They consume the established political, historical, and moral traditions of a country and reproduce them in distorted form, robbing them of their real content and significance. In Russia, totalitarian transformation consumed the Marxist ideology of the Revolution, doing away step by step with its logic, its principles, and its traditions. Stalin in this process transformed himself from a professional revolutionary into a totalitarian leader who has become a substitute for program, thought, and doctrine.

The Comintern reflected these changes during the last phase of its existence. The dissolution decree merely ratified what had already happened: Lenin's doctrine of world revolution and the organization that embodied it were dead.

Manifestoes *à la* 1918 are no longer issued by the totalitarian

Russia of the 1940's. The fundamental political method of its expansion is no longer that of frontal attack but of encirclement of the enemy. Its first task is not to carry to victory a political philosophy of its own, but to destroy its real or supposed enemies. Fundamentally, Stalin's foreign policy rests on one principle—the destruction of the principles of all others. The Stalintern bears witness to this.

Notwithstanding that it announces no principles and doctrine of its own, it has grown at a speed far greater than ever experienced by Lenin's International.

During the three years since the dissolution, the Soviet Republic has developed into the mightiest continental empire of European history. It extends from the Elbe to the Kuriles, from the Arctic to the Persian Gulf, from the North Sea to the Adriatic.

In Europe, Asia, and South America, Communist parties have arisen whose weight is felt in the scales of world politics. In the Slavic southeast of Europe, Communist parties have initiated a totalitarian dictatorship which is a copy of the Russian. In Poland the Communists govern behind the screen of a powerless coalition. In Czechoslovakia they are the strongest party within the government; in Hungary and Rumania, the civilian arm of the Russian occupation. These countries together comprise an area inhabited by more than one hundred million people, nearly one-third of Europe.

In the Russian occupation zone of Germany, the Communist party is fashioned into the monopoly party of the Left. In western Germany the Communist party is offered as a storage facility for the resentment against American and British occupation. In France, the Communists claim a mass following, one and a half million members and more than five million voters—over 20 per cent of the ballot. They control the most important sections of the trade unions. To form a government on a parliamentary basis against their desires has become impossible. In Italy they claim 1,800,000 members and dominate a great portion of the cooperative rural societies in addition to most of the trade unions. In Belgium and Holland the formerly insignificant Communist groups have developed into mass parties. Even in Scandinavia and Switzerland they have become important factors in political life. England is the only European country at whose gate the Communist tide has stopped.

At present there are several Communist parties which exercise a significant international influence because of the specific weight of their organization in their own country. The Communist party of France, for instance, is in a position to prevent a western European block under British leadership. Dimitrov in Sofia can make his power felt as a permanent menace to Ankara and Athens. Tito claims supremacy in the Adriatic. The Chinese Communists have been recognized by the United States as a power in their own right and have been accepted on an equal footing with the national government in Chungking.

Is all this only a continuation of the dissolved Communist International? Is this a resurrection, or are we witnessing the rise of something new? Are the new Communist parties acting on the orders of a central organization in Moscow, as did the dissolved Communist parties? Is there in Moscow an "underground high command" which has the same means at its disposal as the Executive Committee that dissolved itself in May, 1943, and solemnly declared all obligations of the Communist parties in the world extinct?

None of these questions can be answered with a clear yes or no. The Communist movement that originated in the Second World War is not based on a general and universal program—except in its relationship to Russia. It is an instrument everywhere of the expanding power of Stalin's empire.

Yet it does not follow that the present Communist parties are all more or less of the same nature nor that the methods employed by Moscow to guide them are always and everywhere identical. The new Communist movement comprises a great number of different political parties, groups, and front organizations. Their ideologies have as many colors as the rainbow. The Communists of the Stalintern are democrats and ardent believers in dictatorship. They are nationalists and internationalists, militarists and anti-militarists. They defend the rights of some national minorities, and they favor the complete extinction of other nationalities. They are imperialists and anti-imperialists at the same time. They accept all tactical methods of the political and social struggle, regardless of whether they are derived from the Socialist, the liberal or the fascist arsenal.

Moscow's word within the leadership of these multiplex Communist parties is more decisive than it had ever been in the dissolved Third International. But its monopoly position does not express itself everywhere in the same way with the same methods and for the same reasons.

The dissolved Executive Committee ruled the Communist parties by propaganda, money, and emissaries, and by the inexhaustible appeal of the Russian Revolution. In Europe and northern Asia the pressure of the Russian military power has replaced this last factor. Within the new Communist world movement Moscow rules by the complete integration of all these factors with the organs of state power of Stalin's new empire. The subordination of the Communist parties to the Moscow command has become a tacitly recognized institution of international politics. It is no longer possible for any statesman to ask for the noninterference of Moscow in the domestic affairs of other states as a condition of international cooperation with Russia, as did Lloyd George, Poincaré, Baldwin and Laval.

Did Stalin anticipate such a development when he dissolved the Comintern in 1943? If so, he knew how to conceal his thoughts and hopes well, for he said at the time: "The dissolution of the Communist International is proper and timely because it facilitates the organization of the common onslaught of all freedom-loving nations against the common enemy, Hitlerism. The dissolution of the Comintern is proper because (a) it exposes the lie of the Hitlerites to the effect that Moscow allegedly intends to intervene in the life of other nations and to Bolshevize them. An end is now being put to this lie. (b) It exposes the calumny of the adversaries of Communism within the labor movement to the effect that Communist parties in various countries are allegedly acting not in the interest of their people but on orders from outside. An end is now being put to this calumny too. (c) It facilitates the work of patriots in freedom-loving countries in assisting the progressive forces of their respective countries. . . . . I feel that the dissolution of the Comintern is perfectly timely because it is exactly now when the fascist beast is exerting its last strength that it is necessary to organize the common onslaught of freedom-loving countries to finish off this beast and to deliver the people from fascist oppression."

318

The Executive Committee decreeing its own dissolution added two thoughts of its own, the first that because of the increasing differences between conditions surrounding the working class parties in different countries, no longer could an international center assist the labor movement in solving its international problems; the second that the form of organization chosen by the Founding Congress of the Comintern had become an impediment for the full development of the various national working class parties.

The first argument defeats itself, for similar differences between the various labor parties of the different countries have existed since the start of the modern labor movement. In fact, they were never more pronounced than at the time the Comintern was founded.

The second argument has received peculiar confirmation during the last two years in the record of what has happened to some of those who signed the dissolution decree: Gottwald is premier of the Czechoslovakian government; Dimitrov, the dictator of Bulgaria; Kolarov, vice-premier of the Bulgarian Fatherland Front and minister of justice; Manuilsky, People's Commissar of Foreign Affairs of the Ukrainian Soviet Republic, chairman of the Committee for Political and Social Problems of the UN; Pieck, candidate of the German Communists for the head of the coming German state; Thorez, vice-premier of the French government; Ercoli (Togliatti), vice-premier of the Italian government during the first two postwar years; Rakoczi, vice-premier of the Hungarian government.

Do these men all represent the continuity of the dissolved Comintern in the new world Communist movement? As much and as little as Stalin represents the continuity of the equalitarian, orthodox, dogmatic Communist Soviet Republic of Lenin and Trotsky within the new Eurasian empire that is Russia today. These men and the organizations they lead, are national variations of a melody out of Stalin's Eurasian Empire. The Stalintern has been created in emulation of the spirit and the person of its creator. The Stalintern has no tradition transcending the personality of Stalin.

No god appears more divine than the *deus ex machina*. After terrible defeats in the first year of war, Stalin performed a miracle— the resurrection of the Red Army, and in two years of bitter struggle he defeated one of the most powerful war machines of all times.

The battle of Stalingrad marked a decisive turning point. After its victorious conclusion the basic principles of Soviet foreign policy began to appear on the horizon. They contain a Russian variation on a theme of Hitler's, set forth in 1924 in *Mein Kampf:* "Never allow the formation of two continental powers in Europe . . . ." Stalin's glory has become incomparably greater than that of Hitler at the pinnacle of his power.

But to Stalin this glory in international affairs must pale beside what must seem to him his triumph over his dead adversaries—the old guard of Lenin. All of them had warned him that his regime would lead not only to the ruin of the Russian and the international revolution, but also to the transformation of the Soviet Republic into a "capitalist colony." Not a single one of them—the first Commander-in-Chief of the Red Army, Trotsky, least of all—granted him a chance of survival in case of a great war. "The Moscow oligarchy in any case will not survive the war by which it is so thoroughly frightened . . . . Stalin knows that if the U.S.S.R. in alliance with the democracies should emerge from the war victorious, the Russian people would reject the present oligarchy," Stalin's arch-enemy wrote in one of his last articles before his murder.

To a man who fought his way up in a long and desperate struggle against the intellectual and moral elite of the Bolshevik revolution, this victory must mean the last and ultimate confirmation of his own self. Socialism, as he understands it, has been accomplished in Russia. For to him Socialism means the destruction of the old ruling classes, the creation of huge industrial combinations in the hands of the state, the collectivization of agriculture, and the opening up of vast cultural opportunities for the people, impossible under Czarism.

Even more than all his adversaries, Stalin himself regarded "the inevitable clash of the Soviet Republic with the imperialist powers of the world" as the only valid test of his regime and the quality of its leadership. Stalin's Soviet Republic has stood the test. This must have meant even more to Stalin than the potential of power that he wields in Russia where his ideas are law the moment they are expressed.

It is not in Stalin's nature to experience the torment of doubts that assailed Lenin and Trotsky about the outcome of their revolutionary experiment. He is not a world reformer and philosopher. He is a ruler and a conqueror. It is with this Stalin who has arrived at the pinnacle of human power and self-assurance that the world has to deal at a turning point which will determine its destiny for a long period ahead.

The question, "What will Stalin do?" has become a world political problem of the first order. A realistic approach to the foreign policy of the Soviet Union today means a realistic approach to Stalin himself.

The difficulties of such an approach were made apparent in the abrupt turns of Soviet policy in the last years, turns that are understandable only in terms of Stalin's direct and personal interference. For only Stalin's mind could conceive of such an idea as the physical extermination of Lenin's party in Russia, and only his political cynicism could present the pact with Hitler as a supreme accomplishment of statesmanship.

The unlimited nature of Stalin's domestic power accounts for many of the difficulties of approach. On the whole, they are in fact a reflex of the complicated historical personality that is Stalin. This man who has risen from the leading group of the greatest and most radical revolution of history, who has effaced this revolution in its essential principles and aims and has become the creator of a new principle of state power, is frequently misunderstood by his contemporaries even when his conduct has a logical continuity within his own system of thought. Without taking into account the continuity of his thinking, one cannot approach Stalin realistically. To understand him one has to approach him as he interprets himself.

"THE UNBRIDGEABLE CHASM"

Many of the Marxist and liberal opponents of Stalin prove that his theory implies a complete break with that of Marx and Lenin, and there is much to be said for this viewpoint. Yet this does not prevent Stalin from acting as a "Marxist" and "Leninist," as he understands Marxism and Leninism. Whether one likes it or not, world politics and the destiny of millions of men rest on Stalin's interpretations of Marx and Lenin. From them one can learn more about

321

the main lines of his strategy than from all the diplomatic documents of the Soviet Republic.

A study of them by themselves, however, will lead nowhere. They must be read against the background of the doctrine of Lenin, which they elaborate. Stalin always cements and fortifies his political changes of a more fundamental nature with quotations from Lenin's writings. This is not only because of his personal ambition to go down in history as Lenin's best pupil and interpreter. It is also because Lenin's political writings are the main source of Stalin's intellectual and political training. In his own eyes he undoubtedly is the only real interpreter of Lenin and his own policies are the only valid variations of Lenin's theories under historically changed conditions. He calls his theoretical statements "dialectic continuations and developments of the doctrine of Marx and Lenin."

Stalin's elaboration of Lenin's doctrine is focused on the theory of imperialism as handed down to him by the master. A broad outline of the essential features of Lenin's doctrine provides the background for an understanding of the changes that Stalin has introduced.

Lenin held that the capitalist system at the turn of the century had become world wide, embracing all of the old and new civilizations of the globe. For the first time in its history it had established a world market and for the first time in history the competition of capitalist countries for the expansion of their markets could occur only in the form of a conflict between one imperialist power and another for a greater share in the world market. All the conflicts and contradictions in this world system would become threats to its existence. The particular form of its breakdown is the process of world revolution that eliminates one imperialist zone at a time from the global structure of world capitalism, thereby intensifying the contradictions within the remaining imperialist zones and furthering the process of world revolution. The first imperialist zone that historically has been eliminated from the system of world imperialism is that of the Russian revolution, the Soviet Union. It follows that imperialism and the Soviet Republic cannot coexist peacefully for the process of world revolution that has found its first historical realization in the Soviet Union is continuing at an accelerated pace in the remaining imperialist states. They cannot continue to exist under these circumstances. Sooner or later, therefore, either the Soviet Union or imperialism will disappear.

World revolution, according to Lenin, is mainly identified with the disintegration and the ultimate decline of the entire capitalist order. The Soviet Republic may further this process, but it cannot decide its outcome or initiate it by its own action. World revolution represents a chain of proletarian Socialist and colonial national revolutions, interconnected and interallied by the disintegration of the capitalist order in the world, but proceeding on their own within their own national and political frameworks.

Such revolutions can be successful only when they occur at the culmination point of a crisis of a capitalist state or of a group of states, at a time when "the bourgeoisie is not able to rule any longer in the old way and the working class is no longer able to live in the old way." They occur only when "the conscious minority of the working class"—the Communists—assumes the leadership of the majority and is able to neutralize the middle classes; in other words, at a time when the bourgeoisie has either lost its political and ideological influence on the people or is about to lose it.

In this doctrine the Communist Party represents an advance guard but remains an organic part of the working class of its own country, allied through trade unions, cooperatives, and similar organizations with its entire labor movement. It develops its own revolutionary practice from specific national conditions, although it always stays an integral part of the international revolutionary army of the Comintern. The revolution, according to Lenin's doctrine, culminates in an "armed insurrection" and destroys the political machinery of the bourgeois state in order to construct a political machinery of its own.

Stalin's interpretation of Lenin's theory of imperialism and world revolution takes the existence of the Soviet Union as its starting point. It retains the main structural elements of Lenin's doctrine but it changes the pattern of their structure. It retains the essential features while it shifts their emphasis. It states as firmly as did Lenin the inevitable decline of the capitalist order and the "unbridgeable chasm" between the Soviet Republic and the imperialist world surrounding it. But while Lenin subordinated the Soviet Republic to the process of world revolution, Stalin ties the decline of the capitalist order to the existence and the expansion of the Soviet Union.

Lenin said the existence of the Soviet Republic depends in the last analysis only on the victory of the world revolution.

Stalin says Socialism has been victorious in Russia. World revolution in the last analysis depends only on the fortification of our victory.

These two formulas may appear on the surface as too pointed in their opposition, but to ignore their sharp differentiation would mean to block the path towards an understanding of Stalinism and the historical process it represents. For Stalin's formula expresses the entire evolution of Bolshevism from an internationalist and equalitarian movement into a state party of specific Russian imperialist and totalitarian nature.

At no time has Stalin renounced Lenin's doctrine of the "unbridgeable chasm" between imperialism and the Soviet Republic. In none of his speeches or writings is there the slightest trace of such a change. On the contrary, in his own doctrine the thesis of the "unbridgeable chasm" has become exclusive and overrides all other considerations.

Since 1928 Stalin has consistently based all his domestic and foreign policies on the "unbridgeable chasm." In its name he asked the Russian people to take upon themselves the sufferings of the Five Year Plans, of the forced industrialization and collectivization of agriculture. "Either we will pass and surpass the capitalist countries industrially or we will be completely lost." This is the refrain of all Stalin's speeches and writings since 1928.

Stalin has liquidated all his foes within Russia as "imperialist agents." At the Eighteenth Party Congress of the Communist Party of the Soviet Union in March, 1939, he characterized the defeated Trotskyites and Bukharinites in these words: "This Trotsky-Bukharin bunch of spies, murderers and wreckers who kowtowed to the foreign world, who were possessed by a slavish instinct to grovel before every foreign bigwig, and who were ready to enter his employ as a spy— this handful of people who did not understand that the humblest Soviet citizen being free from the fetters of capitalism stands head and shoulders above any high-placed foreign bigwig whose neck wears the yoke of capitalist slavery . . . . . " and so on. He concludes

324

his remarks on foreign policy in this same speech with the challenge "never to forget that we are surrounded by a capitalist world."

Stalin uses all means to imprint on the minds of the Russian masses his doctrine of the "unbridgeable chasm" and of "capitalist encirclement." At the same Congress he raises the question of how it was possible that the espionage and conspiratorial activities of the Trotsky and Bukharin groups had been noticed only so recently, while the evidence indicates that they began in the very first days of the October Revolution. He immediately answers his own question by saying: "It is to be explained by an underestimation of the strength and consequence of the mechanism of the bourgeois states surrounding us and of their espionage organs."

At the same Congress Stalin proclaimed the final victory of Socialism in the Soviet Union: The exploited classes have disappeared, class conflicts have been eliminated, a society without classes has been built. "Now the main task of our state inside the country is the work of peaceful economic organization and cultural education. As for our army, punitive organs, and intelligence service, their edge is no longer turned to the inside of the country but to the outside against external enemies."

As a disciple of Marx and Lenin, Stalin knew very well that his statement about the disappearance of classes in the Soviet Union was in contradiction to the original theories of the masters. The creators of scientific Socialism have always regarded the "withering away of the state" in all its forms as the decisive criterion of the existence of a Socialist society. The existence of the state and its coercive machinery, according to their doctrine, is a striking proof that class conflicts still cleave society into two hostile sections, that classes have not been eliminated, and that Socialism—that is, a society without classes—has not been achieved. Only after economic and social classes and the conflicts arising from their existence and threatening to tear a given society asunder have vanished, will the coercive machinery—that is, the state—no longer be required. The state will then wither away like a muscle that is no longer being used. Marx and Lenin believed that between capitalism and Socialism would come a period of proletarian dictatorship representing a condition for Socialism but not yet a Socialist order of society. Lenin never regarded the Soviet Union as Socialist in respect to its existing social structure, but only in respect to its political philosophy, the forms of its economic administration, and the intentions of its leadership. "Socialism in one country" has no logical place in his or Marx's theory.

While Stalin was proclaiming the final victory of Socialism in the Soviet Union, every Soviet citizen was well aware that the state machinery, particularly the police, had acquired a more and more powerful grip on all aspects of his life and showed not the slightest sign of relinquishing it. Stalin solved the contradiction, however, by formulating a theory that has been praised by Manuilsky as "unsurpassed for its profundity," while other Soviet propagandists have heralded it as a new Communist Manifesto.

The centerpiece of this theory is again "capitalist encirclement." The theory of Marx and Lenin on state and Socialism remains correct after all, Stalin pronounced, but it is impossible to apply it literally to the Soviet Union while capitalist encirclement still threatens its existence. For Marx could not possibly foresee that Socialism would first be realized in a country threatened by capitalist encirclement. Lenin intended to change his doctrine originally derived from Marx in order to make it applicable to the problem of "Socialism in one country." Only death prevented his completing this.

In the Soviet Republic, according to Stalin, although completely Socialist, the state cannot "wither away." On the contrary, it has to grow and become stronger—at least as long as capitalist encirclement has not been eliminated and replaced by what he terms "Socialist encirclement."

Whether Stalin is sincerely convinced of his mission to reform Marxist and Leninist doctrine or whether he is a cynic who regards the doctrine exclusively from the standpoint of its utility for the accumulation of power, is of secondary importance. In all Soviet schools his doctrine is taught as the Bible of political wisdom. Its role is comparable to that of the Declaration of Independence in the United States.

It is of decisive importance that Stalin's interpretation of Lenin's doctrine has moulded the political psychology of the Russian Communists. This interpretation is the answer to all the pressing political questions of the day. It explains to the young generation why the "happy Socialist life" which could be claimed as a birthright cannot yet be enjoyed, and why Russia will reap the fruits of Socialism only after "capitalist encirclement" has been eliminated. It is indubitable that Stalin, in his intention, is and remains an implacable foe of the imperialist order of the West and East, even though he has exterminated in Russia and as far as he could abroad the proponents of a program of world revolution.

This apparent paradox is the source of most of the misjudgments of Stalin's policy, one of the most frequent of which is a democratic interpretation of events in Russia. This, for instance, seemed confirmed when Stalin, at the outbreak of war, took steps toward furthering nationalism and individualism within Russia. The Holy Synod was restored; the managerial authority of the Red directors in the war factories was enhanced; the last privileges of the trade unions and shop councils were eliminated; political commissars in the army were removed; army officers received golden epaulets, high salaries, and personal servants; the accumulation of substantial private fortunes was permitted even during the war, the educational system was reformed in a spirit foreign to that of Communist ideals; and the entire war propaganda was directed towards reviving the ideals of the fatherland and the history of the great Czars and generals of the past.

But even during the war years, those who knew Stalin's Russia could have no illusions as to the significance of the religious changes in Russia: The fact that Stalin placed the Metropolitan Sergius back on his golden throne makes neither Stalin nor the few thousand high ranking officials belonging to his general staff nor the hundred thousand higher "officers"—of the party, the police, the economic administration, and the army—into believers, nor does it change the relationship between church and state in a liberal direction. In a totalitarian dictatorship such as Stalin's, where the state has command over all spheres of life, religion as a private affair is not possible. Whenever the state and nation are deified, God will inevitably be nationalized. For twenty-five years the slogan "Religion is an opiate for the people" had been an official slogan of the Soviet Republic. Perhaps the atheistic dictatorship has now reached the conclusion that an "opiate for the people" is needed for domestic or foreign consumption or for both.

Never in the past have reforms of this or a similar kind seemingly directed towards democracy of the Western type led to the development of a political and cultural atmosphere which would facilitate the "bridging of the unbridgeable chasm." The most important domestic reform of the Soviet Republic, the democratic constitution of the year 1936 which extended the suffrage to the entire population (the chief authors of which were Bukharin and Radek) was followed in 1939 by the most fundamental turn of Stalin's foreign policy, his pact with Hitler.

But this pact with Hitler as well as the subsequent developments of Soviet foreign policy can be properly understood only if viewed from the standpoint of Stalin's basic assumptions: the unbridgeable chasm between the "capitalist encirclement" and the Soviet Union and the requirements of Soviet policy that flow therefrom. This was also a key to Stalin's interpretation of the Second World War. "The bourgeois politicians know, of course," he said in his speech at the Eighteenth Party Congress in March, 1939, "that the first imperialist world war led to the victory of the revolution in one of the largest countries. They are afraid that the second imperialist world war may also lead to the victory of the revolution in one or several countries."

However, the chief reason for the policy of the nonaggressive countries, particularly England and France, of rejecting collective resisttance to the aggressors, was in Stalin's view the collective opposition of the entire capitalist world to the Soviet Union. He cited imperialist policy in the Far East as well as in Europe to prove this point, and the yielding of Czechoslovakia to Germany he interpreted as the price of an undertaking to launch war on the Soviet Union. Up to the time that the Soviet Union was actively participating in the Second World War, therefore, Stalin had not abrogated the basic principle of his foreign policy, the fundamental clash between the Soviet Union and the capitalist world surrounding it.

The keynote of the entire speech was the repetition of the old refrain: The Soviet Union is ready to enter into a bloc with any capitalist state regardless of its internal structure. Such blocs come

328

and go. What remains is the unchangeable opposition to the entire imperialist system.

Perhaps in 1939 when Stalin concluded his pact with Hitler, he recalled Lenin's policy from the year 1918. In the spring of that year Lenin had negotiated with France for armed support against Germany and in the summer, after the peace treaty of Brest-Litovsk, with the Germans about an armed expedition against the English who had occupied Murmansk. Lenin's policy in 1918 and Stalin's in 1939, however, sprang from different fundamental considerations. For Lenin negotiated with the expectation that the coming German revolution would soon render all these agreements obsolete, and, in addition, he did not offer or accept from his imperialist partners any compensation, as for instance a partition of Poland. Lenin rejected the very idea of the Soviet Union's joining with either of the two warring groups.

During the year and a half of his pact with Hitler, Stalin's foreign policy corresponded to his oft-quoted statement about England, made in the year 1927 and cited by Manuilsky in his speech at the Eighteenth Party Congress, right after Stalin left the speakers' platform:

"British capitalism always was, is, and will be the most vicious strangler of popular revolutions. Ever since the great French Revolution of the end of the eighteenth century down to the Chinese revolution that is now in progress, the British bourgeoisie has always stood in the front ranks of the butchers of the liberation movement of mankind. . . . . But the British bourgeoisie does not like to fight with its own hands. It has always preferred to wage war through others."

Actually the war of coalition that Russia has waged against Germany has not caused Stalin to deviate from his basic conviction. In all of his announcements he has recognized as the primary explanation of victory only the heroism of the Red Army, the sacrifices of the Russian workers and peasants, and the accomplishments of Socialist industry and collectivist agriculture. The lend-lease help of the Allies and the fact that the German High Command had to split its forces have been given only a subordinate position. The second front and the coalition with the West have been allotted the honor of having put the finishing touches to a victory already achieved by the Soviet Republic.

During the electoral campaign for the Soviet parliament after the war, in the winter of 1946, all the members of the Politbureau, the most influential body of men in the Soviet Union, repeated the *leitmotifs* of the Eighteenth Party Congress: "We have been victorious. Germany and Japan have been destroyed. Yet capitalist encirclement continues. Without Socialist encirclement the security of the Soviet Union remains contingent, temporary, and incomplete." The basic principle of Stalin's strategy has survived the Second World War.

WORLD REVOLUTION OR "SOCIALIST ENCIRCLEMENT"

If this be basically correct the question arises: Is Stalin, now at the peak of his power, still an adherent of world revolution as he interprets it? Has he perhaps played just a devilish Caesarian game with Russia and the world in destroying tens of thousands of world revolutionaries in Russia? Is it possible that he will now as military victor return to the young dreams of the Russian Revolution?

These questions can best be answered by setting off the theories of Stalin and the various phases of his career against the struggle of ideas within the Bolshevik High Command.

A few days before Lenin returned from his Swiss refuge to Russia he wrote in his "Farewell Letter to the Swiss Workers": "The idea that the Russian proletarian is the chosen revolutionary among the workers of the world is absolutely alien to us. . . . . The Russian proletariat singlehanded cannot bring the Socialist revolution to a victorious conclusion. . . . ." This Lenin expected from a joining of the Russian with the German revolution.

On the morning after the victory of the Russian Revolution, Lenin expressed the hope that "our children or grandchildren may experience the victory of Socialism." A short time before his death Lenin formulated the same idea even more pointedly: "We are not yet civilized enough to pass directly to Socialism!"

Stalin's approach to the problem whether Russia was the chosen country to achieve Socialism by herself and by her own efforts was cautious and devious in the beginning. But not long after Lenin's death

330

he answered the question in a way that differed markedly from that of the dead master:

"What else is our country if not the base of world revolution? . . . . And how can it be a real base of the world revolution if it is not competent to construct a complete Socialist society?"

In this doctrine Stalin gives the world revolution a new content. It becomes fundamentally identical with the victory of Socialism in the Soviet Union. Russia now becomes the chosen country. Revolutionary movements or revolutions in the capitalist countries become its by-products, having to adjust and subordinate themselves to it. The fundamental difference between Lenin's and Stalin's doctrines is illustrated most clearly in the relationship of the Soviet Union to the revolutionary movement in Germany: When the German Communists prepared an armed insurrection in the fall of 1923, the Soviet Republic mobilized its army and was ready to risk its own existence for the sake of world revolution in Germany. Ten years later during the German crisis that resulted in the destruction of the Communist movement in Germany, Stalin proceeded on the lines of a determined nonintervention policy dictated by the requirements of Socialist construction in the Soviet Union.

In 1936, in line with his concept of "Socialism in one country," Stalin branded charges that the Soviet Union was harboring plans for world revolution as a "tragi-comic blunder." Stalin's sensational statement at the time excited much doubt and questioning. Yet it was more than a propagandistic twist for foreign consumption. It was entirely in line with the thesis that he had already expressed ten years earlier about the change of functions between the Soviet Republic and world revolution.

This, however, did not prevent Stalin from writing two years later, in an article about the Red Army: "Our army is an army of the world revolution, an army of the workers of all countries. . . . ."

The removal of Lenin's conception of world revolution from Stalin's system has not left a vacuum. Its place has been taken by a new concept that follows logically from Stalin's position, on one side, that Socialism was realized in one country and, on the other, that between the Socialist country and the rest of the world stretches an unbridgeable chasm.

331

Stalin has given up the idea of world revolution on the pattern of Lenin and Trotsky, but this does not mean that he has given up the thought of utilizing the "organic crisis of capitalist society." The countries outside of Russia have demonstrated their inability according to Stalin, to travel on the road to revolution and Socialism on their own power. "The organic crisis of capitalist society," therefore, acquires a different function. It does not lead as with Lenin to "revolutionary situations" in the capitalist countries outside of Russia. It does not enhance the spontaneous process within the masses of forming Communist parties, but it enhances the process of disintegration within the capitalist order, whose only beneficiary is the Socialist society already born in Russia.

The task that is left to the Communist parties is to channel the benefits that result from the existing process of disintegration into the direction of the Soviet Union. They are no longer permitted to direct their own revolutionary struggles in accordance with the conditions of their own countries. Now they have to conduct themselves exclusively as the requirements of the Soviet Union direct.

"The international army of revolution" has become a Russian army with international battalions. "Socialism in one country"— Russia—excludes Socialism in all other countries until it is made possible by the expansion of power of the Soviet Union. This is the cornerstone of the theory of world revolution in Stalin's interpretation.

The development of Stalin's political ideas in this field did not follow a preconceived theoretical path but grew out of the changing conditions themselves by a process of continuous adaptation to them. From 1924 to 1934, the decisive years of his rise, in all questions concerning the disintegration of the capitalist order and the rapidity with which a Communist revolution could be expected to develop therefrom, Stalin took a more radical stand than did his opponents, Zinoviev, Trotsky, and especially Bukharin.

Marxist economists before Stalin had depicted the life of capitalist society as a cycle turning booms into sudden depressions through crises. Stalin designed a simplified scheme of his own: a permanent crisis of capitalist society. This scheme is one of the sources of his unlimited confidence in his own political and social system and plays

332

a determining role in his appraisal of the revolutionary process in the capitalist countries.

In 1928 Stalin appeared to have a better grasp of the economic situation than his chief adversary Bukharin who was by far his superior in the field of economics. The world economic depression of 1929 seemed to confirm his simplified economic scheme. He heralded the appearance of the economic depression of 1929 as a harbinger of the coming revolution, and he ordered all Communist parties, especially in Germany, to direct their entire policy towards "the immediate conquest of power." (Only after his domestic policies brought on a crisis in Russia in 1930-31 did he call for a sudden turn in Comintern affairs. In accord with this, right after Hitler's rise to power, the Russian-German agreements were extended for a five-year period.)

Even at the beginning of 1934 he still saw in German Fascism only a confirmation of the profound convulsion through which the entire capitalist system in Europe was going. The Nazi purge of June 30, 1934, convinced him that the Hitler regime was there to stay and that no further immediate shocks to the capitalist system could be expected. But he never deviated from the Marxist doctrine that the forces of self-destruction within the capitalist system are inescapable. Every one of his speeches up to the very inception of the war repeats this thought: The crisis of capitalist society is organic and permanent; its consequence is a new series of wars and revolutions.

In his first programmatic speech after the war, Stalin repeated the same thought as the most important lesson of the war: "It would be incorrect to think that the war arose accidentally or as the result of the fault of some of the statesmen. Although these faults exist, the war arose in reality as the inevitable result of the development of the world economic and political forces on the basis of monopoly capitalism. . . . . Our Marxist analysis declares that the capitalist system of world economy conceals elements of crisis and war, that the development of world capitalism does not follow a steady and even course forward, but proceeds through crises and catastrophes."

In this respect there is no difference between Lenin and Trotsky and Stalin. What Stalin adds to the old analysis is the thought that in the Soviet Union a new society, unimpeded by the diseases of the

333

old—depressions, unemployment, and insecurity—has been constructed and exerts a magnetic attraction on the working classes of the old world still plagued by the old sores.

The concept of "Socialist encirclement" in the new scheme replaces world revolution in the old scheme. Stalin applies this term for the first time on a broad scale at the Eighteenth Party Congress of the Communist Party of the Soviet Union, in connection with his new doctrine of the state already mentioned. "Socialist encirclement" in Stalin's terminology is the elimination of capitalist encirclement, the entire surrounding world of capitalism. Only if capitalist encirclement is liquidated and the danger of foreign military attack vanishes can Communism accomplish its goals in the Soviet Union. If, however, according to Stalin, capitalist encirclement is not liquidated and is not replaced by a Socialist encirclement of the capitalist world, Communism in the Soviet Union will remain in danger. "Socialist encirclement," therefore, becomes the last and highest objective of Soviet policy.

In Stalin's theory the self-creative process of revolution within the framework of separate capitalist countries is no longer conceivable. Its place is taken by the military action of the Red Army and the diplomatic action of the Soviet Union, the decisive instruments of "Socialist encirclement." In this sense the Red Army remains an army of the "world revolution."

The Bolsheviks in Lenin's time defended themselves energetically against the accusation that they wished to carry the world revolution forward on the points of bayonets. Tukhachevsky and other new converts who advanced such theories in 1920 were sharply rebuked by Lenin and Trotsky, although they were only repeating what they had heard from Radek and Bukharin: The action of the Red Army beyond the frontiers of the Soviet Republic represented either a "defense against imperialist attacks" or "assistance to a revolution already developing and expressing itself in a victorious determined insurrection within a capitalist country."

In this way they defined their 1919 and 1920 military offensives against Poland and Georgia. In none of their countless speeches and writings is there anything that could be interpreted as a wish to replace the proletarian and Socialist revolutions by military conquests or to substitute for the economic, political, and social processes of revolution military interference.

In Stalin's scheme of things the military action of the Red Army becomes synonymous with the social and national liberation of the occupied country. Lenin found a decisive cause for the defeat of the Red Army before Warsaw in 1920 in the refusal of the great majority of the Polish people to accept the Soviet system. Such an eventuality has no place in Stalin's scheme: The occupation of a country by the Red Army implies the elimination of the bourgeoisie and of the big landowners. Such elimination is identical with the liberation of the people in Stalin's doctrine. Stalin has never accepted as one of the main causes of his first misfortunes in his first Finnish campaign the fact that not only the propertied classes but the majority of the working classes as well, stubbornly refused to accept the Soviet social and political system.

In his view the problem of Socialism is identical with the economic expropriation of the capitalist groups and the introduction of collective state property. Once the old posts of economic, social, and political command have been evacuated and their holders replaced by the representatives of a collectivized state, the essential problems of Socialism have been solved. The organization of a Socialist economy becomes a technical question and, therefore, in his scheme of things, the spontaneous and active support of the masses of men is superfluous, even detrimental: Happiness has to be imposed upon the masses from above, as Romain Rolland said.

THE LEGITIMATE REVOLUTION

Stalin is not sincerely devoted to the liberation of humanity by a Socialist world revolution, as was Lenin. Stalin's theory of Socialist encirclement is an opportunist but not a theoretical substitute for Lenin's world revolution which represented a qualification of the Socialist world federation of Marx. "Socialist encirclement" is not an idealistic end in itself nor a dogma of a perfect solution of all social problems. It represents a means by which the established state power of Stalin's empire expresses its dynamism. The Slavic countries of Europe *are* Socialist encirclement. If ever in France or England a Socialist movement of a non-Russian nature should become victorious, these countries would continue to represent the "vanguard of capitalist encirclement."

Stalin does not consider the Russians a chosen people, as did Hitler the Germans—a superior nation because of their racial origins. Such theories were always a target for his sarcasm. But he is imbued with the idea of the economic and social superiority of the system that he has created over that of all other countries.

In his campaign speech already mentioned which contained a sort of justification of the principles of his policy, Stalin declared: "The point is that the Soviet social system has proved to be more stable than a non-Soviet social system, that the Soviet social system is a better form of organization of society than any non-Soviet social system."

His strategy proves that he regards himself as the legitimate inheritor of Hitler's "new order," for he is convinced that the conservative capitalist order in Europe has collapsed and that not the United States nor England nor the European nations themselves will ever be able to reconstruct it. Outside of Stalin's Soviet Russia there existed in his opinion no power with a feasible system of order for Europe after Hitler's fall. As far as he personally is concerned, his occupation of Hitler's lebensraum is the occupation of a space that had neither master nor order.

Stalin's expectations have apparently been confirmed by events. Bourgeois civil society and order in Europe have disintegrated. Eastern Europe under Russian occupation is being re-formed in the molds of a totalitarian Socialism. Germany has become a power vacuum. Potsdam added another success to Stalin's long series of successes. For here the elimination of private property in the means of production was accomplished not by unilateral Soviet action but with the cooperation of the capitalist West. The self-elimination of the liberal capitalist order imparted to Stalin's conception of democracy in Europe an aggressive and expanding vitality.

From a diplomatic angle Stalin had already accomplished international acceptance of the legitimacy of his expansion at the conferences of Moscow and Teheran. For the first time since the rise of the Soviet Republic did the Allies accept "Soviet democracy" as a complete equal to their own political and social system. Outside of international law there now remains only Fascism. Consequently every nation now has the right to choose between democracy of the Anglo-American type and that of the Soviet Russian type. His emphatic statement after the close of the Moscow conference: "Liberated countries must be allowed to choose their own form of government"—should be interpreted this way.

Since the legitimacy of Soviet democracy has been internationally recognized and the policy of nonintervention in the domestic affairs of European nations accepted as obligatory by both himself and the Allies, Stalin can look upon such acceptance as a de facto recognition of future Soviet expansion in these countries. With a clear conscience, therefore, he was able to sign the famous paragraph six of the Moscow declaration, that reads: ". . . . that after the termination of hostilities they (the Four Powers) will not employ their military forces within the territory of other states except for the purposes envisaged in this declaration and after joint consultation."

Stalin's advantage during the international negotiations since his victory at Stalingrad arose from the fact that his moves took for their starting point the anticipated distribution of power and change in social structure after the defeat of Germany. Whether the Allies had a defined program for Europe or not, their diplomatic strategy did not take into account the fundamental change in social structure that had been taking place. In any case, they have accepted the legitimacy of Soviet democracy within the whole of Europe.

Only those who regard diplomatic tests as the only authoritative commentaries of history can claim that Stalin has kept his world political intentions concealed, that an enigma—Stalin—exists. Twenty years ago he wrote: "For the slogan 'the United States of Europe' we will substitute the 'federation of Soviet republics' of advanced countries and colonies which have fallen out of or are falling away from the imperialist system of economy."

The system of 1944 designed to accommodate such advanced countries is the decentralization and the greater national autonomy granted to the old as well as the new Soviet republics.

Stalin has been consistent and constant in this as in many other respects. Just as twenty years ago he rejected a unification of Europe, so he rejects today a federation on a regional basis as proposed by Churchill.

"Every right-minded person," an editorial in his periodical *War and the Working Class* said in the summer of 1943, "understands that one of the leading roles in the organization of postwar Europe and of the whole world will belong to the USSR Anti-democratic and semi-Fascist elements, however, are striving to prevent the participation of the USSR in the organization of the postwar world, setting up the many fantastic plans in this direction, plans obviously hostile to the Soviet Union. There are quite a few such plans starting with the plan for the creation of a United States of Europe, Pan-Europe, and ending with the plan for creating a Europe divided into various federations, confederations, and regional blocks of states."

Stalin's rejection of a European federation of the Western type has both defensive and offensive purposes: By preventing a new *cordon sanitaire* in all forms, he secures Soviet expansion diplomatically—that is, the elimination of capitalist encirclement—and leaves the door open for federations of the Eastern type, "Socialist encirclement."

CHAPTER XXIII

Totalitarian Pan-Slavism

STALIN'S PILOT IN THE BALKANS

I N A GREAT SOMBER STONE HOUSE IN SOFIA, NOT FAR FROM THE
American legation, are the headquarters of Georg Dimitrov.

Around the building runs a high iron fence. In front of the
heavy wrought-iron doors Red Army soldiers stand on guard. Dimitrov in Sofia is as inaccessible as is the Great Father in the Kremlin.
His house is the Kremlin of the Balkans.

The power Tito wields in Yugoslavia is strong. Yet Tito is only
one of Dimitrov's lieutenants, as are General Hoxha in Tirana,
Rakoczi in Budapest, or Petrascanu in Bucharest. The imposing
palace of the Kara-Georgevitch on the Danube that has become
Tito's domain is but a subsidiary of the mysterious bourgeois townhouse in Sofia.

After the Russian occupation of Bulgaria, Dimitrov held no official
position of state; he is General Secretary of the Communist Labor
Party and a representative in the National Assembly. When, after
the occupation by the Red Army, Dimitrov first appeared in the
old Duma building, the former pilot of the Comintern was given
an unending ovation. Weeks before the event the columns of the newspapers, particularly those of the *Fatherland Front,* were filled with
long articles describing his life in all detail to the people of Bulgaria.
In Bulgarian schools the "life and struggle" of Comrade Dimitrov
has become one of the most important subjects of instruction. A
picture of Dimitrov in intimate conversation with Stalin and Manuilsky can be seen everywhere. The picture is more than ten years old. It
was shot in 1934 when Dimitrov returned to Moscow from the
Reichstag trial.

The old photograph has, as everybody understands, a current
significance: this is Stalin's representative, it says, the only foreigner
who belongs to his intimate circle and to whom he has given the
Order of Lenin.

The General Secretary of the dissolved Comintern understands the paraphernalia of power as a magician his stage tricks. This he demonstrated in 1935 when he stepped into the new office of General Secretary of the Comintern. To merge and unify the Slavic-Southeast of Europe with the Russian Soviet Republic requires that the man entrusted with this task live in an atmosphere of inaccessible and impersonal power. Dimitrov plays this role as effectively as the one assigned to him ten years earlier.

At its inception around the middle of the last century, pan-Slavism was a religious idea merging the fraternal feelings of the Slavs with the Messianic faith of the Greek orthodox church. It was only after the Russian wars against Turkey and the subsequent liberation of Bulgaria from its Turkish oppressors by Russian armies at the end of the last century that pan-Slavism began to take on a militant imperialist character.

After the expulsion of the Turks from the Balkans, pan-Slavism was chiefly directed against the Austro-Hungarian monarchy which included Czechs, Slovaks, Croats, and Bosnians. In these countries, however, the pan-Slav movement did not assume a decidedly nationalistic character. On the whole, in most of these national groups it represented the upper middle classes and their intellectual following. Labor in general preferred the Hapsburg monarchy to the Czarist autocracy.

The Bolsheviks in the early days of their rule fought a determined battle against pan-Slavism. Stalin's pan-Slavism amalgamates the revolutionary and religious aspirations of the Slavic world with the expansionism of the great Russians. This was what Stalin revealed to the Russian people as the significance of their sufferings during the war, when he stated in his victory message:

"The centuries-old struggle of the Slav people for their existence and their independence has been concluded by victory over the German invaders and over German tyranny."

The totalitarian pan-Slavism of the Stalintern merged the spontaneous revolutionary movements of the Balkans with the expanding power of the Red Army. The sudden rise of a man like Tito illustrates this fact.

TITO'S PARTISANS—CHEF D'OEUVRE OF THE STALINTERN

The Balkan revolution that is associated with the name of Tito had all the attributes of the great romantic legends immortalized in the memory of mankind. There was the glorious hero allied with distant omnipotent powers. There were the endless sufferings of the people that merged death and victory. There was the cruel monster and arch foe who finally was brought to an ignominious end in the valleys and woods of the country.

This movement of the Yugoslav people was a real revolution in the midst of a world war. The civil war between Tito and Mikhailovitch was as much of its warp and woof as was the national war against Germany. The Partisans of the Balkans were late successors of the *sans culottes* of the French Revolution, of the militia of the Paris Commune, and the Partisans of the Russian Revolution.

The Russians had as little to do with the outbreak of this popular revolution as they had with the Spanish Civil War, but they were the only power able to utilize it for their own purposes.

In the mind of the primitive peasant who was the foundation of Tito's armies, the invader as well as those groups who collaborated with him directly or indirectly represented the same feudal upper class as had exploited him twenty-five years earlier from Vienna and, later on, from Belgrade. His country is the soil on which he lives and on which his bread grows. The poor Balkan peasant, whether orthodox Serb, Catholic Croat or Slovene, or Bosnian Moslem, hated the Yugoslav feudal dynasty as heartily as his parents hated the Austrian satraps and their Turkish predecessors. His national ideal and his social ideal are one. For this reason he regarded the victory of the Red Armies as a victory over the feudal upper classes, and identified it with his own hopes and expectations. That was why the Red Armies could invade the entire Southeast of Europe as a liberating force.

The peasant revolution was the elementary source of Tito's power. It was the first of the great currents that originated in Russia and that bind the Balkan movement with the Soviet power in Russia. The Balkan peasant knew nothing about Socialism. Russia represented for him the land of peasant liberation. Characteristic of his attitude was a report emanating from Bulgaria in 1944 that after the Russian victory at Stalingrad many Bulgarian peasants began to return from Macedonia to their own villages because they did not want to come too late for the "great distribution."

The second major current whose source was Russia was that of Slavic fraternity which had little to do with the nationalistic pan-Slavism of the last century but much more with similar language, culture, patterns of life, and the memory of the role Russia played in the liberation of the Balkan countries from Turkey. For the last twenty-five years the feudal upper class had blocked Balkan communication with Russia. The military debacle of France and the cruel German occupation again opened all Balkan gates wide for Russia.

The third great current emanating from Russia was the unification of the orthodox churches. With the re-establishment of the Moscow Synod, the absolute dictator from the East appeared to the Balkans in the light of a social liberator and a religious reformer.

All this explains how Joseph Broz, a Croat-Slovenian metal worker known previously only to the police archives of Belgrade and Zagreb and to the cadre division of the Comintern, could overnight have become the leader of a great movement and one of the most talked-of men of his times.

After the split of the Serbian Social Democrats at the end of the First World War, the Yugoslav Communist Party had become one of the strongest parties of the country. The majority of the workers of the country as well as substantial groups of intellectuals followed its leadership. In the constitutional assembly elections it became the third strongest party, with fifty-eight representatives. On the thirty-first of December, 1920, the party was declared illegal, and in the years that followed, the brutal military dictatorship suppressed and eliminated it by all the means of terror known in those days. Its leaders died in the prisons of Yugoslavia, and, those who were able to survive, in Russia.

The report that Manuilsky gave in March, 1939, on the status of the Comintern and its parties has already been mentioned. In this report he characterized the Yugoslavian Communist Party as "ruined by police factionalists" in the same way as the Polish and Hungarian parties. In other words, as far as Moscow was concerned this meant that the Communist Party of Yugoslavia had ceased to exist before the war.

Neither in the minutes of the all-Slavic congresses in Moscow nor in the government of Tito is there a single name of a Yugoslav Communist known from former years. Many of the Yugoslavian Communists were destroyed in the great Russian purges; others were lost in the jails of the Serbian police dictatorship.

In 1939 the remnants of the Yugoslav Communist Party consisted of a loose organization of former volunteers from the Spanish Civil War grouping themselves around the organizer of a Yugoslav regiment, Joseph Broz.

He was a typical proletarian professional revolutionary, trained by the Comintern during the first ten years of its existence. In the First World War he had been a soldier in the Austro-Hungarian army and, later, a war prisoner in Russia; in the Russian Revolution, an organizer of a Yugoslavian division of the Red Guards; in the Hungarian revolution of Bela Kun, a Communist organizer in the Croat Hungarian frontier districts. His entire further life was spent either in underground work in Yugoslavia—interrupted by several terms in jail—or in Moscow where in the various training schools for civil war of the Comintern, he received the military education that now stood him in good stead.

The small Communist group that he gathered around himself in the summer of 1941 was composed of volunteers from the Spanish Civil War. Peter Dapcevic, Vlada Rukovina, Kostja Nagy, and other volunteers later became generals leading divisions and armies of the National Army of Liberation. Tito had the great advantage of knowing nearly every one of these men personally. Although he himself had not participated in the Spanish Civil War, he had acted as a recruiting officer for the Spanish revolutionary army from 1936 to 1938, and in this capacity came into close contact with these volunteers.

The Yugoslav government had been on the side of Franco and had hunted down all would-be volunteers for the Spanish Republic. The agility of a shrewd conspirator was necessary to move a few hundred men illegally across the Yugoslav border to Vienna and

Zurich, where a new organization took charge and sent them to a central office in Paris.

Since his training at the Academy for Civil War in Moscow, Tito had been ready to step forth at any time as officer in a civil war army. But he might never have become a marshal if the situation in Yugoslavia in the summer of 1941 had not required a man with his talents, abilities, and background.

Mikhailovitch, colonel of the Serbian general staff, was a specialist in guerrilla warfare—one of the few Serbian staff officers who had realized that the Yugoslav army did not have the slightest chance against Germany. Long before the actual outbreak of the war, therefore, he had prepared himself for his role as leader of a guerrilla army. The graduate from the Academy for Civil War in Moscow, Joseph Broz, proved to be very much his superior by the time the guerrilla war was a reality.

Mikhailovitch considered guerrilla war a matter of military tactics. His army operated in small mobile units which, because of their precise knowledge of the terrain and their great elasticity, were in a position to fight a very much superior foe. Yet his army grew smaller and smaller and that of Tito kept growing larger, even while Tito still accepted the sovereignty of the Yugoslav government-in-exile in London that had made Mikhailovitch its war minister.

Mikhailovitch had overlooked the fact that a guerrilla army can in the long run neither be led by professional officers nor kept together by military discipline.

Tito realized that a guerrilla army, regardless of its general patriotic zeal, is lost unless it continuously draws its strength from the people and is led by men who have acquired their military ranks fighting. The same principle applies to the strategy of civil war. At the end of 1942 Mikhailovitch put the balance of his army in cold storage, planning to use them only when the Allies opened up a front in the Balkans. Probably this strategy was agreed upon between himself and his British staff officers. Actually, it lost him even his life.

Guerrilla armies have their own laws. They have to be in continuous action or they disintegrate. Their military cohesion holds only in action; it cannot be based on pure military discipline. The passive strategy of Mikhailovitch, therefore, became a source of new energy for Tito, supplying him with many deserters from Mikhailovitch's ranks and ultimately giving him military superiority, so that Churchill, whose personal sympathies were on the side of Mikhailovitch, had to recognize Tito as the only military ally in Yugoslavia.

Mikhailovitch had begun his fight against the Nazis with the federalist program of the democratic opposition in Yugoslavia. But his ensuing struggle against the popular movement of Tito brought him into close alliance with the absolutist Greater Serbian cliques. The Communist Tito, however, who up to the summer of 1941 had probably never exchanged a word with anyone belonging to the bourgeois society of Zagreb and Belgrade, gathered around himself all the democratic and progressive forces in Yugoslavia with the exception of the insignificant Social Democratic groups who remained in Mikhailovitch's camp because they feared Russia.

The chain of events in operation can not be explained solely on the basis of the conditions of national struggle in Yugoslavia. The Yugoslav Communists had had some influence among the intelligentsia after the Russian Revolution, but during the 1930's this influence had been wiped out. At that time the entire intelligentsia of the Balkans regarded Paris as the cultural and political center of the world. But after Munich the faith and confidence that they—and the Czechoslovaks even more—had placed in the West, vanished. The betrayal of Czechoslovakia by Chamberlain and Daladier turned Slav democracy definitely away from the West. The military debacle of the French was to the western Slavs a "Goetterdaemmerung."

It was then that the new pan-Slavic movement was born and Moscow was able to reap its benefits without having contributed directly to its rise. After the overthrow of the Prince Paul regime friendly to Hitler by General Simovitch with the help and connivance of the British embassy, the military assistance that the British promised the new regime in Yugoslavia got stalled in Greece. This did not enhance the reputation of the West in Yugoslavia. When British military help failed to arrive there, the bitter word went round in Belgrade: This is our Munich!

This turn of the Slavic intelligentsia explains why Tito was able to win over so quickly the active Serbian youth organizations, the national sport organizations like the all-Slavic Sokol, and most of the academic intelligentsia. Into his government he gathered some of the best names of Yugoslav democracy.

In Tito's faction were found a great number of orthodox priests who consecrated their own Yugoslav national flag together with the Soviet Star and who fought actively along with the Partisans. When the French Communists "offered their hand" to the Catholics, they were playing a cynical comedy. In the Balkans, however, the attitude of the poor priests towards the Partisans was proof that this movement had sunk its roots deep into the people. A modern atheist movement like that staged by the Communists in Germany and France would have been impossible among the workers of the Balkans who were still tied intimately to the religious faith of their villages and their land.

The Balkan Communists, even in the first years of the Comintern, had never openly advanced an atheistic viewpoint. In the Podkarpatka Russ, the extreme eastern section of Czechoslovakia that was annexed by Russia in 1945, for example, a Jewish Communist deputy had been one of the most popular figures in the period from 1918 to 1923. He had begun all his meetings with the sign of the Cross and with the words: "Blessed be our Lord Jesus Christ." In those areas, mostly populated by poor peasants faithful to their religion, the Communists were the strongest party. Frequently at elections they received absolute majorities.

The Russians realized the importance of this religious factor for the furtherance of their purposes. In September, 1943, Stalin recalled the Patriarch Sergius from his exile in Kasan, the capital of the Soviet Tartar Republic, and solemnly declared himself sympathetic to the establishment of the Holy Synod dissolved in 1918. By this act Stalin attempted a unification of the orthodox church of the Balkans under the direction of Moscow and its coordination with Stalin's Balkan protectorate. This coordination of the Balkans with the Russian sphere of security has been taking place with the blessing of the orthodox church. Its unification may become a strong foundation for Russian expansion.

The Serbian clergy did not take a united stand in the civil war. Yet the cautious attitude of the Patriarch Gavrilov, refusing to condemn Tito and his movement, indicated that it was prepared for all eventualities.

To be sure, the Balkan Federation for which Tito fought was not the alliance of Communist states that was the objective of the Comintern for its first ten years. Tito promised "full democratic rights," "inviolability of private property," provision for "every possible opportunity for individual initiative in industry and economic enterprise" to the Balkan peoples, and expected "no radical changes whatever in the social life and activities of the people. . . . ."

At the same time, however, he demanded the "replacing of reactionary village authorities and gendarmes with representatives chosen by the people who will bear the truly democratic character of the people. All the most important questions relating to social life and state organization of the people have to be solved by the people themselves through representatives who will be properly elected by the people themselves."

Tito's program was one of a *petit bourgeois* democracy, attempting to eliminate the feudal upper classes and their adherents in the rural villages. In former years the peasant parties of the great Croat leader Raditch and of the Bulgarian Stamboulinski had advanced similar programs. But Tito gathered into his hands the power actually to destroy the upper classes.

The masses of the Balkan peoples who shed their blood in the struggles of these years did not regard the announcement of the terror as a breach of the democracy and legality that had been solemnly promised by Tito. They reacted as did the French masses for whom the execution of Marie Antoinette was as an act of revolutionary legality. Tito's revolution was a Jacobin revolution in a world grown one hundred and fifty years older. At the same time, Tito's irreconcilable opposition to the upper classes of the Balkans was a solid foundation for a democratic Balkan Federation.

A democratic federated Yugoslavia could have offered a realistic solution to the Macedonian problem which always faced the authoritarian Yugoslav and Bulgarian governments of the past. Such a solution would have been a great stimulus to a democratic federation of the entire Balkans. Actually, the Yugoslavian constitution introduced after the dissolution of the monarchy instituted a democratic federal system, a system that had been the goal of all Balkan minorities and the common program of all democratic and Socialist movements of the past. Following the Russian example, Tito created a chamber of all nationalities in addition to a parliament, with rights equal to those of the parliament.

Unfortunately, events in Yugoslavia after the war depreciated the progressive constitution to a piece of paper. They demonstrated that in the lebensraum of the Eurasian empire every form of revolution is bound to end in a totalitarian dictatorship. The Jacobins of the Balkans have fought in vain.

STALINTERN PARTY IN BULGARIA

Bulgaria's Tito is a woman—Tsola Dragoitcheva. Bulgarian women have always been known in eastern Europe for their proud beauty. Tsola Dragoitcheva in her younger years was no exception. The secretary of the Fatherland Front, with her heavy, auburn hair and her dark, flaming eyes, had for two decades been one of the idols of the old guard of the Bulgarian Communists. Perhaps now she is their last hope—particularly of those who have returned, after a brief revolutionary honeymoon, to the same concentration camps and jails from which they had been liberated together with Tsola, when the Russian armies approached the frontiers of Bulgaria.

Czar Boris had joined the Axis after the defeat of Yugoslavia, Rumania, and Greece, but he always remained adamant in his decision not to declare war on Soviet Russia. The Russian ambassador stayed on in Sofia. The Bulgarian armies plundered Yugoslavia and Thrace, but no Bulgarian soldier fought on the Russian front. The German occupation was moderate in its demands, and the Germans paid good prices for Bulgarian tobacco. The Bulgarian peasants prospered. Their sons returned from their expeditions with good loot.

Nevertheless, the peasants sympathized with the desperate party war the Communists were waging against the German occupation. They gave refuge to fleeing Communists and restored their spirits with their precious goat cheese and good old red wines. They themselves, however, did not participate in the civil war waged by some thousands of Communist workers. In the Bulgarian concentration camps in the mountains bones were broken and human flesh burned just as in the jails of the Gestapo. Their Bulgarian colleagues had little to learn from the Gestapo.

In the middle of 1944, Tsola, after many years of absence, suddenly re-emerged in Bulgaria. Rumor had it that she had descended from a Russian airplane. Probably things were somewhat less romantic. The old paths of conspiracy of the Comintern in the Balkans that led from Odessa to the Bulgarian shores of the Black Sea were as useful in war as in peace. But Tsola had come from the East, from Father Stalin—she must, therefore, have descended from heaven. She was a symbol of the coming change in Bulgarian affairs.

It was her destiny and personal ill fate always to be a symbol. In 1920 she had been sentenced to death as a young student because she had participated in one of those numerous bombing assaults that were part and parcel of the revolutionary class war in Bulgaria. Hundreds of thousands of people at that time prayed and trembled for the life of the intrepid girl.

Tsola, however, was not only courageous but shrewd. Bulgarian law does not permit the execution of pregnant women. Tsola became pregnant in prison. According to rumors, she had charmed the director of the prison and had won him over to Communism. Her child added new rays of glory to her own halo.

Her return from Moscow in 1944 became the signal for an intensification of the war of the Partisans. Again she was arrested, but this time her life was no longer in danger. The Russians were already fighting in Hungary and Rumania. So with her assistant, Anton Yugov, later to become Minister of Police, she directed the activity of the labor party and of the Partisans from prison. The Communist workers of Bulgaria were preparing a repetition of the Russian October Revolution. Even the peasants no longer vacillated, for a redistribution of the land was being promised. . . . . But neither the workers nor the peasants were aware that Moscow's plans headed in an entirely different direction.

When the Russian army marched into Bulgaria Stalin showed no mercy to the Bulgarian Premier Muravieff, who had not joined Hitler's war against the Soviets and was now trying to save his country's independence by declaring war on the Axis. Stalin answered by declaring war on Bulgaria, forcing out the Muravieff government by this declaration and making way for a new government of his old agents, Georgiev and Veltchev, with whom he immediately concluded an armistice.

Tsola had brought with her from Moscow the order to form a united front of the Communists with the Fatherland Front of Kimon Georgiev and Damian Veltchev. These two men had for years been among the many mysteries of the Balkans.

Conventional political yardsticks are even less applicable in the Balkans than anywhere else. "Yesterday there was no political murder in Sofia." That was one of the headlines in a daily newspaper in Sofia during the 1930's. In such a country terms like "democracy" and "fascism" have little meaning.

Georgiev and Veltchev had led the middle class conservative opposition to the bloody reign of Tsankov, and with support from the officers' corps of the Bulgarian army had succeeded in overthrowing Tsankov in May, 1934. They had been welcomed by the majority of the population in the hope that they would free the country from the exploits of the Macedonian terrorists. The Russians, who, shortly before, had extended the Rapallo agreement with Hitler for five years, had not been disturbed by the fascist facade of the new government. Georgiev and Veltchev resumed diplomatic relations with Russia, ruptured since 1923.

This first Georgiev-Veltchev dictatorship lasted just one year. Yet the diplomatic relations with Russia remained untouched. Georgiev and Veltchev became the most important agents of Soviet influence in Bulgaria.

Bulgaria accepted the new government of Georgiev as a proof that Russia did not expect to interfere in the domestic affairs of Bulgaria and as a guarantee against a Communist party dictatorship. Communist workers looked at the matter as a tactical maneuver. Even before the Red Armies had crossed the borders, workers' and peasants' Soviets were being organized everywhere, taking over authority in local affairs. The Red Army was being welcomed with the old slogans of the October Revolution: "All power to the Soviets," "Land and Liberty!"

The liberal hopes of the middle classes did not last longer than the revolutionary ones of the workers. Both were suffocated in the

350

ensuing totalitarian "coordination." The workers' and peasants' Soviets were suppressed by bloody terror. Those who did not understand the significance of Stalin's revolution from above quickly enough were returned to the old concentration camps. "All power" belonged to the Fatherland Front—a totalitarian merger of the reformed Communist party and the corps of Bulgarian army officers. The transformation of the Balkan revolution into a weapon of the new Eurasian empire had begun.

PLEBISCITE DEMOCRACY

It took the Communist Revolution in Russia three years to achieve its political consolidation, twenty years to accomplish the transformation from a socialist to a totalitarian state.

The revolutions of the West and South Slavs move at much greater speed. The Jacobin revolution in Yugoslavia and the Communist revolutionary upheavals in Bulgaria were submerged before they could develop a life of their own. In Poland and in Czechoslovakia the revolutionary change was not even introduced by a Communist preface. The Russian occupation supplied all the necessary prerequisites of a Stalintern induced transformation.

The totalitarian, one-party organization replaces the revolutionary party with its Marxist traditions, hopes and illusions. A national army fashioned according to the model of the modern Russian army replaces the Red Army originating in cadres of citizens. The NKVD replaces the Tcheka which traced its origins to the Committees of Welfare of Robespierre in the French Revolution. Democracy by plebiscite, acclaimed in the Stalin constitution of 1936 as the most highly developed form of democracy, replaces the Soviet electoral system of 1917 whose fundamental ideas were taken from the experience of the Paris Commune of 1871.

This transition from the original Soviet electoral system to democracy by plebiscite has played a highly significant part in the present Russian expansion in Europe. In Eastern Europe, especially, the new Soviet conception of democracy has become a highly potent instrument for the coordination of these areas into the expanding Eurasian Empire of Stalin.

Believing that democratic elections represent the best "guarantee" against revolutionary change imposed from the outside, the representatives of Western democracy demanded from Stalin at the Conferences of Moscow and Teheran the promise of free democratic elections in those countries to be occupied by the Russian army. Democracy is a word with many meanings. Washington and London were taught this lesson when Stalin illustrated his principle of democracy in Eastern Europe. A knowledge of the transition the original Soviet electoral system had undergone might have saved them this bitter experience.

Originally Soviet elections were neither general nor equal, neither proportional nor secret. Members of the expropriated classes were excluded from the vote. The ward was the factory and the plant. Its workers decided who could vote and who could be elected. The Bolsheviks derived their electoral system from the principle of a proletarian dictatorship in a country with a tremendous rural majority. Five peasants were given equal voting power with one worker. With this measure they secured the Soviets against an inundation by the peasant population of the country. The election was public; candidates were nominated publicly. This original Soviet electoral system knew no voting coercion.

Soviet elections at that time were indicative of the political trends among the "toiling masses," and usually revealed different trends in different parts of the country. During the first five years after the revolution, electoral conflicts and struggle in such campaigns were clearly in evidence. Representatives of opposition Socialist groups were elected even after their parties had already legally been prohibited. Rejection of official party candidates and nomination of new candidates were normal matters, and the recall of Soviet delegates during their official terms was nothing unusual. This was the "proletarian democracy" which had openly and programmatically rejected the principles of western parliamentarianism.

The plebiscite of Stalin's constitution represents a fusion of the old Soviet electoral system with that of western democracy. At the same time it destroys both. Theoretically, every person with civil rights has the vote. Actually the privilege of voting becomes a coercion.

One hundred per cent participation in the elections is guaranteed in advance. The ballot is secret, but it is impossible for the voter to check the results. Theoretically, various electoral candidates are admitted. Practically, opposition is permitted to express itself only in a vote of "no" to the government list. The "opposition" never can become a majority via a plebiscite. The victory of the government list is assured in advance—not by falsifying the results, but by eliminating the alternatives of choice in the very minds of the voters.

Time was too short for the Yugoslav and Bulgarian plebiscites, through which Tito and Dimitrov legalized their power, to approach the Russian perfection. Many Yugoslav and Bulgarian peasants had to be dragged by soldiers and militia to the balloting place. In another few years they will have been taught to drag themselves.

In Yugoslavia the legalized official opposition was given the conspicuous privilege of separate electoral urns. Nevertheless, it received 15 per cent of all the votes cast. In Bulgaria as well as in Yugoslavia the Communist party rules in the form of a "front." Yet even if a legal or semi-legal opposition calls for the boycott of a plebiscite as was the case in Bulgaria, it is unable to supervise its procedure. The boycott is a parliamentary gesture without potency against the ultimate elimination of parliamentarianism.

That Stalin is well aware of the role his democracy by plebiscite is playing in the Balkans was highlighted in an attack on Churchill. "As is well known," he said, "in England at present there is one party which rules the country, the Labor Party. The rest of the parties are barred from the government of the country. . . . ." Totalitarian democracy permits all parties to participate in the government. Therefore it is the perfect expression of real democracy. "Meanwhile Poland, Rumania, Yugoslavia, Bulgaria, and Hungary are governed by several parties. And besides, the opposition, if it is loyal, is guaranteed the right to participate in the government." If it is not loyal, it loses its quality as a party, and with it all human rights.

Stalin's constitutional conceptions may seem unreasonable and illogical viewed from the vantage point of Western individualism. From the standpoint of the Russian system of democracy, western objections are unreasonable and hypocritical. The debate between Russia and the West becomes more and more like a conversation between a blind man and a deaf mute.

POLISH NKVD REVOLUTION

Stalin has frequently confessed that the secret police, the NKVD, is one of the chief pillars of the Soviet state. The political speculations presented by him during the sessions of the Eighteenth Party Congress glorified the NKVD as incorporating a Marxist dogma.

This was a far step from the original theory of state offered by Lenin as the guiding principle for the young Soviet Republic. Lenin's theory embodied two fundamental thoughts. He wanted the Soviet state and the Soviet people to be one. He therefore opposed to the old principle of separation of power his new principle of merger, of fusing the executive with the legislative power. This was the first thought. The second attempted to protect the people against an executive that had merged with the legislative, by building state power from the bottom up and anchoring the fused legislative and executive power firmly in Soviets of the people themselves directly elected by them. Lenin's doctrine has no place for a strong state as an instrument separate and alien from the people.

Stalin has given Lenin's theory a new twist; he eliminated the second part and cemented the first into an all-embracing principle.

In this way the "Vecheka," the "sword of the revolution," of Lenin's period has become the GPU, a state within a state, and the GPU became the NKVD, a superstate. "As for our army, punitive organs, intelligence service—their edge is no longer turned to the inside of the country, but to the outside against external enemies," Stalin declared at the Eighteenth Party Congress as the ultimate implication of this theory of the state.

The first foreign country in which this Stalinite principle was made into a reality was Poland. There the NKVD took over openly all the commanding heights of state power. In Poland there had been no revolutionary preface and no Communist movement preceding totalitarian coordination. For this reason the NKVD had to take over directly. The triumvirate, Beirut-Amsterdam-Radkievicz, that is governing Poland is the Polish division of the NKVD. The Polish NKVD state arose from the Russian-Polish espionage embroglio.

Boleslav Beirut, president of the Polish provisional government, asked by an American correspondent whether he was a Communist,

354

answered: "At a meeting of the National Council of Poland on January 2, 1945, I stated that I was not connected with any political party." There is some truth in this answer. Beirut began his political career in the Polish Communist party. However, from 1930 on he belonged to the only "party" that is not a political party—the NKVD. Krasnodebsky, Bienkovsky, and Rutkovsky were some of the *noms de guerre* used by the young typesetter who during the 1920s had become a professional revolutionary. Party recognition was his, when, together with a few comrades, he succeeded in liberating the party leader Lensky-Lescynsky from prison in Warsaw and in getting him across the border to Russia. This was a master stroke, for Pilsudski's secret police was known to show no mercy to a revolutionary when caught.

After his "graduation," Beirut was taken on by the NKVD. Their foreign division was a Polish monopoly, the chief of it being the Pole Trilisser. Beirut advanced quickly. He became resident in Vienna and Prague, charged with the special task of fighting the Ukrainian nationalist movements. Beirut survived the great purges which liquidated most of the Polish Communists. The most probable explanation for his good fortune is that he was abroad while the purges were circulating in Russia. Beirut chanced to be in Lwow when Poland was being divided between Hitler and Stalin. He organized the pogrom for the Russian occupation, putting a radical end to the Ukrainian nationalist movement. In this way he accomplished his old task and became worthy of the new honors in store for him.

After his return to Moscow he became acting chief of the Polish section of the NKVD, then headed by Stanislas Radkievicz, who is now Minister for Public Security in the Polish government. When the battle of Stalingrad was over he crossed the front lines and went to Eastern Poland as chief of the Russian counter-espionage. When the Red Army conquered Lublin he organized the "Home National Council." In July, 1944, he finally appeared in the public limelight as premier of the Provisional Polish government.

It was in Lublin that Beirut met a third member of the present NKVD triumvirate, Saul Amsterdam, known also as Dunsky, Dunajevsky, Henrykovsky, and Sandecky. Amsterdam, a narrow-chested attorney, has become the most feared person in Poland. The terror

355

that surrounds his name is connected with an episode of recent years. In 1937, Amsterdam, like most other Polish Communists, disappeared from Moscow. The Executive Committee of the Comintern branded him officially a "Polish Spy." Certain Polish Communists living in exile in Paris reported at that time that he, along with the entire Lensky group to which he belonged, had been shot. Others claimed that Amsterdam was living in Warsaw and had become a high official of the Polish secret police. According to them, he had been entrusted with the "purge" of the Polish Communists in Poland by the NKVD. This same source claimed he had become the GPU Asev of the Communist movement of Poland.

There is much to give this version probability. Manuilsky in 1939 had attested that the leaders of the Polish Communists were agents of Polish fascism. Against such enemies every means of combat was permissible.

The Polish NKVD state follows as a logical consequence from Stalin's postwar policy which rests on the idea of a permanent crisis between Russia and her allies of the war against Germany and Japan. Stalin is far too cautious and too shrewd to regard any one of his conquests as completely secure. For this reason liberated Poland has been given a form that will permit it neither to live nor to die. In the East it had to give up an area inhabited by about one-third of its people. In the West it had to incorporate an area from which eight to nine million Germans were expelled and in whose place one million Poles from the East were settled.

During the war Poland lost between five and six million lives. At present it has on approximately the same area as in prewar times only a little more than half of the prewar population. With the manpower available it can not farm its agricultural land and at the same time mine the coal of the conquered mines of Silesia. It has been condemned to an economic and social paralysis. It has been bled to death first by the Germans, then by the Russians, who after they had finished the bloodletting confronted the anemic country with tasks too formidable for its weakened organism. In such a country a Quisling government would be an insufficient guarantee for Russia, for such a government would have been unable to protect the security of Russian military passage to the West. A Russian military government would not have been in line with the fiction of Polish independence maintained for the benefit of the West. The present NKVD regime possesses the terrorist power of a military regime in action. It has the political elasticity of a totalitarian state while it still maintains the semblance of a free alliance of independent parties. From its long and intimate cooperation with Polish Com-. munists, it has drawn the experience necessary to merge its functions as Polish government machinery with that of a Russian police mechanism.

Russia's requirements in Poland call for men who hold everything human as alien and foreign to their natures. That is why Beirut and Radkievicz have become ministers and Amsterdam the terror and mystery of the country.

THE GOOD SOLDIER SCHWEYK, SOVIET EDITION

The good soldier Schweyk spoke thus in 1946: "It is in this spirit of absolutes that people speak of Communist or Socialist totalitarianisms and attack them. A frequent protest is that we have just overthrown one totalitarianism and want to create another. I do not share these fears or this spirit. I conceive the development of present events quite differently. I have three reasons. In the first place, this war has been a world war, and no solution of its problems can be other than on a world basis. In the second place, these problems include the destruction of the Nazi legacy. This is by no means a local or temporary object. It is a world aim independent of time. In substance the Soviet Union also has this aim. You can find exponents of Communism who will defend the necessity for a temporary dictatorship of the proletariat. I assert that in the great majority of countries it is not necessary, that it is against the principles of really progressive democracy, and that it is for this democracy itself to prevent such dictatorship by sensible efforts to improve constantly the social order. Third, the Soviet Union and the Russian Communists themselves acknowledge today that the transformation of a liberal democracy to a higher form, that of a socialized democracy, should and can come about gradually, step by step. I am of the opinion that gradual cooperation of the Soviet Union with the rest of the world will lead to general acceptance of this view. It will be

357

a link between the great powers. It will be a basis for the coexistence of the Soviet regime with other regimes. For the Soviets will continue to develop toward greater and greater individual freedom within the framework of their Socialist state."

And so the good soldier Schweyk decided upon this course of action. He nationalized the entire industry of his country, the mines and railroads, the banks and insurance companies. He organized a state trust in control of three-quarters of the wealth of the country. He froze bank deposits and rationed the use of currency. To the state bureaucracy he gave the power to control the spending of the earnings of its subjects.

He overhauled the state and at its switchboards placed Communists from Moscow returning home with the Red Army. The Ministry of Agriculture, of the Interior, of Propaganda, and the administration of public education he entrusted to their care. Schweyk permitted existence to four parties only—the Communists, the Social Democrats, his own National Social Party, and the Catholics. He prohibited ten others in existence before 1939. Schweyk decided that two parties, one unified labor party and a democratic party, were sufficient for the needs of the population in Slovakia, at the borders of the Soviet Union.

President Benes of Czechoslovakia is a generous man, and he will not, we hope, resent having his words identified with those of Schweyk, for Schweyk was a Czech national hero, created by one of the great writers of Czech fiction. He defeated the authorities of the Austro-Hungarian monarchy by the wisdom of his peasant shrewdness and the persistence of his humble forbearance. Benes-Schweyk cannot prevent the advance of Soviet coordination. For this reason he marches at its head.

When Schweyk rose to power in 1918 he did away with a monument of the hated monarchy on the main square of Prague, erected by an obscurantist church. In 1945 he did away with the monuments of Jacob Boehme, the humanist of old. This is Schweyk's capitulation to the barbaric Socialism of the East.

It is now twenty years since some of the same leaders of Czechoslovakian Communism who are now in charge of the expulsion of 3,500,000 Germans and eight hundred thousand Hungarians from

Czechoslovakia appeared as defendants in Moscow. Their accuser was their party comrade Kreibich from the Sudeten areas, who criticized the Czech comrades sharply for having violated their international duties. According to him they had fought with insufficient energy for the national demands of the German minority in Czechoslovakia. The Czechs promised to improve. But the chairman, Bukharin, was not satisfied with their promises. "I want a statement that you will defend in the Czech parliament the rights of the German and Hungarian minorities to self-determination, including that of separation."

A Czech delegate interrupted Bukharin by asking: "Shall we support the Hungarians if they decide to join up with Horthy, the Admiral who submerged the Hungarian revolution in a blood bath?" Bukharin replied: "If the Hungarian minority decides for this course, we will have to accept the decision. Otherwise we would cease being Socialists and turn into chauvinists."

In 1945 the Communist Minister of Information Kopecky stated in a speech in Reichenberg, the heart of the Sudeten territory: "Liberec will never again be Reichenberg. We will clear Liberec of the German enemies and we will do it so thoroughly that no place will remain for the German seed ever to grow again. We shall expel all the Germans, we shall confiscate their property, we shall denationalize not only the town but the whole area, so that the victorious spirit of Slavdom shall permeate the country from the frontier range to the interior. . . . . We will not allow even some hundreds of thousands of Germans to remain in this country. . . . . We do not want any Germans along our northwestern frontier. We want Czechoslovakia to form one integral Slav territory with Poland and the Soviet Union."

Former Communist theory of self-determination is replaced by the totalitarian pan-Slavism of Stalin. Kreibich who in 1918 had called for an armed resistance against Czech occupation in Reichenberg has now become a herald of the new pan-Slavism. The leader of the German Communists from the Sudeten areas is now driving them out of the homes that have been theirs for hundreds of years.

Surely after six years of barbaric German occupation the expulsion of the Sudeten Germans was in accord with the wishes of broad sec-

tions of the Czech people. But this was not the first time that national
and racial hatred had engulfed the country. Bohemia and Moravia
had been its victims, for instance, in 1899. At that time a Jew by the
name of Hilsner had been accused of a ritual murder and had been
sentenced to death. The fact that all legal evidence was in his favor
made no difference. He was saved from execution by one man,
Thomas Masaryk, who twenty years later became the founder and
the first president of the Czechoslovakian republic. Masaryk then stood
nearly alone against the overwhelming majority of his people and
by his courageous action founded his world reputation as a great
humanitarian. "I did this in order to save the Christians from their
own superstition," he declared later.

Benes, Masaryk's heir, did not follow in the footsteps of his master.
The nationalism condemning three and a half million people as col-
lectively and individually responsible for the misdeeds of Hitler and
his gang found no resistance by the humanitarians of 1945. But
when humanitarianism capitulated to realpolitik and expelled the Germans and Hungarians from Czechoslovakia, they became instruments
of the totalitarian coordination of the country. This was one reason
why Stalin agreed to the expulsion.

The Germans have not only been expelled but expropriated as
well, down to their last shirt. Even before the war, domestic German
and Czech capital was closely fused in the industrial and commercial
companies that played a great role in the economic life of the nation.
During the occupation by the Nazis complete fusion took place,
securing for the Nazis domination over Czech industry. To expropriate the German capitalists meant to expropriate the Czechs with
them. The beneficiary of the nationalization spree could be only the
party whose principle rests on the expropriation of all capitalists.
The expulsion of nearly one-third of the population—to a large
part consisting of industrial workers—results in a chronic deficiency
of labor. This in turn will lead by slower or faster steps to compulsory labor, always the driving force of a totalitarian state. Czech
industry, dependent on exports, will require the strait jacket of a
state foreign trade monopoly, when nationalized. Schweyk in bowing
to the antihuman humanitarianism of the East has introduced into
Czechoslovakia all the paraphernalia of a nascent totalitarianism.

Benes lives in expectation of a miracle: a liberal Soviet republic. Czech Communists are more farsighted. They are negotiating with the Soviet Russian Supreme Economic Council for the "coordination" of Czech industry into the Russian Five Year Plan. "During the present period of the development of our country national and class interests are identical," the Communist leader, Clemens Gottwald, then vice-premier in Benes' cabinet, stated. The statement stresses the word "present." Tomorrow or the day after, the representatives of the national interests will be declared the agents of a British anti-Soviet block, the foes of a merger between Social Democrats and Communists will be declared Fascists, the Catholic Popular party an instrument of the Pope who has dared to call Stalin the "father of the lie."

To commemorate the anniversary of the Russian October Revolution, a popular Catholic priest celebrated a mass in one of the old cathedrals of Prague. . . . . There Schweyk died a final and irrevocable death.

INDIA ON THE DANUBE

The only country in southeastern Europe that went through a revolution according to Bolshevik program, after the World War of 1914, was Hungary. Whether this is why the present Russian military government does not permit the dictatorship of Bela Kun to be mentioned has not been disclosed. The fact that Bolshevism and Bela Kun were synonymous in Hungary and that the former chief of the Hungarian Soviet government was tortured to death in the Moscow Butyrka is of little concern to the Russian generals now ruling in Budapest.

Of more concern is the more factual fact, that Hungary can not be integrated into the pan-Slav block surrounding it. Language and religion make it a stranger among its Slav neighbors. Its strategic importance for Russia, however, is great. Without full control of the Danube, Russia's dominion over the Balkans would be questionable. Russia will not permit any genuine political independence in Budapest, yet Hungary can never become a full member in Stalin's "League of Nations." It has, therefore, been treated as a colonial dependency from the very start. This does not leave room for the kind of political ambitions expressed in Kun's regime.

The commercial agreements that have been concluded between Hungary and Russia, as well as those between Rumania and Russia, are colonialism at its worst. The "mixed" companies, Hungarian-Russian and Rumanian-Russian, exploit the entire economy of their countries. The Russian partners deliver their products to these companies at approximately three times the ordinary prices while they pay for the products received only about one-third of the ordinary prices.

In view of the fact that prior to the Russian entry one could count the Hungarian and Rumanian Communists on the fingers of two hands, the task of the Moscow emissaries, of securing these commercial agreements, was not a simple one. There were few men equal to such jobs. Among them Matthias Rakoczi, Stalin's man in Budapest, is of top calibre. He has little reason to love his country which kept him in solitary confinement for fifteen long years. He has good reason for complete devotion to Russia which has saved his life twice.

The first time was during the winter of 1925. Matthias Rakoczi, at that time Secretary of the Comintern, had been arrested during an underground visit to Budapest. As a former member of Bela Kun's government, he was threatened with sentence of death. According to Rakoczi's attorney, a well-known liberal lawyer, trial before a military court meant certain death sentence, while trial before an ordinary civil court would at least offer a chance of appeal. But safer and more efficient than this legal maneuver would be an extralegal course. A son-in-law of Horthy was in financial difficulties. If the Soviet government was ready to pay good cash for a few thousand horses from his farm, the attorney thought he could guarantee the life of Rakoczi. This extralegal course was actually the procedure taken. The Soviet government purchased the horses, and Rakoczi was sentenced by an ordinary court to twenty years in prison.

The second time that Russia saved Rakoczi was in the spring of 1940. Hungary, then an ally of the Nazis, had recognized the Soviets after the Stalin-Hitler pact. Russia asked for and secured Rakoczi's release as evidence of the newly won friendship.

As a young man Rakoczi received excellent economic training

in Budapest and Hamburg. He knows how to express himself fluently in Russian, French, English, German, and Italian. A charming and experienced negotiator, he moves easily in any society. Small in stature, he looks more like a dependable bank cashier than the mature professional revolutionary he really is.

He will need all his agility, for his Russian masters are still inexperienced and awkward in dealing with their European colonies. Their agreements with Washington and London require the maintenance of certain procedures, like elections with uncertain outcome.

The Hungarian "Agrarian revolution" has been a political failure. The exiled Hungarian Communists attributed their defeat of 1919 to their neglect to distribute the large estates among the peasants. This theory became generally accepted within the Comintern. Every Bolshevik believed that the division of the land, the old dream of the peasants in eastern Europe, would play political leadership into the hands of the Communists.

Actually, however, developments have taken a different course. After the division of the land in eastern Europe, the peasants attached themselves even more strongly to their old parties. The reasons everywhere—in Poland, Hungary, Rumania, Bulgaria, and eastern Germany—were the same. The division of the land was executed everywhere in Russian style; no consideration was given to maintaining sound agricultural units able to carry on production. The new owners were given plots of between five and fifty hectares, frequently without proper shelter and water. As the Red armies had carried off agricultural tools and equipment nearly all over, and had taken between 80 per cent and 90 per cent of the cattle, the great majority of the peasants in eastern Europe had to utilize quickly made wooden ploughs and use themselves or their women as draft animals.

Industry in these countries is working almost exclusively for Russian reparation account. The peasant, therefore, sees little chance of purchasing industrial products or agricultural tools in the near future. The national currency has become worthless everywhere. Therefore, the free market on which he might sell some of this produce after having delivered his quota to the state has little to offer him. The former dependence on a feudal and patriarchal lord has turned into

363

slavery under an all-powerful state apparatus in the hands of a foreign power.

In Rumania, Stalin's coordination took place in the style and manner of a comic opera. Russian espionage in that country first managed to win over Tatarescu, former Foreign Minister and intimate friend of former King Carol, then in Latin-American exile. Constantin Oumansky, Russia's late ambassador to Mexico and Stalin's confidential agent for South America, wove the net that tied together Tatarescu, Carol, the latter's royal son, and the NKVD. From then on everything moved according to schedule. General Antonescu, Rumania's Quisling, was drawn into a trap, or to put it more precisely, was locked up in a royal safe. In the adjoining room Tatarescu and an attorney by the name of Patrascanu were waiting. Patrascanu had been in the services of the Russian espionage for twenty years. Young King Michael appointed him Chairman of the Commission to negotiate the armistice with the advancing Red Army.

In this way Moscow created an "independent government" in Rumania without interference in the domestic affairs of the country, as agreed upon at the conference of Moscow with the Allies.

After this auspicious beginning, Moscow followed up with the customary importation of specialists for the establishment of "peace and order." Two disciples of the Civil War Academy of the Comintern, Georgescu and Dey-Gheorgiu, took the ministries of the Interior and Commerce, together with the management of the railways. The former student of the Lenin Academy, Emil Bednaras, took the job of general secretary to the Premier Petru Groza; Constantinescu Jaczi, former member of the Information division of the Comintern, took the Ministry of Propaganda, and Petrascanu the Ministry of Justice.

In Hungary some of Horthy's marshals, their uniforms covered with the glory of Hitler's medals, hit upon the idea of changing over to the Russians with their armies. Voroshilov welcomed them with open arms. At present they are commanding those Hungarian regiments that have not been sent marching towards Siberia. The representative of the Hungarian government in the Allied Control Commission is General Pokorny who during the First World War had been entrusted with the espionage against Russia on the General Staff of the Austro-Hungarian army. The Hungarian ambassador in Moscow is Julius Szekfü, a historian from the close circle of Horthy.

The peculiar combination of Communists imported from Moscow and former lackeys of the feudal gentry, to whom the marshals of the Red Army entrusted civilian power in the rich Hungarian-Rumanian plains, indicates that there is no social or political combination that cannot be accommodated by the Stalintern. The Stalintern is an organization whose opportunities know of no limit.

To this opinion Georg Lukacz most certainly subscribes. He is the other surviving leader from Kun's dictatorship who returned to his home city, Budapest. He has no official position. Indefatigably and with considerable success, he is carrying his message of "anti-Fascist humanism" to the academic youth of Hungary. Hungarian intellectuals did not move into the Catholic church to seek solace. The God, for whom Lukacz is writing a new theology, is too close and too powerful not to be taken seriously.

CHAPTER XXIV

German Foreign Legion

WILHELM PIECK AND WALTER ULBRICHT

IN NOVEMBER, 1945, THE VICTOR OF THE BATTLES OF MOSCOW AND Berlin, Marshal Zhukov, at a huge festive banquet in Berlin asked his guests to join him in a toast for a "free and democratic Germany." Wilhelm Pieck, the elder statesman of the German Communists, responded in the name of the German officials present: "There are no longer any victors and vanquished. We are all united here in order to prepare a brighter future for the German people."

The Communists lauded Zhukov's toast as "an historical deed." They had reason to celebrate this turn of events, for during the first few months of Russian occupation they had gone through the same hell as the rest of the population. The fury of the victorious Red Army knew no discrimination. The homes of the Communists had been plundered; their wives and daughters raped. The proletarian suburbs of Berlin which had greeted the Red Army with red flags had after a few weeks of occupation become centers of burning hatred.

Wilhelm Pieck, even during the storms of these weeks, undoubtedly remained calm and self-assured. It is these qualities that have made of him one of the show pieces of the Stalintern. He is the only surviving Communist leader of the first hour who, for twenty-seven years, has belonged to each succeeding leadership of the German Communists, each of which denounced its predecessor as Public Enemy Number 1. Whenever his colleagues were close to despair, his clear blue German eyes exuded calm confidence. His hair has turned white, but his face shows few traces of age. His voice, strong as ever, proclaims the latest word from Moscow with unbroken fervor.

Pieck's activity in the German labor movement began fifty years ago in the Social Democratic party. Like many radical members of the party, he had been educated and trained in the school of Rosa Luxemburg and had become her loyal pupil. During the First World

War, as a follower of hers he had been an active member of the Spartacus group. Throughout the civil war that followed the military collapse of Germany, he had remained on the side of Karl Liebknecht, had been arrested with him, and had been spared the same fate only by a fortunate accident.

A second time his name had been connected with a great spontaneous revolutionary movement. In 1920 he had been the delegate of the Communist party to the workers in the Ruhr rising against the German army.

During the next ten years he became an inimitable servant of the powers that be. Within the Communist party he was known for his devotion to order and discipline. The files of his offices were always beyond reproach. On his desk, pencils and pens stood in military array.

Next to capitalism Pieck hated nothing so much as disorder in the party. Disorder included all ideas which had not been passed upon by Moscow. The Comintern rewarded his reliability. He became one of its most trusted representatives in Germany.

Pieck had few political ambitions. At each of the numerous "turns" that invariably left political corpses on the battlefield, he managed to keep in the background He did not aspire to the dangerous and unrewarding post of a "leader." But in the end he became a leader against his wishes, probably because all other aspirants had left the Communist party or had been done to death in Hitler's and Stalin's concentration camps.

For Pieck's seventieth birthday the Russian occupation authorities permitted a celebration in the Berlin state opera in the grand syle. A well-known German actor read a poem composed for the occasion. The mayor of the city of Berlin conferred honorary citizenship on him and nominated him "the first citizen of the anti-Fascist era." Miners from Silesia donated a few carloads of coal; peasants brought a cow. An automobile and many other gifts "from a liverwurst to a plough," as the Berlin radio commentator said, bore witness to the fact that the Germans in the Russian zone realized they again had a fuehrer.

The second strong man of the German Communists is Walter Ulbricht. Like Pieck, he is a former carpenter, about fifty years of age, a typical blond, heavy-boned German. He is unpopular, a poor and boring speaker with the thin and shrill voice of a person afflicted with a throat ailment. In Pieck are merged the good and bad traditions of the German labor movement; in Ulbricht, only the worst. As secretary of the Berlin Communists, he, together with the Nazis, organized the strike of the transport workers union in 1932, facilitating Hitler's seizure of power. As late as December, 1932, he prohibited mass demonstrations of the Communists against the Nazis and directed them against the Social Democracy as the chief enemy. His challenge to uncover the foes of the German-Russian pact in Germany, already mentioned, was consistent with his character.

The influence of Ulbricht in the Russian-German Communist net is great. For many years he has been an intimate collaborator of the GPU, at present the supreme Moscow authority for all Communist parties in eastern Europe. His Russian wife was Zhukov's private secretary. Intrigues lasting for years and costing the lives of many of his colleagues gained him the confidence of Dimitrov and particularly of Manuilsky, who still is Stalin's closest assistant on all Communist party affairs outside of Russia. The German Social Democrat Noske, in the early days of the Weimar Republic, during the months following the murder of Liebknecht and Luxemburg, had said: "The bloody job has to be done and somebody has to do it." Ulbricht too will not hesitate. The Russians will require men like him for the execution of their policies in Germany.

"WANDERERS INTO NOTHINGNESS," A LA STALIN

During the years preceding the German collapse, two German "national committees" attempted to influence the destiny of Germany. The name of one was "Free Germany." It had its seat in Moscow and was a restaging by Stalin of the "wanderer into nothingness" of 1923. The other had no name. Its existence was known outside of Germany only to the Allied governments and their general staffs. The attempt on the life of Hitler of July 20, 1944, was the peak of its activity and its end.

These two national committees were engaged in a hard and bitter war of their own of which little up to the present is known. But one thing is clear—that Stalin's victory in that "war" was not of much less significance than his victory at Stalingrad. Stalin won a poker game where he held nothing but a blank card because his opponents did not have the courage to put their royal flush on the table.

The Free German Committee in Moscow amalgamated the remnants of the General Staff of the German army defeated at Stalingrad with the remnants of the German Communist immigration in Russia. The Free German Committee substituted for Lenin's slogan "Europe cannot live without Germany" a new one: "Germany will either be a Russian protectorate or it will cease to exist."

The experienced Russian directors set their German stage with all the props of propaganda. They were well versed in the lessons of history. Their proclamations cited the example of German officers on Russian soil in 1812 leading the fight for Germany's liberation from there. Just as did the group of officers of 1943, this earlier group had invited the officers and soldiers of the Prussian armies fighting on Napoleon's side against Russia to desert their colors and to organize guerrilla groups.

One should not forget that Russia, because of her long and intimate cooperation with the German Reichswehr, was well acquainted with the personalities of the German commanders. Up to 1933 "Bendler Strasse," the residence of the German war minister, had few secrets from Unter den Linden, the seat of the Russian embassy. This intimate relationship contributed largely to the fateful miscalculation of Stalin in the winter of 1932. At that time he did not give Hitler a chance, for he believed that the German army would come out a victor in the political crisis of those days. After July 20, 1934, Hitler by eliminating most of those officers in the Army command in favor of cooperation with Russia, had raised a curtain of secrecy around the Reichswehr, shielding its leading figures from Russian eyes. Stalingrad lowered the curtain again. For now the Russians had in hand people like Walter von Seydlitz who knew Hitler's marshals, their conflicts and their doubts, as well as they knew themselves.

Even more important was Marshal von Paulus, the chairman of the Free Germany Committee. For von Paulus had himself taken part in the conspiracy of the generals. Russia did not lack information, and it is obvious now why Stalin originally accompanied the

369

propaganda of the Officers League with the promise of a strong army in a new Germany freed from Hitler when, for instance, he said on the seventh of November, 1942: "It is in no way our goal to destroy all military power in Germany. This would not be advisable in view of the problems of the future. Only Hitler's army can and should be destroyed." The Russian dictator gave more serious attention to the inner German conspiracy than did Churchill and Roosevelt.

Pieck and Ulbricht could play but a minor role in the game between the Western and the Eastern conspiracies. At the Russian broadcasting stations they untiringly repeated Stalin's slogans promising Germany the right of self-determination and democracy for tossing out Hitler. This propaganda, however, no longer had an audience in Germany. The underground Communist organization had been eliminated before the outbreak of the war. In 1938 the Communist party in Germany continued to exist only in the German prisons and in the emigration. The German-Russian pact defeated the last chance of a spontaneous resurrection of the spirit of resistance on the part of the Communists.

A change occurred when the probability of defeat became clear. This did not improve the chances of the Committee in Moscow but rather diminished them. For in the meantime the other conspiracy had assumed proportions representing not only a real danger to Hitler but also a danger to Stalin's plans for solving the German problem.

THE WESTERN FREE GERMANS

The history of the conspiracy of Goerdeler, Witzleben, Stauffenberg, Trott zu Solz, Leuschner, and their comrades will some day be told elsewhere. The attempt of July 20, 1944, to assassinate Hitler was not a bloody fight between Nazi gangsters, as Churchill said, but the explosion of an underground movement existing many years and comprising thousands of men and women from all sections of the population. Originating in the spring of 1942, it comprised small groups around the conservative mayor of Leipzig, Goerdeler; the former Social Democratic Minister of the Interior of Hessen, Leuschner; and the former chiefs of the general staff, Ludwig Beck and von Hammerstein. In the summer of 1943, Goerdeler considered himself and his group strong enough to write a letter to Marshal von Kluge, the commanding officer of a German army, challenging him to open action against the dictatorship.

"The hour has arrived to take our fight into our own hands. . . . . To continue the war any longer is a crime. There exists no heroic death for an entire people. . . . ."

In the beginning of 1944 the conspiracy consisted of two groups, a military group preparing the assassination of Hitler, and a civilian one attempting to formulate a common program for a revolutionary government. The movement had been joined by numerous local groups of conservatives, Social Democrats, Protestant and Catholic ministers. Only one group had failed to join the plot, the German Communists who regarded themselves as part of the Moscow Committee. Their role has been described in contradictory detail. But all descriptions agree that a Communist, whose name has not been mentioned, disclosed the secret of the plot in the middle of June, 1944, to the authorities.

The statement of the American National Lutheran Council is general and says only that the Committee committed the blunder of communicating with a group of Communists riddled with Gestapo spies. The account given by Lieutenant Commander Alexander Maley, on February 27, 1946, in *Human Events* is more precise. Commander Maley reports that the Social Democrat Julius Leber, who was to become Minister of the Interior in the coming revolutionary government, met with three leaders of the Communists on July 12, 1944. One of these three disclosed the plan to the Gestapo. Leber was immediately arrested. On July 17 an order of arrest was issued for Goerdeler. This action caused the military division of the plot to move earlier than planned. According to Cyrus L. Sulzberger, the *New York Times* correspondent, a member of the Communist committee of three with which Leber was negotiating was an agent of the Gestapo.

Evidently in the spring of 1944 Moscow had become aware of the danger to the Russian war plans inherent in the success of Goerdeler's plot. In his many attempts to negotiate with the Allies, Goerdeler had sent a representative to Cairo at about this time. The Russian news agency Tass immediately spread a story emanating from Cairo according to which British sources were negotiating with Germany for a separate peace.

The Western conspiracy at its inception had no anti-Russian aspect. One of its most eminent leaders, Adam von Trott zu Solz, negotiated in Stockholm with the Russian minister there, Mme. Alexandra Kollontai. As more and more generals and military men personally involved in Hitler's barbaric campaign in Russia joined in the plot, the conspiracy took an anti-Russian turn. In the beginning the conspirators expected to get an armistice from the Western Allies assuring them some latitude in negotiations with the East. When they found no willing ears either in Washington or London, they were ready to capitulate unconditionally in the West in order to negotiate an armistice with the Russians at Germany's Eastern frontiers.

Active cooperation between the Russian and Allied general staffs and vast amounts of lend-lease did not silence the Russian campaign against alleged separate negotiations of England with Germany. It ceased only with the unsuccessful attempt on Hitler's life and the subsequent elimination of the Western conspiracy. Hitler's victory over Goerdeler opened the gates of Germany wide to Stalin's plans.

STALIN'S WACHT AM RHEIN

Till 1928, Stalin's participation in affairs of German Communism had been only sporadic. After 1928 his strong hand had asserted itself there.

Stalin shared the hate of the Bolsheviks for the German Social Democrats and had contempt for the German Communists. The party of Ebert and Noske, of Otto Bauer and Renner in Austria, was the real *cordon sanitaire* after 1918. Neither the Little Entente of Benes nor Poland would have been in a position at that time to stop the bolshevization of Europe. It was the German Social Democracy that erected an impenetrable dam against Communism. Stalin despises the defeated. The German Communists were victorious in thousands of skirmishes, but they lost every decisive battle. From 1933 on they had nothing to offer but the martyrs of their hopeless underground organization.

Sentimental attachments to Bolshevik tradition no longer had any meaning for Stalin when he formulated his postwar German policy.

372

This is of paramount importance for the present. For Stalin's strategic plans in Central Europe involve the destruction of that class in Germany that had been the revolutionary hope of the Bolshevists in Lenin's time: the working class as an industrial productive factor.

In his election speech already mentioned, Stalin reiterated the thesis announced before the outbreak of the war in 1939: The imperialist system breeds wars among its own members and between the system as a whole and the Soviet Union. The conflict between the Western Allies and the Axis was according to this view a "political," not a "social or fundamental" one. What Stalin thus expressed in a diplomatic way was his real diagnosis of the Second World War: fundamentally a war between Socialism embodied in the Soviet Union and world capitalism. The Soviets succeeded in utilizing the inescapable internal capitalist conflicts, allying themselves once with one side (German-Russian pact), once with the other, and finally emerging as the real victor of the struggle.

In this speech Stalin gives a comprehensive report on his entire war policy and formulates the principles to make victory secure in the political, military, and, particularly, in the economic fields. Stalin fully believes in the supremacy of economics. In this respect he is more Marxist than Marx and more Leninist than Lenin.

The latter tried to solve the problem of Russian industrial backwardness by a union of Russian agriculture with German industry. Stalin seeks a solution in the destruction of the latter and the operation of its surviving parts as an annex to Russian industry. For without this, Russian industrial monopoly in Europe cannot be established. The victim of this solution can be no other than the German working class. Stalin is fully aware that in the final analysis not plants and machines but the productive power of its population represent the industrial potential of a great country. From this viewpoint neither the destruction of war nor the removal of a major portion of the remaining industrial machinery guarantees the permanent industrial impotence of Germany, but only the separation of the German workers from their means of production.

When Professor Varga, the Hungarian economist in Moscow, demanded the labor of ten million German workers for a period of ten years, his program was not accorded the serious attention in the

373

West that it deserved. It revealed one of the basic points of Stalin's postwar policy.

Moscow has not officially made public the number of German war prisoners and civilian deportees in Russia. According to British estimates, the former number between two and three million. Since the end of the war an incessant stream of men from the Balkans, Hungary, Czechoslovakia, and Germany has been flowing into Russia. The scheme of deportation is the same everywhere—employable men towards the East; women, children, the aged, the sick and crippled towards the West. These war prisoners utilized for various tasks in Russian industry, transportation and mines, will not return to their homeland. Exceptions will be few. This represents Stalin's first blow against the German working class as a great productive and industrial force. The second is directed against the Eastern parts of Germany where a deliberate policy of de-industrialization and separation of skilled and experienced workers from their jobs has been initiated. Only a small minority is permitted to maintain their old skills. The others are becoming "down and outers." In less than a generation German workers will have been levelled down to the level of the Russians.

Stalin's German policy is free from ideas of revenge. Denazification in the Russian zone is subordinated to economic goals and has little relationship with democratic re-education. Confessions of collective responsibility of the German people passionately repeated in the Russian zone by Communist poets may be sincere. But Stalin's administrators are skeptics. They do not live in a mystical world of sin and penance. They do not judge the Germans by their feelings of guilt but by their devotion in the service of the Russian state.

The policy of separating the German workers from their means of production is not limited to Russia. In the Western zone a similar process is in operation. The Western zone according to the Potsdam agreement is absorbing those four or five million from the German minorities who have been considered less desirable for employment purposes by the Russian authorities and consequently have been shifted West instead of East. Most of the Germans from Hungary, Yugoslavia, and Rumania who have been moved to Germany are primitive peasants speaking the long forgotten dialects of their ancestors who emigrated centuries ago from Germany. The Sudeten Germans, to a large

374

extent textile and glass workers, peasants, artisans, white collar workers, arrive as beggars, most of the skilled workers screened out for Eastern transit before the shift. France asked for and received a million German workers for use in mines and in construction.* Even throughout the Western zone only a small percentage of workers will find employment in their former occupations.

The disintegration of a producing organism into "human dust" is spreading over the whole of Germany. Russian expansion towards the West, stopped at the river Elbe, is moving in devious ways towards the Rhine.

HEROES WITHOUT HEROISM

Communist psychology is like a labyrinth: it is obscure, it has innumerable paths winding along without end. American Communism is businesslike, uncomplicated, and anti-heroic, registering like a seismograph every impulse coming from Moscow. From a psychological standpoint it offers few complicated problems.

European, particularly German Communism, requires entirely different standards of appraisal.

A German Communist has given an extensive description of Communist activity in the horror camp of Buchenwald. Paul Schreck was one of the last leaders of the underground Communist organization during the Hitler period. Before he was sent to Buchenwald he had been tortured for weeks. He endured these tortures steadfastly like most of his comrades.

"The first problem that confronted the Communists in Buchenwald," Schreck said, "was what form our organization should take. . . . . We formed district and regional branches of the party throughout the camps. . . . . Our next problem was to become block leaders. Each prison had its block leaders picked by the SS. Originally these leaders were all professional criminals set over the politicals. Conflicts developed between criminals and SS, conflicts over a hundred and one trivialities, over who should have the scattered belongings of the last dead or the money and watch of some new arrival in the camp. We Communists took advantage of these conflicts, demonstrating to

---

* England received three hundred thousand German prisoners from the United States for work in the mines.

the SS that robbery was not our motive. In a short time we managed to get ourselves appointed to some of these posts.

"We then began to check up on all new arrivals. I was placed in the cell through which they passed. I had to screen them and place them then in the proper division of the camp. I would begin with casual questioning and then get around to politics. If the man said he was a comrade from Essen, for example, we would check up on him through other Essen party members in the camp. We would put the prisoner into one of three categories: party members were given party work; indifferent elements were handed ordinary jobs, letting them drift as they wished; Nazi stool pigeons were assigned to labor details.

"We undertook actions of international solidarity. In 1941 the first Red Army prisoners were marched in from Minsk to Weimar. They entered Buchenwald with bleeding feet and in rags, while the SS called us out and mocked our liberators. German political prisoners saved their bread crusts and tossed them over the barbed wire to their Soviet comrades. In retaliation the SS put one hundred and fifty of us into a special punishment company, beat us all thoroughly and killed seventeen of the hundred and fifty in the course of the beatings.

"As the flow of prisoners of war increased, I was made responsible for screening of French and Red Army soldiers. Seventeen thousand eight hundred and twenty Red Army officers passed through my hands. We put them in positions with the greatest chance of remaining alive.

"Prisoners of war included the most diverse elements, eight hundred Norwegian students, the French and Czech general staffs, French intelligentsia and many other groups. In all there were forty thousand international prisoners and only two thousand German. We regarded it as essential to build a broad united front of all prisoners, but SS regulations permitting Germans only to hold posts stood in the way of this. One day, therefore, I went up to the SS chief and complained heatedly. 'Why must we Germans clean up the dirt of these foreign swine? Why don't you make them do their own sanitation?' The fool was taken in by this and in a few days international Communists held important posts in the non-German divisions of the camp.

"Serious decisions had to be taken every day. Medical facilities

376

were scarce. The camp suffered an outbreak of typhus with 2,500 ill and injections for 250 only. We decided who should live and who should die.

"On August 2, 1944, Himmler's order to evacuate all prisoners to Dachau reached the camp. The intent of the order was to kill the prisoners on their march. We immediately passed the word around to resist the attempt to move us. Twenty-seven thousand left for Dachau. None reached it. Twenty-one thousand stayed in Buchenwald, most of them Communists. . . . ."

For those who doubt the trustworthiness of this report we reproduce the account of an Austrian Catholic who spent eight years in Buchenwald, which was published by R. H. S. Crossmann in the London *New Statesman and Nation.*

"When the SS got rid of Commandant Koch, the new commandant was easier to deal with. The Communists got themselves into all the key positions which had been held by the criminals. There was a Communist block leader in charge of each block. Communists ran the hospital, the canteen, the kitchen, and, most important of all, the labor office which decided on the movement of prisoners from camp to camp and the imposition of the work commandos. The SS had to leave most of this work to the German inmates, especially when the camp grew in size and thousands of foreigners were brought in. The choice was whether the criminals should have this power or the politicals. Of course anyone who had it had power of life and death; yes, of life and death. As more and more foreigners came in the Communists naturally tended to select foreign Communists to head up the barracks. They had an iron discipline. They did many hard things, but they saved the camp from total extermination. . . . . It was through our positions in the hospital and experimental stations that we were able to save many people from execution. A party of some fifty British, for instance, were brought in one day, mostly parachutists. . . . . One day we got wind that they were all to be executed within a week's time. I talked it over with the Communists in the hospital, and we agreed that we might be able to save four. So we held a meeting and selected the four. The rest knew that they were in for it.

"The most difficult problem was the British C. O. because he was so well known in the camp. The only way to save him was to substitute him for a dying man in the hospital and let him take the dying man's papers. Unfortunately the only foreign language he knew was French, and there were no Frenchmen in the hospital. By luck a transport of Frenchmen arrived two or three days before the execution date, many of them down with typhus. But there was only one who would do.

"I shall never forget that time. The Communist who had agreed to do the job kept on saying to me one little injection will do the trick. If your man is worth saving we can't be squeamish. But the Englishman and I decided we couldn't murder the man, and we hung on till the Frenchman really was dying and the injection would be O.K. That was the day before the execution day.

"After the execution we both got the feeling that perhaps the man hadn't been dying after all, and that we really had polished him off. So we got the address of the Frenchman's wife and we're trying to find her to explain what happened. . . . .

"Anyway it went off all right. After a week in the hospital posing as the dead Frenchman, the Englishman was moved out to a camp where he was less well known. . . . . You're surprised that one had scruples about little things like waiting for a man to be really dying before injecting him. But it was those little things that were the faith that kept me going. The Communists of course didn't mind about them. For them the end justified the means."

This psychological portrait of German Communists should be supplemented by the description of a characteristic incident: In 1933 the Communist reporter Willy Bredel was arrested and clamped into the concentration camp Fuhlsbuettel near Hamburg. There were few Communists who left Fuhlsbuettel alive. Bredel was one of them. He succeeded in fleeing to Moscow where he became an active collaborator of the Free German Committee. One fine day he met another collaborator there—the SS Commandant of Fuhlsbuettel who had been taken prisoner in Stalingrad. The Communist propaganda did not remain silent about this embarrassing meeting. On the contrary, it celebrated the community of the tortured and the torturer as the symbol of the purification of the German people through the Free German Committee. After his return to Germany Bredel was com-

378

pensated for his stoicism by an honorary doctorate from one of the universities in the Russian zone.

Twenty-five years of incessant civil war and fascism, submerging every individual trace in a party that had become a substitute for all other values—family, home, and faith—combined to produce a human product with few equals in the history of humankind. There have been heroes and martyrs aplenty throughout human history. As yet the German Communists are the first to become heroes without heroism and martyrs without martyrdom.

Is this Red fascism? Such a definition would be erroneous. The SS had courage only as a herd. Separated from it they became cowardly and treacherous hirelings. To behave as did the German Communists in Buchenwald, one had to be immersed in a revolutionary tradition to sustain one's strength. To select among comrades in pain candidates for death without turning into a beast oneself, there had to be strength and gentleness in the innermost depths of one's soul. But all these human qualities exist in the German Communists in a way as if they did not exist. They are condemned to an underground existence. In Buchenwald they could find expression because there they arose from the individual acts of free men in revolt against their jailers. Liberated from the camp, the hero submits to the dictates of the party. The tortured begin to torture. The control committees begin their work. The free hero of the camp turns into the potential prison guard without a will of his own.

These German Communists are Stalin's tragic foreign legion in Germany.

SOVIET GERMANY EXPENDABLE

After the fall of the Third Reich, this tragic column of Communists from the concentration camps was met by a column of the Communist Party coming from the East under the commands of Pieck and Ulbricht. Among these were the remnants of the German Communists after long years of exile in Russia, decimated by deportations to the North Russian and Siberian work camps, demoralized by the purges, and picked up behind the Urals where they had been kept during the period of the German-Russian pact.

But these old Communists were only a small minority of the column

379

coming from the East. With them came the newly enlisted recruits of the Free German Committee; active officers of the army and the SS; Social Democrats, liberals, and Catholics; naive believers in a rejuvenation of Germany by the East; and cold-blooded adventurers—all of them carefully screened by the NKVD and trained in special colleges for their coming tasks. The merger of these two columns forms the present German division of the Stalintern.

In the Russian zone and slowly also in the other occupation zones, a "classless society" of the Russian type developed. Such a society demands leaders and organizers like the men who come out of the German concentration camps or those who have returned from Russian exile. That is why the German section of the Stalintern has become a dangerous knife in Stalin's hands.

In their first public manifesto of June 25, 1945, the newly founded Communist Party of Germany came out for "democracy, parliamentarism, and private capitalism," turning against "Sovietization" because the "present situation is not yet ripe."

At the beginning of March, 1946, Pieck tossed out the democratic slogans and announced the birth of the revolutionary era: "Our historic task is to begin the reconstruction of the German state. We will have to solve the problem once and for all. We will have to destroy the state of the big capitalists, the militarist, and of the conservative officials once and for all. . . . . If the capitalists and those who follow them continue to sabotage, we will have to use other means. We will take revolutionary measures against them, and we will break their power by our own. . . . ."

The political coordination of the Russian zone in Germany, announced by Pieck, is a by-product of the transition to a "revolutionary offensive." The elimination of "private property" by the bombing squadrons of the West and by the decisions of Potsdam produced a "classless society" of paupers in the vacuum left after the fall of the Third Reich. For the Stalinite revolution had already been accomplished in March, 1946, in the Soviet zone with the exception of the "Western inlets" of Berlin. The propertied classes had been liquidated, the landed estates divided, the remaining industry nationalized. The "revolutionary offensive" was directed against "the Western part of Germany oppressed by the imperialist powers." "We

380

are learning what democracy means in the three western zones of Germany," declared Pieck, "namely class rule against the working population. . . . ."

UNITY PARTY

During the fifteen years of the Weimar Republic, Communist mass influence had grown continuously until in the fall of 1932 the Communist Party's strength nearly equalled that of its competing party, the Social Democrats. Now the opposite development is occurring. In all elections since 1945, whether for shop councils or for municipal positions in the Russian or in the Western zone, the Communists reached only a small fraction of their pre-Hitler strength. In the Austrian elections the Communists, although in possession of the police and propaganda ministries, were utterly snowed under. Regardless of how one evaluates these parliamentary victories of the Social Democrats, one can be sure they represent a spontaneous movement in opposition to Stalin's "revolution from above."

Twenty-five years ago the Comintern solved the problem of its German mass influence by the split in the Independent Social Democracy that won it hundreds of thousands of members and millions of voters. At that time it was the magic of Zinoviev's world revolution which drew the German workers to the Communists. This time, however, the German masses do not follow the Pied Piper from the East. At the party conference of the Berlin Social Democrats on March 1, 1946, more than four-fifths of the delegates voted against the intentions of the Social Democratic Central Committee to unite with the Communists and decided to submit the question to a plebiscite by the members of the party.

The immediate answer to the vote was the reopening of the old concentration camps in Buchenwald, Oranienburg, and Sachsenhausen. Numerous delegates disappeared from their residences; others—living in the "western" zones of Berlin—found the doors of their apartments decorated with swastikas. On the day before the plebiscite, a decree prohibiting participation was issued in the Russian occupied zone. In the other zones the delegates of the party conference were supported by a majority of more than 90 per cent. Nevertheless the merger took place in April in the Russian zone.

The Social Democracy, in conforming to this decision, has been declared "undemocratic" and its further political functioning has been rendered impossible.

A few months after the merger-by-compulsion, the Unity Party was in full operation. Its membership was a multiple of the separate memberships of the Communists and Socialists before the merger. The membership card guarantees bread, jobs, and relative security in respect to the ever overhanging threat of deportation to Russia.

The political developments occurring in the German Soviet zone have nothing in common with those splits and mergers of former years. They are the growing pains of a political society formed on Stalinite principles. Splits that formerly represented ideological differentiations and gave expression to political objectives are at present synonyms for the totalitarian atomization of German society. The liberal democracy and Christian democracy still in legal existence in the Soviet zone will not escape. They are adopted waifs of the United States not to be "provoked" at present. Their days are numbered.

Germany has become a country without history. Stalin offers it a modest place in the family of nations assembled in his Eurasian empire. Dreams about a return of the old glory are permissible and are even desired. Stalin is not afraid of dreamers.

The West has no program for Germany and regards dreamers as a threat to the peace of the world.

As long as Germany does not regain a soul of its own, its heroes without heroism will have the upper hand. Without mercy for themselves or their kind, and without ideals of their own because they have been ideologically expropriated, ready to sacrifice everything because they themselves have been sacrificed, obedient to the last because every new day of life is an unexpected present from a distant and mythological power, their mission is to plant Russia's flag across the Rhine.

CHAPTER XXV

The Stalintern Order

TOTALITARIAN CENTRALISM

TOTALITARIAN COMMUNIST ORGANIZATIONS FORMED UNDER THE
iron pressure of the Russian protectorate hold sway in Eastern
Europe. West of the Stettin-Trieste line the Stalintern draws
its strength from spontaneous revolutionary movements arising out
of the collapse of the liberal capitalist order in Europe. A similar
process is occurring, if for other reasons, in South and Central
America. In China, peasant rebellion still supplies the Red Armies
with a reservoir of new soldiers. In North America, where no spontaneous movements exist favoring the Communist party, an organizational structure different from most of the others has been
developed.

To understand the role these different party types play within the
Stalintern, it is necessary to turn back to their organizational development before the war.

During the first ten years of the Comintern the rapid up-and-down
fluctuations in the membership of the Communist organizations were
a topic of great concern to the Moscow Executive Committee. In
the numerically largest European party of the Comintern—the German—these membership fluctuations were intensified during the
years of the depression. In 1930, for instance, the German Communist party gained 143,000 new and lost 95,000 old members. The
membership of the French Communist party changed in similar
fashion. Between 1924 and 1929 it decreased from 68,000 to 46,000.
In 1933 it lost nine-tenths of its old members and during the following
years up to 1939 gained more than 200,000 members.

From 1935 on, the Comintern began to look at these membership
fluctuations as indications of inexhaustible strength. This change
of attitude foreshadowed the new conceptions of the Stalintern that
make the numerical strength of the Communist organizations a question of secondary significance. The important thing today is the

ability to maneuver a fluctuating loosely-bound mass, and to use it at will.

The Comintern even before the outbreak of the war was organizationally bankrupt. Manuilsky gave out official membership figures in his last public report on the Comintern at the Eighteenth Party Congress of the Communist Party of the Soviet Union in March, 1939. The Comintern at that time did not have in the entire world as many members as had the parties of Germany, France, and Italy combined between 1920 and 1921. After allocating more than 600,000 members in China, Manuilsky reported only 554,000 for all the rest of the world. In Western Europe he counted 305,000: 270,000 in France, 10,000 in Holland, 7,000 in Belgium, 18,000 in Great Britain. In the Scandinavian countries he mentioned 28,000. Czechoslovakia accounted for 60,000. The Western hemisphere for 161,000: 90,000 in the United States, 18,000 in Canada, 23,000 in Cuba, and 30,000 in Mexico. In South America the Comintern had no worthwhile organization. The Prestes *putsch* in Brazil in 1935 had eradicated the last remnants of party organization there. Actually the Comintern existed as a political factor just before the outbreak of the war only in France and China.

The German-Russian pact of August, 1939, shrank the membership of the Comintern organizations throughout the world with the exception of China down close to zero. The French Communist party, the only mass Communist party left in Europe at the outbreak of the war, lost at least three-quarters of its membership. The same happened in Belgium and Holland. In England at least one-third of the Communists left their party. The disintegration of the Communist parties all over the world was even more marked after the beginning of the Russian-Finnish war. The same membership decrease took place in the Western hemisphere where the Communist parties lost between 30 per cent and 50 per cent of their members. The American Communist party according to a report by Earl Browder had 60,000 members at the beginning of 1944; that is about one-third less than at the beginning of 1939. The Communist party of Great Britain recovered its old numerical strength, but only the Communist parties of Mexico and Cuba multiplied their membership.

An organizational process of a new kind is taking shape in the

Western hemisphere as well as in Western Europe. The Stalintern
with its national organizations draws its strength not from the labor
movement in general, as did the old Comintern organizations, but
from the disintegration of established social groups and classes into
social atoms. Party members, Partisans, and *francs tireurs* are being
recruited from all groups of the population. Among them are still
some who believe in a Socialist salvation coming from Moscow. Some
of them dream that Stalin is moving, though frequently by dangerous
and incomprehensible detours, towards the goals of Lenin. The
majority of its members and followers turn to the Stalintern because
it is wielded by the strong hand of the victor—because the rising
power promises relief in the bleakness of their misery and hope in
the desperation of their helplessness.

What they expect from their respective Communist parties is an
end to their misery regardless of the price they have to pay for it. They
are willing to accept a dictatorship or a democratic regime if it
promises them more bread and a bit more economic security. Of
Communism or Socialism they know nothing but the news fed them in
the Communist party press.

The main gainers from this spontaneous process, the Communist
parties of Italy and France, have since the end of the war won
more members than Manuilsky counted in 1939 for the entire
Comintern. In this shapeless mass the organizational principles of
the Stalintern can be observed in crude operation.

One of the most important is the elimination of party democracy
in the relations between members and leaders: "Leadership only
from the top down, responsibility only from the bottom up." The
present extreme application of this principle and the "democratic
centralism" of the old Comintern are not separated in watertight
compartments. The Comintern purges of the years 1930 to 1932 and
the foundation of the cadre division in Moscow with full authority
over Communist life, that of members and of leaders alike, were
important milestones on the road to the totalitarian centralism of
the Stalintern.

But before the war the Communist parties of Western Europe were
still in a sense working-class parties. Because of the democratic
atmosphere in which they were functioning, they could not eliminate

inner party democracy completely. Only the social landslide during and after the war made this possible.

Now the party hierarchy of all Communist parties is everywhere the same. At the top is the Central Committee instituted and controlled by Moscow, with one or two leaders from Stalin's Iron Guard; around them stands a circle of official functionaries. These groups comprise the real nuclei of the Stalintern parties.

At the circumference of the party nucleus are grouped "Communist mass organizations." They represent a sort of mass protectorate. Even where the Stalintern party has a few thousand members only, it is nevertheless able to mobilize hundreds of thousands of people through these organizations.

Such a system of organization appears impossible under normal circumstances in countries with parliamentary governments. But the Stalintern does not reckon with stable or normal conditions in the postwar period. On the contrary, it envisages an unending crisis, a crisis that will cause inexperienced masses, demoralized by fascism and the miseries of war and peace, to seek an escape from their intolerable existence. With such masses one deals, according to Stalintern philosophy, not by methods of education and conviction but by imposing upon them an apparatus of power wielded by a group of men forged together by iron discipline.

No stairway connects the lower with the top levels of the Stalintern party. A party leader may be demoted—a party member can never rise into the leading circle of the order.

To belong to the inner leading nucleus of the order in the Stalintern becomes, as Stalin said at the Eighteenth Party Congress, a question of life and death. This statement holds true for Russia as well as for the Stalintern sections abroad. To this nucleus belong different types of Communists, chiefly those from the old leading cadres who have successfully weathered the difficult tests of the Moscow trials and of the war, particularly those of the German-Russian pact.

This inner structure of the Communist parties is the decisive answer to the question of how Moscow is able to direct these various Communist parties as securely as a pilot his plane.

Lenin's High Command of the world revolution did not impose

its policy by force on its subordinate parties: it attempted to educate, to persuade, and to convince. After his death, Moscow policy was transmitted to the Comintern parties in the more convulsive form of splits, one to the right, one to the left. It took fifteen years for the totalitarian principle of party and mass control to penetrate into all pores of Communist organizations.

This totalitarian centralism offers Moscow important advantages. Up to 1939 the Comintern had to be directed through an executive committee in Moscow operating by directives from Stalin. Such centralized direction continually created areas of conflict between the Soviet government and nearly all countries with which it maintained diplomatic relations.

The Stalintern offers the Soviet Republic the precious advantage of ruling out frictions of this nature. It needs neither an executive committee nor Congresses nor resolutions to see its policy through. Nor does it require confirmation by plebiscite from its parties abroad. Except for England, the Scandinavian countries, Switzerland, Portugal, and Turkey, the Stalintern participates in some form or other in the government of all European countries. Its former representatives in the High Command of the world revolution have now become its delegates in the various European cabinets. Moscow's intervention in the affairs of the various European countries has now been crystallized into a legitimate institution. Moscow no longer has to send out mysterious agents to direct the various Communist parties. The Russian ambassador in each and every European country has become the internationally recognized representative of the Stalintern whose members are his colleagues in the cabinets and on the diplomatic staffs.

This is the real significance of the statement in the dissolution decree of the Comintern: "The entire course of events . . . . has convincingly proven that the organizational form for uniting the workers as chosen by the First Congress of the Communist International . . . . more and more has outlived itself . . . . and that this form has even become a hindrance to the further strengthening of the national workers parties."

In view of the rise of Russia to the status of a world power, the Stalintern can function without visible central direction. The Narkomindel, intimately connected with the foreign division of the GPU since the beginning of the war, performs this function without running into diplomatic difficulties.

THE STALINTERN ORDER

The leaders of these various Communist organizations form an order. To attempt to understand its psychology in the non-Russian world involves great difficulties. Usually one tries to understand the psychology of a group of men in terms of their common interests, in terms of their common ideas, in terms of their tradition or background. The Stalintern order, outside of Russia, possesses neither common interests nor common ideology. Its individual members are allied to each other by nothing. On each and every one of them the central power in Moscow presses with such intensity as to exclude all spontaneous personal expression of solidarity.

Stalin cannot deliver a dissident member of his English or American staff over to the "authorities" as in Russia, in order to extinguish his civil or physical existence. Yet he accomplishes similar results abroad by other means.

Different members have arrived at the point of their moral self-destruction on different paths, but all have one thing in common: During the course of their activity within the Comintern they have utterly abrogated faith, philosophy, and conviction. They are neither Socialists nor Communists. They are modern nihilists, atheists of every form of belief.

Between an American or English member of the Stalin order living the comfortable life of a political official on the one hand, and a European or Asiatic member of the order whose life is in constant danger, there exists a significant difference. Yet in respect to the central power in Moscow they are all in the same position. It grants them material existence only. They expect nothing of Moscow, not even the protection of their own lives.

All understand the merciless logic of Stalin's machine of power. Nobody knows any means of escaping it when it moves against himself. They regard their "community" as an incessant struggle for sheer existence where everyone must protect himself against everyone else.

In Europe a major part of the staffs of the Stalintern consists of former refugees, of men without homes and country for many years. The Stalintern has become their only home—their only country, the bread they eat and the protection they secure for an unknown period before the inevitable end. All its members are aware that the power of the Soviet Republic is the only foundation for their existence and their activity. They are aware that outside of the pale of this power they would be pariahs. Moscow shares this knowledge.

Out of the order of the Stalintern, from time to time, individual personalities like Tito or Mao Tse Dun arise for a moment of history. Yet their independence is transitory and illusory. The closer the increase of their own power moves them to the top of Stalin's pyramid of power, the more tightly do they become bound by the iron law of his order that makes membership in the order a matter of life and death.

THE CASE OF EARL BROWDER

The Stalintern order and the functioning of its totalitarian centralism is spotlighted in the history of the fall of Earl Browder in 1945.

After the Teheran conference in the winter of 1943, the Communist party of the United States extended its superpatriotic turn, which originally began on June 22, 1941, eliminating all Communist principles of all preceding variations. Its culmination point was the party Congress in the summer of 1944 when the American Communists dissolved themselves as a party and proclaimed themselves an association. This turn was in fact the sharpest in the history of international Communism. Later it became known that Foster had written a memorandum criticizing this turn. Nevertheless, the Teheran policy was accepted unanimously by that party Congress and Browder solemnly elected as president of the new association and chief editor of the *Daily Worker*.

For a whole year Teheran policy was proclaimed all over the country. In Communist parlance, "enemy of Teheran" became an epithet even worse than "Trotskyite."

Suddenly during the summer of 1945, an article of Jacques Duclos criticizing the Teheran policy of Browder and sharply attacking his association was published in a periodical of the French Communists. The Frenchman Jacques Duclos, cause of the palace revolution among the American Communists, is a very talented and shrewd man. He knows no foreign languages except a few words of German brought back to France after the First World War. He does not know America nor was he ever occupied with anything but French affairs during the period of the dissolved Comintern. Nevertheless he was selected by Moscow to instruct the American Communists in the ABC's of Stalintern policy within their own country. A short time later his article was run word for word in the *Daily Worker* after a New York paper had publicized the impending split. The national committee convened and decided to open a general discussion on the subject.

What happened after that is material for a tragedy in the Greek style. The protagonist of the drama was suddenly completely deserted and alone. Nobody could be found on his side in the arena. Only a few days before the appearance of the article, the association had celebrated Browder's fifty-fourth birthday and the national committee had declared, "We express what all of us feel so deeply about you, beloved leader of our movement. Your bold mature Marxist leadership . . . . You are one of the great leaders of the people . . . . We have the highest confidence that under your firm guidance we shall continue to make an honorable and vital contribution . . . ." etc.

The first reaction of the beloved leader expressed clearly the fact that he was aware of the purpose of the new turn and willing to accept any role assigned to him. Soon he became completely silent and was only an object of discussion. Then all members of the national committee entered the arena and announced themselves guilty and ready for the return trip to real Communism. Everybody manifested his sense of guilt by a more or less vitriolic attack on the defendant. Then the "activists" entered the arena and repeated the self-accusation of the national committee. The longer the discussion lasted the more violent became the language against the silent protagonist. In the end the entire discussion turned into a choir of raging indignation against the "renegade," the "agent of capitalism and imperialism." Finally in February, 1946, Browder was as unanimously expelled as he had been elected president of the association the year before. Not a single collaborator of his remained loyal to him.

What had happened? Earl Browder is not one of those rebels of the Communist movement fighting for their convictions, and expelled for this reason. He had become a member of the Stalin order and had graduated into its ranks when he became fuehrer in the early 1930's. Without doubt the Teheran policy that brought on his downfall had been prescribed to him verbatim by Moscow.

Browder himself could not lead the fight against Browderism. For him there was no compromise solution as there was for his intimate political friend, Robert Minor, who was removed only from his leading positions. Regardless of his personal attitude, Browder had to be the scapegoat.

No member of Stalin's order is immune from such blows of fate. The permanent readiness to offer oneself as a victim after having been a leader is the risk that each exposes himself to. Litvinov after his elimination from the Narkomindel in the spring of 1939 was reprimanded for having "neglected his duties." For five years after Hitler's rise to power he had fought for collective security—a British-French-Russian military alliance. Nobody in the world could attribute to him the slightest responsibility for Munich. But according to the inner logic of the Stalin order, this was of no consequence. To be unsuccessful, regardless of the reason, means to have neglected one's duties. Within the ranks of this order there is no place for the defeated.

The elimination of Browder may have caused a few hundred or thousand Communists to leave their party. But such desertions do not weaken the totalitarian party control. On the contrary, they are desirable. The symbol in power, be it Browder, Thorez, or whoever else, controls the rank and file. It pushes uncertain elements to the periphery and beyond. As long as the control itself remains secure, the acquisition of new members remains a secondary problem. Within the many front organizations there is always a sufficient number of new candidates for membership—repelled or attracted by the symbol in power—Browderism or anti-Browderism.

Earl Browder's fall was followed by an epilogue even more grotesque than the spectacle of the fall itself. To the horrified surprise of the American Communists, Browder was called to Moscow just a few months after his expulsion from the party. The Central Committee of the American Communists, just purified from the mortal sin of Browderism, was thrown into a fit of convulsion and confusion.

William Foster, Browder's successor, offered as guide out of perplexity this explanation: "It was Browder who dissolved the Communist Party, and a greater service than this no man can do to capitalism. It is also Browder who is trying to give a coloration of progressivism to American capitalism . . . . . The most sinister aspect of this whole furore about Browder's 'case' being taken up in Moscow by an imaginary Comintern is that the war mongers are using it as a war provocation."

Browder was given a friendly reception in Moscow by high government officials who disregarded the growls of the American Communists, and returned to the United States as general representative of the Russian state publishing company. Several weeks after his return the Central Committee stated: "Communists will do nothing certainly to interfere with Mr. Browder's circulation of Russian books in America. But there is every indication to make us believe that he is continuing to propagate in substance the same line he had before . . . . ."

Browder in retirement serves as the pan-American symbol of the struggle against monopoly capitalism. If his services are needed again on the open stage, he can be heralded as the apostle of a long-range peace program between the United States and Soviet Russia.

The directors of the Stalintern did not have to ask Browder to the Kremlin to give him their instructions. Their intention seems to have been to secure for the renegade some very noisy publicity. Browder was the apostle and the victim of the Teheran policy. As such he undertook his trip to Moscow. He came back to the United States as a witness to the possibility of a return to Teheran, a witness with excellent attributes. Calumnied by the wagers of radical class war, yet equipped with the new Moscow halo, Browder is the carrot while Foster is the stick. The roles can be changed. A good audience is assured.

The Browder case is one of those episodes typical of the Stalintern order, not explicable by normal standards of psychology. Confronted with the power without limit which rules them, Browder and Foster are as nothing—no longer men with a claim to the respect of others and of themselves. They are the property of the "master of all things" whose name they dare not utter when his lightning strikes them. The Lord giveth and the Lord taketh away: blessed be the name of the Lord!

STALIN'S MASTER OF CEREMONIES

Dimitri Zacharovitch Manuilsky is the master of ceremonies of the Stalintern order. All his personal qualities—his shrewdness which has become legendary in Moscow, his ability to improvise and find formulas which say one thing and mean another—bloom in the Stalintern.

During the passage of the years Manuilsky has turned from a versatile teller of stories into a brutal cynic. Characteristic of him was his reply to a colleague in the Executive Committee of the Comintern when asked to intervene in favor of a German Communist arrested by the GPU: "But, my dear friend, the man has confessed and signed an affidavit that he is a spy. What value would such a fellow have for the party even if he were innocent? How would he bear up in a Gestapo prison after showing such weak powers of resistance in Moscow?"

Manuilsky was Stalin's right hand in the Comintern from 1929 to its dissolution. At present he is Vice Premier and Foreign Minister of the Ukrainian Soviet Republic and its chief delegate to the council of the United Nations. The weight of all these posts does not count for too much in the present structure of power in Russia. Nevertheless he is now at the pinnacle of his career, one of the most powerful men in the Soviet Union. He is the only member of the present Russian Central Committee who has been personally connected with most of the Communist leaders in Europe for many years and has an intimate knowledge of the Communist parties abroad.

Manuilsky is now sixty-three years old. Among the straightlaced and glum Stalinite leaders he cuts a peculiar figure. He is the only one in Stalin's circle belonging to the old Bolshevik generation, who spent years abroad before the October Revolution, and "Manu" has lost nothing over the years of his French elegance and quick wit. His youth and early manhood were similar to those of most Russian professional revolutionaries. Son of a fairly wealthy priest, he attended the University of Petrograd and was soon drawn into the whirl of the revolutionary movement. He joined Lenin's group in 1903. After the defeated revolution of 1905, he was exiled to Siberia but escaped from there and lived in Western Europe, chiefly in Paris, until 1917.

For the first years following the October Revolution he was employed for third rank functions only. Lenin's inner circle considered him without principles and reckless. But personally he was well liked for his great charm and special gift at telling stories. When Radek, master of political satire, became silent, Manuilsky succeeded him in the Comintern of 1924. The initiative for this move came from Stalin who, after Lenin's death in 1924, had begun to build up his own group within the Comintern.

The rest of Manuilsky's history has been recorded in earlier chapters. A great part of his present power in the Stalintern rests on the fact that most of the Communist politicians in Europe have belonged for many years to his personal faction. Dimitrov is the product of his political shrewdness. In 1928 he saved Ercoli-Togliatti who at that time belonged to Bukharin's group. It was Manuilsky who smoothed his way to Stalin. The leading French group of Thorez, Marty, and Duclos owe their power to his personal influence. The Czech Communist ministers owe him a debt of gratitude. Their leader Gottwald fled with his colleagues to Moscow even before the Germans had occupied Czechoslovakia. This behavior, contrary to Communist tradition, gave rise to sharp criticism. Manuilsky defended the Czechs and placed them in positions in his own entourage. In every Communist government of Eastern Europe are some of his personal agents. The Hungarian Minister of Transport Geroe was one of his many secretaries. To his able and agile hand Moscow owes the direction, smooth and soundless, of the various Communist parties. He directs the Communist propaganda music throughout the world. When the propaganda section of the Comintern eliminated all foreign Communists in 1941, Manuilsky replaced them with a group of young Russian Red professors who have now become the editorial staff of the *New Times,* official organ of the Russian trade unions in place of *War and the Working Class* originally used for the purpose.

Manuilsky, last of the Europeans in Moscow, is the father confessor of the newly created Communist excellencies. Into his ear they can pour their troubles without having to tremble lest the organs of surveillance of the NKVD receive immediate information. Rakoczi can complain about Gottwald when the latter creates trouble by expelling the Hungarian minority from Czechoslovakia. Gottwald

394

can complain about Beirut when the latter refuses to loosen his grip on the Czech-Polish frontier town of Teschen. Tito can complain about Togliatti when the latter is not doing his bit for the Yugoslav annexation of the Italian city of Trieste.

Manuilsky's function as delegate to the United Nations symbolizes the penetration of all international institutions by the actors and agents of the Stalintern.

CHAPTER XXVI

Dual Power on the Atlantic

FRANCE'S NEW ROBESPIERRE

MAURICE THOREZ AND PALMIRO TOGLIATTI-ERCOLI, STALIN'S satraps on the banks of the Seine and the Tiber, are on the threshold of the great decision: the French and the Italian Communist party will either establish monopoly power or go under. A third way—a permanent coexistence with other parliamentary parties—is out of the question. A Communist party that has reached the present strength of the Italian and the French must fight, whether it wills to or not, for the monopoly of power, or be destroyed as a mass party. Twenty-five to 30 per cent of Communist votes in a democratic country do not mean simply that one-quarter or one-third of the citizens wish a proportionate Communist representation in its government. They indicate that the political and social conflicts are of such a nature as to exclude a parliamentary compromise. Only arithmetically speaking do the Communists represent a minority. Politically they are bound to act as the majority of the coming day.

The parties of Togliatti and Thorez for the first time in the history of the Communist movement have accomplished a goal long fought for: the political conquest of the majority of the entire working class. The Italian trade unions are now altogether in the hands of the Communists. At the last Congress of the French trade unions they received four-fifths of the votes cast. They could proclaim a general strike any day they wished, bringing economic and social life to a standstill. But they do the opposite. They come out so strongly for an increase of production that the Syndicalist representatives protest: "Do the Communists wish the miners to take their beds with them into the mines?"

Present Communist policy in France and Italy is a Western totalitarian variation of Lenin's dual power practiced between February and October, 1917. During this period, against the expectations of the Bolsheviks and of the other parties, Soviets of the workers, peasants, and soldiers arose spontaneously as a parallel power to the provisional government. The Duma was diminishing in strength while the Congress of Soviets was augmenting its strength.

Immediately after the war it appeared as if the French Communists were going to copy this policy by putting in place of the Soviets the *Comités de résistance*. Thorez, however, after his return from Moscow in the spring of 1945, put an end to this strategy. Again the strategists from Moscow, with Manuilsky at their head, showed their master hand.

Their policy in France had been extremely elastic during the war period. In the summer of 1941 they had seized the political opportunity offered by the résistance without harboring any illusions about its military quality. André Marty, civil war specialist of the French Communists, declared at that time from London: "The French people know that liberation does not come from the outside . . . . . All conditions are present for the creation of numerous groups of *francs tireurs* who, while maintaining contact among themselves in town and countryside, will wear down and weaken the Hitlerites, at the same time carrying out acts of justice against the traitors. In this way they will create support points for the formation of a new French anti-Hitler army on the territory of France proper."

General de Gaulle at this time still clung to the conception that he had proclaimed after the military collapse of the summer of 1940: "*La force militaire que je constitue ne fait pas de politique.*" De Gaulle planned to recruit an unpolitical French army abroad with an espionage and sabotage annex in France. Acting on the basis of the same orders from Moscow as Tito had, Marty considered metropolitan France herself the center of liberation from the Nazis. He conceived of a modern army of *sans culottes* around which a new, a fourth republic would be constructed. Although his slogan of liberation of France without allied help never was more than demagogy, it permitted the Communists to emerge from their existence as a defeatist sect and achieve first place in the movement of resistance against the German conquerors.

De Gaulle changed his policy when he became aware of the political strength of the resistance movement. But neither he nor their other competitors were able to overcome the advances made by the Communists in the meantime. The political army of the Communists was the strongest power in the French mass movement. After the retreat of the German armies they organized a militarily insignificant but politically extremely important "battle of Paris" which gave the French the illusion of having regained their own capital by their own force.

When de Gaulle in the spring of 1945 granted amnesty to Thorez, a deserter during the war and sentenced by a military court to six years imprisonment, he sold one of his basic political principles for a mess from Moscow. The return of Thorez from Moscow to Paris was a condition for the treaty with Moscow.

Paris quickly forgot and forgave Thorez the military sin he committed. Frenchmen in general had less faith in the resurrection of imperial France via a mystical balance between Moscow and Washington than did de Gaulle. They were aware of their poverty, and this time they really wanted peace *a tout prix*. Thorez represented their revenge for Munich, for the *drôle de guerre,* for the backwardness of the French ruling groups who had for twenty-five years considered themselves safe in back of the Maginot Line and the sacks of gold of the Banque de France. The program of the French Communists exerts so great an influence on the French masses because it is realistic—it accepts the French defeat as a fact. Its motivating thought is self-help and "the poor man has no friends." All other parties rely on the rich uncle across the Atlantic. The Communists say: take what you can get but rely on yourself. Undeniably they express the French situation more accurately than their Catholic, Democratic, and Socialist adversaries.

For this reason dual power in their hands has become such an explosive and expanding weapon. They have made no attempt to use the resistance as revolutionary competition with the parliamentary institutions. Their policy aims at dissolving these institutions from within, infiltrating into the executive power from the Post Office to the staffs of all ministries, and atomizing the French middle classes by economic, social, and political means. They are in absolute control of the state administration of the nationalized mining and electrical industries. They have power over a great part of the bank and railroad administrations. Through their influence on the armament ministry

398

they have penetrated into the military arsenals and armament industries, and there can be little doubt that many thousands of their members have retained their weapons from the times of the resistance. . . . . They have eighteen generals in the French army. . . . . It is undeniable that never yet has a Communist party had as much power before the conquest of power as the French. They voted with the Socialists for the reduction of the military budget, causing the retirement of de Gaulle. Yet they employed for their organization and propaganda hundreds of dismissed officers who have joined them in the hope of regaining their military insignia in a new army. Their political propaganda, penetrating into even the smallest villages of France, is an able copy of the technique employed by the Nazis before their conquest of power. A Swiss journalist described it in a report from Provence:

"In nearly every French village and hamlet the Communists have occupied the stores formerly belonging to collaborationists and have turned them into propaganda centers. In the show-window where before the war you could inspect cabbage heads, lettuce, and carrots, you look now at pictures or statues of Stalin, Thorez, or Marty. In the small and medium-sized cities of the South there are frequently four, sometimes five and even ten, such propaganda centers. Here you can read the latest speeches of Duclos or of the local Communist leaders; you can regard well-displayed exhibits; brochures are sold, short movies shown, records are played. The Communists know how to satisfy the rural population's desire for amusements and pleasures. They arrange dances, festivals for the young people, meetings for women, excursions. Their main newspaper in southern France, *Midi Rouge*, does not try to attract new readers by political slogans, but by serial detective stories. No other French party can equal the propaganda machinery of the Communists."

According to Communist propaganda, Thorez has already reached the heights of infinite wisdom and goodness and the infallibility of a destiny-sent leader. Louis Aragon calls him "the tested revaluator of all French values who will re-evaluate France."

Totalitarian coordination produces its different protagonists in different countries. The Nazis took Frederick the Great as their inspiration, the French Communists the *"philosophes"* of the French revolution. Optimists always claimed the French spirit would never capitulate to the Fuehrer deification of totalitarianism. Aragon, who has been heralded as "the French poet of the Resistance," declared: "Will people understand me if I say that in every one of my acts, in moments of danger as well as when I sit down to write, I always asked myself: what would Maurice Thorez think of this? For I have but a single idea—to be worthy of him in order to be worthy of France."

And finally Aragon expressed his deeply felt gratitude for the fact that Thorez had liberated him from "the disorderly thinking and the confusion of our former ideas."

A French syndicalist attributed their success to their technique and discipline. Master in this field is Jacques Duclos, regarded by many as the "little Stalin" of France. Compared to "Stalin the Great"—his official title since the end of the war—every other Communist leader is small. But the adjective "small" is a personal description of Duclos, for he is just a little more than five feet tall, and, being also very fat, he resembles a human globe. When he used to march at the head of a demonstration, Parisians would shout "Here comes our Jacques rolling along." But this unimpressive looking little man is full of explosive energy and expansive ambition. Within the French Communist party he represents more real power than the Fuehrer-candidate Thorez and the resistance-general Marty.

These two fled, in the winter of 1939, but Duclos remained in Paris during the German occupation; this required more than average courage. Duclos saw the heads of Pierre Semard, Gabriel Peri, and many another Communist leader fall. Doriot's henchmen who hated Duclos personally more than any of his other former Communist colleagues, were after him. After the execution of Marcel Gitton, Duclos' former chief who had gone along with Doriot, the latter placed a high price on the head of his enemy. Duclos spent years in a small room in a working class suburb.

The man possesses iron nerves and has a sharp quick wit. During the debates with de Gaulle he often succeeded in silencing the emotional general. In November, 1945, while the Communists were threatening to step out of the de Gaulle government, he asked de Gaulle: "Are there two categories of Frenchmen, one to be executed, the other to govern?" But it was only a few minutes later that he announced in the Chamber, in an indifferent voice, that the Communists accepted de Gaulle's conditions, which implied their elimination from the political ministries. The telephone call and decision from Moscow had arrived at the very last minute. Its tactical significance was for the Communists to become a governmental and oppositionist party at the same time. This is the road to power in a country that has lost its soul.

Jacques Duclos has made sure that when Moscow calls Paris headquarters the call will find him on the other end of the wire. At the beginning of the '30s Duclos became head of the Department of Information. At the time this was an exceedingly unpopular division to head, for it involved the secret supervision of party members for the Moscow cadre division. In the course of the years the Department of Information of the French party became more and more powerful and influential, as in all other Communist parties. It grew parallel with the power of the NKVD in Russia, whose foreign division began to exercise an even more rigid control. Stalin showed little confidence in the Executive Committee of the Comintern where the direct fight against spies and Trotskyites was concerned.

Before the outbreak of the war the information departments had concentrated in their hands control over all communication from and to Moscow; through their office were channelled all financial subsidies. In France this department has become a state within the state. It maintains a huge apparatus of its own, equalling the secret agencies of the French government itself. The department now controls potential enemies not only within the ranks of its own members, but within all other parties as well. If the balance sheet of the "dual power" works out favorably, the baker Jacques Duclos, will crown the bald dome of his head with the cap of Robespierre.

STALIN'S MACHIAVELLI IN ROME

The Communist division of the Italian government has its roots in the general staff of the International Brigade of the Spanish civil war. Ercoli-Togliatti was the chief of the Comintern delegation in Spain; Fausto Gallo, present Minister of Agriculture, was Inspector General of all brigades; Mauro Scoccimarri, Inspector of the Italian.

Ercoli-Togliatti is the most outstanding member of Stalin's present international team. He is a statesman in his own right who has merged within himself the tradition and the culture of the Latin West with the Asiatic shrewdness and unscrupulousness of Moscow. Like many young intelligent men from good families, he had joined the Italian labor movement in the years before 1914. Cleverness and unscrupulousness he acquired in a war against himself that led frequently to the brink of despair. When he graduated from the Comintern he had mastered all the intrigues of the Stalin order.

At the beginning of the First World War the young law student was a passionate Socialist pacifist. In Turin he met Antonio Gramsci, who became his teacher and friend, later the leader of the Italian Communists. After securing his doctorate, Togliatti became editor of one of the Socialist dailies fighting for an unconditional merger with the Communist International. When the Socialists split at Leghorn in 1920, he was with Gramsci on the side of Bordiga and Terracini, the hot-blooded foes of Serrati and Turati. Factional struggles followed during the next few years, and then bitter years of emigration in Moscow's Hotel Lux, interrupted by trips to the Italian border.

During the Comintern crisis of 1928, Ercoli separated from his closest comrade and friend of these years, Tranquilli-Silone. But even this did not save him entirely from the suspicion of opportunist sympathies with Bukharin. *"Ercoli ha surpasso la colonna del opportunismo d'Ercole,"* Heinz Neumann, then Stalin's favorite in the Comintern, exclaimed menacingly. When Hitler seized power in Germany, Ercoli found it emotionally difficult and intellectually intolerable to continue his loyalty to the Comintern. It was Bukharin who finally convinced him that all other roads ahead were closed and no other decision compatible with the tradition of his past life was possible but capitulation to Stalin.

The rise to power of Dimitrov, himself formerly suspect as an opportunist, brought Ercoli into the inner circle of the Comintern. At the Seventh World Congress he developed Communist strategy and slogans of the struggle against the approaching war. His speech was a *chef d'oeuvre* of demagogy, underlining orthodox Bolshevik dogma without neglecting the requirements of Russian foreign policy.

402

When Stalin agreed to entrust him with the leadership of the Comintern delegation in Spain, he had stepped up onto the highest Communist platform. In this capacity Ercoli represented the supreme Comintern authority in Spain. In the last days of the battle for Madrid, the generals of the Popular Front, Miaja and Casado, who had come to an agreement with Franco, arrested Ercoli. Casado would surely have delivered him up to Franco had not a division of the International Brigades stormed the prison and freed him. He escaped to France. From there he returned to Barcelona, the last "trench" of the Republic. Again he remained to the last instant to make his escape in a plane to Morocco, for the road to France had already been cut off by Franco's troops. From North Africa he went to Paris. There, as surprised as lesser Comintern dignitaries, he received word of the German-Russian pact.

But Ercoli no longer had conflicts of conscience. He had succeeded in subduing his own self. After a short stay in prison he managed to return to Moscow.

His hour struck with the fall of Rome and the arrest of Mussolini by Badoglio. To the amazement of the world, Stalin recognized the Badoglio government. The Italian republicans were indignant. Moscow's move ended their hopes at that time of bringing the Italian monarchy along with Mussolini to an end. Stalin's move was based on well-considered reasons. The recognition of Badoglio was the door to "dual power" in Italy. The Allies who had occupied the south of Italy permitted Ercoli's return as willingly as did Ludendorff that of Lenin in 1917.

Even the master of ceremonies at the court of the Italian king could have found no fault with Ercoli's discharge of his ministerial duties. He paid his proper respects to the crown prince and reverently kissed the hand of the Pope. "There are no fortresses that cannot be taken by Bolshevik audacity," is one of the better known Stalin slogans.

After the fall of Mussolini Communist party organization was formed under the leadership of Dr. Scotti, a subordinate of Ercoli in Spain. But only after Ercoli's arrival from Russia did the Communist party expand on a big scale. Probably no more than a few hundred of the old experienced Italian party members were left after twenty years of exile, innumerable factional struggles, and the losses suffered during the Spanish civil war. Yet Ercoli knew how to use his small party as a nucleus for mass expansion. In the years that preceded Mussolini's conquest of power he had realized the extraordinary significance of the rural cooperatives in Italy. For this reason he insisted on the Ministry of Agriculture, handing it over to his most intimate collaborator, Fausto Gallo. Whoever holds the Ministry of Agriculture controls the Italian peasants. Before the Socialists knew what was happening, the newly founded trade unions were headed by Communists. Dozens of front organizations penetrate into all the pores of Italian society. That has been Ercoli's work during his two years in Italy.

One of his main antagonists is Ignazio Silone who has returned after fourteen years of refuge in Switzerland. At the beginning of the war Silone began to organize a Socialist underground in Italy. After Mussolini's fall he emerged as the leader of a spontaneous Socialist movement.

The immediate object of the struggle between Ercoli and Silone is the "Socialist Unity Party." To establish it would crown Stalin's dual power in Italy. Silone succeeded at first in turning Pietro Nenni's initial majority (Nenni had been a Socialist leader commanding an Italian brigade in Spain) into a minority. But this may be a passing, not a decisive success in the struggle. For the organizational form of the conflict conceals its real import.

Italian and French Socialism can save itself only by saving Europe. It is impossible for a greater part of Europe to remain Russian and totalitarian and the rest democratic and Socialist. The Stettin-Trieste line has a military but not a political and social significance. Western Europe cannot exist in permanent dependence on the United States and England. The division of Europe decided upon at Potsdam is as much a catastrophe for France and Italy as for Germany. Socialism in Western Europe is afraid to proclaim a European program, although without such a program it is condemned to a slow death.

To divide Europe into two worlds will make the crisis in its Western part permanent and hopeless. In that situation the uncertain and flickering light from the East will turn into a message of a new dawn. The Eastern solution offers Europe participation in the vast raw material resources and markets of the new Russian empire. Its price in exchange is surrender of national, social, and moral sovereignty.

The costs of a totalitarian coordination of Europe by Russia would be far greater than those of the German attempt, for this was backed by the economic and organizational experience of the most efficient and powerful industry of the Continent.

Masses of people will not go under without attempting escape on some last path of solution: If the Socialist parties of Europe do not dare lift the iron curtain dividing the continent into two compartments, they will become prisoners of their totalitarian competition. With the iron curtain lowered permanently, the number of those in Western Europe who "die tomorrow gaily in order to have eaten yesterday" will become legion. Only when the Socialist parties realize that a democratic program in Europe fundamentally implies a European solution of the German problem and face up to this fact with courage and determination will they be able to extricate themselves from the iron grip of the Stalintern party. Germany cannot be cut into four parts and German industry eliminated without affecting Europe to the quick. The Socialist parties of the West are not ready to face this problem, and, therefore, they become unwilling allies of the Eastern European program.

Every move on the part of the French Socialists to solve the Rhine and Ruhr problem in the direction of a democratic European federation meets with the Communist choir demanding a French separatist solution, which in reality implies the totalitarian organization of a European chaos.

In Trieste Italy touches the Soviet Union. Here Moscow controls the exit into the Adriatic. Ercoli's victory in Rome would be as dangerous a threat to the British imperial lifeline as Rommel's march towards Cairo. Thorez and Duclos in power in France would turn the British-American zones in Germany into helpless islands against which the tides of the totalitarian sea would beat ceaselessly. The dual power of the Stalintern in France and Italy is aimed at the heart of Europe. Stalin's order knows this, and this is its strength. Its adversaries do not want to see the truth. This is their weakness.

CHAPTER XXVII

Stalintern of the Western Hemisphere

PRESSURE GROUPS

IN THE SUMMER OF 1935 LUIS CARLOS PRESTES, FORMER CAPTAIN
of the Brazilian army, supported by a few regiments of soldiers
and the small Communist party of Brazil, attempted to seize
power in that country. The attempt was brutally suppressed after a
few days, and for the next ten years Brazil enjoyed the undisputed
dictatorship of Vargas.

This unsuccessful *putsch* has had great significance for the entire
Communist movement in the Western hemisphere. It convinced the
Comintern that the Communist parties of America could be used
for better purposes than mere propaganda outlets. It demonstrated
the value of the Communist parties in South and North America
for the global objectives of Soviet policy.

Prestes unintentionally discovered the continent of South America
for Moscow. His strange career opened Moscow's eyes to the substantial opportunities of political infiltration into a continent whose
specific weight in world politics is rapidly increasing.

Luis Carlos Prestes was born about fifty years ago in a little town
in the State of Rio Grande de Sul in the extreme south of the country. He comes of a Catholic family and as the son of an army officer
was sent to a military school. Among his schoolmates were some of
the Brazilian officers who during the last two decades have acquired
a strong influence in Brazilian politics. These officers were active in
a series of insurrections more or less periodic up to 1930, culminating
in the revolution of 1930 which brought Vargas into power.

Prestes made his political debut in 1924. At that time he took
up arms against the federal government and after the defeat of this
insurrection continued a guerrilla fight with a gang of his soldiers.
In this way he became a national hero. The opposition press made
him into a legendary figure. In the end, however, he had to leave
the country and established himself across the border in Buenos

Aires. All revolutionary groups of Brazil vied for his favor. The Communists outbid all their competitors, and during the revolution of 1930 Prestes came out with a manifesto in which he denounced the bourgeois opposition and advocated an agrarian and anti-imperialist revolution according to the then current prescription of the Comintern. After that he became associated with the South American bureau of the Comintern with headquarters in Montevideo.

In 1931-32 with Vargas firmly established in power, Prestes was called to Russia from where he returned to South America only when the Comintern established its popular front policy of 1935. Under strict orders from Moscow, which was alarmed by a vision of an alliance of the capitalist countries against the Soviets, Prestes staged the quickly suppressed insurrection in 1935. He himself was arrested in 1936 and not released until April, 1945, when Vargas turned to the Communists for support, giving them in exchange the release of Prestes from prison and a free hand for their propaganda and action. In this way the Brazilian army captain Prestes has become the leader of a Marxist mass party.

"If Brazil should decide to fight Russia, I will organize guerrillas and fight for Russia," Prestes declared. Diego Rivera, the famous Mexican painter and former intimate friend of Trotsky, who has returned to the fold repentant, expressed the same thought even more drastically: "Communists in South America will wage war against all South American governments if they would join the United States in war against the Soviet Union. This position is patriotic, not treason. . . . . Workers of Latin America and Canada, as well as of the United States, would sabotage hemisphere communications and eventually destroy supplies of raw materials destined for an Anglo Saxon war effort." A similar statement was made by Lazar Pena, leader of the Cuban Communists.

The frank statement of Prestes' after his election to the Brazilian senate should not be interpreted too literally: the chance of a conflict between Brazil and Russia is infinitesimal. Prestes' pronouncement defines the aims of the Stalintern on the entire South American continent: If the United States decides to fight actively against Russia, then the South American Communists will organize guerrillas against pan-American cooperation. Prestes formulated the transformation of the formerly insignificant Communist propaganda groups south of the Rio Grande into Russian pressure organizations with sharply defined objectives.

The Western hemisphere is in Stalin's mind the "heartland" of capitalist encirclement. Here the industrial power of capitalism is concentrated in a country as yet not affected by the general disintegration evident in the older capitalist countries. Until 1939 the Comintern repeated in all countries of South America its slogans of an anti-imperialist democratic revolution directed against the oppressive powers of the north. The Stalintern demands from its Latin-American adherents no revolution, but participation in power, be it ever so small. Its pressure groups are advised to utilize all means that will serve the purpose; to enter into any combination with political or military groups, be they democratic, fascist, or Socialist. They are absolutely free to move as it seems best to them on one condition—a common minimum program of direct or indirect support of Russia's acts and activities in the Western hemisphere.

Moscow demands little and offers much. The elastic anti-fascist programs of the South American Stalintern parties permit them to work with Vargas or Batista or to form a coalition with the Mexican governmental party. Peron's victory in Argentina with the help of a labor party and radical democratic slogans again demonstrates the unlimited possibilities of an anti-Fascist Fascism or of an anti-Democratic Democracy or an anti-Communist Communism.

The anti-American turn of the Stalintern in the summer of 1945 was received at all Communist conventions in South America with genuine jubilation. The struggle against "Browderism," accepted unanimously everywhere, has become a symbol of the South American struggle against Yankee imperialism.

The Cuban Communists dominate the trade union movement of the island. In Mexico the Communist trade union federation under the leadership of Lombardo Toledano strongly supports the government party. Toledano and his Cuban colleagues using the growing commercial and economic influence of Russia, have become a power throughout Central America. Trade union leaders installing presidents, as did Toledano in Ecuador and Costa Rica, are symbols of the turn events have taken.

The North American section of the Stalintern is operated in a similar fashion, as a Communist totalitarian pressure group. No Communist party in either Europe or Asia has identified itself so completely with Russia as has the American. One of the most telling illustrations of this is a statement made by William Foster after Churchill's anti-Soviet speech at Fulton, Missouri: "It is imperialist aggression and a menace to international peace when the United States monopolizes the atom bomb and brandishes it before the world. It is similar aggression when President Truman proposes that we have a navy and air force bigger than those of all the rest of the world put together, and also a huge army based on universal military training. It is aggression when the United States holds naval and air bases stretching from Europe to China. It is aggression when administration spokesmen with the President's tacit consent openly advocate a get-tough policy with Russia and encourage such speeches as Churchill's. It is aggression when American political leaders systematically whittle down the Yalta and Potsdam agreements to the advantage of the Fascist and Anglo-American monopolists. It is aggression when the United States maintains armed forces in China and lends active aid to reactionaries there. It is aggression when Anglo-American leaders try to force notorious reactionaries into the new democratic governments in the Balkans. It is aggression when the United States, Great Britain, and other capitalist nations consistently gang up against the USSR in the United Nations and vote down its constructive proposals."

If Foster had simply said: Every step of the United States in the foreign field that does not have the approval of the Narkomindel is aggression, he would have been less diplomatic but more precise. Foster indicated that the American Communists in case of a conflict with Russia would side with the latter. There is no reason to doubt their good will. Their ability is another question. It seems much more probable that the Stalinist pressure group in the United States would be unable to withstand the pressure of a war for it lacks the tradition of civil-war experience possessed by most of the European Communist parties.

American labor unions are associations of a purely trade nature and maintain no close political affiliations as did the European. This makes it easier for a closely knit political group to corner important key positions within the unions. To utilize them, however, for extremist political purposes, is an entirely different proposition. It is one matter to proclaim defeatism in a country with freedom of speech and press in times of peace, as Foster did; a different matter to practice it in war. The Stalintern obviously attempts, as did the Comintern, to create in its followers the willingness to sacrifice themselves for "the fatherland of the toilers of the world." The Comintern succeeded in this direction with European Communists who placed themselves outside their own country and whose loyalty to internationalism was stronger and more exacting than the loyalty to their own country. The mass of the American Communists, while they are good Soviet patriots, manage to be American patriots at the same time. A war would destroy this happy coordination of American and Soviet patriotism. Unquestionably some individual Communists might participate in the net of Russian espionage. But the Stalinist pressure group in the United States as a whole is neither an espionage nor a civil-war organization. It utilizes all the potentialities of American civil and political liberties for Russian purposes. Organically, it is unfit to transgress the limits defined by American political institutions.

Only after the victory of the Labor Party could British Communists of the Stalintern make their weight felt as a pressure group. With a membership of less than 50,000 they succeeded in winning over one-third of the unions of the Labor Party to their demand for admission as an organization into the British Labor Party. The Communists were favored by a number of objective reasons. During the war the British trade unions had to enroll several hundred thousand new members with little tradition or experience. The Labor government was unable to effect an overnight change in the working conditions in the British coal mines. The Communists conquered the leadership of the Mine Workers' Union with 417,000 and of the Amalgamated Engineers Union with 136,000 members. They won over the National Union of Railwaymen and the National Union of Distributive and Allied Workers for their acceptance into the Labor Party. Only a fraction of the masses in these unions, even of those

410

actively directed by Communists, belong to the group of active and organized sympathizers.

The same is true of the left wing of the parliamentary faction of the Labor Party which follows Communist ideas in many of their political activities. The radical opposition to Attlee and Bevin attempts to accelerate nationalization. If the Communists and their followers succeed in these attempts, the end of the labor government will be the ultimate outcome of their activities. The urban middle classes who helped Attlee and Bevin into power will scarcely continue to follow the lead of a Labor party that has suffered a Communist blood transfusion and has become tainted with the suspicion of the foreign affiliations of the Communists.

Such consequence of pressure group action might, it appears, not be welcome in Moscow, for it would again put the conservatives into power. But this is of no great consequence. The Stalintern is completely disinterested in what happens to the British masses. It is not a working class international but the international instrument of Russian expansion. Its British sector has one task only—that of breaking England's resistance to the consolidation of Stalin's victory in Europe. As long as Bevin continues the foreign policy of the conservatives, it makes no difference to Moscow whether the conservatives or the Labor Party are in power in London.

Sir Walter Citrine, president of the British unions and a close friend of Bevin, probably had no such contingency in mind when he participated in the foundation of the World Federation of Trade Unions. But the two events have a close interconnection. If the British trade unions are able to unite with the Russians in an International, why should it not be possible to admit the small British Communist party into the Labor party, the political organ of the trade unions?

Logic is on the side of the oppositionists asking such questions. Citrine fortified the new organization with many statutory and organizational protective measures, willingly accepted by his Russian partners. The Communists dominate nearly the entire European and Asiatic as well as a great portion of the South American trade union movement. The purpose of the new organization was the invasion of England and the international isolation of the A. F. of

L. Both purposes have been successfully accomplished with the involuntary assistance of Citrine and Bevin.

In addition, the World Federation of Trade Unions represents an international propaganda center of great significance for the Stalintern, pumping a large volume of propaganda material into all countries of the globe. In all member unions the WFTU blocks discussion of the Russian trade unions. For the newly founded organization rests on the fiction that the Russian compulsory organizations are free associations of workers. Any union member raising the question of slave labor in Europe and in Siberia would be put under moral quarantine. The WFTU destroys the very foundations of a free trade union movement in all countries of the world. In the WFTU the Stalintern holds western democratic trade unionism in a dangerous embrace.

FELLOW TRAVELLERS OF THE STALINTERN, VINTAGE 1945

In eastern Europe fellow travellers no longer exist. The totalitarian state does not need them and does not tolerate them. Once totalitarian coordination has been achieved, the fellow traveller has the alternative of becoming a vocal partisan within the totalitarian party or a silent spectator.

In western Europe the fellow traveller who had been in hibernation during the Stalin-Hitler pact had a glorious reawakening. Thousands of writers, artists, and scientists have converted themselves to a new faith, Communism, as they understand it. André Gide's adventures are being relived a thousand times, only that André Gide in the end could save himself on the lonely island of his art. The western European fellow traveller, vintage 1945, can no longer escape. Totalitarianism has him in its grip.

The French continue where they left off in 1939. The Italians, however, lived for twenty years under Fascism. Even Ignazio Silone fled into a religious glorification of Socialism as an escape from the iceland of totalitarian coordination. Small wonder then that the naive Italian intelligentsia which had experienced a magical shift from an obscure dream existence into a mysterious inexplicable light seeks a synthesis between religious mysticism and Communism. A Swiss periodical published an interview with Ello Vittorini, one

412

of the most famous poets of modern Italy. In this interview Vittorini formulates with precise intensity these latest illusions of the Italian fellow traveller: "The Communist party of Italy," Vittorini said, "has outgrown its Marxist origin. It attracts youth not only because it is the only party which had already fought underground against the fascist dictatorship. . . . . From all sides youth is drawn to us. We attract the followers of Croce. We attract Catholics, faithful and attending service every Sunday. We no longer demand a Marxist or materialist credo. The party as a whole no longer possesses any unified ideology.

"What is the British occupation army doing in our country? It favors the Fascists everywhere; in office, in the newspapers, in industry. And why? In order to keep Italy a vanquished state. Even the victory of the Labor party has made no change. The English workers are an aristocratic class which shows no solidarity toward us Italians."

When the interviewer injected a question whether the Russians were any better with their demands on North Italian industry and Tripoli, Vittorini answered: "The first was only a rumor. As for the second, we are completely indifferent to that. We lose little and receive a counterweight against British imperialism."

When the interviewer asked the poet about the relationship of the Italian Communists to the Catholic Church, Vittorini replied: "We are more favorably disposed to her than she to us. The Italian worker is not an enemy of Christianity. On the contrary. But he sees in Jesus Christ not the mystical god-man, but primarily the Socialist; and while the Church promises its believers felicity in heaven only, we want to realize it right here on earth. I used to be a believer myself. When I was a child I attended mass and confessed regularly. The last time twenty years ago. Then I ceased believing in the divinity of Christ in order to turn to Him as a human being. I regard Him as the greatest man who has ever lived on earth, and I feel that He has not lost anything of importance but on the contrary has gained. Formerly His words were revelation for me. Today they are truth, science, experience. Formerly His teachings were a message of salvation, something for myself alone, showing me the road from me to Him. Today they smooth the path between me and

413

other human beings. Today they have a meaning for all men. We have to fight for these teachings to become a historical reality.

"I know that there is much evil also within myself. But I seek to overcome it by fighting it outside of myself. Hitler is also within *me;* I know it. The fight I wage against oppressors and exploiters is a fight against this Hitler within me, and every obstacle that I erect against him in the outside world I erect within myself against evil."

The interviewer asked Vittorini whether this fight uniting the Cross with the sickle and hammer would lead humanity on to new paths. "Yes," the poet said, "the millions of dead children in the ruins of century old cities, the dead of Maidanek and Buchenwald, they are witness to the end of a culture that taught us the dignity and inviolability of man, of a culture that had its origins in Greece, the Christian Middle Ages, and the Renaissance, and that now reaches into the world of Thomas Mann, Benedetto Croce, Huizinga, Unanumo, Valéry, and Berdyaev. If fascism has committed all the crimes which this culture has for so many hundreds of years taught to hold in contempt, is it not necessary to search for the reasons in this very culture itself? They are clear. It has had no educational influence on human beings. It has influenced the intellectual life but not the whole of man. Today it appears as if Greek classicism and the Christian idea had served only to mask the barbarism of men, to justify it and to lead to destruction with ever more perfect methods. This culture has preached only and taught. It has developed principles and values. It has discovered continents and constructed machines. But it has never identified itself with human society. It has never ruled its governments nor led its armies. Man has always suffered within society and suffers to this very day. And what does culture offer to suffering man? It seeks to give him solace. In this limitation lies its weakness. Because of this nature it had no social power to prevent the rise of fascism in Germany and Italy. It had no guns, tanks and airplanes. . . . .

"Will we never have a culture that helps him to escape exploitation and suppression?"

Fellow travellers, vintage 1945, in Western Europe exhibit the wounds and the sores of a civilization fallen prey to a sickness unto death. Their souls are inflicted with a disease that requires new hori-

414

zons for its cure. Are American fellow travellers inflicted with the same malady?

In America all the outward characteristics of a material crisis are absent. American fellow travellers live peacefully at the hearth of the richest and most powerful country in the world. They are nourished in the western tradition of liberty. Compared with the fellow travellers of Europe they are economically secure. All the sources of information and education are open to them. The storms that have shattered Europe are still distant from American shores. Nevertheless, nowhere else in the world is fellow travellership so widespread and deeply anchored an institution of the Stalintern as in the U.S.A. "The strange hypnotism of a doctrine so condemned by experience as Russian Communism still remains to be explained," Norman Angell wrote. "Why should so many be prepared to bow the knee and bend the will to the secular pope in Moscow, especially when he makes so little secret of the purpose to which he proposes to apply their strange abnegation and abject submission?"

The following observations do not try to answer Norman Angell's question but attempt only to round out the picture of the "Stalintern."

The American fellow traveller should not be identified with the blind adorers of the Soviet government. The professional political agent, journalist, or radio commentator who serves Russian politics for financial compensation is not a fellow traveller, strictly speaking. The exploitation of power and corruption are not monopolies of the Stalintern nor its discoveries. They were present at all times. Even less is an American journalist in Moscow a fellow traveller, whose profession requires that he report what he is permitted to hear and see, and who would lose his job if he attempted to report more. He does not become a fellow traveller even in violating the tradition of his profession and joining up with others in a statement of protest against a colleague who has dared to have heard more and seen more than is permitted. This also is nothing particularly new and has frequently happened in this and similar fields in the past.

Even the eccentric, be he a millionaire, his son, or the inventor of a sure remedy for all the maladies of humankind, is not necessarily a fellow traveller. He substitutes one hobby for another. Tomorrow he may be a Buddhist, an adherent of the Dalai-Lama, or the collector of something no one has ever before collected.

Even the coldly calculating union boss who does business with the Communist party on a shorter or longer basis and is willing to pay ideological interest is not necessarily a fellow traveller.

The real American fellow traveller is a volunteer. He is altruistic, ready to torment and flagellate himself. He is the fetishist of an ideal produced within himself. This is the source of his peculiar strength and of his ability to become an American institution. He has the strength of faith.

A classical illustration of his peculiar psychology is the well-known statement of a former American ambassador to Moscow, who acknowledged the moral right and privilege of the Russians to appropriate the secrets of the atom bomb by means of espionage in view of the American government's unwillingness to deliver up the secret voluntarily.

This statement contains the entire "program" of American fellow travellership. First, the most burning problems of humanity can be solved only with the help of the Soviet Republic. (If you wish to eliminate the horrible threats resulting from the discovery of atomic energy, confide in Moscow. Then the plague will become a benediction.) Second, Moscow is beyond good and evil. For this reason it has moral privileges not ordinarily accorded any other country in the world. (Espionage is an unmoral institution. Applied by Moscow it is elevated to the rank of a moral one.) Third, the natural prerogatives of your own country lose their pre-eminence when they come into conflict with those of Moscow, particularly when the latter's "principles of security" are threatened.

The peculiarity of this way of thinking is that it does not originate in a revolutionary or totalitarian negation of the "own country" as it does with orthodox Marxists or modern Stalinists. The fellow traveller is essentially a bourgeois, the living negation of everything revolutionary. His ideal as far as the United States is concerned is stability, harmony, and progress within the framework of law. Yet in everything concerning the Soviet Republic he sheds the criteria of the well-behaved citizen. In respect to Russia he abandons the normal processes of logic and is willing to forgive everything, to excuse everything, and to defend everything.

416

In line with his education and training as well as the intellectual tradition of his country, he demands when confronted with a problem in his own American world facts, figures, statistics. As soon as he approaches Russia his factual curiosity ceases. He is satisfied with the results of political propaganda which he treats with suspicion otherwise. He tries to dissolve not doubts but doubters. He wants to burden the doubter with a moral responsibility for the doubt.

A few illustrations from everyday discussions suffice for this point: "It is pretty improbable that all the close collaborators of Lenin with the exception of Stalin were foreign spies, as the prosecutor of the Moscow trials claimed." "The war has justified the trials and the executions. Had Bukharin, Zinoviev, etc. remained alive, they would have formed a Russian fifth column, for they were Stalin's foes. This proves that the prosecution was right."

"Stalin had Ehrlich and Alter, two Jewish Socialists from Poland, executed as agents of the Nazis. Is it probable that a Jew and a Socialist from Poland, where Hitler murdered three million Jews, would come to Russia in order to act there as Hitler's agents?" "Certainly it is possible, for Trotsky was a Jew, too, and negotiated with the Nazi, Hess."

"The entire Russian policy is founded on the doctrine of the infallibility of Stalin. This may be necessary as far as Russia is concerned, but how can one accept such infallibility as far as the United States is concerned?" "I reject this just as you do."

"Can you name a case where Stalin has blundered?" "Certainly, for Stalin himself declared that Russian leadership has committed many blunders during the war."

And so on ad infinitum and ad nauseam.

Suppose that the fellow traveller is an American historian who has written a voluminous book on recent Russian history. One of the most crucial problems of Russia's recent past and present is the question of slave labor. Does it exist in the country of accomplished Socialism? If so, in what form? What does it mean for its economic and social structure? Out of six hundred pages our professor devotes two to this question to develop the following proposition: The Soviet government has good and satisfactory reasons to remain silent on this question. Several authors have estimated the number of slave laborers

417

in Russia in 1938 at between fifteen and twenty million. How ridiculous, for: first, the country is so tremendous that no one in Russia or outside can give a proper estimate; second, in the United States there occur annually approximately two million criminal cases. There may exist a similar number in the Russian labor camps. Nevertheless, this also is only an estimate; third, an author hostile to the Soviets claims that the mortality in these labor camps amounts to nearly 30 per cent per annum. According to our professor, therefore, sixty million people must have died in these camps within ten years— one-third of the entire Soviet population. (As if anybody had claimed that in 1928 there had been twenty millions in these Russian labor camps!) Finally, all these estimates are drowned in a quotation from a book of another author who claims that the whole Russian people live in a "moderately well-run penitentiary."

Suppose the fellow traveller is a former priest. Then his Russian problem is solved in the following fashion: "The New Testament's teaching that every child by being born into the great human family has equal rights with all others to the abundance of life and is a joint inheritor of the earth and all its treasures, I find is unconditionally upheld by the Communist constitution and principles of action. I look in vain for the same in the platforms and pledges of what are called the leading political organizations in the United States. How then should a minister of religion not rejoice to find such spiritual fellowship as this?"

Yet seemingly the devil had his finger in this conversion. For the Communist who persuaded this minister of religion to become a fellow traveller was Louis Budenz, editor of the *Daily Worker,* who himself, one year after this conversion, became converted to Catholicism and declared Communism to be the work of the devil.

The fellow traveller has good reason to be fearful of a factual presentation of the Soviet Union. Few human beings adore what they know well. Mystery is frequently the source of adoration.

As long as the Soviet Union embodied the rational social and political slogans of a proletarian world revolution, it created few fellow travellers. Only when world revolution finally abdicated to a dictator equipped with infinite power could it become an "individual answer to a collective demand."

418

This collective demand in the United States arises from a fear of life flowing from its power and its wealth. Power and wealth overwhelming in relation to the rest of the world have tossed into the lap of the United States a moral responsibility that is beyond her present intellectual and moral capacity. In an individualist society the individual feels individually responsible for the collective moral irresponsibility of the society to which he belongs. To dissolve these doubts and the fears that arise from them by the application of reason and understanding is at best an uncertain and arduous task. It contributes little to an immediate alleviation of doubt and fear.

"World government is either world revolution or world illusion," wrote the Swiss economist Roepke. The fear-obsessed individual of the Western hemisphere who has taken into his consciousness the idea of "one world" is perforce accepting the only solution that solves everything—the totalitarian. Philosophy he regards with the God-given contempt of the faithful. Only a mystery to which one can submit without having to think, which permits one to participate with eyes closed and brain estopped, offers peace and rest. American fellow travellership is one of the outstanding political neuroses of the modern age.

The efficacy of the mystery increases proportionately to the distance of the faithful from the tabernacle. The priests know the tricks. They are aware that the American fellow traveller would be horrified if the mystery were to become an American reality. They eagerly preserve his spiritual double existence.

The party member moves according to the iron laws of totalitarian mass control. The fellow traveller who receives the message of salvation directly from the tabernacle as an individual carries himself with pride and dignity. He cannot be tossed out of the party. For him the Communist party is only a medium for his adoration of the Soviet tabernacle. Whether Browder or Foster is the leader in his own country is of no concern to him. He represents an American institution. This is his great political significance. To be a fellow traveller does not involve disqualification. In the United States it is not possible for a Communist to become a high official of state. But no court in the country could find a legitimate reason to disqualify a fellow traveller. Nevertheless it is no exaggeration to claim that the

419

influence of fellow travellership in American foreign policy represents a power to be reckoned with. In a country where public opinion changes spontaneously and suddenly, the fellow traveller represents a stable center of an undeviating and conforming influence. Fellow travellership as the loose association that it is, is an ideal arrangement for this purpose. It has no offensive function: It defends the United States against every move of foreign policy not agreeable to Moscow. The implication is that any price is low for American-Russian harmony—including a Russian hegemony in Europe and Asia.

Fellow travellers exist in all classes and professions but chiefly among the well-to-do and intellectuals. Workers demand material security. Their fear of life is natural. The bourgeois fellow traveller for whom freedom from want is normal rebels against his own security in view of his own aimlessness. The adoration of the tabernacle in the end is a fight with his own self. The fellow traveller before his conversion usually had little traffic with Socialist or any other well-defined political philosophy. Frequently he is a scientist for whom science substituted for philosophy. Now when all philosophy is being examined in the final court of history, he rebels against the vacuum in himself. Stalinism attracts him because it rejects critique as a method of thinking. Stalinism can be acquired without much cost to the innocent.

The Bolsheviks used to cultivate the work of disintegration in their enemies' back as a special art of warfare. Fellow travellership, a product of disintegration, required little labor on the part of the Stalintern. It is a present from the gods of American democracy to the Russian organs for "the struggle against counter-revolution outside of the Russian frontiers."

CHAPTER XXVIII

Chinese Army Party

PRELUDE

THE RESULT OF THE STRUGGLE WILL DEPEND IN THE END ON the fact that Russia, India, China, etc, constitute the gigantic majority of the population of the world. But the certainty of an ultimate Socialist victory for all time does not guarantee our immediate success.

"To assure our existence until the approaching armed conflagration between the counter-revolutionary and imperialist West and the national revolutionary East; that is, between the most civilized states in the world and the revolutionary states, backward as are all Oriental states—this majority must have time to civilize itself. . . . ."

These words Lenin wrote in one of his last articles restating the world historical perspective that he had given to the Second World Congress of the Comintern.

Years after Lenin's death, the Bolsheviks returned again and again to these words. Bukharin planned to devote the Seventh World Congress of the Comintern to these last thoughts of the deceased leader. . . . .

The defeat of the Comintern in the East, however, was as devastating as in the West.

In 1927 the last hopes for a revolutionary victory in China had vanished. The Chinese labor movement of the coastal areas in the great port cities had gone under in Chiang Kai Shek's blood baths. The Communist party of China became a peasant party with a thin proletarian and intellectual upper group. By 1937 all the old tacticians of the Far East had disappeared from Moscow: shrewd Michael Borodin who had permitted himself to be taken in by Chiang Kai Shek, the Indian Manabendranath Roy who had predicted the Comintern catastrophe in the Far East, Lominadze, Heinz

Neumann, and Pogany-Pepper, and many other small China "experts."

By 1938 the executive committee of the Comintern in Moscow had been deprived of all authority over the Chinese Communists. The Far East division of the Comintern had been dissolved, its representatives in China withdrawn. The net of underground communications of the Communications Division of the Comintern (OMS) had been transferred to the foreign division of the GPU.

The Communist party of the United States was the first Comintern party to secede formally from the central direction of the Comintern. But the Communist party of China had already been removed, two years earlier, in 1938, from all interference by the politicians of the Comintern. It had become the first non-Russian Communist party to be annexed directly by the Russian state apparatus. Stalin himself with his own secretariat made all the decisions relevant to the Chinese Communists, who were made subordinate to the general staff of the Far Eastern Red Army at Chabarovsk.

General Grigori Stern became Stalin's most trusted executive in the Far East. Stern is a former Austrian war prisoner and officer in the Austrian army who joined the Red Army in 1917, advanced quickly in the academy of its general staff, directed the insurrection of the Hamburg Communists in 1923 under the name of Georg, became one of the Russian commanders to administer a crucial defeat to the Japanese at the battle of Lake Chasan in 1935, fought in Spain as General Kleber, and was elected to the central committee of the Communist party of the Soviet Union at its Eighteenth Party Congress.

General Grigori Stern plays a much greater role in the Red Army of Mao Tze Dun than the famous General Bluecher-Galen played in Chiang Kai Shek's armies during the latter's military rise. General Stern is not an adviser; he is commander-in-chief.

In 1939 all Chinese universities and military academies were transferred from Moscow to the Siberian provinces, particularly to Irkutsk and Novosibirsk. At the same time the construction of an automobile road from Alma-Ata through Sinkiang (Chinese Turkestan) across the Gobi Desert into the North Chinese province of Kansu dominated by the Chinese Communists, was begun. This road as well as the air facilities in the area have been built by the forced labor of hundreds of thousands of inhabitants of Siberian concentration camps and of Mongolian tribes.

MAO TZE DUN

When Mao Tze Dun, a Chinese student of peasant birth, became a Communist around 1920, he was about twenty-eight years old and uncertain what course to follow. Today, at fifty-four, Mao is head of the Chinese Soviet government, ruling a population of eight to ten million, and general of an army of several hundred thousand soldiers. He is a man of medium height, solidly built with a broad, serious face; thick, black, hair; and dark, searching eyes. His manner is mild and amiable. His friends, poor peasants of the Soviet areas, and the barefoot soldiers of his armies adore him.

Mao Tze Dun stands between Stalin and Chiang Kai Shek. Whatever the policies the Russian dictator and the Chinese generalissimo pursue with or against each other, Mao has to mesh them into gear.

Mao owes his position not only to his personal qualities. He has been lucky too. He has leapt over many of the traps of Comintern policies and intrigues that caught dozens of his friends, and hundreds of times he has escaped Chiang Kai Shek's executioners.

But all his good luck would have availed him nothing had he not adhered steadfastly and deliberately to three principles. First, Chinese wisdom is more profound and more farseeing than Comintern wisdom. Second, make the source of your strength not the Chinese workers in the coastal areas but the millions of peasants who inhabit the interior of the country. Third, stay at home and visit Moscow as rarely as possible.

Just as Mao Tze Dun refused to accept a fellowship offered by the French government in 1920 to study at the Sorbonne, so did he turn aside from Moscow's invitations to the Far Eastern university. Throughout the entire twenty years that Mao has belonged to the high command of the world revolution, he has gone to Moscow only three or four times and then only for a short stay.

At various times the Comintern made up its mind to give the promising young revolutionary the necessary training in Moscow. But Mao always managed to be unavailable. Once he happened to be involved in a peasant rebellion; another time the message failed to reach him. His power grew not at the court of the high command, but in China itself. For that reason it became real power.

In 1923 Mao was elected to the central committee of the Chinese Communist party and at the same time became a member of the Kuomintang. He was cautious enough not to be personally involved in the intrigues of the Chinese central committee. To the representatives of the Comintern, Michael Borodin and, later on, Manabendranath Roy, he showed utmost and sincere respect. But he knew how to keep his distance. In any case he felt more secure in his own province of Hunan, and he did not commit the European mistakes of Chen-To-Hsin, the chief leader of the Communist party at the time.

"The Comintern asks an independent policy of us," the leader complained, "and does not permit us to retire from the Kuomintang. There is no way out of this dilemma. I cannot continue my work."

Such dramatic utterances were not to Mao's liking. The principles of Confucius were more deeply infused in his blood than the methods of debate introduced from Moscow. He knew that in affairs of state one should not show one's real face. He kept silent and did not express an opinion on the relationship with the Kuomintang. When the actual decision was made by the party authorities to step out of the Kuomintang, he kept just as silent. And again in August, 1926, when a new leadership was installed by Heinz Neumann and Lominadze under the tempestuous Li-Li-San, it was but natural that Mao Tze Dun was included in this new leadership. But he kept in the background. His friend Chou-En-Lai, descendant of an aristocratic old Chinese family, well trained in the ways of the West at French, English, and German universities, reported to him on the goings on. He personally did not participate in the insurrection of Canton, being too preoccupied with his peasant Soviets in Kiangsi. Moscow became fully aware of Mao after the latter had succeeded in consolidating the peasant Soviets of Kiangsi into a sort of Soviet government and had in addition, without help from the Russians, organized a Red Army of barefoot soldiers that defeated Chiang Kai Shek's troops in several clashes.

Even after the defeat of Canton, Stalin continued to insist on his

424

slogan of Soviets in China. Nobody in Moscow believed, however, that the Chinese Communists after the dreadful blood baths they had suffered would be sufficiently strong for serious action. This was certainly correct in the coastal areas where the industrial workers were the foundation of the Communist party. In the peasant Southeast, the realm of Mao Tze Dun, however, new sources of energy for Communist action arose.

Mao did not talk much about revolution and Socialism, but dispersed the landlords and distributed land to the peasants. With their sons, victims of famine and refugees from the inundation areas, he filled the ranks of the Red Army. Bitter factional strife broke out in the leadership group of Li-Li-San, installed into power by Heinz Neumann and Lominadze; so bitter that not only did the central committee meetings become the scene of shootings but that the leaders of the various factions waged actual war against each other.

Mao Tze Dun stood aloof from all this. In 1931 he and Li-Li-San were called to Moscow. Li-Li-San became a permanent refugee among the "impure" at the Hotel Lux.* Mao returned to China as victor.

Stalin had received him personally, an honor seldom accorded a foreign Communist. After this reception he had said to Molotov: "This one Chinese is worth more than all the beggars of the Machavaya put together."

Mao went back to the Soviet district of Kiangsi crowned with all the authority of Moscow. But Stalin could not be of much help to his chosen one. Rarely was it possible to smuggle through arms from the coastal cities to Kiangsi. Few agents of the Comintern successfully penetrated into Mao's section. Chiang Kai Shek made short shrift of Communist agents, Chinese or European. He beheaded them. For three years Mao with his barefoot army braved all the military expeditions of his Chinese adversary. He proved himself a real leader, not one of Stalin's making alone.

In July, 1934, Mao Tze Dun was elected president of the Chinese Soviet government. A short while later he was again called to Moscow. This time he went without hesitation. There could no longer be any surprise in store for him.

* News reports of 1946 have it that Li-Li-San is now in Manchuria.

But the surprise that awaited him here was one to stagger his imagination. Stalin proposed to transfer his Soviet government and his Red Army to Cheng-Si, from the south of China to the farthest Northwest. Even the stoic Mao lost heart when he heard this proposal. From Kiangsi to Cheng-Si is thousands of miles. The way leads through desert country, high mountains, and roaring rivers. Mao felt sure his Red Army would perish on such an expedition. Nevertheless he agreed.

Stalin had a simple reason for this fantastic idea. He had just suffered a decisive defeat in Germany and wished to avoid a similar catastrophe in China. Mao's Red Army had successfully weathered four assaults of Chiang Kai Shek's. But to a fifth or sixth it was bound to succumb.

With the transfer of the Chinese Red Army to Cheng-Si, two objectives could be attained. The areas of friction with Chiang could be reduced and an additional military force in the flank of the Japanese army created.

Against all expectations the transfer of more than one hundred thousand men was accomplished. On the march that lasted over a year, tens of thousands perished. Other tens of thousands of hungry peasants joined. In this way the Soviet Republic of Mao Tze Dun's in Chengsi and Kansu came into being—the most advanced post of Stalin's power in the Far East; a thorn in the flesh of Chiang; a red arrow aimed at the heart of China, but also an independent revolutionary Chinese power more popular among many of the Chinese peasants, workers, and intellectuals than Chiang Kai Shek's government.

THE VICTORY OF THE STALINTERN IN MANCHURIA

The sudden end of the war in the Far East created a new military, political, and psychological situation for Mao Tze Dun's army party. For ten years the slogan of an active national and anti-imperialist war had attracted new forces to the Chinese Communists and strengthened their political order in Yenan. Now they lost the drawing power of this slogan. The Americans liquidated the Japanese invasion and occupied Tokyo. The British no longer inspired fear in the Orient. Manchuria fell into the lap of the Russians. Stalin accepted the easy fruits of victory in the Far East. His troops have carried off the industrial equipment of Manchuria. His administrators have expropriated all movable property and destroyed the concentrated industry of the country. The anti-imperialism of Lenin's International has now bowed out of China and the Far East and has ceded its place to the Soviet imperialism of the Stalintern. Communist anti-imperialism in China no longer can draw on the tradition of the Russian revolution as a source of strength.

Nor does Mao any longer enjoy the advantages of distance from Moscow. His Chinese Soviet Republic of the Northwest rubs shoulders with detachments of the Russian Far Eastern Army. His capital Yenan finds itself in the same situation as Warsaw. Mao's cunning is no longer of much avail.

Chiang Kai Shek has returned to Nanking, Hankow, Shanghai, and Pekin. He has a more modern and more numerous army than in 1936 and relies heavily on political support from the United States in the unstable balance of power in the eastern Pacific. This is the main reason why the Japanese war did not turn immediately into a general civil war. The uncertain armistice between Mao Tze Dun and Chiang Kai Shek is one of the formulas of an American-Russian *modus vivendi* in the Far East.

Both for the Kuomintang and the Chinese Communists the situation is fraught with incalculable danger. The total victory of the United States over Japan has returned the Russians to Port Arthur and Dairen, from where they face the Japanese islands directly. The United States has become the center of "capitalist encirclement" of the Soviet Republic in the Far East. As long as it is not willing to leave all of Asia to Moscow or share the Far East with Russia on terms acceptable to Stalin, the United States will remain the spearhead of "capitalist encirclement."

The Yalta agreement granting Russia the privileges she lost in 1905 and in the 1930's has not bridged "the unbridgeable chasm." But it delivered Chinese independence up to the Soviets. Stalin was well aware of the implications of Yalta when in his agreement with Chiang in August, 1945, he acknowledged the sovereignty of the Chinese National government over all of China including Manchuria and recognized the principle of nonintervention. On the **very** same day, Mao Tze Dun submitted his plan for the pacification of China and its national reconstruction. During the months that followed, Stalin's and Mao Tze Dun's strategy were equally well synchronized.

The negotiations between the Kuomintang and the Communists aimed at an initial merger of the armies of Chiang with those of Mao. As far as the Communists were concerned, their objective was to gain time. The longer the negotiations interrupted by various artificial crises lasted, the more secure became Stalin's occupation of Manchuria, and when the Russian occupation was finally completed and the danger of American intervention had passed, the second part of the maneuver began. While the Russians were carrying away the industry of Manchuria and establishing themselves in its ports, the Eighth and the new Fourth Army of Mao began a strategic withdrawal to the rear of the Russian Red Army, and allied itself with the Manchurian people's "democratic army." Now the moment for unity in Chungking had arrived and for Stalin to make good on his promise to withdraw his armies from Manchuria. But as the Russian Red Army withdrew through one exit of a city, the Communist troops entered at the other side, in order to occupy the town or to wage war against Chiang's divisions. Early in February, 1946, the great majority of Manchurian cities was in Communist hands.

The cooperation between General Grigori Stern in Mukden and Chou-En-Lai in Chungking has had a glorious outcome. The surprising thing in regard to this maneuver was not its success but the surprise it caused. For since 1936 the synchronization of Stalin's China policy with the strategy of the Chinese Communists has been clear for anyone to observe. In the period between 1936 and 1939 when Russian-Japanese relationships were at their worst, the Chinese Communists elevated national unity in China to their supreme aim. From 1937 to 1939 the Chinese Communist armies fought actively against Japanese invasion. With the German-Russian pact, the political and military strategy of Mao Tze Dun changed abruptly. He declared that "with the liquidation of the Nazi anti-Soviet, anti-Comintern policy, the distinction formerly drawn between the fascist and democratic countries lost its validity." His Communist armies no longer sought open clashes with the Japanese but embarked on a very

428

elastic guerrilla war. Their attacks against Chiang, who still expected a Russian-Japanese war, became more and more pronounced. When the Russian-Japanese pact was signed in April, 1941, Japan ceased to be their imperialist arch foe.

Throughout the duration of the Russian-Japanese pact, that is up to April, 1945, no Japanese offensive against Yenan was undertaken, although this city was only about one hundred miles from the Japanese lines. The Chinese Communists estimated their armies at one-half to one million. This figure was probably exaggerated. But it is certain that only a small portion of their troops actively participated in the Chinese war against Japan. The other part was a reserve of Russia's Far Eastern Army.

Nevertheless, the Chinese Communists have won a place in the national resurrection of China. Chiang attempted for too long a time to reach a compromise with Japan. The Communist regime in Yenan has been more democratic—in the sense of proximity to the masses —than has Chiang's.

Now the happy years of isolation are past. The Chinese Soviet Republic has become an advance post of "Socialist encirclement." Here the hope of conquering the leadership of the nation with the active help of the entire people has been put aside. The Stalintern has made the Chinese Communists, probably against their own expectations, into a foreign legion, like the German Communists.

Frequently Stalin's expansion in the Far East has been compared with that of the Czar's. Yet it is not the same historical process that is happening now. After the October Revolution, Russia found herself still more in a position of defense and resistance in the East than in the West. When the transition to a policy of imperialist expansion occurred, Stalin could avail himself of the new revolutionary forces created by the disintegration of the old imperialist colonialism. Without them his first *rencontre* with American power in the Pacific might have ended with a devastating Russian defeat. In Manchuria, Stalin has given unmistakable demonstration of his version of an alliance of the Soviet Republic with the "suppressed peoples of the East."

GATE TO THE SOUTHERN PACIFIC

To the south of Yenan, Mao Tze Dun's capital, a new center of

Stalintern power is rising in Hanoi, capital city of Tongking, northern province of French Indo-China.

In March, 1944, an autonomous republic comprising Tongking and the northern provinces of French Indo-China up to a latitude of 16 degrees was created under the name of Viet-Nam and solemnly recognized by the Japanese and the Pétain government in France. Bao Dai, the last emperor of Anam, was made president of the new republic by the Japanese. In August, 1945, Bao Dai stepped out, a people's republic was proclaimed and on January 6, 1946, Ho Chi-Minh, alias Song Mantschao, alias Nguyén-aï-Quôc, was elected president of the republic Viet-Nam. With this new president the Stalintern raises its flag for the first time on the shores of the Indian Ocean.

Nguyén-aï-Quôc has been one of Moscow's most loyal, shrewd, and agile agents in the Far East during the last twenty-five years. If possible, he will prevent the British, the Dutch, as well as the French, from re-establishing their colonial empires in the Indian Ocean. The colonial diplomats of France must have felt this determination when he arrived in Paris in the spring of 1946, to negotiate a *modus vivendi* with the French. He and the delegates accompanying him were showered with more honors than were ever shown an emperor of Anam: private railway cars, royal suites in the most exclusive hotels of the capital, honor guards of the Republic, state banquets. The President of Viet-Nam was as little moved by these gestures of respect as he was amused by the memories served him by some of his hosts about his own life, twenty-five years earlier, as an employee of a photographic studio in the Parisian suburb of Clignancourt. Nor was the French Colonial Minister, Marius Moutet, more successful, when he reminded him of their former common membership in the French Socialist Party.

Nguyén-aï-Quôc had grown up with bitterness and hate against French colonialism as a family tradition. His father had belonged to many of the secret conspiracies attempting to regain independence for Anam. Anam's most exclusive college where Nguyén-aï-Quôc and other sons of Mandarin families studied was a fertile soil for conspiracy against the French. In later years, he described the French colonial administration in one of his numerous pamphlets in these words: *"On dirait que la colonisation c'est un vol—nous ajoutons: un viol et un assassinat."*

430

France maintained in Indo-China a colonial administration as numerous as the British in India proper, with its population of hundreds of millions. Most of the French officials were corrupt, cruel and vicious. The natural resources of the country were exploited without consideration of the needs of the population. French companies were supplied by the military with ample slave labor. Sale of opium and alcohol were monopolized for the benefit of the French and the colonial officials. "In France nothing is prohibited but opium. In Anam everything but opium is prohibited," Nguyén-aï-Quôc wrote in one of his attacks on the French.

Along with French colonialism, the young revolutionary hated its collaborators in his own country, the aristocrats of Anam. In 1911 his entire family, his father, brother, and sister, were imprisoned by order of the Emperor. Nguyén-aï-Quôc evaded arrest by joining a ship's crew and sailing for distant parts of the world. At that time he was nineteen years old. It was only at the end of the First World War that he returned home. France was then trying to compensate for her losses on the battlefield by enlisting colonials—most of whom had to be forced into the French army. Those who deserted or escaped service were the recruits for Nguyén-aï-Quôc's first revolutionary organization. Soon he had to decide again whether to be imprisoned or to flee. He was now a sophisticated man of the world. He knew English well, having visited New York; and spoke French fluently. He decided to flee to Paris. There he worked in a photographic studio just long enough to earn the few francs required for his living. Most of his time he spent in the lecture rooms of the Sorbonne, the reading room of the Bibliothèque Nationale, and in the halls of the innumerable political discussion clubs. One of these Socialist clubs chose him as its representative for the party congress in Tours in 1920, where the controversy between the followers and the foes of the Third International was to be carried to a decision. There was no hesitation on the part of Nguyén-aï-Quôc: he joined the party that had promised to wage war on colonial imperialism at its recent Congress at Baku. Nguyén's address, accusing the imperialists of crimes against humanity, brought him an invitation to Moscow. This invitation was the fateful turn of his life. The unknown revolutionary from Anam was elected to the presidium of the Third World Congress of the Comintern where he sat side by side with Lenin, Trotsky and Zinoviev. Nguyén became the comrade of Manabendranath Roy, at that time idol of all the revolutionaries from Asia. Moscow became his second home. For him it was no cheap catchword, as it was for many others.

The Russians realized full well that he represented only himself. Yet their confidence in the magic of the world revolution was so strong that they regarded every one of these revolutionaries from Asia as a potential leader.

Nguyén became a member of the "Eastern Secretariat" of the Comintern forming the leading staffs of all the revolutionary movements of the East. His friendly and modest manner made him well liked everywhere. Although now a man of thirty, with a somewhat short upper lip and protruding teeth, he still gave the impression of a delicate young boy. He became one of the main organizers of the famous University of the East in Moscow where sixty-two different groups of colored peoples were initiated into the mysteries of the profession of professional revolutionary. Nguyén was teacher and disciple in one— learning from the Russians all branches of their Leninist science, teaching them the psychology of the Asiatic peoples. After a short time he had acquired a knowledge of Russian in addition to French, English, and some experience in the Cantonese dialect of Chinese. He was a most dependable interpreter for the Russians to their students from Asia. Here he organized the first members of his revolutionary group from Anam—the Communist Seamen's International brought the men from Asia to France without cost, and from there Russian ships took them to Leningrad. After finishing their courses they were returned home the same way. His party in Anam, although prohibited and brutally persecuted, grew slowly and early learned the laws of conspiratorial life.

The "Eastern Secretariat" maintained branch offices in Paris and Canton between 1922 and 1939, and up to 1933 in Berlin. The Berlin office concerned itself with the British colonies exclusively. Because of frequent protests and threats, the British section of the Secretariat was given the protection of Willy Muenzenberg's parliamentary immunity. In Paris Jacques Doriot, later leader of French fascists, conducted the Communist campaign in the French colonies. Canton housed the "Front Office" for Southern China and the entire Pacific area. Nguyén was active continuously in these offices up to the outbreak of the Second World War—interrupted only by some years in Burmese, Siamese, and Malayan prisons. His working energy was inexhaustible, his equanimity during the innumerable crises of the Comintern unassailable. Stalin's rise to power never endangered his supreme position in the organization of the Far East. In 1930, in accord with the policy of the Comintern of that year, he attempted an armed uprising. But he suffered a quick and bloody defeat. Many of his followers died on the gallows with the cry "Viet-Nam, Viet-Nam" on their lips. During the years that followed, the Communist movement in the countries of the Pacific seemed to have disappeared completely.

When the Second World War started Nguyén-aï-Quôc was again in Canton—officially a translator of the Russian Consular Offices. After the Japanese occupied Indo-China he reappeared for the first time in twenty years legally in his home country. His party was still prohibited but the Japanese who knew him well allowed him the freedom of the land, although he maintained a cool detachment from Bao Dai's government installed by them. Probably the Russian-Japanese neutrality pact as well as an expectancy of winning over this representative of Indo-Chinese independence were guiding motives of Japanese behavior. Even more important must have been the intimate contacts between Nguyén and Sandra Bose, the former President of the Indian National Congress who was now calling from Hongkong and Singapore for an Indian war of independence on the side of Japan against Great Britain. Bose never had been a Communist and Nguyén never had entertained great respect for the Congress party of India. But he did respect the wisdom of his "elder brother" and was willing to assist him in his fight against the imperialists of the West. Their defeats and humiliations could give him nothing but deep satisfaction. In his eyes Bose was certainly not a traitor—although Indian Communists, after Hitler's attack on Russia, had come out for an allied victory. Nguyén played his cards close—between 1941 and 1945 he must have succeeded in creating a big organization. For only a few days after the Japanese capitulation there emerged in most villages and cities of Northern Anam a militia with red arm bands and frequently with Soviet stars, armed with Japanese guns. This militia was soon organized into an army under the command of Nguyén-aï-Quôc. The new

433

commander-in-chief waged war for eight months against the troops of Chiang Kai Shek who had ventured forth into Indo-China, forcing them out of the country and compelling the French to recognize the autonomy of the Northern provinces. In this war he won a double victory. In past times Chinese war lords had frequently tried to conquer Anam. These bloody attacks were not forgotten. Their memories were preserved in legends and heroic poems. So Nguyén became the successor to the heroes of Anam in the defense of the "land of the South"—Viet-Nam. He could not prevent the French from landing an army in Hai-phong with the help of battleships. But they did not dare occupy the capital Hanoi and finally had to agree to withdraw their troops completely from Nguyén's territory. Since 1862 when the Indo-Chinese princes were made vassals to France this is the first victory Anam had won. As a symbol of its gratitude the new republic coin shows a portrait head of Nguyén-aï-Quôc, the master pupil of the revolutionary academy in Moscow.

Does Nguyén, now nearly sixty years of age, still follow the lead of Moscow as loyally as twenty-five years ago? The compromise with France achieved after interminable negotiations seems to indicate an affirmative answer. Originally he demanded complete independence for Viet-Nam with inclusion of Cochin-China. When the French refused the latter categorically he refused further negotiation, whereupon the guerrilla war in Cochin-China mysteriously flared up anew. Yet ultimately he gave in and compromised this essential point of his program.

Stalin's representatives have denounced British and Dutch colonialism vehemently and passionately during all the recent international meetings and conferences. But they have kept a stubborn silence about the re-establishment of French colonialism in Indo-China. They support Arabian movements against England, yet the Algerian one against France does not delight their eyes. The reasons seem obvious. Open warfare in Indo-China would seriously endanger the position of the French Communists. Should they sabotage such a war—as they promised in former years innumerable times—they could no longer share in the French governmental power and they might lose the support of millions of citizens for whom the "France d'outre mer" is still a symbol and a hope of the France of past glory. Should they, however, decide to support such a war, they would lose large sections of the French workers, particularly in the South. Nguyén-aï-Quôc saved them from this dilemma, notwithstanding the fact that he held more aces than the French government and that his renunciation of Cochin-China caused great opposition within the ranks of his own followers. He sacrificed his own national interests in order not to endanger the Stalintern's struggle for power in France. If this struggle is successful Nguyén will expand his rule to the Gulf of Siam. If the French Communists are decisively beaten, an all-out war against the French colonial administration will be waged. . . . .

Therefore one has to assume that the "man who loves his country" (which is the English translation of his name), loves his second home and the principles it represents even more. What the relationship between Moscow and the Far East will be, should the Mao Tze Duns and the Nguyén-aï-Quôcs actually become the leaders of the entire teeming and mysterious Orient, is a problem of a different nature.

The big problem for the Far East is whether the Soviet Republic will be able to fashion out of the disintegrating Western imperialism in India, Indo-China and the Dutch East Indies, instruments of expansion similar to those that made Mao Tze Dun's army party such a valuable asset in China.

That Russia is making such efforts is undeniable. Its powerful broadcasting stations in Moscow and Baku talk in all languages of the Orient. At all strategic points in Asia, from Tibet to the Persian Gulf, Russian missions are working full speed.

CHAPTER XXIX

Era of Stalinism?

ASIATIC SOCIALISM

BOLSHEVISM WAS A RUSSIAN CHILD OF THE EUROPEAN WEST. Its philosophy originated in the Marxism of the nineteenth century, stemming from British political economy on the one hand and from French and German philosophy on the other.

Lenin's concept of world revolution was a variation of the "universal revolution" heralded seventy years earlier by Marx and Engels as the ultimate end of the capitalist era of human history. The intellectual leaders of the Bolshevist revolution, Lenin, Trotsky, Bukharin, and their circle, were imbued with the culture of the European West; and they wished to imbue Russia with the cultural heritage of the West. This was and remained to them one of the most essential cornerstones for a Communist edifice in Russia.

It may not have been Stalin's deliberate intention, but when he eliminated Lenin's world revolutionary party in Russia he also turned Europe out of Russia and gave the ensuing transformation a peculiar anti-European twist. "Socialism in one country," Stalin's substitute for world revolution, again closed Russia's windows on Europe. Yet the Russian renascence preserved from the Western Marxist ideology that preceded it the insight into the significance of a strong modern industry for the sustenance of political power. To accomplish in ten years what Russia had failed to accomplish during the last hundred, became its atheistic religion.

The execution of this program in a messianic spirit, interpreted by its managers as Socialism, introduced into Russia a new order of society resting on the foundation of modern technology and at the same time on Asiatic methods of labor. This new order required for its maintenance forced and slave labor. Russian revolutionary society, which had attempted to free itself and the world, had become a prisoner of its newly developed ways of production. Productive man in Russia no longer was a freely acting productive agent but had changed into a passive means of production, into a living piece of machinery. That is the social content of Stalin's dictatorship, of the Asiatic Socialism established in Russia.

This transformation telescoped two different social eras into one: the twentieth century with its large-scale mass production industries, and age-old Asia with its inability to discriminate between human labor power and the primitive machines and tools that serve it. In Russia all the institutions of a modern society have been developed —schools, laboratories, transportation and communication systems, and hospitals. Alongside these modern institutions lies the wild barbarism of Asia; alongside the intricate complicated industrial plant, the concentration camp of forced and slave labor; alongside a progressive legal constitution, the lawlessness of the period of Ivan the Terrible who had his Boyars whipped just like his serfs; alongside a diplomacy operating with all the equipment of modern communications, the age-old Asiatic slyness of Attila of whom it says in an ancient legend that he showed great hospitality and kindness to the emissaries of foreign countries wishing to conclude pacts of non-aggression, saying: It is better to have an alliance than war. I am a man of peace but those who oppose me foolishly I will wipe off the face of the earth.

It seems as if the entire foreign policy of Stalin is being guided by the vision of the pan-Slavist Tyutchev of the nineteenth century, who wrote: "The three sacred capitals of the Russian empire are Moscow, St. Petersburg, and Constantinople. Where are her frontiers in the North and East, in the South and West? Destiny will show us that the path of the future will lead us to the seven inland seas and to the seven great rivers, from the Nile to the Neva, from the Elbe to the Yangtze, from the Volga to the Euphrates, from the Ganges to the Danube—this is the Russian empire and it will last through the centuries. . . . ."

The ideological driving force of the industrial transformation in Russia was tremendous. Architects and supervisors of the new structure drove themselves and others on in the fanatical belief that success in this greatest of all historical experiments would solve all the pressing problems of humanity. Soviet youth of the day viewed itself as the pioneer of a new society without classes. Millions of men were consumed in the fire that they lighted. What did it matter? Russia's riches cannot be measured. Her soil is overflowing with promises. The fecundity of her women is greater than that of the women of Europe. No sacrifice could be too great for a beacon light guiding all men to the promised land.

There is no more dramatic illustration of the hypnotism exerted by the idea of "Socialism in one country" than the discussions in the Siberian prisons during the first Five Year Plan, reported by the surviving participants. There Stalin's political victims, Socialists for more than a generation, debated among themselves whether the master of their jail was leading the country towards Socialism or not. Many of them answered the question in the affirmative—just before their execution.

The convulsions Russia experienced in the period from 1928 to 1938 accomplished the totalitarian transformation of the Russian revolution of October, 1917. Stalin probably believed that he was acting in the interests of this revolution when he destroyed the peasantry of the country and subjected its agriculture to the absolute control of the city and of industry. After the victory of the revolution, Lenin had again and again emphasized that the danger for the revolutionary party in Russia was the small peasant, many times outnumbering the industrial working class. Yet at the same time he had always warned against attempts of a coercive socialization of agriculture for he knew that Socialist industry would not be able to supply a socialized agriculture with machines and industrial products for a long time. Within Russia he had seen no solution to this problem. An alliance with a revolutionary industrial Germany was his solution for this seemingly insoluble problem of the Russian revolution.

Stalin pursued a different line of thought. Agrarian economy had recovered from the revolution and the civil war more quickly than had industrial production. Cities and industrial centers not able to give the peasant economy anything in exchange for their produce were threatened by a grain strike. Stalin's answer was the vivisection of the Russian peasantry: forced collectivization of agriculture. Villages were turned into collectives dominated by a net of tractor stations. But Socialist collectivization ended, as Bukharin had predicted in

438

1928, with a militarist subjugation of the peasantry by the industrial monopolies and trusts of the Soviet state.

Industrialization itself, paralleling the collectivization of agriculture, was undertaken without giving the economic and human reserves of the country their due consideration. Machines had to be imported from abroad. Supplies of gold and foreign exchange being soon exhausted, these imports could be financed in no other way than by exporting food. This resulted in a terrific famine. Gigantic industrial trusts were forced out of the steppes of Siberia like flowers in a hothouse. To develop at the same time an industry able to satisfy even the most modest requirements of the population was impossible. The entire economic and social equilibrium of the country was sacrificed to the plans of the ruling party. The workers in the cities became paupers in the same way as the peasants. The coercive machinery of the state had to increase its pressure on them more and more in order to prevent a collapse of the Five Year Plans. The Communist party in these years turned into an organization of terrorist exploitation of labor. The coercive machinery of the police had to be expanded on an ever-increasing scale in order to direct the transfer of millions of human beings to Siberia and the areas beyond the Urals, in order to collect the grain deliveries from the collectives, in order to maintain labor discipline in industrial plants, offices, and on the farms. At the end of this transformation there was no trace of either economic or political democracy left.

At the head of the Russian state an autocracy arose whose claim to power knows no limit. Like every newly developing class, the Russian autocracy required a political code and a philosophy to impose on its members self-discipline and cohesion. "Socialism in one country" fulfills this function. Its economic significance reflects the material interests of the young autocracy that has identified itself with the state and exercises monopolistic power over it. "Socialism in one country" signifies that the means of production are the property of the state and that the distribution of the social product remains securely in the hands of the autocracy. As far as the Russian people are concerned, "Socialism in one country" combines a threat and a promise of Utopia: At some time in the future all citizens will be

439

common beneficiaries of collective property. To doubt this future now is incompatible with loyalty to the state.

As the power of the autocracy expanded, it set itself off more and more from the rest of the people. Its members as well as the bureaucracy that surround them enjoy material benefits from which the rest of the population is rigidly excluded. The stabilization of victorious Socialism therefore required a stabilization of the rule of the directors of production over the producers. The equalitarian tendency of the first ten years after 1917 was made the main enemy of the new regime. Instead of a society without classes, a division into classes developed, sharper and deeper than in any other industrial country.

The new governing class of Russia had its roots directly in the working class and the peasants of the country. A great majority of its members have themselves been either workers and peasants or come from such backgrounds. This is the characteristic that distinguishes the Russian social structure from that in other countries.

During the first ten years of the transformation of the original plebeian Soviet Republic into a monopolistic state trust, a large part of the Russian people was still closely tied to the autocracy by their belief in "Socialism in one country." Hope for a "happy Socialist life" was still strong and sweet in the beginning of the great experiment. It was only later that it turned bitter and became a spiritual desert for the Russian people.

Stalin was thoroughly aware of this. During the first two years of the war he kept away from all forms of Socialist propaganda. The Russian people were not asked to defend the country in the name of Socialism but in the name of eternal, sacred Mother Russia. Only after the military crisis had passed did the "Socialist Fatherland" again put in an appearance.

Full reconstitution of Socialist ideology was deferred to the report Stalin gave during the Soviet elections of early 1946 in which he outlined the program of the victorious dictatorship. The autocracy will not and can not yield in regard to this ideology. This "Socialism" systematizes the collective disposition of the productive machinery of the country and justifies the individual benefits that flow from it. As the social distance between the autocracy and the mass of the people increases, the need for such a collective ideology acquires a

440

greater urgency. To yield in respect to this theory of "Socialism in one country" would mean that the Russian Vesuvius was preparing for new eruptions.

ECONOMY OF PURGE

The day after its triumphant military victory the Soviet Union finds itself in the throes of a new crisis. Its military is in inverse proportion to its economic power. Huge Soviet armies stretch their columns from Port Arthur to the River Elbe and Trieste, erecting a real *cordon sanitaire* against "capitalist encirclement." The Ukraine, the old industrial and agrarian center of Russia, is an economic desert. The industrial center of gravity has been shifted to beyond the Urals. Agriculture in European Russia has lost its backbone of iron. More than one-third of its tractors and combines have been destroyed. Most of the animal tractive power has been wiped out. Twenty-five to 30 per cent of the petroleum industry on which agriculture has become dependent has been destroyed. Russia's human losses during the war have been tremendous, probably eight and 10 per cent of the total population. In Leningrad alone approximately one and a half million people died during the siege.

These war losses have pressed heavily on the rest of the population. All Russian plants have been operating under martial law. Many were completely militarized. Female and child labor has been exploited in a way unknown until this time. It is but natural that the Russian people, after these superhuman efforts, long for rest. But their urge for rest clashes with the economic and social requirements of the autocracy.

This urge for rest is one of the fundamental factors in the present Russian crisis. It puts its own questionmark on all the economic plans of the dictatorship. One of the most characteristic events in this respect took place shortly after the close of the war. During the war approximately ten million people from the Ukraine and central Russia had been shifted to Western Siberia. According to a Soviet decree they were to remain there after the war. Nonetheless, immediately after the expulsion of the German armies, millions started to migrate toward their home areas. The migration could not be broken up by coercive measures, Moscow warned, painting a terrifying picture of the desolation at home. There were many bloody conflicts with divisions of the NKVD. But all this failed to check the flow. Some of the barrack cities of western Siberia have been completely emptied.

The importance of this first spontaneous mass movement in present-day Russia is extraordinary. It demonstrates that even the most centralized dictatorship has its limits. Here a small portion of the Russian people fought for its own "breathing spell," voting "with its feet" against the new grandiose industrialization plan even before it was officially announced.

If this movement is an indication of the present psychology of the people, Stalin will no longer be able to rely on the enthusiasm of the Russian working class as he could during the first cycle of his Five Year Plans. Such an urge for rest will urge him further to sharpen the cutting edge of his coercive machinery—if he wishes to see his industrialization program through.

Stalin's report in the spring of 1946 was a renewal of his arguments against the party opposition of fifteen years earlier. Stalin probably has reason to believe that in the coming years the "opposition" will comprise a great part of the people. On no other grounds can the gesture of the dictator be explained, who declared on the morrow of the greatest victory: Yes, our victory has been tremendous. What we have accomplished has been magnificent. But it does not amount to very much. For tomorrow we will be confronted with an even more serious test.

Even if Stalin were convinced that Washington and London are occupied with nothing else but the preparation of a war against Russia, the psychology of his argument remains strange. Stalin rarely loses his head. In 1927 after the break of diplomatic relations with Great Britain, Russia experienced a genuine war panic. At that time Bukharin gave official recognition to this feeling in a public speech. Stalin, who privately entertained an even more grave view of the situation than Bukharin, stated officially: There will be no war! and said to Bukharin in private: You are a fool. The worst thing one can do in a serious situation is to create panic.

It seems to us that Stalin's alarm of 1946 can be explained only by the pressure that the crisis in Russia is exerting on his own dictatorship.

The capitalists, he said in his report, have had sufficient time to develop their heavy industry. Therefore their path has been an easy one, first creating a light industry and then, from their accumulated profits, a heavy one. We had to take the opposite path.

At the same time he repeated the story that his adversaries during the period 1928 to 1938 had advocated a capitalist path of construction. Actually the differences between Stalin and his opponents of that time concerned the speed of the industrialization process, the proportion between heavy and light industry, and the relationship of the Bolshevik party to the peasantry. In that period the dictatorship was in a position to choose between two roads of construction. Now there is no longer a choice.

The masses who returned from western Siberia to the Ukraine attempted to construct homes without permission by the authorities. In their own way, therefore, they countered the plans of the government: first plants, then residences; first machines to produce machines, then consumer goods. If in the present situation the dictatorship were to give in to the desire of the people for rest, it would have to give up the principle of its existence. Its absolute monopolization of the means of production would be replaced by a decentralized and semi-planned economy. Its planned economy would be crossed by spontaneous and uncontrolled processes. It is heavy industry with its huge and concentrated plants and the resulting concentration of easily controllable workers that is and remains the backbone of the Russian dictatorship. The autocracy can never permit the rise of consumer industries with their geographical dispersion and independence. The system of terroristic control securing the power of the central authorities over production and productive methods would disintegrate, mass movements against coerced and slave labor might emerge from such a situation. These movements might finally express political demands and prove the beginning of a "counter-revolution" with unpredictable consequences. Stalin is bound to the economy of force and coercion as Prometheus to his rock. "Capitalist encirclement" is a prerequisite of his dictatorship, the inescapable stimulus of his monopoly power. The struggle for "security," that is, the struggle for the domination of Europe and China, is a struggle for the security of totalitarian dic-

443

tatorship. This is the reason why the victor himself deprecates his own triumph and accomplishments.

So things will move in their preordained pattern. In Eastern Europe and Asia millions of Russian workers and peasants in uniform hold watch over "capitalist" or "Socialist encirclement," while at home the tragic years of 1928 to 1939 are threatening to repeat. But this new tragedy is surrounded by many more risks for the dictatorship. For this time Stalin can not supply himself with the human material for his Five Year Plans from the huge pools of primitive peasants with their unlimited resources of strength. He must turn to a population that has already drawn on its last resources and that has paid the price for the industrialization of Russia in an army of millions of state slaves.

SLAVES OF SOVIETS

These fifteen to twenty million slaves are a living memorial of the everlasting crisis that is Russia under Stalin's dictatorship.

The Russian state slaves originated in a totalitarian negation of a humanitarian principle and in an ultrarevolutionary principle. The humanitarian principle was the progressive one of correcting and improving criminals by having them participate in productive labor. A few years after the October Revolution, Moscow could boast of some penal institutions that were a cross between a trade school and a boardinghouse. The Soviet courts of that day were inclined to explain all criminal actions by the social milieu of Czarist Russia. The corrective institutions of the Bezprisornyi, the lost waifs, performed wonders.

The ultrarevolutionary principle was most clearly expressed by Bukharin, Stalin's antagonist in the first years of the totalitarian transformation. Bukharin wrote, in 1920: "Coercion is no longer limited to the former ruling classes and their groups. In the period of transformation it is shifted to the workers themselves who have become the ruling class. One of the main forms of coercion operating within the sphere of the working class itself is forced and military labor. From the vantage of a higher historical standpoint, proletarian coercion in all its forms including executions and forced labor, paradoxical as it may seem, represents a method to mould a new

444

Communist humanity from the human material of the capitalist epoch. . . . ."

Lenin refused to accept Bukharin's and Trotsky's demand for the organization of labor armies under military discipline that were to overcome the economic chaos after the civil war. It was Stalin who ten years later put into effect this ultrarevolutionary slogan from the period of war Communism. But Bukharin's paradox did not result in the development of a "new Communist humanity," which to him meant a harmonious society without classes, but in the elimination of the rights of man.

Even after the long civil war in Lenin's time the population of the Russian penitentiaries amounted to less than sixty thousand. Yet shortly after Lenin's death a sharp increase occurred. The camps began to augment and multiply, though for the time being remaining institutions of correction with limited sentences. It was only after 1929 that slaves as an estate began to develop. This process parallels the transformation of the dictatorship into a monopolistic state trust. When the purges of 1936 to 1938 put the finishing touches to this trust, state slavery had become one of the most important institutions of the Soviet Republic.

The first great mass of slaves was drawn from the peasants during the first period of forced collectivization. Hundreds of thousands of peasants were shot down by NKVD troops and millions were deported to Siberia. Such act did not require juridical justification. Yet even the liquidation of law calls for a form of law. The developing state slavery found it in the paragraphs of the Criminal Code of 1922 devoted to the "Defense of Socialist Property." According to Paragraph 11, neglect or irresponsible conduct on the job can be punished if a slow-down of work results. According to Paragraph 128, waste or irresponsible conduct of business may be punished. According to Paragraph 128A, delivery of inferior or incomplete production is punishable. According to Paragraph 107, purchase and sale of products of agriculture and articles of mass consumption for purposes of profit is punishable. According to Paragraph 10, people are liable for prosecution not only if they act deliberately, but also without taking necessary precautions.

When this Criminal Code was published, a campaign was waged

for "revolutionary lawfulness" with the purpose of protecting the citizens against the power of the state. The law makers of the time were afraid of their own paragraphs which made every Russian citizen a potential criminal. Stalin's contribution to the Criminal Code consisted in the application of the paragraphs of 1922 against whole classes and groups of people. This was the foundation for the power of the GPU which became the executive organ of state slavery.

The first Five Year Plan was followed by a crisis of economic and political origin. The dictatorship no longer was confronted with a "class enemy." The resistance of the peasants had been broken. But the cry of the agricultural district for consumer goods had not become less. The productivity of the new workers who had been peasants the day before was low. The new industries were operating with tremendous deficits. Their products were inferior and expensive. Even with the best intentions the consumer goods industry had to remain a secondary consideration of the state, the capital goods industry consuming ever-increasing investments. The villages now collectivized could no longer strike. The tractor stations instituted by the Soviet state had woven them into a tight net of public control. The increasing amount of food required by the industrialization process could not be supplied by the agricultural population. For this reason again the apparatus of control had to be augmented, thereby increasing the general expense of production.

Stalin solved this first great crisis of "completed socialist society" in the purges that put all the blame for the difficulties on the shoulders of an imaginary counter-revolution. The purges accomplished the fusion of the party with the state bureaucracy. Expenses of production were lowered by measures of utmost severity. The most important social result was the creation of an army of millions of workers, originating in the purges and no longer receiving wages—the state slaves. The state slave is the theoretical ideal of the Soviet citizen. He gives the state everything and receives nothing in return.

This army of state slaves was an organic growth developing over a long period. Many years went by before it assumed the nature of a state institution fundamental for present-day Russian society. Even in 1934 after the completion of the canal between the White and the Baltic Sea, seventy-two thousand forced laborers were set free. Since

446

then, however, it has not been possible for a slave to become a wage worker. The transition from "correction by productive work" into slavery had been accomplished. The labor camps which had been publicized as political assets up to that date are no longer mentioned in official publications. Reliable witnesses and a substantial number of foreigners who for one reason or another have escaped have described these camps sufficiently to present at least a rough sketch of the life and death of these Soviet slaves.

All Soviet slaves regardless of age, sex, nationality, or profession have one thing in common: they are forever deprived of their freedom. They receive no wage and are not permitted to found or to continue a family. According to the law of 1937, retention in the camps can be extended to twenty-five years. That means life for practically all the inmates. Only the hardiest, most cruel, and shrewd can expect to survive twenty-five years.

The slaves are recruited from all professions, trades, and skills; they are frequently worked in their former occupations. Among the Siberian slaves, therefore, a sort of hierarchy soon arose. The lowest and most numerous group consisted of those who were occupied in construction work. This group received for its labor only a portion of the food necessary to maintain its labor power. The compensation for its work is the continuation of its life from day to day. In many of these slaves every instinct that can be called human has vanished. Killing and pilfering are the daily phenomena of their struggle to maintain their physical existence. The stake in a card game may be a priority to murder a comrade who is still the owner of a shirt.

Accidental differences of climate and vegetation determine the differences between these slaves. There are camps in the North of Russia and in Northeast Siberia—to be committed to one of them is equivalent to a death sentence. There are others in more fortunate climes where life can be preserved for months and years. The slave aristocracy consists of engineers who continue to work in their old profession, of physicians permitted to treat the NKVD personnel, and of criminals entrusted with the supervision of the others. The "aristocracy" receives a greater amount of food, better clothes, and has better sleeping quarters. Their wage is an allowance of sufficient energy to maintain hope for an improvement.

447

Obviously production under such circumstances, with the continuing heavy losses in human beings, is economically not very satisfactory. But this problem is of no great concern to the dictatorship. Slavery was not an institution based on a pre-established plan. It arose out of the forced industrialization and collectivization of agriculture and, because of the speed of the process, became a necessity for the Soviet state. Industrialization in the past depended on Siberian raw materials; at present they are even more essential. They must be available under all conditions. The new industries had to be erected in close proximity to raw-material centers. All this created a demand for men and their labor power that could not be supplied in a natural and normal way. Of their own free will Russian workers and peasants would not work in the mines or on the new Siberian construction jobs. The coercive machinery of the state had to take charge of the supply of labor power, else the entire policy of industrialization would have broken down. This is the ultimate reason for the identity between the mass purges and the institution of slavery in the anatomy of the Stalin dictatorship. The purges "cleanse" the bloodstream of totalitarian economy. They free it from the political and social poison that accumulates in its system, and they turn it into slave labor producing without cost. During the last years before the war the demand for human labor was intensified by the construction of railways, flying fields, and bases, frequently undertaken in areas without a trace of human habitation. In the course of the war the tremendous losses in human life created a demand for more and more slaves. Entire peoples like the Volga Germans and the Tartars of the Crimea were reduced to slavery. In the official population lists of the Soviet Republic they no longer exist. During and after the Hitler-Stalin pact millions of slaves from the Baltic republics and Poland were added. After the war many of the German minorities in Hungary, Czechoslovakia, and the Balkans followed them into the camps. How many slaves from Germany are being used in the Soviet Union is not known. The Soviet authorities have never published statistics on the number of war prisoners. They have always kept the number of men deported to the camps a state secret.

From the start of the war to date the Soviet Union has annexed directly twenty-five million people, the populations of Esthonia,

Lithuania, Lettland, Eastern Poland, and Bessarabia. One hundred million in Europe and an equal number in Manchuria, Inner Mongolia, and Northern China have come under the indirect control of the Soviet Union. There is no doubt that Stalin will try to draw upon these peoples for new and more slaves. With his new program for industrialization, his need for them is limitless. In its first cycle, devoted to the "victory of Socialism" in Russia, its victims were primarily Russians. Is it probable that Moscow will be more humane towards these vanquished peoples than it has been to its own countrymen?

The numerical relationship between free and slave labor in Russia can be estimated only approximately, but the trend of development is clear and definite. The losses Russia suffered during the war have been probably compensated for by the importation of slaves. By this very fact the specific weight of slave labor has increased. The first cycle of industrialization demonstrated that the demand for slave labor augments with the speed of the industrialization process. If Stalin attempts to approximate the goals announced for his next three Five Year Plans, he will require a far greater supply of labor than in the period from 1928 to 1939. The natural Russian increase has become smaller; therefore the importation of slaves will become an ever greater requirement. If Russian developments follow in line with Stalin's plans, it seems probable that some time during the coming fifteen years slave labor will outweigh wage labor in the Russian economy.

Usually the importation of foreign labor has pressed on the level of domestic wages. Such experience is even more probable in an economy like the Russian, that does not permit its workers to fight for the improvement of their wages by legal means. Strikes are prohibited, and any worker guilty of slow-down or sabotage can be sentenced to death. As slave production expands in volume the value of wage labor will decrease and more work will be demanded by the state for the same wage. A Russian plant manager whose compensation increases as his plant surpasses a set level of profit and who employs both free and slave labor, will be a poor advocate for increasing wages paid to the free workers. The gigantic NKVD trust, resting exclusively on the foundation of slave labor, offers permanent competition to the other industrial trusts, which have to pay out a much larger portion of their receipts in wages to their workers.

The terroristic effect of the institution of slave labor is obvious. Every single Soviet citizen is threatened with sinking down into the morass of this "institution." Therefore every single citizen tries to protect himself by working more, by being more submissive, by denouncing his fellows. Slave labor atomizes the mass of the people on the one side, and on the other stabilizes the omnipotence of the autocracy.

All countries in Russia's "lebensraum" have already introduced forced labor, the first step to slave labor. The Czechs, Stalin's best disciples in Central Europe, have introduced slave labor for a few hundred thousand Sudeten Germans. German war prisoners in Western Europe, used for forced labor under whatever pretense, are spearheads for the invasion of Europe by Stalin's Asiatic institution.

The United States under Lincoln had to decide whether it wished to be free or slave. Europe, devastated by a ruinous war, cannot exist half free, half slave. Russian imperial expansion with the Stalintern as its instrument places this problem in the foreground of decision.

THE GREAT QUESTION MARK

Stalin chose to proclaim the principles of his postwar policy not at a party congress nor in the Soviet parliament. After many months of absence from Moscow he made his announcement at an election meeting. A newsreel gives an impression of the event: the great golden hall of the Bolshoi Theatre is packed; between the ramp and the stage a dense crowd of uniforms; in the rear of the stage, row upon row of gold-bemedalled dignitaries. The chairman of the meeting, a simple civilian, stands among them in the first row. When the floor is Stalin's, he puts in his appearance from a side stage entrance. His steps show fatigue; his posture—in his ill-fitting marshal's uniform with its too long sleeves—is awkward. The picture taken from the gallery emphasizes the distance between the dignitaries in his rear and the audience before him. A rousing, roaring enthusiastic applause drowns the hall in a sea of sound. With a gesture of his hand, Stalin calms it into silence. His face, revealing clear traces of age, is in strange contrast with the spirit of his speech.

450

Again the sixty-seven-year-old dictator concentrated more power into his own hands. He created a Commissariat of Defense, uniting under his direction all branches of the army and navy. He strengthened his control over the NKVD by deposing its chief, Marshal Berya, and elevating the commander of his Kremlin guard, Kruglov, to this all-important post.

Stalin is not a dictator patterned on Hitler or Mussolini. He incorporates in his own person the most important institution of Russia. Broadcasts by the Moscow radio of practically any day will bear this out: There is a speech celebrating an anniversary of the Leningrad Academy of Science, according to which the "scholars of the entire globe" are streaming towards the "scientific center of the world," in order to express their devotion to the "man who has enriched scientific knowledge as no man before him." Or there is a report on the discovery of coal seams somewhere in Siberia. The report lasts one and a half minutes. The follow-up instructing the listeners that Stalin is the founder of the Russian coal mining industry and that no one has greater knowledge of the technology and economy of coal mining, lasts three minutes. Or the radio announces that the state publishing company is printing a new edition of Plato, not forgetting to add that the Generalissimo is the best living expert on Greek philosophy. Every speech, every article by Stalin is translated into twenty different languages and published in millions of copies. Annually millions of copies of Stalin's collected works are sold. The English magazine *Railway Gazette* reported in its edition of October 26, 1945, that the gauge of the entire railway net East of the Vistula and right up to Berlin had been changed to accord with the Russian standard gauge for Stalin's trip to Potsdam, and that after his return to Moscow the European standard gauge was again established. Whether the radio announces the sale of a new perfume with the brand name "Stalin's Breath" or the message of the Patriarch calling Comrade Stalin "our leader sent by God"—the broadcast is delivered in a voice solemn enough to be that of God himself giving his Commandments to Moses on Mt. Sinai.

Stalin is approaching the biblical age. Nothing very certain is known about his health, such knowledge being guarded as a supreme state secret. It is more than sixteen years ago that information about the state of Stalin's health became public abroad. That was in 1930 or 1931 when the well-known German specialist, Professor Z., now living in London, was called to attend him. After his return from Moscow one of his assistants failed to observe the rules of professional secrecy. Since then Stalin has been very cautious in consulting foreign physicians.

Regardless of how many more years Stalin's life may last, his policy indicates that he does not wish to create a successor. None of his most intimate collaborators fills a role in Russian propaganda that would designate him as Stalin's heir. Of the members of the Politbureau, recently enlarged to fifteen, several seem out of the running either because of circumstances or their personalities. Voroshilov's name has been under a dark cloud since the defeats of the first war years. Mikoyan, the minister of food, is a gay favorite of Stalin's, loving drink and dance, but never active in political affairs. Lazar Kaganovitch, Stalin's energetic and industrious trouble-shooter, is a Jew and has little chance in the new nationalist atmosphere of Russia. Krushkov has had a hand in Ukrainian affairs only. Berya is now a provisional member of the Politbureau but has lost the chairmanship of the NKVD. Shvernik, acting member of the Politbureau, formerly chairman of the trade unions and now successor to Kalinin as chairman of the Soviet Executive, is of second rank. There remain Andreyev, chairman of the Party Control Committee and chief of the Ministry of Agriculture; Zhdanov, the leader of Leningrad; and Malenkov who is now a member of the Politbureau and holds a position as chief of the office organization of the Central Committee and vice-president of the Soviet Executive, a key position. In addition there are Vosnezensky, who heads the Office of Planning, and Boulganin, who made a name for himself as defender of Moscow and is now active in the Ministry of Defense. And finally there is Molotov, Stalin's Foreign Minister.

Among these, Zhdanov appears the most powerful figure. Stalin gave him a high military rank, called him to Moscow, and entrusted him with the party control over the army. Zhdanov as "defender of Leningrad" possesses military glory of his own not shared by any other member of the Politbureau. Malenkov's personal influence is increasing. He has risen from the anonymous position of Stalin's private secretary to that of a personnel chief of the Bolshevist party. Molotov has emerged from the obscurity of his former bureaucratic career. Yet all this has little bearing on the choice of candidate whom Stalin's inscrutable wisdom will designate as his heir and successor. No man among them is in a position to organize independent power for himself while Stalin is alive. No man among them has a personal history of note. They are all clay in their creator's hand.

Stalin will probably emulate Lenin and leave a last will and testament. But at that point the similarity ceases. Lenin's testament addressed itself to the Bolshevik party of the October tradition. He warned of dangers threatening, and called the assets and weaknesses of his collaborators to the attention of the party. Lenin designated no successor, but discussed the two strongest men of his leadership: Trotsky and Stalin. The election of his successor was left to the party. Stalin cannot follow such a method. His party today is organically incapable of selecting a successor, being constituted only to receive and execute orders, but not to move on its own initiative. It will have to receive the new leader from above—it cannot create him. Stalin fought for his monopoly position in the five years following Lenin's death by a combination of methods: once a grain of the coup d'état and a pound of persuasion; the next time a pound of the one and a grain of the other. Many reasons can be given for the rise of Stalin. One of the decisive ones was the fact that his main competitor—Trotsky—eliminated himself when he refused to utilize the methods of the October Revolution for his own quest of power, in those decisive days and months after Lenin died. This was a most striking victory for Stalin, who thus succeeded in winning to his side the majority of the old Bolsheviki.

No successor of Stalin can secure his position of power by the same methods. A conflict on ideological grounds is no longer possible. Should Stalin's successor regard his position as endangered or as insufficiently secure, the only procedure open to him would be that of a coup d'état.

Stalin's dictatorship rests on three supports: the NKVD, the army, and the unorganized but very influential group of industrial managers. It has been secure due to its ability to unify and balance these centers of power. This equilibrium of power can be maintained only

453

by Stalin's hands, for he is their creator and their common example. Each successor of Stalin's will have to re-establish the balance upset by the vacuum left after the death of the omnipotent. No successor will be able to do so, for a new totalitarian leadership erected by one of the support columns of the dictatorship will have to be imposed and reimposed on the other two.

This is characteristic of all absolute dictatorships. When the despot dies or when he fails to keep control, the anarchy submerged by the dictatorship rises to the surface, the concealed struggles come out in the open, and the struggle for the inheritance of power unfolds. Stalin's death or weakening in office will set such a chain of events in motion.

First, the security of the Eurasian empire during the present economic crisis demands a super-Stalin, while his death will cause the opening up of a political vacuum not to be filled by any successor. One cannot inherit the "institution Stalin" which it has taken twenty-five years to create. The life of this institution cannot be prolonged beyond the life of its creator. The heir will have to fight for his inheritance.

Second, the fight to fill this vacuum will have to begin immediately upon the morrow of Stalin's death, because the elimination of his omnipotence and his omniscience will create a near collapse in the apparatus of power that he has constructed. The successor will have to operate under the imperative necessity of emerging from this collapse as speedily as possible. Every new day will again confront him with the inescapable ultimatum: Become Stalin or vanish!

Third, the existing "institution Stalin" does not permit a successor to develop while Stalin is alive. Therefore all the disinherited will look upon the actual successor as a usurper. Stalin's testament will be no more than a piece of paper. The more absolute the power of the dictator alive, the less effective it is with the dictator dead. Lenin had ruled as the first among equals during his dictatorship. His moral influence had, in fact, been extraordinary. He had not yet been buried when his contending inheritors began a struggle to the death.

Fourth, as long as the three power groups are united in Stalin's hands, conflicts between them are immunized as they arise. When the struggle to fill the vacuum after the dictator's death begins, this will no longer be the case, for they will have to participate in the conflict in their own right. Each of these three groups has accumulated tremendous resources of power; its leaders have stored up corresponding aspirations. There is a community of interest between these three groups in regard to "capitalist encirclement" and in regard to the Russian people. Nevertheless, their interests are not homogeneous. The industrial bureaucracy is perhaps the most conservative of the three groups. It demands legal stabilization of its power, legal security of its social position, and a stabilization of the country on a foundation of peace with the outside world. The imperialist ideology is represented among the young marshals of the Red Army, who are excluded from Stalin's most intimate circle. They enjoy a greater publicity in the United States than in Russia itself. Both groups maintain common interests against the NKVD which holds both of them in its grip and is a military and economic power in its own right.

The masters of these three power groups will suddenly find themselves in a situation of unaccustomed independence after the disappearance of the "institution Stalin." Even were they angels of patience and Christian love, they would be bound to clash in conflicts among themselves. All of them have been reared in the doctrine promulgated by members of the Politbureau during the campaign of the victory elections: You are weak, so you are wrong; you are powerful, so you are right.

Yet in the background of all these considerations lurks the overriding question: What will the Russian people as a whole do when the power vacuum after Stalin's death develops? The answer will ultimately decide the outcome of the greatest crisis Stalin's Eurasian empire will have to face.

KEY ISSUE

The defeat of Germany and Japan shifted the center of gravity in world affairs to the political relationship between Washington and Moscow. Stalin won the first round of a struggle that causes the world to tremble. He won for himself positions that put political initiative for the coming moves into his hands. Probably this was inescapable after Roosevelt's great plan of reconciliation between Russia and the West broke down. Roosevelt did not desire to repeat the errors of Lloyd George and Poincaré who blocked Europe and Asia off from

Russia after the First World War. He expected to draw Russia into Europe and to assimilate it as a victorious nation with equal rights. This plan, however, would have collapsed even with Roosevelt as its executor, for it rested on a misconception of the internal structure of the Soviet Union. Its initial success—the dissolution of the Comintern and the first Moscow conference, for instance—turned into defeat for its initiators.

It is nevertheless undeniable that Roosevelt had reason for expecting a compromise with Stalin. This is evidenced in the policy pursued by Stalin at the end of 1943 when he came out for a modified repetition of the famous Genoa plan of Lenin's, from the year 1921.

Immediately after the Russian civil war, Lenin had begun his new economic policy. This policy succeeded the war-Communism that governed the first phase of the revolution. It was due to the necessity, as Lenin said, of a "breathing spell" after the stabilization of the new regime and the defeat of the first revolutionary wave in postwar Europe. Lenin's plan carried the turn much farther than was ever accomplished in practice. In addition to the Socialist sector of the economy, he visualized one of private capitalism under state supervision. This sector he expected to develop on a grand scale with the assistance of foreign capital. Industrial and agrarian concessions were to be managed by foreign capital, together with the Soviet government, on terms of equal partnership. This plan was to be offered to the world not only as a help to Soviet economy and a profitable business for big enterprises, but also as a means of overcoming the world-wide depression of the postwar period. Chicherin offered Lenin's plan at the conference of Genoa in April, 1922. Lloyd George refused to accept the plan, however.

Stalin's Genoa plan never took a form that permitted open discussion of it in Russia with all its pros and cons—as had been the custom in the first years of Lenin's regime. Stalin's Genoa plan was publicized through the Teheran policy of the American Communists who offered American capitalism economic and political stabilization of the world as an asset of the partnership with the Soviet Union. The price which Earl Browder, Stalin's mouthpiece at the time, demanded was large credits to the Soviet Union and a division of the markets in the Far East between the United States and Soviet Russia.

The end of the war brought the Teheran policy to a speedy finish. At Yalta, military developments had already secured Stalin against all unpleasant surprises in the West. Annexation of Eastern Poland by Russia had been internationally accepted. Russian supremacy in the Balkans with the exception of Greece was uncontested. The River Elbe had been decided upon as a line of demarcation in Germany. His victory was probably greater than he himself had even imagined.

After Yalta, Roosevelt died. American international policy viewed from Moscow became a big question mark. When the Russian armies finally arrived at the River Elbe, Russia itself was psychologically and politically more remote from Europe than at any other time of her recent history.

The barbaric struggle that Hitler had forced on Russia intensified its barbaric socialism. The Red Army could not turn into an army of liberation. Its innate urge for revenge blended with the politically instilled hatred toward the West. The "liberation" of the Slavic countries, particularly in the beginning, proceeded not very differently from the subjection of Germany. A power that had arisen from a most brutal process of industrialization could seek reparation for the losses suffered only in just as brutal a de-industrialization of the vanquished. Humane considerations had no place in its vocabulary. In the debates on the volume of German reparations that followed, the logic of facts was on the side of the Russians. The collective responsibility of an entire nation for the decisions and doings of its leadership involves the inclusion of its entire economy in the concept of war potential. What significance could such a formula have but to hold each single individual citizen responsible with his property and his labor power for reparations? Roosevelt and Churchill hesitated in Yalta before they accepted Stalin's claim to reparations in the form of human labor. But when they finally acceded to the demand they disregarded one of the fundamental principles of their own civilization, namely the inalienable right of each individual to dispose of his own labor. They opened the doors of Europe to a principle that in the final analysis is the foundation of the dictatorship in Russia.

The years to come will show whether it is possible for the United States and England to disengage themselves from the Yalta and Potsdam commitments without causing the final destruction of the

457

culture that was Europe. Stalin expects to make the present crisis permanent by a definitive division of Europe or to solve it by transforming the entire continent into an annex of the Russian empire. His minimum expectations include the political incorporation of the Slavic countries into the Soviet Union and the international recognition of the River Elbe as the Russian frontier. His maximum expectations involve the inclusion of West and Southwest Europe into the lebensraum of Russia, the military and diplomatic withdrawal of the United States from Europe, and the separation of England from the continent.

American policy might accept a Western European bloc as a long term compromise. Its sensibilities may not be shocked by the discovery that such a bloc is nothing but a Western name for Stalin's minimum expectations. Europe could view such a solution only as another form of a slow end. Its Western parts cannot live without an organic connection with its Central and Eastern parts.

Stalin has won the first round of this struggle. Yet even the co-ordination of Eastern Europe, with the exception of Czechoslovakia, is based on the bayonets of the Red Army. Before the peace of totalitarian stability and its graveyard stillness settle down on Eastern Europe, tempestuous convulsions will shake this part of the continent for a long time. In Western Europe the period for solutions in Stalin's direction become shorter and shorter. The crisis in Russia itself, which is only beginning, may involve the entire international position of Stalinism and subject it to dangerous tests.

These tests will decide the destiny of the Stalintern. The totalitarian Stalinist mass parties of the Stalintern in Europe require "quick solutions." Regardless of the social expectations attached to them, they have to win out quickly or be defeated. Tactical compromises entertained by the Stalintern parties of the West are possible for short periods only. The Stalintern parties of the West can never be assimilated into a democratic order of the Western type. German Communism as it exists today is a result of the Russian occupation. A retreat of the Russian armies would involve a rapid disintegration of the Stalintern party in Germany. In China also the present situation, a division of power between the national government and the Communists, is impossible as a permanent solution.

However one approaches the historical role of Lenin's International, it is undeniable that its leaders acted in the spirit of a dogmatic conviction and its masses with the fanatic devotion of a strong faith. Both leaders and masses desired to eliminate the roots of the devastating wars they had experienced, and wanted to create a harmonious society. This explains their powers of resistance during a tumultuous twenty-five years.

The Stalintern rests on force, suppression, and despair—not on hope and expectation. It is an end unto itself. It does not represent a socialist alternative to the breakdown of a capitalist order of society. It is a form of disintegration of human society.

Because it has no ends beyond itself, the Stalintern will ultimately end in the extinction of the Communist parties that compose it. Those which operate within the physical and geographical proximity of Stalin's empire will be transformed into mere appendices of the Russian State apparatus. The contradiction between obedience to the requirements of Moscow and the conditions essential for their political existence in their own countries will defeat the others.

If, on the other hand, the crisis in Russia proper results in convulsions threatening the European and Asiatic expansion of Moscow, the likelihood is that then the parties of the Stalintern will vanish into the dark more quickly than they rose into the limelight of recent events.

The Stalintern has no future and will produce no successors.

Index

461

INDEX

D